EDUCATING THE
DEMOCRATIC MIND

SUNY Series, Democracy and Education
George H. Wood, Editor

EDUCATING THE DEMOCRATIC MIND

WALTER C. PARKER

State University
of New York
Press

Published by
State University of New York Press, Albany

© 1996 State University of New York

All rights reserved

Production by Susan Geraghty
Marketing by Theresa Abad Swierzowski

Printed in the United States of America

For information, address the State University of New York Press,
90 State Street, Suite 700, Albany, NY 12207

Library of Congress Cataloguing-in-Publication Data

Educating the democratic mind / [edited by] Walter C. Parker.
     p. cm. — (SUNY series, democracy and education)
   Includes bibliographical references.
   ISBN 0-7914-2707-2 (hc : acid-free paper). — ISBN 0-7914-2708-0
(pb : acid-free paper)
    1. Citizenship—Study and teaching—United States. 2. Democracy—
Study and teaching—United States. 3. Civics—Study and teaching—
United States. 4. Education—United States—Aims and objectives.
I. Parker, Walter. II. Series.
LC1091.E385 1996
370.11'5—dc20   94-49551
                                                CIP

10 9 8 7 6 5 4 3 2

To Marie Wirsing, Sally Geis, and Lyle and Sydelle Ehrenberg, who taught me something about philosophy, sociology, and teaching, respectively, each at just the right time.

TABLE OF CONTENTS

FOREWORD

James A. Banks

Walter Parker's new volume is a welcome collection of essays, old and new, on the idea that democrats are not born but educated, and that their education can and should be deliberate. "Democrats" here means men and women who are committed to ways of living together that are marked by popular sovereignty rather than authoritarianism, genuine cultural pluralism rather than oppression in the name of political unity, and a fundamental commitment to liberty, law, justice, and equality as the moral ground of social life.

In a postmodern world characterized by competing interests, a lack of civility, and enormous diversity, democracy is an extraordinarily ambitious and difficult ideal. The development of democratic citizens is an ideal that is in many ways inconsistent with human history and with the ways in which human beings are socialized in most societies and cultures. History is replete with oppression and injustice, and most human societies are stratified along racial, ethnic, gender, and social-class lines. Most societies also consist of groups that are stigmatized and regarded and treated as the Other.

Yet democracy and inclusion are elusive and difficult ideals that we must pursue in the postmodern age. Without the pursuit of the democratic project by the schools and the larger society, the contradiction between our democratic ideals and the racial and social-class inequality within our society will intensify, thus creating disillusioned and ineffective citizens. The democratic project pursued by the Civil Rights movement of the 1960 and 1970s is testimony to the effectiveness of deliberate attempts to make our society more just and humane. In the pre–Civil Rights years, apartheid was institutionalized throughout the South and racism and discrimination were rampant throughout the United States. Students were taught about the equality of men and women in the classroom and experienced blatant discrimination both within segregated schools and within the larger society.

I grew up in Arkansas in the forties and fifties in a society marked by racial segregation that was supported by both laws and customs. We learned about liberty and justice in school, and said— repeating the Pledge of Allegiance in our segregated school each morning—that our nation had "liberty and justice for all." As a child who took school and my teachers seriously, I internalized that notion. However, much in society told me that liberty and justice was for some but not for all.

My African American teachers and my parents, who were practicing democrats within a racially segregated society, taught me that I was somebody, that I must believe in myself, and that if I worked hard, kept the faith, and kept my eyes on the prize I could become anything I wanted to be. They taught me that things would not always be easy, and there would be hard times, but that I must keep the faith and persevere. They also taught me that no matter what I achieved, I had an obligation to my people, to my community, and to my country. My achievements, they taught me, were not to be measured by how many material things I attained, but by how much I gave to those in need, how much I helped others, and how much I helped to make society better for me, my children, and my children's children.

The faith that my parents and teachers had in democratic ideals and in the possibilities of a democratic society—and the ideals of freedom that were promoted by the Civil Rights movement as I was coming of age—were decisive factors that enabled me to live in an apartheid society and yet believe in the possibilities of a democracy. The democratic work done by my teachers in the segregated communities of Arkansas in the 1940s and 1950s is a cogent example of the important work that can be done by schools and teachers in a society that has democratic ideals, even when many of its institutionalized practices contradict them.

As the work of my Arkansas teachers and the chapters in this book make clear, the struggle to educate democrats is not new, nor is it unworkable. As we read Dewey, Griffin, Taba, Kohlberg, Newmann, and Apple, for example, we see a lineage of democratic educators committed to the practice of freedom, albeit from sharply differing vantage points and interests. Some tried to take pluralism seriously; others ignored it, assuming a unity that simply did not exist. Parker's *Questions for Discussion,* given at the beginning of each of the book's four parts, encourage a critical reading of each work. Readers can greatly benefit from using the data-retrieval chart at the end of the Introduction to work through the questions for each chapter.

The authors in this collection are a disparate lot. And the new works in the final section reveal that the reflections on these works are equally diverse. Yet each of them has something to say about the key question of our time, as Walter Parker puts it so aptly in his introduction: "What does it mean to educate children in such a way as to fashion them for the demands of an increasingly diverse society, one that is in Toni Morrison's terms 'wholly racialized,' and that is organized and struggling, on and off, to realize the democratic ideal? Briefly, how are we to educate children to embrace difference and maintain a common life?"

To function effectively in a democratic society, students must understand the nature of knowledge, how it is constructed, and how it frequently serves to reinforce structural inequality, sexism, and racism. In their recent book *The Bell Curve,* Richard J. Herrnstein and Charles Murray argue that lower-income groups have less native intelligence than upper-income groups. This argument, which is reminiscent of the theories developed by phrenologists about race and intelligence near the turn of the century, indicates that there is still a strong relationship between science and politics, and that this relationship often poses a serious threat to democracy.

The publication of books such as *The Bell Curve* is an important reminder of the significance of the work that Walter Parker is doing to promote democracy in the nation's schools. This thoughtful and creative collection of articles will enable its readers to ponder seriously the democratic work that schools need to undertake to understand the reasons why such work is essential for the survival of our nation, and to become acquainted with creative ways to make our schools democratic, just, and moral communities.

INTRODUCTION:

SCHOOLS AS LABORATORIES

OF DEMOCRACY

Walter C. Parker

The notions *community* and *mind* have been paid a great deal of attention over the years. These are unstable ideas, their meanings shifting both across and within discourses. Many lights have been shed on them from an array of vantage points without converging— from Aristotle to Hannah Arendt, for example, or Plato to Dewey, James Madison to Langston Hughes, Sojourner Truth to bell hooks, Confucius to Black Elk. The differences are not subtle: Plato's universalism is anathema to Dewey's pragmatism; the celebrated, secular mind of Europe's Enlightenment is Zen's "drunken monkey in a cage"; the Confucian approach to community life would be an Orwellian nightmare, awful and incomprehensible for many North Americans.

This book explores just one facet of this sprawling conversation: the concern to prepare citizens for a loosely defined genre of political and social community called "democracy." The volume is concerned especially with the views of one group that more than most others has cause to pay serious attention to democracy: educators. Featured mainly are educators interested in the school curriculum, for here lies much of the concentrated and concrete work on the topic. This volume, then, is a collection of inquiries, old and new, joined on the central question of our era: What does it mean

1

to educate children in such a way as to fashion them for the demands of an increasingly diverse society, one that is in Toni Morrison's terms "wholly racialized," and that is organized under and struggling, on and off, to realize the democratic ideal? As Chantal Mouffe writes,

> [T]he challenge that we are facing today is precisely that of developing a view of citizenship which is adequate for multi-ethnic and multi-cultural societies. We have to accept that national homogeneity can no longer be the basis of citizenship, and that pluralism must allow for a range of different ethnic and cultural identities. (1992, p. 8)

In this introduction to the volume, I will broach and support the notion that schools are fitting places for democratic education. I could do this by delving into the argument that education for democracy has moral primacy over other purposes to which schooling might be put in a democratic society. That has been done well elsewhere, however, and tends to be neither a novel nor terribly pressing point among educators already committed to education for democracy, especially those, I suspect, who read this book. It is, to be sure, a critically important argument, and one with which I stand in full accord. I shall use this space, however, to develop an argument that is likely to be consequential for educators who labor in the curriculum field, whether is central offices of school districts, state departments of education, classrooms, or the academy. In other words, I will *assume* the moral primacy argument—that the schools' first moral obligation is "to give all children an education adequate to take advantage of their political status as citizens" (Gutmann, 1987, p. 288)—and concentrate instead on how schools might actually accomplish this.

I will rely on the associationist view of democracy and its meaning for curriculum. On this view, closely linked with Dewey's and Toqueville's analyses of democratic life, we are able to see that schools generally possess easily and naturally, which is to say they *already* possess without first needing to be transformed, the bedrocks of democratic living—diversity and mutuality. As well, we are able to conclude that these are two practical and elegant standards against which curriculum plans for educating democrats can be examined.

I will begin with an examination of the associationist view, which should help us distinguish between strong and weak forms of education for democracy, then explore briefly the consequences of that view for schooling in general and the school curriculum in particular. Finally, I will introduce readers to the plan of this volume.

I. ASSOCIATED LIVING

The idea of educating the children *for democracy* as opposed to, say, educating them for authoritarianism or theocracy is central to the rationale for public education in the United States. It has not been the only rationale, to be sure. Educating a stratified labor force for domestic productivity, keeping children off the streets, and greasing the tracks of social mobility have also been central. Yet, the democratic mission has been resilient: Educators have argued that public schools provide a singular civic apprenticeship, an education for liberty, that a fledgling democratic society snubs only at great risk to its growth and longevity. Democratic experiments are *all* fledgling, to be sure, and typically they are short-lived. They do not have the advantage of citizens who are naturally democratic, for the democratic mind is not natural. It does not arise spontaneously but in institutions—democratic institutions—and then only with difficulty. Recall that egocentricity and ethnocentricity are primary forces in humans and, like breathing, take no special training. Democracy, on the other hand, consists of habits and competencies that require cultivation without which they will not sprout in the first place, or sprout then wither quickly. Barber (1992) is explicit:

> The literacy required to live in civil society, the competence to live in democratic communities, the ability to think critically and act deliberatively in a pluralistic world, the empathy that permits us to hear and thus accommodate others, all involve skills that must be acquired. . . . Empower the merely ignorant and endow the uneducated with a right to make collective decisions and what results is not democracy but, at best, mob rule: the government of private prejudice and the tyranny of opinion—all the perversions that liberty's enemies like to pretend (and its friends fear) constitute democracy. (pp. 4–5)

Rationalizing public education in and through the democratic ideal is hardly new. Consider these widely cited statements making essentially the same point, the first as the republic was beginning, the second as free public education was being considered in Boston:

> Every government degenerates when trusted to the ruler of the people alone. The people themselves are its only safe depositories. And to render even them safe their minds must be improved to a certain degree. This indeed is not all that is necessary, though it be essentially necessary. An amendment of our constitution must come here in aid of the public education. The influence over government must be shared among all the people. (Thomas Jefferson, 1785)

> The great moral attribute of self-government cannot be born and matured in a day; and if children are not trained to it, we only prepare ourselves for disappointment if we expect it from grown men. . . . As the fitting apprenticeship for depotism consists in being trained to despotism, so the fitting apprenticeship for self-government consists in being trained to self-government. (Horace Mann, 1846)

The civic value of education was apparent not only to European immigrants such as these but to the Africans who were in chains when both men spoke. W. E. B. Dubois's disagreement with Booker T. Washington is telling. A full half-century after the Emancipation Proclamation, Washington wished patience and "realistic expectations" on black people. He argued that prosperity would come in time but only in proportion to the freed Africans' willingness to embrace common labor. He urged them to forget their minds and instead to put their hands to work on farms and in factories. Agitating for social and political equality wasted valuable time that could otherwise be spent on the hard-won opportunity to work for a living without chains.

The implications for education were clear. "Booker T. Temptation" (West, 1993) was advocating for African American men training in the industrial arts, that is, vocational education for labor at the bottom rungs of the occupational ladder. DuBois railed against this movement, considering it nothing more than appeasement to the former slave-owning class. He wanted access to the civic realm, to the franchise, and, beyond this, to liberal education and what could be for people recently enslaved only the *imagined* possibilities of freedom to develop one's potential.

Is life not more than meat, and the body more than raiment? And men ask this today all the more eagerly because of sinister signs in recent educational movements. We shall hardly induce black men to believe that if their stomachs be full, it matters little about their brains. The tendency is here, born of slavery and quickened to renewed life by the crazy imperialism of the day, to regard human beings as among the material resources of a land to be trained with an eye single to future dividends. Race-prejudices, which keep brown and black men in their "places," we are coming to regard as useful allies with such a theory. . . . (1903/1982, p. 126)

John Dewey took the argument for a liberatory democratic education further than anyone before or since has done. Not only did he clarify the object of the apprenticeship, he specified its method. Dewey recognized that the aim of democratic education could be conceived in two very different ways. One, the weaker, nominal view, was expressed by Jefferson and Mann and is found in many school-district mission statements. It appreciates that the election of governors requires educated voters: "Since a democratic society repudiates the principle of external authority, it must find a substitute in voluntary disposition and interest; these can be created only by education" (Dewey 1916/1985, p. 93). A stronger conception. Dewey reasoned, understood democracy to be a kind of living together. More than a form of government, it is "a mode of associated living, of conjoint communicated experience." This mode is distinct in two ways.

First, the interaction among a group's members entails numerous and varied interests that are consciously shared. Second, the interplay between and among groups is wide-ranging and unrestricted. Any group, therefore, must refer its own actions to the actions of other groups, and the existence of these groups as well as the interplay among them are encouraged by the mores and institutions consciously shared by the *broader* public—the *bigger* public, the *commonwealth* that contains these little publics. In this way, common interests and multiple reference points are joined and nurtured. To clarify, Dewey has us ponder life in a criminal gang:

[W]e find that the ties which consciously hold the members together are few in number, reducible almost to a common interest in plunder; and that they are of such a nature as to isolate the group from other groups with respect to the give and take of the

values of life. Hence, the education such a society gives is partial
and distorted. (1916/1985, p. 89).

It is partial and distorted precisely because the gang is ingrown. Its
shared interests are too few and unvaried (recall the first distinction), and they partition this one group from the diversity and
reciprocity that define civic life (the second distinction). Such an
education is inherently bigoted.

Dewey was no dreamer. The "give and take" of associated
living that he wanted badly and thought deeply about is fundamental, not a luxury, and its necessity is derived from objective conditions of the industrial era—hallmark conditions such as increasing
prosperity and personal freedom untethered by tradition, but also
the sudden impossibility of isolation without ethnocentrism, ghettos, and alienation. Isolation dissolves multiple reference points in
favor of ignorance because one's particular experience becomes
the sole reference point. Simultaneously, common interests are ex-
changed for private interests. In the industrial age, isolation breeds
pathology.[1]

Diversity plus common interests, then, compose the bedrock of
a democracy strong enough to cope with modernity. These require
in turn the dissolution of "barriers of class, race, and national
territory" (Dewey 1916/1985, p. 93) which are precisely what
prevent populations both within and among nations from clarifying and pursuing broadly shared interests: housing, food, trade
policy, land policy, equal opportunity, labor relations, child care,
environmental stewardship, health care, and so on. None can be
handled alone by the "little publics," whether gangs, churches,
professional associations, college faculties, ethnic or residential en-
claves, sports clubs, diet clubs, the Chamber of Commerce, or
nation states.

Dewey goes still further. He ties not only civic vigor but self-
development to the commonwealth. The "situatedness" of identity-
formation is rapidly becoming conventional wisdom among intel-
lectuals, of course; Vygotsky and Foucault have seen to that. But
Dewey's approach remains direct and unique: The same barriers
to association that prevent concerted, public action also prevent
people from understanding their own activity and choosing their
own lives. The hard-won, panoramic view of one's situation that
might be derived from a "widening of the area of shared concerns"

provides the conditions for "the liberation of a greater diversity of personal capacities" (p. 93). Brazilian educator Paulo Freire argued roughly the same point decades later using the concept "conscientization": To awaken, to see themselves, humans must sever their adherence to and immersion in the world. They must be not merely *in* and *of* the world, as are nonhuman animals, but *with* it—both in and of the world and distant enough from it psychologically to allow self-knowledge of the world. "Only beings who can reflect upon the fact that they are determined are capable of freeing themselves," he wrote. "Conscientization is viable only because man's consciousness, although conditioned, can recognize that it is conditioned" (1985, p. 68–69).

Alexis de Toqueville's work, published at about the same time that Horrace Mann was speaking to the Boston school committee, demonstrates that the strong, associationist view of democracy was not new with Dewey. Toqueville argued that nothing more deserves attention in the study of democracy "than the intellectual and moral associations" among people. "In democratic countries *knowledge of how to combine* is the mother of all other forms of knowledge; on its progress depends that of all the others" (1848/1969, p. 517, emphasis added). He was astounded by and evidently took great delight in Americans' penchant for association. Not only do they associate for political purposes, as in the town meeting, but for countless civil purposes as well: sales and other business associations, financial, religious, charity, leisure, travel, courtship, health, labor, educational, not-in-my-backyard, large, small, serious, silly:

> Americans combine to give fetes, found seminaries, build churches, distribute books, and send missionaries to the antipodes. Hospitals, prisons, and schools take shape in that way. . . . In every case, at the head of any new undertaking, where in France you would find the government or in England some territorial magnate, in the United States you are sure to find an association. . . .
>
> The first time that I heard in America that one hundred thousand men had publicity promised never to drink alcoholic liquor, I thought it more of a joke than a serious matter and for the moment did not see why these very abstemious citizens could not content themselves with drinking water by their own firesides.
>
> In the end I came to understand that these hundred thousand

Americans, frightened by the progress of drunkenness around them, wanted to support sobriety by their patronage. . . . One may fancy that if they had lived in France each of these hundred thousand would have made individual representations to the government asking it to supervise all the public houses throughout the realm. (pp. 513 and 516)

To the associationist foundation laid by Toqueville and Dewey was added the varied work of numerous twentieth-century social scientists. Walter Lippmann argued in *The Good Society* (1937) that new modes of association spawned by the industrial era—notably, division of labor and market-directed economies—presented genuinely new possibilities for social life. He was right. These associations made people mutually dependent on others not of their circle, the consequence of which potentially was a broadening of the commonwealth as shared interests became more varied and diversity among groups more pronounced. In fact, however, the commonwealth was in many ways weakened. New or revised support structures were not sufficiently in place to keep up with the new interplay. Labor often was treated mercilessly by owners; cultural and racial minorities were systematically excluded from power and privilege; the new comprehensive high schools quickly became diploma mills, specializing in requiring no one to learn; the bigger public adopted consumption as a major life project; and voting, democratic minimalism's version of popular sovereignty, became almost too much to ask. The bigger public rapidly was handing citizenship over to politicians and retreating from the common weal.

Edward Banfield's study in 1958 of an impoverished village in southern Italy provided vivid case data on the difficulty of bringing little publics into a working commonwealth. Here was a village that, on the associationist view, fairly could be described as dead. There was no organized action whatsoever in the face of striking local problems. And these were *felt* problems. Locals complained bitterly about them, but they did nothing. There was no hospital, no newspaper, only five grades of school, no charities or welfare programs, no agricultural organizations. The only "association," so to speak, was the nuclear family. Banfield concluded that the villagers' inability to improve their common life was best explained by their inability and unwillingness to combine, that its, to associate outside their families. They were unable "to act together for their common good or, indeed, for any end transcending the immediate, material interest of the nuclear family" (1958, p. 10). Banfield called this *amoral familism* and gave its ethos as "Maximize the material, short-run advantage of the nuclear family; assume that all others will do likewise" (p. 83). Several hypotheses follow logically:

1. In a society of amoral familists, no one will further the interest of the group or community except as it is to his private advantage to do so.

2. In a society of amoral familists, only officials will concern themselves with public affairs, for only they are paid to do so.

3. In a society of amoral familists, there will be few checks on officials, for checking on officials will be the business of other officials only.

4. In a society of amoral familists, organization (i.e., deliberately concerted action) will be very difficult to achieve and maintain. (pp. 83–86)

More recently, the work of Robert Bellah and his colleagues (1985, 1991), Harry Boyte (1989), Carol Gould (1988), Amy Gutmann (1987), Karl Hess (1979), Ann Phillips (1993), Charles Taylor (1993), and Robert Putnam (1993) elaborate and specify the expansive, associationist view of the factors that constitute civic life. Running through them, and serving as a nutshell representation of their argument, is a devastating critique of the citizen's penultimate act in weaker accounts of democratic education: voting. Voting is seen on this view to be woefully partial—a minor, nonassociative act when set against the interactive, buzzing, and inescapably political practices that define strong democracy and strong democratic citizenship. Hess (1979) is quite bold on the matter, stating that a person is simply not a citizen if his or her only function is to vote. For such a person is electing the people who act like citizens. It is they who deliberate about public problems and try to work out policy:

> People who argue for their positions in a town meeting are acting like citizens. People who simply drop scraps of paper in a box or pull a lever are not acting like citizens; they are acting like consumers, picking between prepackaged political items. They had nothing to do with the items. (p. 10)

Voting is not mocked in this view, I should stress, but its limitations are not hidden either. Voting is an act of a "minimal self" (Lasch, 1984), producing a nanosecond of popular involvement in government followed almost without pause by a relapse into dormancy. It is citizenship, to be sure, but of the thinnest and weakest sort. Some argue that it is enough (James Madison, for example), but logically and morally it is not adequate for just and satisfying living in modern, culturally diverse societies. To educate for it, therefore, is to set a standard for citizenship that is lower than the times can tolerate.

II. CONSEQUENCES FOR SCHOOLS

The upshot of the associationist view of democracy for curriculum deliberation is an affirmation of the long-held vision of public schools as laboratories of democracy. Public schools are in key ways ideal for this project because the two characteristics that mark the associationist view are indigenous to them. First, numerous and varied interests are consciously shared. Unlike in a criminal gang or the amoral family, many ties potentially connect members of the school community, faculty and students alike. These bonds potentially include studies, the daily routine, local norms of civilized interaction, the school mascot, and the goal of "making it through." They also include cohorts, classrooms, courtship activities, play groups, cooperative study groups, athletic and other extracurricular clubs and events, counseling, health assistance, perhaps some school-policy decision-making, and the like. For teachers, the ties include curriculum planning across grades, courses, and departments, perhaps school governance deliberations, parent and paraprofessional contacts, relationships with noncertified staff, unions, professional associations, community networking, and myriad conversations with one another in coffee klatsches, meetings and so on.

Second, the interplay among groups—students, teachers, ethnic and racial groups, males and females, administrators, counselors, parents, nurses, police, guests, the media—potentially is quite vigorous. Public schools are the only public spaces encountered by virtually all children, and this makes them, if not ideal sites and certainly not the only ones, nonetheless *promising* sites for a genuine civic apprenticeship. Public schools are places where the bigger public congregates, where the array of little publics gathers and engages in common activity. At least this is the possibility public schools afford. The problems that arise in them (academic, interpersonal, within-group, and between-group) around which discussion is made necessary and becomes a supreme associative practice, are precisely the sorts of problems through which a diverse body of young people gradually can be initiated into democratic community, which is to say into increasingly critical levels of civic competence: into wondering and worrying together about how we ought to live together.

But citizenship education has suffered too much utopianism and too much lip service. Schools are *potentially* ideal sites: this is their *possibility*. Realizing this dream is quite another matter. Democracy has not seriously been undertaken as a curriculum project in this society. The democratic aim of public schooling has been tucked safely away in the rationale and mission statements of school-district curriculum guidelines. Beyond the establishment of free public schooling, surprisingly little has been done to educate children for democracy. Curriculum plans have been laid, to be sure, as the chapters in this volume attest. But they have remained always on the outskirts of educational practice.

Two traditions in particular stand in the way of strong citizenship education. One prevents congregations, the other fails to take advantage of them. Tracking, racial and ethnic tensions, sexism, and ability grouping, for example, keep the little publics from congregating. Now that access to school buildings has been pretty much achieved (ignore for the moment their differential quality), grouping practices *within buildings* turn schools into clusters of discrete neighborhoods. The little publics are kept separate. Gangs, recalling Dewey's meaning, are *nurtured*. While these practices have received considerable attention as threats to equity in education, they persist at all grade levels and their implications for the broader project of democratic education has been all but ignored.

Second, just as obstructive as segregationist practices are those that fail to capitalize on difference where it is found. Consider that student bodies rich in ethnic, gender, racial, class, and school achievement differences are increasingly the norm in American public schools, and that this diversity is increasingly found within classrooms, the first tradition not withstanding. Yet, curriculum planning that takes seriously this heterogeneity is not common. The mere provision of playgrounds, lunchrooms, gymnasiums, heterogeneous classrooms, and extracurricular activities falls short of the associationist vision of commonality *where within and among these settings problems of common living are identified and mutual deliberation and problem-solving activity is undertaken as a routine practice of school life.* Ironically, conflict resolution, "tolerating diversity," and even "multicultural education," often function as discourses of avoidance, encouraging school people mistakenly to act against conflict, muffling or preventing it or rushing to put it out when it flames up, rather than seizing upon it to nurture diversity while working out the practices of democratic living. They are not at odds.

III. CURRICULUM DEVELOPMENT

Such concerns are concentrated in the social studies field (Parker, 1991; Saxe, 1992). Social studies broke with academic disciplines at the turn of the century on the belief that history and the social sciences should not be learned for their own sake (even if that was possible) but used, or in today's terms *situated*. Further, their use should be in artful combination (*integrated*), and the target of their use should be human betterment and figuring out what human betterment means. But reforms came slowly. Harold Rugg (chapter 2, this volume) complained in 1921 that progressive administrators and teachers were "impatient with the further perpetuation of non-essential material in our public school courses." The culprits, he charged, were "college professors of history, geography, political science, economics, and established teachers in our larger high schools" who were working through committees of the American Historical Association, the American Political Science Association, and the American Sociological Society. These groups had dominated social studies reform for the thirty years before Rugg set out these sentiments, and they had failed to respond to the sea change that Dewey and Lippmann and countless others, including Mark Twain, Charles Peirce, William James, Carter Woodson, and George Herbert Mead, were endeavoring to grapple with: modernity.

On Rugg's view, essential subject matter entails three things: history brought to bear on important current problems, generalizations concerning social institutions, and knowledge of diverse cultures. This was hardly the muddleheaded fluff that latter-day critics (e.g., Rickover, 1959; Ravitch, 1985) liked to hang on the social studies mantle. A sample of the problems Rugg had in mind will illustrate:

1. Crucial matters of land; the history and critique of land policies.
2. Problems of the market economy and its historical development.
3. The history of labor problems; movements for the increase of cooperation between capital and labor.
4. How the press developed its influence at various times in our growth.
5. The history of experiments in government so organized as to give a critique of the relative fitness of various forms of government.

In addition to these three objects of a reconstructed social studies curriculum, Rugg saw "training children in the process of testing evidence" as the centerpiece. Here we come to the intentional cross-fertilization of challenging intellectual processes with challenging academic content that marks a thoughtful school curriculum at any grade level, distinguishing it from the lists of topics that dominate high school curricula and the lists of skills that grip elementary education. The study of problems, institutions, and cultures, on Rugg's view, could be accomplished in and through an intellectually lively and rigorous process of problem clarification and problem solving. The apprenticeship Rugg had in mind thus included simultaneously an initiation into social understandings and habits of reasoning.

This comingling of academic content and higher-order thinking is critically important in precollegiate education. It has become too clear over the decades that in elementary and secondary schooling, perhaps unlike in advanced levels of study, having their noses rubbed in content does not automatically engage students in reasoning with and about it, not even in learning it in some minimal way. Deliberate, planful attention is needed to both reasoning and content worth reasoning about, the result being what Resnick and Klopfer (1989) call the "thinking curriculum." While Rugg's work proves this is not a new idea, recent work in cognitive psychology has clarified it.

A thinking curriculum is one in which declarative and procedural knowledge are taught as one thing, not two. They are *conceived* as one. Higher-order forms of thinking (e.g., argument analysis, manipulation of data, dialogical reasoning) are designed into lessons, thereby converting them into higher-order tasks geared to the production of higher-order understandings. For example, students gather and interpret numerous sets of data and diverse viewpoints in the course of grappling with a public controversy. In this way, students need not wait to use their heads until the facts have been "covered"; rather, gathering the facts, deciding which of them to gather, interpreting and analyzing them, and putting them to work on something that needs doing all are components of a meaningful and complex task. In Hunt and Metcalf's famous phrase, "the content of learning may be regarded as the data of acts of reflective thought. . . . In a very real sense, knowledge does not exist before learning begins" (chapter 5, this volume).[2]

This reconceptualization of curriculum-making counters the common instructional method of laying in a thick foundation of background information *before* inviting learners to reason. Rarely do students typically get around to thinking about information because the pressure and desire to cover yet more information is so great. Students get loads of background but experience no foreground, no laboratory in which the background *becomes* background. The point here is straightforward: A curriculum of deliberation and problem-solving invites a different sort of intellectual and civic life than a curriculum of lists. In a thinking curriculum, knowledge therefore is regarded as the *culmination* of higher-order thinking, not, as Bloom (1956) got educators wrongly in the habit of thinking, the first measly step.

Not all democratic education projects since Rugg's have been concerned to locate the cultivation of reasoning processes in academic learning. A good number have sought to shape the reasoning itself, making it the subject matter and leaving content to others or to another time. The propaganda-resistance movement just before the Second World War, for example, wanted to teach students techniques for detecting attempts to alter their opinions on controversial issues (chapter 3). Teaching and learning these critical thinking techniques was to be added to the routine school curriculum. Even Kohlberg's moral reasoning work (chapter 10), aimed at developing students' sense of fairness by bringing them to intimate dialogue on matters of common living, was not embedded in the school curriculum but added on in the form of the "just community."

Whether embedded or freestanding, higher-order thinking has been considered a basic building block of democratic education throughout the century. The rationale, as Dewey saw, is a blend of the pedagogical and the political. The Right traditionally has viewed democracy as a set of institutions already achieved; the Left considers it a project—Lincoln called it a "proposition." On this view, democracy is more aspiration or path than accomplishment. The Right wants the Founders' truths, their answers to the great questions of common living, to be grasped by students and then applied. The Left wants the Founders' reasoning on these questions to be examined and their answers evaluated. It wants students to engage—to *experience*—the questions themselves. Allan Griffin (chapter 4) honed this idea in the 1940s, arguing that democracy depends upon the "development of people who are capable of steadily modifying their beliefs in terms of their adequacy for explaining a steadily wider range of experience. . . ." This in turn depends upon the diversity Dewey spoke of, without which this broadening of experience cannot obtain (television's evening news not withstanding), and upon common interests, without which diverse publics have no impetus for congregating. Griffin included but pushed beyond these categories, stressing the needed intellectual training. His history curriculum centered on two points: "(1) improving and refining the reflective capacities of our population, and (2) breaking through the hard shell of traditional sanctity which encrusts many deeply rooted and emotionally charged beliefs."

In short, the Right emphasizes the already-constructed understandings that compose the democratic ideal; the Left emphasizes humans' shell-breaking deliberative capacity that might generate these understandings anew, or better ones.[3]

Deliberation-oriented democratic educators appear in roughly three forms. The first emphasizes the rational negotiation of private interests. On this view, citizens need to be critically minded participants in democratic procedures, especially electoral politics, and wary watchdogs of duly elected representatives. The second wants more: a vigorous participatory democracy that is strong in the associationist sense described above. Here the main objective is to revitalize civic life and fashion a commonwealth for modern times, and the chief method is grappling with one another's views on the public controversies that arise naturally in civic life. The third form is more ambitious still. These educators want schools to be sites of social transformation where students are encouraged to uncover cultural and political taken-for-granteds and to contest social forces that, left alone, perpetuate entrenched patterns of domination, thus preventing democratic living. These educators are leery of any form of democratic education that dismisses or ignores underlying power relations.

Of course, democratic educators of all stripes want schools that foster thoughtful citizens, but the Right stresses socialization and the Left critique. There is not, despite appearances, a tremendous gap between the two positions. More like opposite sides of a coin, or a paradox, both socialization and critique are essential to education for democracy. Attempts to devise a theory that overcomes the natural tension between the two are futile and unnecessary.

IV. PLAN OF THE VOLUME

This book enters this messy terrain with an historical and critical interest. In the first three of its four parts are seminal works from the twentieth century on the problem of educating democrats. These parts are arranged chronologically, each surveying in turn the early, middle, and recent years of the century. The chapters in each part are a disparate lot, displaying a remarkable diversity of interests, conceptions, and intents. New works prepared for this volume compose the fourth part. Each reflects on the work to date, taking stock, providing criticism, and proposing new directions.

Questions to guide readers' discussion of these chapters are given at the beginning of each part and are the same throughout. I hope they encourage critical reading, for the value of these works to those of us laboring in the curriculum field today is their function as springboards and stimulants. I do not apologize for this utilitarian approach. Our creative, imaginative thinking together today about the purposes of schooling and its relationship to the kind of society we want to construct—this is what matters to me.

This is why these earlier works are important. Accordingly, the *Questions for Discussion* invite readers to focus their attention first on the authors' sense of problem: To which problems are they choosing to attend? Concurrently, which problems are being neglected or denied? Second, readers are directed to the historical contexts of these authors' work. This is by way of encouraging readers to look into the reasons why a particular construction of a problem came to be, who believed it to be a problem, and why. For this reason, A United States or world history text or other historical references would be helpful companions to this volume. The third question goes to the authors' conceptions of democracy and, particularly, to the ways in which they articulate the twin concerns of diversity and mutuality (if they do this at all). The fourth question encourages readers to flip back and forth through the book, comparing the chapters. A data-retrieval chart, such as the one shown in figure I, could be useful for comparing the chapters based on these questions and others that readers may generate.

Works in the first part, "Early Years," range from Rugg's problem-centered curriculum to Wayland Osborn's attempt to teach high school students to resist propaganda. Both works were deeply embedded in their times, of course. (All of the chapters in this volume are "period pieces"; they could not be otherwise.) Rugg's chapter was a letter written in response to a speech given before the Secondary Education Club of New York City; Osborn's research built on the considerable work done by educators working in the highly volatile 1930s to make young people less susceptible to unscrupulous influences on their opinions. The era's brightest intellectual beacons arguably were two texts by John Dewey: *How We Think* and *Democracy and Education*. A key chapter from the latter is featured here, for it clearly lays out the associationist conception of democracy. But the former is equally pertinent to the education of democrats because it helped launch the teaching of thinking as a durable and central theme of democratic education. A selection of Allan Griffin's elegant work closes this section, adding an exclamation mark to the sentence Dewey was writing thirty years before and bringing his work into the heart of the social studies field.

Works in the second part, "Middle Years," were drawn more or less from the New Social Studies efforts of the 1950s and 1960s.

FIGURE I.
Comparing the chapters using the *Questions for Discussion*

	Question 1 Problems	Question 2 History	Question 3 Democracy and Diversity	Question 4 Comparisons
1. Dewey				
2. Rugg				
3. Osborn				
4. Griffin				
5. Hunt and Metcalf				
6. Engle				
7. Taba and Elzey				
8. Oliver and Shaver				
9. Apple				
10. Kohlberg				
11. Newmann et al.				
12. Gagnon				
13. Mathews				
14. Bernard-Powers				
15. Whitson and Stanley				
16. Angell and Hahn				

At this point, the project to educate for democracy took two distinctly different forms: issue-centered education and inquiry. The first, found here in Hunt and Metcalf's, Engle's, and Oliver and Shaver's work, was akin to Rugg's: Educate the population to reason capably, to embrace individual freedom and human dignity, and to tackle genuine public problems loaded with value conflict. The inquiry approach was different in assumptions and intent. Represented here only in Taba's work, it was rather more scientized and aimed less at the moral imperatives of schooling than at academic disciplines themselves. This work nonetheless concerned itself with the cultivation of reflective minds and, hence, if indirectly, minds suited to the demands of popular sovereignty. What this approach ignored, however, was the democratic training that association-rich schools might afford. It generally held itself above the fray.

Works collected in the third part, "Recent Years," sample the 1970s and 1980s. Principles of psychology, philosophy, and sociology were joined in programs as different as neo-Marxist emancipatory pedagogy (chapter 9) and Kohlberg's moral development project (chapter 10). Newmann and his colleagues delineated an interdisciplinary high school curriculum designed to teach students to exert influence in public affairs, arguing that without this competence "the inalienable right to do so. . . . cannot be exercised" (chapter 11). Finally, historian Gagnon brings us full circle, back to Rugg's response to the American Historical Association, by arguing that historical study is sufficient (chapter 12). At century's end, education for democracy is a noncollapsible array of visions and methods, some weak and some strong, some related directly to education for democracy, others arguably so indirect as to fall barely within the project.

The new chapters composing the fourth section of the volume reflect on these works. Each problematizes key features of the project. David Mathews asks civic educators to redefine *politics* and *citizenship* in such a way that deliberation—talking with one another about problems held in common—becomes the centerpiece of a curriculum for democracy. Jane Bernard-Powers asks why public life generally has excluded women, almost by definition. James Anthony Whitson and William Stanley "re-mind" readers that a discredited, dualistic conception of mind still governs progressive education discourse. Finally, Ann Angell and Carole Hahn take us from North America to Denmark, Japan, and England for cross-cultural comparisons of democratic education.

Taken as a whole, the collection stands as an inquiry on what remains today an open question: How should young people be educated for democratic living in culturally diverse societies? Assuming there can be no democracy without democrats, and that democrats are made, not born, this is a sobering question. An education has not yet been attempted in this century, not on a broad scale anyway, that does not take the weaker of the two roads to democracy and, in tandem, that does not marginalize diversity.

Education for democracy is a program waiting to happen. The common school movement of the nineteenth century was democratic in its impulse and aspiration. It brought many of the little publics together. Beyond this foundation laid early in the century, however, educators have not ventured, at least not in ways that made an institutional difference. Mass and common schooling was a fundamental move, to be sure, but a more ambitious program awaits invention. We could call it by the clumsy name, "Civics, Now That We Have Public Education," thereby emphasizing that the project's point is to take advantage of the diverse congregation afforded by the common-school movement, and to use these associations as the ground of democratic education. It is an idea long overdue if *e pluribus unum* and *popular sovereignty,* which is to say democratic political community *with* cultural pluralism, are to have meaning in this and other lands in the twenty-first century.

NOTES

1.   In *The School and Society* (University of Chicago Press, 1899/1956), Dewey clarified the need for a new education to match the imperatives of modernity. He wrote of an "intellectual revolution" in which learning was no longer guarded by priests. Instead, "learning has been put into circulation . . . it has been liquefied. It is actively moving in all the currents of society itself" (p. 24–25).

2.   Just as thinking cannot wait for the facts to be "covered," neither can democratic politics wait until formal education has ended. "Without recourse to democratic politics," Gutmann argues, "there would be no acceptable means to educate adults and no acceptable means of educating children outside the family" (1987, p. 287).

3.   Recently, the Right has set up deliberation-oriented social studies educators as the *cause* of students' poor grasp of democratic knowledge (e.g., Cheney, 1987). This is not an entirely silly charge. Perhaps some understandings are best learned by memorizing them and then contemplating them until some sense is made of them. Still, it is typical of the Right's remedy for ignorance.

REFERENCES

Banfield, E. C. (1958). *The moral basis of a backward society.* New York: Free Press.

Barber, B. R. (1984). *Strong democracy.* Berkeley: University of California Press.

————. (1992). *An aristocracy for everyone.* New York: Ballantine.

Bellah, R. N., Madsen, R., Sullivan, W. M., Swidler, A., & Tipton, S. M. (1991). *The good society.* New York: Knopf.

————. (1985). *Habits of the heart.* Berkeley: University of California Press.

Bloom, B. (1956). *Taxonomy of educational objectives: Handbook I: The cognitive domain.* New York: David McKay.

Boyte, H. C. (1989). *Commonwealth: A return to citizen politics.* New York: Free Press.

Cheney, L. V. (1987). *American memory.* Washington, D.C.: National Endowment for the Humanities.

Dewey, J. (1916/1985). *Democracy and education: The middle works of John Dewey, 1899–1924.* Vol. 9. J. A. Boydston (Ed.). Carbondale: Southern Illinois University Press.

DuBois, W. E. B. (1903/1982). *The souls of black folk.* New York: New American Library.

Freire, P. (1985). *The politics of education.* New York: Bergin and Garvey.

Gould, C. C. (1988). *Rethinking democracy.* Cambridge: Cambridge University Press.

Gutmann, A. (1987). *Democratic education.* Princeton: Princeton University Press.

Hess, K. (1979). *Community technology.* New York: Harper and Row.

Lasch, C. (1984). *The minimal self.* New York: W. W. Norton.

Lippmann, W. (1937). *The good society.* Boston: Little, Brown.

Morrison, T. (1992). *Playing in the dark: Whiteness and the literary imagination.* Cambridge: Harvard University Press.

Mouffe, C. (1992). Democratic politics today. In C. Mouffe (Ed.), *Dimensions of Radical Democracy* (pp. 1–14). London: Verso.

Parker, W. C. (1991). *Renewing the social studies curriculum.* Alexandria, VA: Association for Supervision and Curriculum Development.

Phillips, A. (1993). *Democracy and difference.* University Park: Pennsylvania State University Press.

Putman, R. D. (1993). *Making democracy work.* Princeton: Princeton University Press.

Ravitch, D. (1985). *The schools we deserve.* New York: Basic.

Resnick, L. B., & Klopfer, L. E. (Eds.). (1989). *Toward the thinking curriculum: Current cognitive research.* 1989 A. S. C. D. Yearbook. Alexandria, VA: Association for Supervision and Curriculum Development.

Rickover, H. G. (1959). *Education and freedom.* New York: E. P. Dutton.

Saxe, D. W. (1992). Framing a theory for social studies foundations. *Review of Educational Research, 62*(3): 259–277.

Taylor, C. (1993). *Multiculturalism and the "politics of recognition."* Princeton: Princeton University Press.

de Toqueville, A. (1848/1969). *Democracy in America.* G. Lawrence (Trans.). J. P. Mayer (Ed.). Garden City, NY: Anchor.

West, C. (1993). The new cultural politics of difference. In C. McCarthy & W. Crichlow (Eds.), *Race identity and representation in education* (pp. 11–23). New York: Routledge.

PART 1

Early Years
1916–1942

. . . in which John Dewey clarified the meaning of democracy,
Harold Rugg attempted to turn the school curriculum toward
practical public problems, Wayland Osborn showed how difficult it
was to immunize students against propaganda, and Alan Griffin
wrote on the proper teaching of history in democracies.

QUESTIONS FOR DISCUSSION

1. What problems are emphasized? Neglected?
2. What was happening in North America and the world that
   might have shaped how these problems were articulated?
3. How is democracy defined? How are diversity and mutuality
   (difference and unity) treated?
4. What are similarities and differences across the chapters?

CHAPTER 1

The Democratic Conception In Education

John Dewey
1916

For the most part, save incidentally, we have hitherto been concerned with education as it may exist in any social group. We have now to make explicit the differences in the spirit, material, and method of education as it operates in different types of community life. To say that education is a social function, securing direction and development in the immature through their participation in the life of the group to which they belong, is to say in effect that education will vary with the quality of life which prevails in a group. Particularly is it true that a society which not only changes but which has the ideal of such change as will improve it, will have different standards and methods of education from one which aims simply at the perpetuation of its own customs. To make the general ideas set forth applicable to our own educational practice, it is, therefore, necessary to come to closer quarters with the nature of present social life.

1. THE IMPLICATIONS OF HUMAN ASSOCIATION

Society is one word, but many things. Men associate together in all kinds of ways and for all kinds of purposes. One man is concerned in

From *Democracy and Education: John Dewey, The Middle Works, 1899–1924*, vol. 9: 1916, edited by Jo Ann Boydston. Copyright © 1980 by Southern Illinois University Press. Reprinted by permission of the publisher.

a multitude of diverse groups, in which his associates may be quite different. It often seems as if they had nothing in common except that they are modes of associated life. Within every larger social organization there are numerous minor groups: not only political subdivisions, but industrial, scientific, religious associations. There are political parties with differing aims, social sets, cliques, gangs, corporations, partnerships, groups bound closely together by ties of blood, and so in endless variety. In many modern states, and in some ancient, there is great diversity of populations, of varying languages, religions, moral codes, and traditions. From this standpoint, many a minor political unit, one of our large cities, for example, is a congeries of loosely associated societies, rather than an inclusive and permeating community of action and thought.

The terms society, community, are thus ambiguous. They have both a eulogistic or normative sense, and a descriptive sense; a meaning *de jure* and a meaning *de facto*. In social philosophy, the former connotation is almost always uppermost. Society is conceived as one by its very nature. The qualities which accompany this unity, praiseworthy community of purpose and welfare, loyalty to public ends, mutuality of sympathy, are emphasized. But when we look at the facts which the term *denotes* instead of confining our attention to its intrinsic *connotation*, we find not unity, but a plurality of societies, good and bad. Men banded together in a criminal conspiracy, business aggregations that prey upon the public while serving it, political machines held together by the interest of plunder, are included. If it is said that such organizations are not societies because they do not meet the ideal requirements of the notion of society, the answer, in part, is that the conception of society is then made so "ideal" as to be of no use, having no reference to facts; and in part, that each of these organizations, no matter how opposed to the interests of other groups, has something of the praiseworthy qualities of "Society" which hold it together. There is honor among thieves, and a band of robbers has a common interest as respects its members. Gangs are marked by fraternal feeling, and narrow cliques by intense loyalty to their own codes. Family life may be marked by exclusiveness, suspicion, and jealousy as to those without, and yet be a model of amity and mutual aid within. Any education given by a group tends to socialize its members, but the quality and value of the socialization depends upon the habits and aims of the group.

Hence, once more, the need of a measure for the worth of any given mode of social life. In seeking this measure, we have to avoid two extremes. We cannot set up, out of our heads, something we regard as an ideal society. We must base our conception upon societies which actually exist, in order to have any assurance that our ideal is a practicable one. But, as we have just seen, the ideal cannot simply repeat the traits which are actually found. The problem is to extract the desirable traits of forms community life which actually exist, and employ them to criticize undesirable features and suggest improvement. Now in any social group whatever, even in a gang of thieves, we find some interest held in common, and we find a certain amount of interaction and cooperative intercourse with other groups. From these two traits we derive our standard. How numerous and varied are the interests which are consciously shared? How full and free is the interplay with other forms of association? If we apply these considerations to, say, a criminal band, we find that the ties which consciously hold the members together are few in number, reducible almost to a common interest in plunder; and that they are of such a nature as to isolate the group from other groups with respect to give and take of the values of life. Hence, the education such a society gives is partial and distorted. If we take, on the other hand, the kind of family life which illustrates the standard, we find that there are material, intellectual, aesthetic interests in which all participate and that the progress of one member has worth for the experience of other members—it is really communicable—and that the family is not an isolated whole, but enters intimately into relationships with business groups, with schools, with all the agencies of culture, as well as with other similar groups, and that it plays a due part in the political organization and in return receives support from it. In short, there are many interests consciously communicated and shared; and there are varied and free points of contact with other modes of association.

I. Let us apply the first element in this criterion to a despotically governed state. It is not true there is no common interest in such an organization between governed and governors. The authorities in command must make some appeal to the native activities of the subjects, must call some of their powers into play. Talleyrand said that a government could do everything with bayonets except sit on them. This cynical declaration is at least a recognition that the bond of union is not merely one of coercive force. It may be said, however, that the activities appealed to are themselves unworthy and degrading—that such a government calls into functioning activity simply capacity for fear. In a way, this statement is true. But it overlooks the fact that fear need not be an undesirable factor in experience. Caution, circumspection, prudence, desire to foresee future events so as to avert what is harmful, these desirable traits are as much a product of calling the impulse of fear into play as is cowardice and abject submission. The real difficulty is that the appeal to fear is *isolated*. In evoking dread and hope of specific tangible reward—say comfort and ease—many other capacities are left untouched. Or rather, they are affected, but in such a way as to pervert them. Instead of operating on their own account they are reduced to mere servants of attaining pleasure and avoiding pain.

This is equivalent to saying that there is no extensive number of common interests; there is no free play back and forth among the members of the social group. Stimulation and response are exceedingly one-sided. In order to have a large number of values in common, all the members of the group must have an equable opportunity to receive and to take from others. There must be a large variety of shared undertakings and experiences. Otherwise, the influences which educate some into masters, educate others into slaves. And the experience of each party loses in meaning, when the free interchange of varying modes of life-experience is arrested. A separation into a privileged and a subject-class prevents social endosmosis. The evils thereby affecting the superior class are less material and less perceptible, but equally real. Their culture tends to be sterile, to be turned back to feed on itself; their art becomes a showy display and artificial; their wealth luxurious; their knowledge over-specialized; their manners fastidious rather than humane.

Lack of the free and equitable intercourse which springs from a variety of shared interests makes intellectual stimulation unbalanced. Diversity of stimulation means novelty, and novelty means challenge to thought. The more activity is restricted to a few definite lines—as it is when there are rigid class lines preventing adequate interplay of experiences—the more action tends to become routine on the part of the class at a disadvantage, and capricious, aimless, and explosive on the part of the class having the materially fortunate position. Plato defined a slave as one who accepts from another the purposes which control his conduct. This condition obtains even where there is no slavery in the legal sense. It is found wherever men are engaged in activity which is socially serviceable, but whose service they do not understand and have no personal interest in. Much is said about scientific management of work. It is a narrow view which restricts the science which secures efficiency of operation to movements of the muscles. The chief opportunity for science is the discovery of the relations of a man to his work—including his relations to others who take part—which will enlist his intelligent interest in what he is doing. Efficiency in production often demands division of labor. But it is reduced to a mechanical routine unless workers see the technical, intellectual, and social relationships involved in what they do, and engage in their work because of the motivation furnished by such perceptions. The tendency to reduce such things as efficiency of activity and scientific management to purely technical externals is evidence of the one-sided stimulation of thought given to those in control of industry—those who supply its aims. Because of their lack of all-round and well-balanced social interest, there is not sufficient stimulus for attention to the human factors and relationships in industry. Intelligence is narrowed to the factors concerned with technical production and marketing of goods. No doubt, a very acute and intense intelligence in these narrow lines can be developed, but the failure to take into account the significant social factors means none the less an absence of mind, and a corresponding distortion of emotional life.

II. This illustration (whose point is to be extended to all associations lacking reciprocity of interest) brings us to our second point. The isolation and exclusiveness of a gang or clique brings its antisocial spirit into relief. But this same spirit is found wherever one group has interests "of its own" which shut it out from full interaction with other groups, so that its prevailing purpose is the protection of what it has got, instead of reorganization and progress through wider relationships. It marks nations in their isolation from one another; families which seclude their domestic concerns as if they had no connection with a larger life; schools when separated from the interest of home and community; the divisions of rich and poor; learned and unlearned. The essential point is that isolation makes for rigidity and formal institutionalizing of life, for static and selfish ideals within the group. That savage tribes regard aliens and enemies as synonymous is not accidental. It springs from the fact that they have identified their experience with rigid adherence to their past customs. On such a basis it is wholly logical to fear intercourse with others, for such contact might dissolve custom. It would certainly occasion reconstruction. It is a commonplace that an alert and expanding mental life depends upon an enlarging range of contact with the physical environment. But the principle applies even more significantly to the field where we are apt to ignore it—the sphere of social contacts.

Every expansive era in the history of mankind has coincided with the operation of factors which have tended to eliminate distance between peoples and classes previously hemmed off from one another. Even the alleged benefits of war, so far as more than alleged, spring from the fact that conflict of peoples at least enforces intercourse between them and thus accidentally enables them to learn from one another, and thereby to expand their horizons. Travel, economic and commercial tendencies, have at present gone far to break down external barriers; to bring peoples and classes into closer and more perceptible connection with one another. It remains for the most part to secure the intellectual and emotional significance of this physical annihilation of space.

2. THE DEMOCRATIC IDEAL

The two elements in our criterion both point to democracy. The first signifies not only more numerous and more varied points of shared common interest, but greater reliance upon the recognition of mutual interests as a factor in social control. The second means not only freer interaction between social groups (once isolated so far as intention could keep up a separation) but change in social habit—its continuous readjustment through meeting the new situations produced by varied intercourse. And these two traits are precisely what characterize the democratically constituted society.

Upon the educational side, we note first that the realization of a form of social life in which interests are mutually interpenetrating, and where progress, or readjustment, is an important consideration, makes a democratic community more interested than other communities have cause to be in deliberate and systematic education. The devotion of democracy to education is a familiar fact. The superficial explanation is that a government resting upon popular suffrage cannot be successful unless those who elect and who obey their governors are educated. Since a democratic society repudiates the principle of external authority, it must find a substitute in voluntary disposition and interest; these can be created only by education. But there is a deeper explanation. A democracy is more than a form of government; it is primarily a mode of associated living, of conjoint communicated experience. The extension in space of the number of individuals who participate in an interest so that each has to refer his own action to that of others, and to consider the action of others to give point and direction to his own, is equivalent to the breaking down of those barriers of class, race, and national territory which kept men from perceiving the full import of their activity. These more numerous and more varied points of contact denote a greater diversity of stimuli to which an individual has to respond; they consequently put a premium on variation in his action. They secure a liberation of powers which remain suppressed as long as the incitations to action are partial, as they must be in a group which in its exclusiveness shuts out many interests.

The widening of the area of shared concerns, and the liberation of a greater diversity of personal capacities which characterize a democracy, are not of course the product of deliberation and conscious effort. On the contrary, they were caused by the development of modes of manufacture and commerce, travel, migration, and intercommunication which flowed from the command of science over natural energy. But after greater individualization on one hand, and a broader community of interest on the other have come into existence, it is a matter of deliberate effort to sustain and extend them. Obviously a society to which stratification into separate classes would be fatal, must see to it that intellectual opportunities are accessible to all on equable and easy terms. A society marked off into classes need be specially attentive only to the education of its ruling elements. A society which is mobile, which is full of channels for the distribution of a change occurring anywhere, must see to it that its members are educated to personal initiative and adaptability. Otherwise, they will be overwhelmed by the changes in which they are caught and whose significance or connections they do not perceive. The result will be a confusion in which a few will appropriate to themselves the results of the blind and externally directed activities of others.

3. THE PLATONIC EDUCATIONAL PHILOSOPHY

In the remaining portions of this chapter, we shall consider the educational theories which have been evolved in three epochs when the social import of education was especially conspicuous. The first one to be considered is that of Plato. No one could better express than did he the fact that a society is stably organized when each individual is doing that for which he has aptitude by nature in such a way as to be useful to others (or to contribute to the whole to which he belongs); and that it is the business of education to discover these aptitudes and progressively to train them for social use. Much which has been said so far is borrowed from what Plato first consciously taught the world. But conditions which he could not intellectually control led him to restrict these ideas in their application. He never got any conception of the indefinite plurality of activities which may characterize an individual and a social group, and consequently limited his view to a limited number of *classes* of capacities and social arrangements.

Plato's starting point is that the organization of society depends ultimately upon knowledge of the end of existence. If we do not know its end, we shall be at the mercy of accident and caprice. Unless we know the end, the good, we shall have no criterion for rationally deciding what the possibilities are which should be promoted, nor how social arrangements are to be ordered. We shall have no conception of the proper limits and distribution of activities—what he called justice—as a trait of both individual and social organization. But how is the knowledge of the final and permanent good to be achieved? In dealing with this question we come upon the seemingly insuperable obstacle that such knowledge is not possible save in a just and harmonious social order. Everywhere else the mind is distracted and misled by false valuations and false perspectives. A disorganized and factional society sets up a number of different models and standards. Under such conditions it is impossible for the individual to attain consistency of mind. Only a complete whole is fully self-consistent. A society which rests upon the supremacy of some factor over another irrespective of its rational or proportionate claims, inevitably leads thought astray. It puts a premium on certain things and slurs over others, and creates a mind whose seeming unity is forced and distorted. Education proceeds ultimately from the patterns furnished by institutions, customs, and laws. Only in a just state will these be such as to give the right education; and only those who have rightly trained minds will be able to recognize the end, and ordering principle of things. We seem to be caught in a hopeless circle. However, Plato suggested a way out. A few men, philosophers or lovers of wisdom—or truth—may by study learn at least in outline the proper patterns of true existence. If a powerful ruler should form a state after these patterns, then its regulations could be preserved. An education could be given which would sift individuals, discovering what they were good for, and supplying a method of assigning each to the work in life for which his nature fits him. Each doing his own part, and never transgressing, the order and unity of the whole would be maintained.

It would be impossible to find in any scheme of philosophic thought a more adequate recognition on one hand of the educational significance of social arrangements and, on the other, of the dependence of those arrangements upon the means used to educate the young. It would be impossible to find a deeper sense of the function of education in discovering and developing personal capacities, and training them so that they would connect with the activities of others. Yet the society in which the theory was propounded was so undemocratic that Plato could not work out a solution for the problem whose terms he clearly saw.

While he affirmed with emphasis that the place of the individual in society should not be determined by birth or wealth or any conventional status, but by his own nature as discovered in the process of education, he had no perception of the uniqueness of individuals. For him they fall by nature into classes, and into a very small number of classes at that. Consequently the testing and sifting function of education only shows to which one of three classes an individual belongs. There being no recognition that each individual constitutes his own class, there could be no recognition of the infinite diversity of active tendencies and combinations of tendencies of which an individual is capable. There were only three types of faculties or powers in the individual's constitution. Hence education would soon reach a static limit in each class, for only diversity makes change and progress.

In some individuals, appetites naturally dominate; they are assigned to the laboring and trading class, which expresses and supplies human wants. Others reveal, upon education, that over and above appetites, they have a generous, outgoing, assertively courageous disposition. They become the citizen-subjects of the state; its defenders in war; its internal guardians in peace. But their limit is fixed by their lack of reason, which is a capacity to grasp the universal. Those who possess this are capable of the highest kind of education, and become in time the legislators of the state— for laws are the universals which control the particulars of experience. Thus it is not true that in intent, Plato subordinated the individual to the social whole. But it is true that lacking the perception of the uniqueness of every individual, his incommensurability with others, and consequently not recognizing that a society might change and yet be stable, his doctrine of limited powers and classes came in net effect to the idea of the subordination of individuality.

We cannot better Plato's conviction that an individual is happy and society well organized when each individual engages in those activities for which he has a natural equipment, nor his conviction that it is the primary office of education to discover this equipment to its possessor and train him for its effective use. But progress in knowledge has made us aware of the superficiality of Plato's lumping of individuals and their original powers into a few sharply marked-off classes; it has taught us that original capacities are indefinitely numerous and variable. It is but the other side of this fact to say that in the degree in which society has become democratic, social organization means utilization of the specific and variable qualities of individuals, not stratification by classes. Although his educational philosophy was revolutionary, it was none the less in bondage to static ideals. He thought that change or alteration was evidence of lawless flux; that true reality was unchangeable. Hence while he would radically change the existing state of society, his aim was to construct a state in which change would subsequently have no place. The final end of life is fixed; given a state framed with this end view, not even minor details are to be altered. Though they might not be inherently important, yet if permitted they would inure the minds of men to the idea of change, and hence be dissolving and anarchic. The breakdown of his philosophy is made apparent in the fact that he could not trust to gradual improvements in education to bring about a better society which should then improve education, and so on indefinitely. Correct education could not come into existence until an ideal state existed, and after that education would be devoted simply to its conservation. For the existence of this state he was obliged to trust to some happy accident by which philosophic wisdom should happen to coincide with possession of ruling power in the state.

4. THE "INDIVIDUALISTIC" IDEAL OF THE EIGHTEENTH CENTURY

In the eighteenth-century philosophy we find ourselves in a very different circle of ideas. "Nature" still means something antithetical to existing social organization; Plato exercised a great influence upon Rousseau. But the voice of nature now speaks for the diversity of individual talent and for the need of free development of individuality in all its variety. Education in accord with nature furnishes the goal and the method of instruction and discipline. Moreover, the native or original endowment was conceived, in extreme cases, as nonsocial or even as antisocial. Social arrangements were thought of as mere external expedients by which these nonsocial individuals might secure a greater amount of private happiness for themselves.

Nevertheless, these statements convey only an inadequate idea of the true significance of the movement. In reality its chief interest was in progress and in social progress. The seeming antisocial philosophy was a somewhat transparent mask for an impetus toward a wider and freer society—towards cosmopolitanism. The positive ideal was humanity. In membership in humanity, as distinct from a state, man's capacities would be liberated; while in existing political organizations his powers were hampered and distorted to meet the requirements and selfish interests of the rulers of the state. The doctrine of extreme individualism was but the counterpart, the obverse, of ideals of the indefinite perfectibility of man and of a social organization having a scope as wide as humanity. The emancipated individual was to become the organ and agent of a comprehensive and progressive society.

The heralds of this gospel were acutely conscious of the evils of the social estate in which they found themselves. They attributed these evils to the limitations imposed upon the free powers of man. Such limitation was both distorting and corrupting. Their impassioned devotion to emancipation of life from external restrictions which operated to the exclusive advantage of the class to whom a past feudal system consigned power, found intellectual formulation in a worship of nature. To give "nature" full swing was to replace an artificial, corrupt, and inequitable social order by a new and better kingdom of humanity. Unrestrained faith in Nature as both a model and a working power was strengthened by the advances of natural science. Inquiry freed from prejudice and artificial restraints of church and state had revealed that the world is a scene of law. The Newtonian solar system, which expressed the reign of natural law, was a scene of wonderful harmony, where every force balanced with every other. Natural law would accomplish the same result in human relations, if men would only get rid of the artificial man-imposed coercive restrictions.

Education in accord with nature was thought to be the first step in insuring this more social society. It was plainly seen that economic and political limitations were ultimately dependent upon limitations of thought and feeling. The first step in freeing men from external chains was to emancipate them from the internal chains of false beliefs and ideals. What was called social life, existing institutions, were too false and corrupt to be entrusted with this work. How could it be expected to undertake it when the undertaking meant its own destruction? "Nature" must then be the power to which the enterprise was to be left. Even the extreme sensationalistic theory of knowledge which was current derived itself from this conception. To insist that mind is originally passive and empty was one way of glorifying the possibilities of education. If the mind was a wax tablet to be written upon by objects, there were no limits to the possibility of education by means of the natural environment. And since the natural world of objects is a scene of harmonious "truth," this education would infallibly produce minds filled with the truth.

5. EDUCATION AS NATIONAL AND AS SOCIAL

As soon as the first enthusiasm for freedom waned, the weakness of the theory upon the constructive side became obvious. Merely to leave everything to nature was, after all, but to negate the very idea of education; it was to trust to the accidents of circumstance. Not only was some method required but also some positive organ, some administrative agency for carrying on the process of instruction. The "complete and harmonious development of all powers," having as its social counterpart an enlightened and progressive humanity, required definite organization for its realization. Private individuals here and there could proclaim the gospel; they could not execute the work. A Pestalozzi could try experiments and exhort philanthropically inclined persons having wealth and power to follow his example. But even Pestalozzi saw that any effective pursuit of the new educational ideal required the support of the state. The realization of the new education destined to produce a new society was, after all, dependent upon the activities of existing states. The movement for the democratic idea inevitably became a movement for publicly conducted and administered schools.

So far as Europe was concerned, the historic situation identified the movement for a state-supported education with the nationalistic movement in political life—a fact of incalculable significance for subsequent movements. Under the influence of German thought in particular, education became a civic function and the civic function was identified with the realization of the ideal of the national state. The "state" was substituted for humanity; cosmopolitanism gave way to nationalism. To form the citizen, not the "man," became the aim of education.[1] The historic situation to which reference is made is the after-effects of the Napoleonic conquests, especially in Germany. The German states felt (and subsequent events demonstrate the correctness of the belief) that systematic attention to education was the best means of recovering and maintaining their political integrity and power. Externally they were weak and divided. Under the leadership of Prussian statesmen they made this condition a stimulus to the development of an extensive and thoroughly grounded system of public education.

This change in practice necessarily brought about a change in theory. The individualistic theory receded into the background. The state furnished not only the instrumentalities of public education but also its goal. When the actual practice was such that the school system, from the elementary grades through the university faculties, supplied the patriotic citizen and soldier and the future state official and administrator and furnished the means for military, industrial, and political defense and expansion, it was impossible for theory not to emphasize the aim of social efficiency. And with the immense importance attached to the nationalistic state, surrounded by other competing and more or less hostile states, it was equally impossible to interpret social efficiency in terms of a vague cosmopolitan humanitarianism. Since the maintenance of a particular national sovereignty required subordination of individuals to the superior interests of the state both in military defense and in struggles for international supremacy in commerce, social efficiency was understood to imply a like subordination. The educational process was taken to be one of disciplinary training rather than of personal development. Since, however, the ideal of culture as complete development of personality persisted, educational philosophy attempted a reconciliation of the two ideas. The reconciliation took the form of the conception of the "organic" character of the state. The individual in his isolation is nothing; only in and through an absorption of the aims and meaning of organized institutions does he attain true personality. What appears to be his subordination to political authority and the demand for sacrifice of himself to the commands of his superiors is in reality but making his own the objective reason manifested in the state—the only way in which he can become truly rational. The notion of development which we have seen to be characteristic of institutional idealism (as in the Hegelian philosophy) was just such a deliberate effort to combine the two ideas of complete realization of personality and thoroughgoing "disciplinary" subordination to existing institutions.

The extent of the transformation of educational philosophy which occurred in Germany in the generation occupied by the struggle against Napoleon for national independence, may be gathered from Kant, who well expresses the earlier individual-cosmopolitan ideal. In his treatise on Pedagogics, consisting of lectures given in the later years of the eighteenth century, he defines education as the process by which man becomes man. Mankind begins its history submerged in nature—not as Man who is creature of reason, while nature furnishes only instinct and appetite. Nature offers simply the germs which education is to develop and perfect. The peculiarity of truly human life is that man has to create himself by his own voluntary efforts; he has to make himself a truly moral, rational, and free being. This creative effort is carried on by the educational activities of slow generations. Its acceleration depends upon men consciously striving to educate their successors not for the existing state of affairs but so as to make possible a future better humanity. But there is the great difficulty. Each generation is inclined to educate its young so as to get along in the present world instead of with a view to the proper end of education: the promotion of the best possible realization of humanity as humanity. Parents educate their children so that they may get on; princes educate their subjects as instruments of their own purposes.

Who, then, shall conduct education so that humanity may improve? We must depend upon the efforts of enlightened men in their private capacity. "All culture begins with private men and spreads outward from them. Simply through the efforts of persons of enlarged inclinations, who are capable of grasping the ideal of a future better condition, is the gradual approximation of human nature to its end possible. . . . Rulers are simply interested in such training as will make their subjects better tools for their own intentions." Even the subsidy by rulers of privately conducted schools must be carefully safeguarded. For the rulers' interest in welfare of their own nation instead of in what is best for humanity, will make them, if they give money for schools, wish to draw their plans. We have in this view an express statement of the points characteristic of the eighteenth-century individualistic cosmopolitanism. The full development of private personality is identified with the aims of humanity as a whole and with the idea of progress. In addition we have an explicit fear of the hampering influence of a state-conducted and state-regulated education upon the attainment of these ideas. But in less than two decades after this time, Kant's philosophic successors, Fichte and Hegel, elaborated the idea that the chief function of the state is educational; that in particular the regeneration of Germany is to be accomplished by an education carried on in the interests of the state, and that the private individual is of necessity an egoistic, irrational being, enslaved to his appetites and to circumstances unless he submits voluntarily to the educative discipline of state institutions and laws. In this spirit, Germany was the first country to undertake a public, universal, and compulsory system of education extending from the primary school through the university, and to submit to jealous state regulation and supervision all private educational enterprises.

Two results should stand out from this brief historical survey. The first is that such terms as the individual and the social conceptions of education are quite meaningless taken at large, or apart from their context. Plato had the ideal of an education which should equate individual realization and social coherency and stability. His situation forced his ideal into the notion of a society organized in stratified classes, losing the individual in the class. The eighteenth-century educational philosophy was highly individualistic in form, but this form was inspired by a noble and generous social ideal: that of a society organized to include humanity, and providing for the indefinite perfectibility of mankind. The idealistic philosophy of Germany in the early nineteenth century endeavored again to equate the ideals of a free and complete development of cultured personality with social discipline and political subordination. It made the national state an intermediary between the realization of private personality on one side and of humanity on the other. Consequently, it is equally possible to state its animating principle with equal truth either in the classic terms of "harmonious development of all the powers of personality" or in the more recent terminology of "social efficiency." All this reenforces the statement which opens this chapter: The conception of education as a social process and function has no definite meaning until we define the kind of society we have in mind.

These considerations pave the way for our second conclusion. One of the fundamental problems of education in and for a democratic society is set by the conflict of a nationalistic and a wider social aim. The earlier cosmopolitan and "humanitarian" conception suffered both from vagueness and from lack of definite organs of execution and agencies of administration. In Europe, in the Continental states particularly, the new idea of the importance of education for human welfare and progress was captured by national interests and harnessed to do a work whose social aim was definitely narrow and exclusive. The social aim of education and its national aim were identified, and the result was a marked obscuring of the meaning of a social aim.

This confusion corresponds to the existing situation of human intercourse. On the one hand, science, commerce, and art transcend national boundaries. They are largely international in quality and method. They involve interdependencies and cooperation among the peoples inhabiting different countries. At the same time, the idea of national sovereignty has never been as accentuated in politics as it is at the present time. Each nation lives in a state of suppressed hostility and incipient war with its neighbors. Each is supposed to be the supreme judge of its own interests, and it is assumed as matter of course that each has interests which are exclusively its own. To question this is to question the very idea of national sovereignty which is assumed to be basic to political practice and political science. This contradiction (for it is nothing less) between the wider sphere of associated and mutually helpful social life and the narrower sphere of exclusive and hence potentially hostile pursuits and purposes, exacts of educational theory a clearer conception of the meaning of "social" as a function and test of education than has yet been attained.

Is it possible for an educational system to be conducted by a national state and yet the full social ends of the educative process not be restricted, constrained, and corrupted? Internally, the question has to face the tendencies, due to present economic conditions, which split society into classes some of which are made merely tools for the higher culture of others. Externally, the question is concerned with the reconciliation of national loyalty, of patriotism, with superior devotion to the things which unite men in common ends, irrespective of national political boundaries. Neither phase of the problem can be worked out by merely negative means. It is not enough to see to it that education is not actively used as an instrument to make easier the exploitation of one class by another. School facilities must be secured of such amplitude and efficiency as will in fact and not simply in name discount the effects of economic inequalities, and secure to all the wards of the nation equality of equipment for their future careers. Accomplishment of this end demands not only adequate administrative provision of school facilities, and such supplementation of family resources as will enable youth to take advantage of them, but also such modification of traditional ideals of culture, traditional subjects of study and traditional methods of teaching and discipline as will retain all the youth under educational influences until they are equipped to be masters of their own economic and social careers. The ideal may seem remote of execution, but the democratic ideal of education is a farcical yet tragic delusion except as the ideal more and more dominates our public system of education.

The same principle has application on the side of the considerations which concern the relations of one nation to another. It is not enough to teach the horrors of war and to avoid everything which would stimulate international jealousy and animosity. The emphasis must be put upon whatever binds people together in cooperative human pursuits and results, apart from geographical limitations. The secondary and provisional character of national sovereignty in respect to the fuller, freer, and more fruitful association and intercourse of all human beings with one another must be instilled as a working disposition of mind. If these applications seem to be remote from a consideration of the philosophy of education, the impression shows that the meaning of the idea of education previously developed has not been adequately grasped. This conclusion is bound up with the very idea of education as a freeing of individual capacity in a progressive growth directed to social aims. Otherwise a democratic criterion of education can only be inconsistently applied.

SUMMARY

Since education is a social process, and there are many kinds of societies, a criterion for educational criticism and construction implies a *particular* social ideal. The two points selected by which to measure the worth of a form of social life are the extent in which the interests of a group are shared by all its members, and the fullness and freedom with which it interacts with other groups. An undesirable society, in other words, is one which internally and externally sets up barriers to free intercourse and communication of experience. A society which makes provision for participation in its good of all its members on equal terms and which secures flexible readjustment of its institutions through interaction of the different forms of associated life is in so far democratic. Such a society must have a type of education which gives individuals a personal interest in social relationships and control, and the habits of mind which secure social changes without introducing disorder.

Three typical historic philosophies of education were considered from this point of view. The Platonic was found to have an ideal formally quite similar to that stated, but which was compromised in its working out by making a class rather than an individual the social unit. The so-called individualism of the eighteenth-century enlightenment was found to involve the notion of a society as broad as humanity, of whose progress the individual was to be the organ. But it lacked any agency for securing the development of its ideal as was evidenced in its falling back upon Nature. The institutional idealistic philosophies of the nineteenth century supplies this lack by making the national state the agency, but in so doing narrowed the conception of the social aim to those who were members of the same political unit, and reintroduced the idea of the subordination of the individual to the institution.

NOTES

1.   There is a much neglected strain in Rousseau tending intellectually in this direction. He opposed the existing state of affairs on the ground that it formed *neither* the citizen nor the man. Under existing conditions, he preferred to try for the latter rather than for the former. But there are many sayings of his which point to the formation of the citizen as ideally the higher, and which indicate that his own endeavor, as embodied in the *Émile*, was simply the best makeshift the corruption of the times permitted him to sketch.

CHAPTER 2

Reconstructing the Curriculum: An Open Letter to Professor Henry Johnson Commenting on Committee Procedure As Illustrated by the Report of the Joint Committee on History and Education for Citizenship

Harold O. Rugg
1921

My dear Professor Johnson:
Your address to the Secondary Education Club,[1] which was not
debated because of the lateness of the hour, provides the occasion
for an open letter on current issues in the teaching of social
sciences. I am writing in the hope of initiating a thorough
discussion of needed change in the reorganizing and teaching of
the social studies in our elementary and secondary schools.

Two schools of thinking are developing with respect to the reorganization and teaching of the social studies—history, geography,
civics, economics and related subjects. The first is contributed to
largely by college professors of history, geography, political science,
economics, and by established teachers in our larger high schools;
the second by students of the school curriculum and miscellaneous

From *Historical Outlook*, 12 (May 1921), 184–189.

group of progressive school people, administrators and teachers. These latter are impatient with the further perpetuation of non-essential material in our public school courses, and desire to see the courses *completely* reconstructed. The first group has controlled for thirty years the reorganization of our courses. This has been done largely through committees of the American Historical Association, the American Political Science Association, the American Sociological Society and through national and regional bodies in the field of geography, etc. I personally believe that the wide-spread adoption of reconstructed courses can be effectively brought about only by representative committees of national prestige. But, to the present time, such committees have distinctly failed to bring about scientific and relatively permanent reconstruction of the school curriculum.

For example, a careful study of the reports of the committees of the American Historical Association, since the Committee of Ten in 1892, leads to the belief that thorough reconstruction of the historical curriculum will hardly come from this group. Some gains have been made in the elimination of non-essential political details, and through the greater emphasis upon the modern periods in history as opposed to the methodical, analytical treatment of ancient times. But the fact remains that the course of study still largely fails to acquaint children with the development of current institutions and problems. And that, of course, is the avowed purpose of public school instruction in history.

The second school of workers would set up an entirely different procedure in making over the social studies curriculum. They would ignore, at least in the initial stages of curriculum-making, the content of the existent course. They would start new, set up a thorough program of principles, of criteria for subject-mater. They would conduct investigations of social needs as to what ought to be taught. They would establish careful experimental studies of most effective methods of organizing instructional material. In short they would substitute scientific, objective methods for opinionated and empirical ones.

Need for complete reconstruction. There can be no doubt of the need for a *complete reconstruction* of the materials of our historical curriculum. Let me illustrate. Would we not agree that the history which is taught in public schools first should deal with important current problems; second, should give children constant practice in drawing important generalizations concerning their environment and how their institutions developed, and third, should acquaint them with the established modes of living. I have recently made a careful study of the extent to which our existent curriculum in history, geography and civics deals with certain vitally important problems of contemporary life. Four of the newest and most popular grammar grade U. S. histories have been canvassed from cover to cover to determine the extent to which each of a selected group of problems was treated. The aim was to find out whether the treatment of these problems was extensive enough that children could be expected to understand and develop an appreciation of problems of present interest. You will note that most of these problems are economic and industrial. The same conclusion follows, however, concerning the treatment of crucial social and of political matters.

I give next a list of the illustrative problems for which the books were analyzed.

1. Crucial matters of land; the history and critique of land policies; the importance of land questions in helping to explain the development of farm tenancy and the like.
2. Problems of the "market" and its historical development; railroad rates and rebates; public vs. private ownership, operation and control of railroads, terminal facilities, grain elevators, and the like.
3. The control and operation of "credit" facilities.
4. The history of labor problems; movements for the increase of co-operation between capital and labor; problems of wages, hours, living conditions.
5. The operation and control of "key" industries.
6. The development of centralization and concentration in industry and business.
7. How our distributing agencies grew—railroads, merchant marine, public utilities, agencies for communication, etc.
8. The cost of living—historical and current.
9. How the press developed its influence at various times in our growth.
10. The story of "how America developed agencies" for the formation of public opinion.

11. The history of experiments in government so organized as to give a critique of the relative fitness of various forms of government with which society has experimented to secure adequate expression of either popular opinion or most intelligent opinion.

The investigation supplies data for the conclusion that commonly used textbooks in history provide such a meager treatment of these crucial problems (many of them ignored altogether) that a grasp of these vital economic and industrial matters and of their historical backgrounds, *is totally impossible.*

As early as 1916 Professor Bagley and I published a report of a tabulation of the contents of 23 United States histories.[2] This report showed that American history always has been and still is predominately political and militaristic history. It showed too that a perceptibly heavier emphasis is laid upon facts of economic and industrial developments in the more recent books. However, five years after, we find such an inadequate treatment of vital current matters that it is little wonder that children who leave our schools at the end of the eighth or ninth grades are thoroughly unacquainted with, and have little or no appreciation of the outstanding economic, social and industrial "laws" and the great problems of contemporary social life. You can expect to see a vigorous and constructive attempt on the part of students of the curriculum ("education" men) to take an active part in the reconstruction of the social studies curriculum. That activity is going to move emphatically in the direction of putting into the curriculum a thoroughly new type of material. To accomplish this, this group of workers is convinced that a new method of making the curriculum must be employed. The title of this article and the above introduction points to the first great issue between the two schools of thinking, on which I am commenting.

Armchair Opinion Versus Scientific Method in the Reconstruction of the Social Studies. The curriculum has been devised to the present time by what we may term committee procedure. To the present time it has been a method of the most unscientific sort. The method has exhibited an armchair philosophy and in it the opinion and apriori judgment of a small group of specialists in subject-matter have predominated. I shall ask the editor of *The Historical*

Outlook to publish a careful study of the personnel, methods and recommendations of each committee of the American Historical Association since the Committee of Ten in 1892, which will completely substantiate these statements. Details cannot be given in this letter, space in which must be devoted to other matters.

Lack of a program for curriculum-making. Contrasted with such a method it is feasible at the present time for us to reconstruct the curriculum by more objective and scientific means. First and foremost, we must rest all our work on a definite program for procedure. This seems to me precisely the most serious defect in the procedure of the New Committee of Eight—the complete omission of a program. We felt in hearing your address, and I have been confirmed after a careful reading of your report in the April issue of *The Historical Outlook,* that although the committee has recommended specific materials for each of the school grades, yet no criteria are given by which we can measure the validity of the materials which they have selected. They do not state specifically *why* various courses are presented, *why* particular materials are to be presented in the different grades, or *why* they are organized as they are within the different grades.

This is precisely the vulnerable point in the entire procedure which historians have employed in making the course of study since the Committee of Ten in 1892. I have recently made an exhaustive study of the procedure of all the national committees in history and in the other social studies beginning with the Committee of Ten. In no one of these reports is there stated definitely a scheme of criteria against which the validity of subject-matter can be checked. They all make recommendations as to the materials to be taught—nation and period to be studied—*but no fundamental discussion of the basis of selection and of the placement of materials is given.*

This, the curriculum maker today regards as an essential first-step, and he feels that "committees" should be stopped from recommending materials without a complete statement of criteria and organizing principles and before the materials have had a controlled and *measured* trial in a considerable number of public schools. The student of the curriculum takes the stand that committees of educational associations are doing more harm than good when they recommend courses of study before those courses of study have been thoroughly experimented upon. Furthermore, this does not mean mere trial with a few classes by the authors of this report, so that it is known that given materials *can* be taught in particular grades and by the recommended methods. Rather, it means *controlled and measured experimentation,* objective measured results obtained from a considerable number of schools.

WHAT IS A SCIENTIFIC PROGRAM FOR CURRICULUM MAKING IN THE SOCIAL STUDIES?

I am publishing in the next issue of the *Elementary School Journal* a complete statement of what I regard as a sound program. I will abbreviate that program here, enumerating the steps. Lack of space will prevent me from giving important fuller discussion.

A committee can improve school practice largely by acting in three capacities. First, as a deliberative body of specialists—as specialists in the validity of subject-matter, but also as specialists in the science of curriculum-making. As such a body it should set up educational aims and definite criteria for the selection and arrangement of subject-matter against which it measures each item proposed for the curriculum. In the *second* place the committee should *set up a complete investigational program.* It should substitute objective analyses of human needs and activities for opinion as to what children need to be taught. More specifically I believe it should do the following things: (1) It should determine the exact status of the present teaching of history and related subjects in our public schools—it should set forth the aims and scope of the courses, time allotments, and make detailed analyses of the textbooks and reference books used. (2) It should evaluate critically and constructively the scientific investigations of curriculum-making in social studies which are already available, either published or unpublished. (3) It should make and publish an exhaustive analysis and interpretation of representative examples of "experimental" or innovating courses. (4) It should test by standardized measures of attainment results obtained from the study of history and the related subjects as now taught. (5) Most important of all, it should make scientific investigations of what ought to be taught in our schools. (Examples are given in the article to which I referred.)

Now, as an investigational body it appears that the Committee of Eight has failed completely. So far as reported, no investigations of any kind have been made. Materials have been selected and recommended for teaching in the public schools of America without an objective and basic analysis of economic, industrial and social life.

Third, the committee should act as a great clearing house and as a forum, stimulating controversial discussion of both its own and other proposed programs. After some years of debate, clear thinking and experimentation will make possible a wide-spread agreement of fundamental matters. It is safe to conclude that this committee, although it has given much publicity to its report, has not secured a real exchange of views or constructive criticisms.

Finally, the committee should act as a continuing body. It should study the application of its recommendations in public schools; collect reactions of school people, and test results obtained. Since the committee has been discharged this, of course, cannot be done. A new standing committee has been appointed by the American Historical Association, of which you are chairman. I would urge upon your committee the fundamental importance of inaugurating a movement for the scientific study curriculum-making in history and related subjects.

The committee's report is a set of hypothetical programs by individuals. Probably the most significant comment one can make of this report of the Joint Committee on History and Education for Citizenship is that it is a set of hypothetical programs by individuals. Your own scheme has been employed by the committee for the first eight grades, the outlines and materials organized recently by Professor Shafer and Miss Morehouse for the ninth grade, Dr. Knowlton's material for the tenth. Thus, the course recommended for each grade is the program of a single worker, not the carefully matured recommendations of a great body of historians and educators. As hypothetical programs I regard your suggestions for the first eight grades as important. I am convinced that we should give them careful consideration. But, at the same time, we should be clear that they are largely hypotheses concerning what we ought to teach and how we ought to arrange the material. They are not courses experimentally tried, the consideration of evidence concerning which has led to their wide-spread recommendation by historians and students of the school curriculum.

ON WHAT BASES SHALL MATERIAL BE INCLUDED
IN THE CURRICULUM?

We have before us, then, the first issue: Shall we use a scientific method in the reconstruction of the curriculum? Can sound and permanent reconstruction come in any other way? How can we determine soundly what materials to teach our children in this important and intangible field of social activities unless we sweep the board clean and start new, setting up carefully thought-out hypotheses of selection of material, which are based upon the principle of social worth? My own procedure would be to ignore the fact that we have today a curriculum in history, geography and civics; start afresh and define clearly the scope, functions and objectives of the course by this criterion of "social worth." This criterion necessitates that to be included in the course the material must contribute: (1) To a grasp of the great economic, social and political relationships or "laws"; (2) to an understanding of established modes of living; (3) to an interest in and appreciation of the outstanding "problems" and "issues" of contemporary civilization. If this is done, a considerable body of material will be included that now forms part of our social studies curriculum; we will include very much that is not now in the course and we will eliminate fully one-half, probably more than half, of the administrative and political content in current courses.

To illustrate such a procedure I shall publish during the next year some half-dozen studies made during the past year and a half. These studies consist of careful analyses of nationally used histories, geographies and civics books—some 40 altogether. They include also investigations of the units of material which outstanding thinkers in economics, politics, social reform and industry would include in the curriculum which is to be required of all boys and girls through, say, the ninth grade. Elaborate statistical analyses of allusions found in representative newspapers and magazines will also be reported. The study referred to in an earlier paragraph, of the extent to which our curriculum deals with important problems of contemporary life, will be published in full. Finally, a report will be made of an investigation of what the great frontier thinkers of the day regard as the outstanding economic, industrial, social and political "problems" of contemporary civilization. In its endeavor to construct a sound curriculum, our own research group is turning to the writings of these leading thinkers. From some 70 books on politics, industry, economics, anthropology, sociology and the like—many published since the armistice—statements are being made of these problems and issues.

Such investigations as these after several years of scientific work should enable us to put together a course of study that will stand the most rigorous tests of social value. It is our thesis that the existing curriculum and in a large part the one proposed by the Joint Committee on History and Education for Citizenship will not pass such tests of social validity. Certainly, the committee should set forth its program for curriculum-making—that is, the basic principles of selection and organization of material in order that school people may critically test it.

By this illustration I have tried to show how a scientific program for curriculum-making makes use of the criterion of social worth. The crux of the matter is that we need investigations, not opinion.

ON WHAT PRINCIPLES SHALL THE CURRICULUM BE GRADED AND ORGANIZED?

So much for the content of curriculum. What about the organization, grade placement of materials and arrangement within the grades? The New Committee of Eight has stated no criteria for these important matters. Yet materials are assigned to grades and illustrations are given of methods of presenting material, which appear to me to be at variance with conclusions of psychological validity.

Two distinct issues face us here. The *first* deals with the division of material into school subjects. The *second,* with important matters of presenting informational subject-matter and of providing adequate practice in analytical thinking.

One composite social studies course versus three or more separate subjects. We are dealing, in this matter, with two different problems, one the imperative need of cutting down the number of school subjects, the other an urgent pedagogical and psychological need of insuring that teachers will teach in close relationship all materials which are related in character. As for the former, I am confident that we shall see in the near future the wide-spread demand for fewer school subjects. *More activity on the part of* children, but fewer compartments in the curriculum is an impressive need.

Next let us consider the task of providing that untrained teachers, teaching large classes of children who exhibit very wide individual differences, shall bring into close relationship materials which are related. I am setting up the hypothesis that *it is more in accord with the way in which children learn* to teach related materials in one body of subject-matter than in separate compartments on "subjects." *One subject rather than three is the high point in our theory.* This hypothesis is close to the aim of the old correlation movement. That movement failed, I conclude, for three reasons: (1) For want of systematic supervision of teaching; (2) because our elementary school teachers were, and are, so untrained in both subject-matter and in the psychology of learning that they are unable to do more than to stick to the thread and detail of the textbooks and organized references material which their pupils read; (3) because there were no systems of textbooks in which the "correlation" was worked out.

Rather than have teachers attempt the almost impossible task of "correlating" history, geography, civics, economics and sociology (taught as separate subjects), we postulate that more effective outcomes will be secured by weaving together lesson by lesson the facts, movements, conditions, principles and social, economic and political "laws" that depend upon one another *and that can be fully comprehended only when they are woven together.* From one point of view this *is* "merging history, geography and civics." True enough, in the product of such instruction it is very difficult to distinguish what is history from what is geography, and in turn from other subjects. But if we consider more carefully we will see that this procedure is not *merging* the school subjects at all. It is not "correlated" or "combined" or "fused" social science (to borrow terms for the recent movement in mathematics and science). Rather, it is a whole new and scientific technique of making courses of study by building from the ground up. It ignores the content of current courses in its initial stages at least.

How shall we present information and provide for practice in generalization? I proceed next to other important problems in organization; namely, those of assigning subject-matter to grades, of providing adequate practice through repetition of principles and facts, of giving pupils a clear grasp of information, and of stimulating the interests of children through providing human detail. The problem can be made clear by stating definitely two questions which need to be answered. *First,* how shall information be acquired by pupils? *Second,* how can we accomplish our purpose of training pupils in the power of judgment, teaching them to draw generalizations, to form sound conclusions?

It is regrettable that in 1921, after thirty years of development in the science of psychology, we have practically no evidence upon which to make up a detailed "psychology of the school subjects." We must frankly say today that we do not know what historical and social materials should be taught in the different grades of our public schools. Indeed, it seems that the most intelligent conclusion that we can draw at the present time is that no one scheme of organization can be proven to be the best. Certainly no one scheme available today has been proven to be so.

CURRENT METHODS OF ORGANIZING SOCIAL STUDIES MATERIAL

Investigation will show that there are at least five different methods of organizing social studies material now employed in our public schools. The first, and most typical, is to organize history by periods, by nation and epoch to be studied, and geography by continents, regions and topics. We assign American history to the close of the Revolution to one grade; that from 1783 to date to another grade; medieval history, from 800 to the French Revolution, to another grade; American history from 1609, perhaps, to still another. The significant fact is, however, that no collection of results which is obtained from such an organization has been made to show the relative worth of this method.

A *second method* of organization is to classify subject-matter in accordance with human needs and human activities which satisfy them. With this scheme one would recognize such units as: physical needs and resources, human resources, industrial and governmental organization and the like. This has been done in devising such courses as the Speyer school scheme, the material having been assigned to four subjects, history, geography, economics and industrial arts. The material has been organized around a threefold scheme of food, shelter and clothing. In each grade the material is presented under these three captions, with the industrial arts as the correlating subject.

A *third method* of grading and organizing materials, and one which makes use of the needs and activities of people, has been to assign the work of each grade to different kinds of activities. For example, a part of the year is devoted to industrial life, another part to a discussion of the composition of the people, a third deals with crucial physical needs, a fourth with matters of government, etc.

A *fourth method* of organizing the curriculum might be called the family-community-nation-world scheme. It has been suggested (more recently by your Joint Committee of Eight) that material be organized on a basis of the size of the social group of which the child may be regarded as the center. The arrangements of such material in the primary grades of American schools is chiefly on this family-community basis. Apparently, this is in accord with the best psychology that we know today. The basis of the work in these lower grades is made up of excursions, observations and much activity. In the family and in the local community it is physically possible to organize instruction helpfully on this basis. Beyond the local community, since excursions and traveling are prohibited for our public school grades, and since we must resort to pictures, lantern slides, motion pictures and reading, then the notion that we must gradually expand the social group, to include, first, the nation and then the world, probably breaks down. Perhaps, however, some form of the family-community organization of material should be used in which, from the fourth grade up, material is woven together into the course which will help children to understand their present environments, *irrespective of physical location or time location.* That is, by a sufficiently concrete illustration, either the remote or the near in time or place can be made intelligible. The proposed curriculum of the New Committee of Eight is in large part based upon this family-community-nation-world scheme. I think, however, one can discern the use of another principle of organization.

This is *a fifth method*; namely, that of using great principles upon which social life is based as the guiding themes of organization. It has been suggested, for example, that great social principles, like coöperation, ideas of liberty, provision for individual initiative under current methods of social organization should be used to determine the assignment of subject-matter to various grades. After carefully determining concrete situations for our different levels these great notions can be taught. A suggested principle of grade placement is therefore that of preparing a list of these great social principles and of selecting subject-matter which will contribute to understand them, and of assigning to various grades situations which will contribute to this understanding, the level of the discussion being adapted to the learning of the children.

ANOTHER BASIS OF ORGANIZING SOCIAL STUDIES MATERIAL

I wish to suggest a new basis for organizing social studies material. Aside from the development of important attitudes, probably the most essential outcome to be looked for from the study of history and related subjects is a clear grasp of the great economic, social and political "laws," movements, casual relations. We are primarily interested to train pupils, through years of practice, in meeting thinking situations, to see causal relations, to compare and analyze complex situations; in brief, to understand the great "laws." The crux of human thinking is the ability to see relations clearly. Our training needs center on analysis, on comparison, on selective thinking. If this be true, is it not necessary to set up as the great outcome from teaching the ability to understand and to express the great "laws" in the fields of economics and industry and in social and political life.

Working on this principle one finds a criterion for the organization of factual material in the social studies. It is to employ in each grade those factual situations which will contribute year by year to a growing appreciation and understanding of the great central generalizations in each of these fields. It is one of the chief defects of our historical, geographical and civic instruction that the course has consisted largely of the encyclopedic presentation of facts, with little or no emphasis upon application of these facts to the understanding of great fundamental relationships. We have preached the latter, but our practice has failed to keep pace with the theory. This other point of view would maintain that the task in no grade is the mere giving of information. The real task is the presentation of concrete situations, with such generalizations, comparisons, emphasis upon interrelations and causal connections, that relationships will begin to stand out even in the lower grades—grosser ones first, their refinement developing only with the higher grades.

But the second problem is as important as the first; namely, *how hall we give sufficient practice in thinking to develop a real power of thought?* One of the chief hypotheses underlying my own curriculum research in the social studies is that *in order for children to be able to generalize is handling social situations, they must have constant practice in generalization.* In order for them to understand great movements, they must be faced constantly with such movements and practice continually in interpreting them.

In order for them to understand causal connections, they must deal with them each day of their school career. In our experimentation, we present big, broad movements, relations, causal connections, in constantly *recurring* but varied situations in the attempt to develop a rich, interpretative background. We believe that information should be acquired in this way—that is, by gradual accretion, by the accumulative recurrence of primary facts in greatly varied situations. In our work, therefore, we deliberately present great relationships in the class discussion day after day, believing that for them to be permanently mastered, a pupil must see them illustrated in many diversified settings. Thus, *repetition* of causes, big movements, relations, is imperative to bring about real mastery. *Repetition,* to be effective, must involve the making of many interconnections—not mere drill upon isolated topics, events, conditions, personages, etc.

To provide adequately for thinking and practice in *thought,* we believe it is necessary to do two things which our present textbooks and recommendations of committees do not do: *First,* definitely organize our courses around problems, relations, causes and effects; in brief, around the great "laws"; *second,* make these relationships recur in many school grades and so frequently within a school grade that mastery steadily grows, both of "laws" and the information contributory to them. How far this principle of organization will carry us only the experimentation of the next few years will show. Whether it will be necessary to repeat these "laws" and causal connections in each grade, *i.e.,* whether we must adopt some form of "layer" organization, remains to be seen.

But the important point is this: repetition of "laws" and facts must be provided for and this is in distinct opposition to the present practice of organizing the history curriculum. Chronological sequence opposes "problem" or unitary organization. Fact-giving predominates over problem-solving as an organizing principle. Arranging history by "periods" and "years" holds forth over scientifically determined repetition of fundamentals. Encyclopedism and paragraphic treatment in text-making render impossible the grasp and retention of vital principles of human relationship, which depend for mastery on wealth of detail and human interest, and upon adequate repetition. *Practice in thought is necessary to develop power of thought.*

NEED FOR A NEW TYPE OF NATIONAL COMMITTEE WITH A SCIENTIFIC PROGRAM

What can a committee confidently recommend, then, with respect to these intricate problems of grade placement and organization of subject-matter? My answer is: *"Nothing, at the present time."* The only sound course a committee can take now is to initiate careful experimentation upon several proposed schemes of organizations. The psychological experimentation of the past thirty years has contributed certain fundamental laws of learning which certainly can be recognized, and to which one should conform. The most promising lead, it appears, would be to draw up hypotheses concerning methods of organizing and presenting material which are based upon known laws of learning, and set up detailed and carefully controlled and measured experiments to determine their validity.

In the meantime, let us get underway an important movement for scientifically determining the content and arrangement of the social studies curriculum. Furthermore, let us begin now to look forward to three to five years from now, when we may have the appointment of a different type of committee—a national committee, which will set up a procedure on the order of that discussed at the beginning of this article, which will be adequately financed and permitted to employ two or more high-grade secretaries, who are active professional workers in the field. In the meantime, let us refuse a hearing to any group of workers appointed by a national association which brings forward recommendations concerning what materials should be taught or in what grades and by what methods, unless that group presents a complete, scientifically-founded program and thorough-going evidence to support its recommendation.

NOTES

1.   Address made by Professor Henry Johnson, on the report of the Joint Committee on History and Education for Citizenship, to the Secondary Education Club of New York City at the Faculty Club, Columbia University, February 7, 1921.

2.   Bagley, W. C., and Rugg, H. O., *The Content of American History as Taught in the Seventh and Eighth Grades*. Bulletin No. 16. University of Illinois, School of Education, Urbana, Illinois, p. 59.

CHAPTER 3

An Experiment in Teaching Resistance to Propaganda

Wayland W. Osborn
1939

INTRODUCTION

The Problem of This Study

Today the school is being increasingly called upon to teach resistance to propaganda. Social studies teachers in particular are expected to develop in their pupils habits of critical thinking with respect to controversial social issues. If social studies teachers aim to immunize their pupils against propaganda, they must organize effective curricular materials for classroom use. This study reports the results of one attempt to organize such curricular materials, and to determine their effectiveness experimentally.

The purposes of this investigation were to determine: (1) the effectiveness of a unit of instruction designed for use in teaching high school social studies pupils to resist propaganda, (2) the degree to which knowledge concerning a selected controversial social issue is associated with attitude toward that issue and also with shift of attitude toward that issue stimulated by reading a selection designed to shift that attitude, and (3) the degree to which intelligence is associated with attitude toward the selected controversial

From *The Journal of Experimental Education,* 8 (September 1939), 1–17. Abridged. Notes appear as in original.

social issue and also with shift of attitude toward that issue stimulated as described above.

Unique Aspects of This Study

While separate experiments have dealt with individual phases of the problem studied in this investigation, there appears to be no study which has made the same approach as this one or which has included all three phases of the problem in the same study. Biddle,[1] like the present writer, attempted to teach critical thinking directly by leading pupils to study the forms in which propaganda commonly appears. His study, while closely related to this experiment, varied from it in several particulars. For instance, he expressed the feeling that a clear measure of the degree of understanding of the lessons possessed by the pupils would have helped him in the interpretation of his study; he did not make a direct study of opinions or attitudes; and he gave prior instruction to the experimental group concerning the propaganda devices commonly employed in connection with the very social issue which he used as the basis of his testing. Anderson[2] has suggested the desirability of a direct study of opinions. Others, while showing that attitudes can be shifted and that such shifts tend to persist, made no attempt to immunize pupils against the effects of propaganda designed to shift their attitudes.

Definitions

Attitude and *opinion:* These two words are common in everyday speech and they are often used synonymously. Thurstone and Chave[3] use the word, "attitude," "to denote the sum-total of a man's inclinations and feelings, prejudice or bias, preconceived notions, ideas, fears, threats, and convictions about any specific topic." They[4] take the word, "opinion," to "mean a verbal expression of attitude." When opinions were measured in this study, it was assumed correct to consider such measurement as the measurement of attitude.

Attitude variable: This term was used in this study to refer to the specific issue concerning which it was wished to secure a measure of an individual's position along a linear scale ranging from a negative attitude extreme through a neutral or indifferent attitude to a positive attitude extreme.[5]

Propaganda: The literature on propaganda reveals a wide variety of definitions. For purposes of this study the writer has defined propaganda by this statement: "Propaganda is the expression of opinion or action by a single person or a group of persons in such a way as to influence the opinions or actions of one or more other persons." This definition does not hold that propaganda is either good or bad. It also provides for both intentional and non-intentional influences. Strong[6] suggests a shorter definition which appears to be in complete accord with the above definition when he says of propaganda: "It is a synonym for influencing." The definition, as above defined for use in this study, is an extension of the following one formulated by the staff of the Institute for Propaganda Analysis:[7]

> As generally understood, propaganda is expression of opinion or action by individuals or groups deliberately designed to influence opinions or actions of other individuals or groups with reference to predetermined ends.

The ability to resist propaganda: In this study the ability to resist propaganda was understood to be the ability to identify expressions of opinion or action which influence one to favor or oppose a given opinion or action, and to hold one's judgment or action in abeyance until the desirability of the proposed opinion or action from one's own point of view is determined. The ability to resist propaganda can never be absolute. We can never hope to escape being influenced, to a degree at least, by propaganda.

Knowledge or understanding of attitude variable: The score on an objective achievement test constructed by the writer was the only measure of knowledge or understanding of the attitude variable utilized in this study.

Intelligence: The intelligence quotient of each pupil, as reported by the school officials, or as secured by the writer where the school did not have such records, was used as the basis for defining intelligence. Since several different commercially available intelligence tests were obviously involved, it was necessary to assume that these tests all yielded comparable intelligence quotients. This assumption is correct to a degree at least. It is well known that intelligence quotients based on scores from such tests do vary, but they are usually quite highly correlated positively.

Difference between education and propaganda: While education and propaganda overlap in many respects, meaningful differences between them can be distinguished. Lasswell[8] has provided a distinction between education and propaganda.

> . . . the processes by which such techniques as those of spelling, letter forming, piano playing, lathe handling and dialectics are transmitted may be called education, while those by which value dispositions (hatred or respect toward a person, group or policy) are organized may be called propaganda. The inculcation of traditional value attitudes is generally called education, while the term propaganda is reserved for the spreading of the subversive, debatable or merely novel attitudes.

Unit of instruction used in this experiment: A complete description of this unit of instruction is presented in a later portion of this article. It should be made clear, however, that the time devoted to the teaching of the unit, and the conditions under which this teaching was done, are essential parts of a complete definition of this unit. If, then, the results of this experiment show the unit to be effective or non-effective in achieving its purposes, such a conclusion will not necessarily be considered valid for all time allotments and for all conditions. It is possible, however, that the correlation between knowledge concerning propaganda devices and resistance to propaganda will prove to be negligible. Such a fact would make the provision of increased time allotments for a study of the methods of the propagandist a procedure of doubtful value.

Method Used in This Study to Develop Pupil Ability to Resist Propaganda

Opinions vary as to the most effective method of education against propaganda. Two general methods have been suggested. The first method of teaching critical thinking is based on the conviction that there are no short-cuts whereby an individual can develop resistance to propaganda. According to this method, resistance to propaganda would be achieved through developing in the individual, throughout his school experience, habits of approaching conflict situations from the intellectual, problem-solving point-of-view. Content would be emphasized.   •

The second method of teaching resistance to propaganda would make a direct study of the tricks or techniques of propaganda, and of how they appeal to our emotions and lead us to uncritical acceptance of opinions or suggested actions. Here the emphasis would be on "form" instead of "content."[9] A considerable body of curricular literature is available suggesting student activities whereby this second method can be put into operation. Because of the recent popularization of this method in our schools, it was used in this study.

PROCEDURE

The Design of the Experiment

The pupils enrolled in the eleventh and twelfth grades in twenty pairs of social studies classes, with one teacher for each pair, in seventeen Iowa high schools participated in this experiment. By means of chance, one class in each pair was designated as an experimental class and the other as a control class. The pupils in each of the twenty experimental classes studied, for six days, a unit of instruction entitled *Public Opinion and Propaganda*. During this six-day period, the pupils in each of the twenty control classes carried on their regular class work, and were assigned no work on the subject of propaganda.

On the closing day of the fourth full week following the beginning of the six-day instructional period, all pupils in both the experimental and control groups in attendance were given, in a single sitting of forty-one minutes working time, the following exercises: (1) an initial measurement of attitude toward capital punishment, *Attitude Toward Capital Punishment, Form A,* by Ruth C. Peterson and L. L. Thurstone;[10] (2) an achievement test, *Knowledge Concerning Capital Punishment,* prepared by the writer; (3) a propaganda reading selection, *Why Capital Punishment is Necessary,* prepared by the writer and in part adapted from a similar selection written by Richard M. Bateman;[11] and (4) a post-measurement of attitude toward capital punishment, *Attitude Toward Capital Punishment, Form B,* by Ruth C. Peterson and L. L. Thurstone.[12] The interval of approximately three weeks between these two phases of the experiment was allowed for two reasons. First, it was desired to mask the connection between these two phases of the experiment, and second, the writer felt that this delay would be a test of the permanence of the learning resulting from the instructional period.

On the closing day of the sixth full week following the begin ning of the six-day instructional period, all pupils in both the experimental and the control groups in attendance were given a delayed measurement of attitude toward capital punishment, *Attitude Toward Capital Punishment, Form B,* by Ruth C. Peterson and L. L. Thurstone.

Within the current school year, at no time prior to or during the six-week period were any of the pupils given instruction concerning capital punishment as a social issue.

Within a three-week period following the first six-week period just described, a mental test, *Otis Quick Scoring Mental Ability Test, Gamma Test, Form A,* by Arthur S. Otis,[13] was given to approximately all pupils in the experiment for whom the local schools did not have recent mental test results on file.

Preparation of Instructional Materials

The Institute for Propaganda Analysis has issued a considerable body of instructional materials designed for use in teaching resistance to propaganda. These materials have been judged valuable by teachers who have used them. Since there was no provision in this experiment for extensive tryout of the materials prior to use, the suggestions included in the Institute's publication, *Propaganda, How to Recognize It and Deal With It (Experimental Unit of Study Materials in Propaganda Analysis for Use in Junior and Senior High Schools),*[14] were used freely in the unit prepared by the writer, *Public Opinion and Propaganda (A Self-Study Booklet Containing a Unit of Study Materials in Propaganda Analysis for Use in Senior High School).* The Institute readily gave permission for use of its materials in this unit. Auxiliary aids to the self-study booklet were bound in five separate booklets: (1) *Readings I—Articles Which Present One-Sided Views on Important Public Issues;* (2) *Readings II—Articles Which Lead Us to Look on Both Sides of Public Issues, and Which Help Us to See How the Propagandist Works;* (3) *Summary I—Interests to Which Propagandists Appeal;* (4) *Summary II—The Tricks of the Propagandist;* (5) *Examination—Public Opinion and Propaganda.* In addition to these materials, each teacher was provided with a mounted exhibit of commercial advertisements selected to illustrate the points made in the instructional materials.

The unit of instruction consisted of four lessons, each of which included one or more parts. Each part of a lesson included these divisions: Discussion, Student Activities, and Notes for Class Discussion. It was deemed desirable to keep teacher procedures from experimental class to experimental class as uniform as possible. The reference materials and directions for student activities were useful in achieving this uniformity.

In an attempt to provide for a wide range of pupil ability, considerable optional reading material was included. An attempt was also made to impress the teachers with the fact that the same amount of work was not expected of all pupils.

The examination was prepared to serve as an aid in summarizing the learnings of the unit, and not primarily as a measurement device. The teachers were requested to spend a brief time on the seventh day in discussing the responses to the items included in the examination.

Coincident with the preparation of the instructional materials for pupil use two aids for teacher use were developed: (1) *Teacher Reference Materials,* and (2) *Teacher Procedures for Presenting the Unit of Instruction.* In addition directions were included for the preparation of a *Teacher's Log.*

The unit was tried out under actual classroom situations by two teachers prior to its final issuance for use in this study. On the basis of these preliminary trials, the instructional materials were revised. The materials entitled, *Teacher Procedures for Presenting the Unit of Instruction,* were prepared on the basis of these trials.

The Test and Propaganda Battery

The reader will remember that, in the first phase of the experiment, the emphasis was placed upon the immunization of pupils in the experimental groups against the effects of propaganda. In the second phase of the experiment, the pupils in both the experimental and control groups were confronted with an attitude variable which was a new situation in that there had been no prior class study concerning it within the current semester. As previously stated, this attitude variable was attitude toward capital punishment. Particular care was taken to provide this new situation, since the whole object of the instruction was to give the pupils in the experimental groups the understanding of a set of principles which they could use to resist propaganda for or against any social issue. If the objective of the unit of instruction had been to teach a critical attitude toward propaganda for or against a specific social issue, propaganda, as it commonly appears in connection with that issue, would have been studied directly during the first phase of the experiment. It will be recalled that this is just what Biddle did in his experiment.[15]

Although the word *propaganda* did not appear in the second phase of the experiment, no direct attempt was made to hide the fact that only one side of the argument was presented in the propaganda reading selection. The propaganda was actually hidden to a degree, however, in that the pupil was given the responsibility for any transfer that was made. The selection was introduced by saying, "Below is a selection which gives information which will help you to see why capital punishment is considered necessary. Please read it carefully because an understanding of this article will help you on the rest of the test."

This attempt to capitalize on the prestige which text material usually occupies in classroom and test situations is subject to the criticism that the pupils were put under a "pressure situation" in which they responded as they thought they were expected to, irrespective of their recognition of the propaganda tricks used in the selection.

The writer's answer must be that the instruction aimed to develop immunity to propaganda. If the experimentals accepted a statement equally as often as did the controls, chiefly on the basis of the prestige of the situation in which it was offered, they had not developed the quality of suspended judgment to the degree that it could be distinguished from that exhibited by the controls. Since both the experimentals and the controls were confronted with the same propaganda situation, any superiority in immunity possessed by the experimentals had a chance to be demonstrated by a smaller shift in attitude.

Even though the propaganda selection itself did not admit that there was a tenable case for opposing capital punishment, the directions to the pupils stated clearly that opinions toward the use of capital punishment do vary. In addition, each teacher told his pupils that the results of the tests would not count on their school marks. Thus it is clear that no "pressure" was applied to the pupils as they registered their initial attitudes. The propaganda definitely aimed to exert "pressure" toward a more favorable response to the use of capital punishment on the post-test of attitude. If the experimentals were relatively more immune to the effects of this propaganda, here was the chance for them to show their resistance by refusing to alter their initial attitudes.

The names of the parts and the order of their presentation in the "test and propaganda battery" were given earlier in this article. The entire battery was given in a single sitting of forty-one minutes working time. Seven minutes were allowed for each of the two attitude tests, and for reading the propaganda selection, and twenty minutes were allowed for the achievement test. These time limits were based upon observations made during the preliminary trials.

It was considered desirable to administer the "test and propaganda battery" in a single sitting in order to make it impossible for the results of the post-test of attitude to be affected by discussions of the attitude variable or of the propaganda selection either among the pupils of the same or both groups or among pupils and parents, pupils and teachers, or pupils and others. In order to avoid the effect on attitude which might possibly operate as a result of taking the achievement test, the initial attitude test was placed first in the battery.

The Delayed-Test of Attitude

The delayed-test of attitude was used in order to reveal the persistency of the attitude-shift resulting from the propaganda reading selection, and to reveal the differences between experimentals and controls after a two week interval had given opportunity for discussion of the second phase of the experiment. The cooperating teachers were instructed to refrain from formal classroom study of the "test and propaganda battery" during this two-week period.

RESULTS REVEALED BY A STUDY OF STUDENTS' WORK AND TEACHERS' REPORTS

An attempt was made to form a judgment concerning the degree to which the unit of instruction, *Public Opinion and Propaganda*, was effective for use in teaching resistance to propaganda, as revealed by its use with the experimental group. Three types of materials were available as bases for this judgment. First, each pupil did all his written work in the study booklet which contained all the directions considered essential for studying the unit. Second, each pupil was given an examination near the close of the instructional period. This examination covered the important points with which it was desired that each pupil would become familiar as a result of his study. Third, each teacher submitted a log in which he recorded, in anecdotal form, certain experiences encountered while teaching the unit. The following statements constitute a subjective evaluation of the effectiveness of the unit of instruction based upon analyses of the three types of materials listed above:

1. In general, the unit of instruction, *Public Opinion and Propaganda,* proved suitable for use in eleventh and twelfth grade social studies classes with respect to its interest appeal, range of difficulty, and organization.

2. The responses to the suggested student activities and to the essay questions in the unit examination support the conclusion that, after the instructional unit had been completed, a large majority of the pupils in the experimental group had developed the ability to make satisfactory verbal descriptions of the common propaganda devices, and to enumerate steps to take in resisting propaganda. Each of the items in the unit examination possessed some power to discriminate between high and low scoring pupils.

3. The teachers felt that more effective results would have followed had more time been allowed for class discussion. Possibly an additional time allotment would have improved pupil ability to resist propaganda. Later in this article the degree of correlation between knowledge concerning the devices of propaganda, as measured by the unit examination and the magnitude of attitude-shift in response to propaganda, will be reported. The size of this correlation should help to indicate whether or not more time given to a unit of this type would be profitable.

4. Certain teachers reported that their experience with the unit had led them to doubt whether pupils could detect propaganda devices unless they had a background of information concerning the problem at issue. However, as stated above, the written work of the pupils in the experimental group presented convincing evi-

dence that a large majority of them were able to make apparently adequate verbal statements concerning common propaganda devices, and to enumerate steps to take in resisting their effects.

RESULTS OF THE TESTING PHASE OF THE EXPERIMENT AND THEIR STATISTICAL TREATMENT

Objective Standard of Effectiveness

The second standard for judging the effectiveness of the unit of instruction used in this experiment was based on objective test results. The unit of instruction was to be judged effective according to the objective standard only if the mean shift in attitude in response to propaganda on the part of the experimental group was less than that of the control group by a statistically significant amount. Answers were sought to these questions: (1) Was the immediate shift of attitude on the part of the control group statistically significant? (2) Was the delayed shift of attitude on the part of the control group statistically significant? (3) Was the immediate shift of attitude on the part of the experimental group statistically significant? (4) Was the delayed shift of attitude on the part of the experimental group statistically significant? (5) Was the difference between the experimental and control groups in immediate-attitude-shift statistically significant, and what group did it favor? (6) Was the difference between the experimental and control groups in delayed-attitude-shift statistically significant, and what group did it favor?

Correlation coefficients were used to answer the question involved in the second and third purposes of the problem. This question may be stated as follows: How were both knowledge and intelligence, respectively, correlated with initial attitude, with deviation from neutral in initial attitude, with immediate shift of attitude, and with delayed shift of attitude on the part of the control and the experimental groups considered separately?

As this experiment progressed, an additional basis for a partial evaluation of the effectiveness of the unit of instruction was considered. It was thought that it would be interesting to know whether scores on the unit examination, made by the pupils in the experimental group, were in any way correlated with immediate or delayed shift of attitude. If a marked degree of negative correlation were found, it could be used to support the argument that the greater the understanding of the content of the unit the greater would be the immunity to propaganda.

Statistical Techniques Used to Determine the Reliability of Differences

The twenty pairs of classes in this experiment collectively constituted a small sample. Each pair of classes was split at random, one class being assigned to the experimental and the other to the control group of classes. The exerimental group then consisted of twenty "cases" and the control group likewise included twenty "cases."

The initial and post-attitude-scores were available for each pupil both in the control and experimental groups. The significance of any difference in initial and post-attitude-means for either the experimental or control groups considered separately was determined by a method outlined by Fisher.[16] The difference between the initial and post-attitude-means for each of the twenty pairs of means was found; the mean of these differences was then computed. Finally it was determined whether or not this mean difference differed significantly from zero. The same procedure was followed to determine the significance of any difference between initial and delayed-attitude-means for each group separately.

The test of significance, employed to determine whether mean differences were greater than those which could be attributed to chance, was "Student's" t-test. "Student's" "t" is the ratio resulting from dividing the difference by which the mean of a small sample differs from any given value by its estimated standard error.

Comparison of Attitude-Shift for Control and Experimental Groups, First Testing Period

The results support two conclusions. First, the propaganda reading selection was effective in causing an immediate shift in the mean-attitude-scores of both the control and the experimental groups to a statistically significant degree in the intended direction. Second, the mean difference between the control and experimental groups in such shift was not statistically significant.[17]

Comparison of Attitude-Shift for Control and Experimental Groups, Second Testing Period

Delayed-attitude scores resulted from the administration of the delayed test of attitude in the second testing period. It will be recalled that this second testing period followed the first after a two-week interval.

The results support two conclusions. First the propaganda reading selection was effective in causing a shift in the mean-attitude-score of both the experimental and the control groups to a statistically significant degree in the intended direction when the end attitude was measured after a lapse of two weeks from the time the selection was read. Second, the mean difference between the control and experimental groups in such shift was not statistically significant.

The Relation of Knowledge and Intelligence to Attitude and Attitude Shift

For the experimental and control groups separately the *within* class correlations were determined between: (1) achievement and initial attitude,[18] (2) achievement and immediate-attitude shift,[19] (3) achievement and delayed-attitude-shift,[20] (4) intelligence and initial attitude,[21] (5) intelligence and immediate-attitude-shift, (6) intelligence and delayed-attitude-shift, (7) achievement and deviation from a neutral score on initial attitude test, and (8) intelligence and deviation from a neutral score on initial attitude test.[22] In order to eliminate the effect of school differences and determine the correlation *within* classes, these correlations were computed by the method of analysis of co-variance, described by Fisher.[23] All the correlations were negligible in magnitude.

Relationship Between Scores on Unit Examination and Attitude Shift on the Part of Pupils of the Experimental Group

The correlation between the scores on the unit examination and immediate-attitude-shift, and the delayed-attitude-shift, were computed on the basis of all pupils in the experimental group for whom the necessary scores were available. The analysis of co-variance as described by Fisher[24] was employed to determine each of these correlations. The correlations were .042 and .114 respectively. These are *within* class correlations.

These negligible correlations support the conclusion that possession of information concerning the tricks of propaganda at the level measured by the unit examination does not result in increased resistance to propaganda.

CONCLUSIONS

The results of this experiment were highly consistent, and they strongly support the following conclusions:

1. The unit of instruction, *Public Opinion and Propaganda,* was suitable for use in eleventh and twelfth grade social studies classes with respect to its interest appeal, range of difficulty, and organization.

2. Even though there was strong evidence to indicate that the pupils in the experimental group did develop an increased awareness of the methods of the propagandist, the objective standard of effectiveness used in this experiment showed that the study of the unit of instruction, *Public Opinion and Propaganda,* did not prove to be effective in developing resistance to propaganda on the part of these pupils.

3. The negligible correlations between measures of knowledge concerning propaganda devices and measures of immediate and delayed shift of attitude in response to propaganda, as found in this study, strongly suggest that attempts to teach resistance to propaganda with respect to social issues by emphasis only on the "form" in which propaganda commonly appears will be unlikely to succeed. It seems *unlikely,* therefore, that even a longer time allotment for the unit of instruction used in this experiment would have developed greater resistance to propaganda on the part of the experimental group than on the part of the control group.

4. To the extent that pupils' reactions toward propaganda with respect to capital punishment, as found in this study, can be accepted as a basis for generalization, attitudes of senior high school social studies pupils toward social issues can be shifted in a predetermined direction by means of propaganda in the form of a literary selection even when careful study of methods of resisting propaganda has been completed by these pupils less than one month prior to their being subjected to such propaganda. In the absence

of additional propaganda with the same or a counter emphasis, such shift of attitude tends to be relatively permanent as shown by the fact that, in this study, the shift was still statistically significant after a delay of two weeks. This tendency for a new attitude to have permanence has special significance when it is considered in the light of this study. That the experimental group did not differ in attitude from the control group after this two-week delay, is additional evidence that a study of the "tricks" of the propagandist alone will not develop effective resistance to propaganda on the part of senior high school social studies pupils.

The fact that attitudes can be shifted and that such shifts tend to be permanent substantiates what previous investigators have concluded.

5. The low correlations between knowledge concerning a social issue and attitude toward that issue, obtained in this study, constitute strong evidence that measures of knowledge concerning a social issue possessed by high school pupils are inadequate for use in predicting which extreme of a social issue such pupils will tend to favor. The same conclusion holds for measures of intelligence, so far as this study is concerned, since the obtained correlations between intelligence and attitude were also negligible in magnitude for both groups.

6. The low correlations between knowledge concerning a social issue and deviation from neutral in attitude toward that issue, obtained in this study, provide strong evidence that measures of knowledge concerning a social issue possessed by high school pupils are inadequate for predicting the extent to which such pupils will have definite convictions toward that social issue. The same conclusion holds for measures of intelligence, so far as this study is concerned, since the obtained correlations between intelligence and deviation from a neutral attitude were also negligible in magnitude for both groups.

7. The low correlations between knowledge concerning a social issue and immediate or delayed-shift of attitude toward that issue in response to propaganda on the part of high school pupils, as revealed in this study, present strong evidence that measures of the knowledge concerning a social issue possessed by high school pupils are inadequate for predicting ability to resist propaganda. The same conclusion holds for measures of intelligence, so far as

this study is concerned, since the obtained correlations between intelligence and attitude-shift were also negligible in magnitude for both groups.

NOTES

1. William W. Biddle, *Propaganda and Education*. Contributions to Education. No. 531. New York: Bureau of Publications, Teachers College, Columbia University, 1932.

2. H. R. Anderson, "Classroom Evaluation of the Awareness of Propaganda," Seventh Yearbook of the National Council for the Social Studies, *Education Against Propaganda*, pp. 171–182. Lawrence Hall, Cambridge, Massachusetts: The National Council for the Social Studies, 1937.

3. L. L. Thurstone and E. J. Chave, *The Measurement of Attitude: A Psychophysical Method and Some Experiments with a Scale for Measuring Attitude Toward the Church*, pp. 6–7. Chicago: The University of Chicago Press, 1929.

4. Ibid., p. 7.

5. Ibid., p. 11.

6. Edward K. Strong, *Psychological Aspects of Business*, p. 268. New York: McGraw-Hill Book Company, 1938.

7. Institute for Propaganda Analysis, "Announcement," *Monthly Letter*, I (October, 1937), 1–4.

8. H. D. Lasswell, "Propaganda," *Encyclopedia of the Social Sciences*, XII (November, 1937), 522.

9. Biddle (op. cit., p. 18) has suggested the terms "form" and "content" as a useful general way of distinguishing between the two methods.

10. Chicago: University of Chicago Press, 1931.

11. Richard M. Bateman and H. H. Remmers, "The Relationship of Pupil Attitudes Toward Social Topics Before and After Studying the Subjects," *Bulletin of Purdue University*, XXXVII (December, 1936), 27–42.

12. Chicago: University of Chicago Press, 1931.

13. Yonkers-on-Hudson, New York: World Book Company, 1937.

14. 132 Morningside Drive, New York: The Institute for Propaganda Analysis, 1938.

15. William W. Biddle, op. cit.

16. Ronald A. Fisher, *Statistical Methods for Research Workers*, pp. 132–133. London: Oliver and Boyd, 1936.

17. In this study a difference was considered statistically significant if the t-value for the difference was equal to or in excess of the value

required for the 1% level of significance for the number of degrees of freedom involved.

18.   Achievement was measured in terms of scores on the capital punishment achievement test.

19.   Immediate-attitude-shift refers to the shift of attitude resulting from the reading of the propaganda selection. The immediate shift for each pupil was found by subtracting his initial attitude score from his post-attitude score. Post attitude was measured by Form B of the capital punishment attitude test.

20.   Delayed-attitude-shift for each pupil was found by subtracting his initial attitude score from his delayed attitude score. Delayed attitude was measured by re-administering Form B of the capital punishment attitude test two weeks following the first testing period.

21.   The intelligence quotient for each pupil was used.

22.   The neutral score on both forms of the attitude test was 5.50. The signs of the deviations were ignored.

23.   Ronald A. Fisher, op. cit., pp. 275–290.

24.   Ibid.

CHAPTER 4

Teaching in Authoritarian and Democratic States

Alan F. Griffin
1942

If the role of education in a democracy cannot be simply the inculcation of specific habits or attitudes, what then? The purpose of this chapter is to emphasize the unique role, in a democracy, of that kind of learning into which information enters and out of which it is generated. The emphasis, naturally enough, will be upon the function of the teacher inside this process.

The most obvious statement of the teacher's function (qua teacher) is that he should foster learning on the part of his students. Any society in which teachers exist and are recognized as teachers would accept this formulation. To say more than this—even to make the meaning of the verb "to learn" more explicit—is possible only within the framework of a social philosophy.

A totalitarian state (as the most extreme example of authoritarian control) may take the position that the teacher ought to cause students (1) to adopt or "take on" certain very specific attitudes; (2) to develop a number of fairly specific habits acquired through a multitude of prescribed activities; (3) to accept the orthodox pattern of beliefs and values, in terms of which the approved habits and attitudes fit together and make sense; and (4) to

From chapter 4, "The Unique Function of Information in a Democracy," *Alan F. Griffin on Reflective Teaching: A Philosophical Approach to the Subject Matter Preparation of Teachers of History* (Washington, D.C.: National Council for the Social Studies, 1992), 29–36. © National Council for the Social Studies. Reprinted by permission. [Originally the author's doctoral dissertation, Ohio State University, 1942.]

become aware of a body of facts carefully selected (or myths carefully constructed) to give evidential support to the accepted set of beliefs.

There is nothing vague or even very difficult about preparing teachers for so clearly defined a task as the foregoing; only the question of methods has any element of indeterminacy, and even here evaluation is so simplified by the clear and unequivocal character of the objectives that results of research can be handed on quite directly to practitioners, somewhat as in the field of medicine, without urgent need to make them understand the process through which the "better way" was developed and tested.

Education (and therefore teacher preparation) may be made thus simple and efficient whenever a society is prepared to set forth a hierarchy of preferred values and habits, a collection of unquestionable beliefs, a set of orthodox attitudes, and a selection of "things children ought to know" (a term which as here used is intended to suggest recognition and deliberate suppression of its opposite, "things children ought *not* to know"). Individuals are not lacking in America who are prepared to do precisely this thing, often in the name of democracy itself; fortunately, they tend at the moment to cancel each other out. They disagree sharply with one another upon the appropriate specific content for each of the foregoing categories, and each can see that to allow the other fellow to put *his* program into effect would be to contravene the democratic ideal.

But if democracy has no hierarchy of values—indeed, no preferred values at all—and if democracy does not suggest the specific attitudes an individual ought to adopt, the beliefs he ought to hold, and the particular body of facts he ought to "know," then the problem of teaching becomes an exceedingly intricate one, and the problem of teacher preparation is even more complex.[1]

Democracy and authoritarianism alike place upon teachers the obligation of modifying the beliefs, habits, attitudes and values of students. Authoritarianism can state quite clearly the specific changes it is trying to bring about. Democracy has no such specific wares to sell; for this reason many are inclined to accept operationally, even while they reject it verbally with some vigor, the proposition that the democratic ideal is bankrupt. If teachers are asked to bring about changes in pupils, and if they are forbidden to set up and work toward the specific changes they want to bring about, it would appear that we have laid upon them an utterly hopeless task.

It may help somewhat to repeat that the democratic ideal has been abstracted from a culture pattern—that we made it up as a meaning for activities which were going on within our experience. Widely divergent cultures may be characterized as "democratic" in several aspects, but it is quite impossible either to give specific content to "democracy" apart from a culture pattern, or to deduce the specific character of culture from the word "democratic."

The apparent absence from the democratic ideal of distinctive and positive content is, however, only apparent. It results from a trick of language which has furnished footless entertainment to men of all generations. This is the trick involved in the formulation, "If a man says 'I lie,' and tells the truth, he lies; but if he says 'I lie,' and lies, he tells the truth." It is the trick which provides the quality of apparent self-contradiction that characterizes all possible answers to the ancient question, "Is the class of all classes that are not members of themselves a member of itself?"

We need to realize that whenever a word such as, "true," "false," "know," "believe," "value," (as a verb) and the like is used, our language has moved to one level beyond that in which we express whatever is "known," "believed," "valued," or held to be "true" or "false." The man who says "I lie" cannot possibly refer to the words he is then uttering; he refers to some formulation at a lower level of abstraction, if he refers to anything.[2]

The picture of authoritarianism asserting boldly "Here are my specific, preferred values that men can live by. Where are yours?" and of Democracy piping plaintively, like Simple Simon, "Indeed, I haven't any," is exactly such a trick. A more accurate response would be "Democracy has no specific values *at the level of intellectualization at which all authoritarianisms operate.*"

When we have said that democracy has no preferred values, no orthodox beliefs, no official creed, we have correctly stated the case at one level of language—the level from which authoritarianism derives its sanctions and above which authoritarianism never goes, and dares not go. That is to say, authoritarianism can never stand off and examine or appraise the content of an accepted hierarchy of values, because it has nowhere to stand. The specific values *are* the frame of reference, and to move out of it, even for a peek, is to smash it.

But democracy can and does permit the intellectualization of its own position—indeed, democracy must insist upon that process in order to achieve a positive frame of reference at all. So long as democracy is held at the same language level at which authoritarianism asserts its values, the situation looks like a choice between a frame of reference with values and a frame of reference without values. No view of life could survive the acceptance of this latter status; a frame of reference devoid of positive values is no more than a blank sheet upon which each individual may write what he pleases.

This state of affairs is precisely what we ought to expect, so long as we remain at that level of abstraction which is the highest possible one for any authoritarian scheme. But a new level of language enables us to see the democratic refusal to espouse a hierarchy of preferred values as a positive insistence that values originate out of human experience, that standards arise through the common experiences of people living and working and thinking together, and that authoritarianism is simply the arresting of the process through which values and standards are generated. Authoritarianisms stop the process at different points and in different ways, but in every case they either deny that the process ever went on, or insist that it has now permanently ceased to operate. The values and standards upon which they fix are claimed as timeless and eternal, or as created somewhere outside the world of use and wont and imposed by a Supreme Being or a universal force.

In this sense, then, democracy asserts positive and definite values, which escape being called "preferred" only because at the level of intellectualization where democracy takes on its specific content there are no competing values over which the democratic values can be preferred. When democracy moves to a point of vantage for judging the ways in which values and standards originate and are maintained, authoritarianism can only call from its lower level, "You have no business to go up there!"

In a sense, therefore, it is quite unrealistic to talk about enabling an individual to "choose between" democracy and authoritarianism, as if these ways of life stood side by side. What we do, rather, is to help an individual to lift himself, at least momentarily, above the particular tradition out of which he has developed, and to let him see how his own and other sets of fixed standards have arisen in experience. As soon as he has stood inside the democratic frame of reference long enough to become conscious of its nature and of the commitments it involves, he is ready for the choice, "At which level do I propose to live the rest of my life?"

The man who has never faced this question can still participate in democratic living, but he cannot deliberately and purposefully make the democratic ideal his guide. In cases of conflict between groups, we easily lose him; he can, without consciousness of iniquity, ascribe final validity to his group's values of the moment, and join with others to hold those values as absolute. He is not committed to the widening of the group and the steady extension of common concerns as the method of democracy.

Nor is there any way of "indoctrinating" him in the democratic ideal. Indoctrination necessarily takes place at a level of intellectualization below the point where democracy takes on its specific and positive content. We could, indeed, indoctrinate *against* the values of any particular authoritarianism, but that would be to leave our victim at the mercy of the next plausible fixed system that came along. Commitment to the democratic ideal obviously involves much more than intellectualization, but it is quite impossible of achievement *apart from* intellectualization. The decision against indoctrination, within the democratic frame of reference, is therefore not a decision at all, but a recognition of what is possible. The reason why democracy cannot do business in that way is neither a sentimental squeamishness nor a pusillanimous dread of violent action, but rather the simple fact that the democracy has no offices on that particular floor.

A culture pattern at any moment, whether it tends in an authoritarian or a democratic direction, has and must have central and directing values of a fairly specific kind. Any authoritarian scheme sets forth clearly what these directing values must be. Democracy is concerned, not with the specific character of the directing values of the culture in which it is imbedded, but rather with the way in which central values come into being and are maintained or modified.

It is necessary to recognize, at the outset, that, *so far as any single individual is concerned,* the earliest acts of prizing or valuing grow out of and are built upon sheer animal preference. The human infant feels pleasure and pain, so far as we can tell, in about the same way as any other animal. Pleasure and pain get into his experience long before the process of carving objects out of his experience and identifying them has made any headway.

It must likewise be admitted that no method is known for purposely giving a particular direction to the behavior of little children except the method of conditioning, and that the development of certain personal and social habits which are indispensable both to the comfort and safety of the child and to the well-being of those who have to live with him can come about only because and insofar as the child's environment rewards the adoption of these habits and penalizes variations from them.

In the same way, the earliest beliefs of children are necessarily taken on, quite uncritically, out of the narrow environment that closely envelops little children in any society, democratic or authoritarian. Indeed, it is probably safe to say that, although the flavor of the relationships among adults in the democratic home may be sensed by a child long before he is capable of reflection, and although the very intent to develop self-direction in the child may strongly influence the precise methods employed by adults in conditioning him, the distinction between authoritarianism and democracy inside the experience of very young children will be at best an extremely subtle one.

A sharp practical distinction between authoritarianism and democracy as principles of social organization arises over the question, "Upon what shall we rely to secure that degree of agreement, both with regard to central values and with regard to fundamental beliefs, which all complex societies require in order to maintain themselves?"

The authoritarian answer is very clear. Authoritarianism relies upon the suppression or minimizing of *occasions for doubt*. As a consequence, the specific content of the beliefs and values taken on uncritically in infancy becomes a highly important matter. Uniformity among all the children in the state with respect to these beliefs and values, as well as consistency between them and the central values and preferred beliefs of the whole culture, is necessary if doubt is to be fully eliminated.

Equally necessary to authoritarianism is the creation of a climate of ideas in which expressions of doubt about fundamental beliefs or rejection of approved values are socially unacceptable forms of behavior. People must be taught to wear ignorance like a medal, and to say proudly, "I assure you I know nothing about such matters," or "Really, I prefer not to think about things of that kind." Steel whips and concentration camps are not the basis of authoritarianism, but only an exceptionally unpleasant consequence of it. The basis is the reliance by leaders, teachers, parents, or other authorities upon ignorance as a guide to the conduct of followers, pupils, or children. Social coherence and unity are guaranteed by (1) instilling preferred values and beliefs, (2) holding these values and beliefs as above or beyond question, and (3) carefully keeping out of people's experience any knowledge which might be seen as casting doubt upon the soundness of any preferred belief.

The foregoing paragraphs are not intended to suggest that authoritarian leaders have an easy time of it. Men think as naturally as they breathe, when occasions arise; and no one can wholly eliminate occasions for thinking from the experience of any individual. Even the process of minimizing such is beset with difficulties; but it will, after a fashion, do the job. It will unify and order nearly all the activities of nearly all the people in a state, giving them in some degree a sense of belonging, of commitment, even of security.

Democracies need these things quite as much as authoritarian societies need them. But democratic societies could in one emphasis be defined as societies which have found reliance upon the deliberately cultivated ignorance of the common man, as a method of social control, increasingly distasteful. In America, the areas which are held as above or beyond examination have dwindled to a very small number, and even these tend to open up whenever they limit practical action. Even beliefs about economics, religion, sex, and race, so far as these beliefs actually direct conduct, are not entirely protected from scrutiny. And certainly, although many would wish it otherwise, there is at present no carefully guarded core of uniform and consistent convictions around which our culture is built.

Upon what, then, may democracy rely for that degree of agreement which is indispensable to stability? How can men act together except in terms of common commitment to common convictions? And how can men hold to common convictions if they refuse to regard at least a few basic beliefs as settled, and to withhold them from critical examination? Can a man be fully loyal to that which he doubts, however slightly? Many a man has given his life under the banner "That the truth may prevail"; can men be expected to die for the slogan, "That the some-what-more-probable may be preferred over the rather-less-likely"?

To the question "Upon what does democracy rely for securing a sufficient uniformity of belief to permit common action to go forward?" this writer proposes the reply, "Upon knowledge." The answers to the other questions in the foregoing paragraph depend upon an elaboration of this point.

As a precautionary measure, it would be well to disclaim at the outset the notion that men in a democracy acquire most of their beliefs through the process of examining the evidence for them. Nothing could be less realistic. We need to act far too quickly and far too often for that.

When the taxi pulls up in front of my house, I do not run over in my mind the evidence for my belief that the man operating it is in fact an employee of the cab company and a reasonably normal citizen. As a confirmed reader of mystery novels, I am not unacquainted with the remote possibility that the cab has been stolen by a homicidal maniac who is now systematically following up the driver's call-list. But this possibility never occurs to me as I step confidently into the cab; I accept the belief that this man is the regularly assigned cab-driver simply because I have no reason for doubting it. If I insist upon trying to marshal evidence in support of every belief in the light of which I act, I shall almost certainly be spotted within a day or two as a hopeless neurotic.

In one sense, of course, this illustration is unrealistic, because I do not in fact formulate any belief about the cab-driver at all; I just get into the cab. But this is true of all behavior in which no elements of doubt are involved; we simply "take in" the situation at the level of recognition, so that there is no need even to formulate beliefs about it, let alone to examine them.

The very concept of "evidence for", or affirmative evidence, is ordinarily forensic rather than psychological. The evidence *for* any proposition, as marshalled by a debater or a lawyer, is simply a reorganization, for purposes of persuasion, of the range of experience which the proposition seems adequately to take into account. Only when beliefs are held consciously as hypotheses does affirmative evidence actually appear inside the reflective process. The process of inference may perhaps be regarded as a sudden identification of certain factors in a situation as "evidence for" the proposition inferred, but if so, its evidential quality is momentary and (in the form in which it is perceived) incommunicable. What we rely on is rather the *absence of negative evidence*, an absence which becomes steadily more significant as we extend the range of experience against which a given belief is tested. We can, and indeed must, accept out of the culture, without rigorous examination, an enormous number of beliefs for use in action; and so long as they are not controverted by some sort of negative evidence, we hold on to them. In this respect democracies and totalitarian states are alike.

Many men have reacted to the fact that we take on beliefs quite uncritically by protesting that we ought to do otherwise. Trotter, for example, writes:

> If we feared the entertaining of an unverifiable opinion with the warmth with which we fear using the wrong implement at the dinner table. . . . then the dangers of man's suggestibility would be turned into advantages.[3]

James Harvey Robinson is of a like opinion:

> *We vary rarely consider, however, the process by which we gained our convictions.* If we did so, we could hardly fail to see that there was usually little ground for our confidence in them. Here and there, in this department of knowledge or that, some one of us might make a fair claim to have taken some trouble to get correct ideas of, let us say, the situation in Russia, the sources of our food supply, the origin of the Constitution, the revision of the tariff, the policy of the Holy Roman Apostolic Church, modern business organization, trade unions, birth control, socialism, the League of Nations, the excess-profits tax, preparedness, advertising in its social bearings; but only a very exceptional person would be entitled to opinions on all of even these few matters. And yet most of us have opinions on all these, and on many other questions of equal importance, of which we may know even less. We feel compelled, as self-respecting persons, to take sides when they come up for discussion.[4]

It seems to the present writer that the two demands implied in the foregoing quotations, namely, (1) that men shall refuse to accept beliefs unless they have been "verified," and (2) that they shall abandon all claim to opinions on matters they have not carefully investigated, is an unreasonable and paralyzing demand.

Anyone who sets about the business of "considering the process by which he gained his convictions" is certain to discover that most of them have simply been picked up willy-nilly, in what Robinson calls a "careless and humiliating manner.[5] The effect of this discovery, especially if the discoverer regards it as "humiliating," is one of profound shock. This might be wholesome enough, if it were not for the fact that the person thus suddenly persuaded of his own complete inadequacy may fail to recognize his own situation as the common condition of all mankind.

There is no more reason for being ashamed of sharing with everyone else the common, nonreflective origin of our earliest convictions than there is for being ashamed of the circumstances which have invariably surrounded conception or birth. We accept beliefs uncritically because as children we can do nothing else. Apart from the process of wallowing in a culture and picking up what they can from it, children cannot arrive at the point where reflection is possible. To demand the privilege of choosing our earliest beliefs reflectively is no more practical than insisting on our rights to have some choice about our ancestry.

The distinction between democracy and authoritarianism lies neither in the specific content of the beliefs taken on from the culture in childhood, nor in the fact that they are accepted without examination, but rather in the degree and quality of the reliance which the society in question places upon them. An authoritarian society will be intensely concerned that these beliefs shall be the "correct" ones, because it rests its hope for stability and security upon insuring the uniform specific content of many of the beliefs of its members.

In the United States, we tend to concern ourselves much less about the specific content of a child's initial beliefs than about his ability to modify these beliefs appropriately later on. I am not here referring to the attitude of any parent toward his own youngster, because a great majority of parents assuredly do adopt an authoritarian reliance upon fixing very firmly, and, so far as intent is concerned, for life, the child's "right" initial beliefs, especially in the ticklish areas of religion and so-called moral standards. I refer rather to the attitude of the American public toward American children in general. No devout Lutheran would care to see his child brought up as a Roman Catholic, or a Unitarian, or a Baptist, but he is not ordinarily disturbed about the fact that millions of children in America are so brought up. The concept of heresy as a high crime, of "incorrect" belief as worthy of the death penalty, is an exclusively authoritarian concept.

It is in this sense that democracy places its final reliance for securing commitment to common goals upon common knowledge, and upon the development in each individual of the capacity for generating knowledge out of his experience.

Men may easily become impatient of the so-called "cultural lag"—that unhappy state of affairs in which the mass of the population continues to lend its support to the maintenance of social arrangements which, in the light of the knowledge that has been built up within the experience of experts, are palpably inadequate for modern conditions. But we cannot ask men who are full participants in a democratic society to direct their judgments in terms of knowledge they do not possess. To say that "sufficient knowledge exists" to justify sweeping changes in our social order makes very little sense if we mean by it only that a handful of men control that kind of knowledge.

So far as the ordinary man is concerned, the "knowledge acquired by experts" is simply another statement which claims to be authoritative and asks his support. He is bombarded by such claims and requests from all sides. Other things being equal, he is likely to prefer the beliefs he has already accepted without examination to new beliefs which he is in no better position to examine. In this preference he is clearly justified.

The development of people who are capable of steadily modifying their beliefs in terms of their adequacy for explaining a steadily wider range of experience depends upon two things: (1) improving and refining the reflective capacities of our population, and (2) breaking through the hard shell of traditional sanctity which encrusts many deeply rooted and emotionally charged beliefs. Whether these two jobs can be adequately done anywhere is a real question, testing more sharply than did the events of Lincoln's day whether any nation conceived in liberty and dedicated to the proposition that all men are created equal can long endure. The task has become in a real sense a race against time, and no man can wholly predict its outcome. One thing, however, is certain: the public schools are strategically the best-placed agency for getting the job done, and there is no time to lose. We have compromised and temporized too long, with the result that in the face of desperate crisis we are forced to waste valuable time and weaken morals in order to effect new compromises with the absolute authoritarian values we have tolerated and often fostered. This time the chips are down; the issue between democracy and authoritarianism is more clearly posed than it has ever been. To believe in democracy "with certain reservations," or "in due time," or "as an ideal, but of course it's impractical to act on it" is no longer a tenable position, if indeed it ever was.

Because teachers are people, they too have soaked up out of the culture certain unexamined beliefs and values which they sometimes hesitate to expose to critical examination, even by themselves. Under any decent conception of teacher training, these teachers have almost certainly had a chance, with some help, to stand off and realize that theirs are only some of the many sets of convictions which people have adopted without examination; that their own sets would assuredly have a different content if they had been born of another family or in a different locality; and that insistence on the validity of accidental and uncritical acceptance as a method for securing truth not only gives comfort to but actually justifies the Nazi ideology. They are, or should be, capable of realizing that whenever we hold any conviction in the light of which men act to be above or beyond examination, we urge the case for an irrational basis of conduct, for faith maintained by refusal to test, rather than by successful meeting of tests, and for deliberately cultivated ignorance as the method of preventing doubt. They have been, or should have been, led to face the question: "Is your fundamental loyalty to the democratic ideal, or to your own accidentally acquired habits?"

The foregoing paragraphs are in no sense an attack upon any specific belief which anyone may have happened to pick up. They urge simply that in a democracy all beliefs must be held on terms consistent with democracy—that they must be held as proper subjects for examination by the method upon which democracy places its basic reliance. The test of a belief is its capacity to explain and to organize human experience. Every belief must on demand[6] accept the role of hypothesis and prove its adequacy to explain and to order such relevant facts as may be adduced to test it. For example, anyone who asks his fellow-men to go on acting in the light of the belief that our economic system is self-regulating and can be trusted in times of peace to provide for the maximal welfare of all has the clear obligation to explain the events of 1929 in terms of his thesis.

The problem may now be summarized as follows: The ordinary high school student has accepted most of his beliefs uncritically, out of the culture. He could not have done otherwise. The inadequacy of his beliefs for enabling him to grapple effectively with the problems of today is appalling. Yet he has a "right" to his beliefs, in the sense that he cannot be expected to react to the injection into his experience of different possible beliefs by abandoning the old ones and taking on the new. From where he sits, the new beliefs differ from the old only by being less familiar—so far as their authoritarian character is concerned, they are identical.[7] We can communicate new beliefs to him only as ideas, or bits of purported knowledge. Unless he himself becomes able to carry forward effectively the process of "active, persistent, and careful consideration of a belief or supposed form of knowledge in the light of the grounds that support it and the further conclusions to which it tends,"[8] he and we are both helpless. And the carrying forward of this process requires that the student must locate within his own prior knowledge, or within such purported knowledge as he is able to dig up for the purpose at hand, the grounds on the basis of which belief may properly be vouchsafed to (or withheld from) any suggested proposition or idea.

It may be argued, quite correctly, that the "knowledge" which the child uses in testing a belief, whether it comes from his own prior experience or from research undertaken *ad hoc,* is still only "purported knowledge" and needs to be tested in its turn. This argument is valid as against an attempt to secure absolute certainty; it places unshakable assurance at the far end of an infinite regress. But if your goal is steadily more adequate beliefs, rather than eternal verities, the argument has no force. The student who has located, as grounds for believing a purported form of knowledge, other purported knowledge which he regards as *rather less doubtful,* and who has successfully used the belief under examination to explain and organize the purported knowledge which he later takes as evidence for the belief, has thereby, so far forth, rendered, *both the belief under examination and the supposed knowledge used to test it* relatively more certain. They have been arranged into a framework of mutual support. All of human knowledge gets its title to that name from its membership in some such framework.

Knowledge, then, has a special role to play in a democracy. So has the reflective process, through which knowledge is created and reconstructed. For these reasons, that which is often (and at times somewhat slightingly) referred to as "information" has likewise a unique role in democratic life.

The complexity of modern culture makes it quite impossible for everyone to explore intimately and at first hand all of the institutions and agencies that affect his daily living. No one can hope to acquire extensive personal familiarity with more than a fraction of the matters with reference to which decisions have to be made—decisions in which he ought to participate to the extent of his ability. He is therefore compelled to use as evidence, within the reflective process, assertions of other men about matters of fact—assertions which he accepts as factual, but which may, of course, whenever it seems necessary, be examined on their own account.

All sorts of valid charges may be leveled at history text-books and reference books; it cannot be denied, however, that they are loaded with potential information.[9] The word "information" and especially the expression "functional information" have been a source of confusion to educational thinking because of certain kinds of vagueness and ambiguity. The point of the present chapter has been made if the special role of information in a democracy is seen to consist in its use within the reflective process for the purpose of testing the adequacy of the beliefs in the light of which men live.

NOTES

1.   To anyone who cares to argue that democracy *can* do these things, I can only reply that in that case I find no differences between a democratic society and a totalitarian state; differences in the *specific content* of the value hierarchy will not support any such distinction, since they are common enough as *between* any two dictatorships.

2.   Cf. Russell, Bertrand: *An Inquiry into Meaning and Truth*, Chapter iii.

3.   Trotter, William: *Instincts of the Herd in Peace and War*, p. 45.

4.   Robinson, James Harvey: *The Mind in the Making, The Relation of Intelligence to Social Reform*, pp. 58–59.

5.   Ibid., p. 60.

6.   By "on demand" is here meant "whenever the belief is actually called into question either by the facts of a given situation or by a conflict

with another belief which suggests a different course of action," rather than "whenever anyone asks us to examine our beliefs."

7. It is, of course, possible for an authoritarian state to wrap the new beliefs in a special set of emotional appeals so intense that they will supplant beliefs of longer standing; but this process can scarcely be used on a large scale more than once in a generation. In any case, this possibility is at best a last desperate resort, so far as democracy is concerned.

8. Dewey, John: *How We Think*, p. 6.

9. Whether much of it can be converted from "potential information" into knowledge is a question on which men may easily differ *a priori*. The attempt to accomplish this conversion, undertaken on a large scale, would presumably answer the question, and at the same time determine whether there is a place for history in the school curriculum.

REFERENCES

Dewey, John. *How We Think*. Boston: D. C. Heath, 1910.

Robinson, James Harvey. *The Mind in the Making: The Relation of Intelligence to Social Reform*. New York: Macmillan, 1911.

Russell, Betrand. *An Inquiry Into Meaning and Truth*. New York: Norton and Company, 1940.

Trotter, William. *Instincts of the heard in Peace and War*. New York: Macmillan, n. d.

PART 2

Middle Years
The 1950s and 1960s

. . . in which Maurice Hunt and Lawrence Metcalf took Rugg's problems approach further—to society's *taboo* subjects; Shirley Engle proposed decision-making education as the heart of democratic education; Hilda Taba and Feeman Elzey narrowed the focus to teaching strategies that would stimulate productive and creative thought; and Donald Oliver and James Shaver widened the focus to building a relationship in students' minds between higher-order thinking and enduring public value conflicts.

QUESTIONS FOR DISCUSSION

1. What problems are emphasized? Neglected?
2. What was happening in North America and the world that might have shaped how these problems were articulated?
3. How is democracy defined? How are diversity and mutuality (difference and unity) treated?
4. What are similarities and differences across the chapters?

CHAPTER 5

Rational Inquiry on Society's Closed Areas

Maurice P. Hunt and Lawrence E. Metcalf
1955/1968

In every society, education is regarded as the transmission from one generation to another of that part of the culture which is considered of ongoing value. Although a culture has material as well as nonmaterial aspects, it is chiefly the nonmaterial with which education is concerned: attitudes, beliefs, knowledge, values, concepts, ideas, myths, skills, techniques, and habits. Education is the process by which the young are helped to develop or acquire the ideational and symbolic equipment believed necessary by adults to carry on a chosen way of life.

Almost every social-studies teacher believes that preservation of the cultural heritage is one of his chief purposes. But simply to say that the American heritage is to be preserved leaves many questions unanswered. Under this slogan, social-studies education can take many forms. Teachers may vary widely in the content they emphasize and the methods of instruction they employ. Such variety is almost certain to be the case in a society such as ours, with conflicts over the meaning of the good life as one of its defining traits. In an abstract sense, an appropriate education depends upon what kind of society is desired in the future. Without clarity on this question it is not possible to say what features of present culture possess continuing value. In our conflict-ridden society, teachers and other adults differ in their perception and understanding of present-day culture, and in their definitions of what would constitute cultural improvement. Teachers differ among themselves as much as they differ with lay publics.

It now appears to be the case that great uncertainty has developed in the United States over the kind of education we should have. Some of our most hotly debated and least intelligently considered issues relate to curriculum and methods of teaching in our schools. So great is the confusion that many Americans at this point in the twentieth century favor educational practices which would destroy those aspects of the culture which they claim to prize most highly. Like moths impelled by their tropisms to fly into a flame, they seem bent on destroying the very things they say they cherish.

PROBLEMATIC AREAS OF AMERICAN CULTURE

Certain aspects of American culture are especially relevant to any discussion of social-studies education. It has come to be granted that American culture is beset with problems. Problems seem to accumulate at a rate faster than we can solve them. It is our contention that this problematic aspect has not been well understood. It has not been understood that problems of social conflict exist not only as issues between individuals and groups, but also as sources of confusion within individual personalities. Neither has the existence of *closed areas* as one of the attributes of a problem area been widely recognized. It is one thing to say that American culture includes a "race problem." But it says a great deal more to observe that this problem exits not only between Negroes and whites, but within each, and that rational solutions are difficult to achieve because race is treated in the culture as a closed area. In our curriculum proposals, we argue for reflective studies of the problematic aspects of American culture, including elements of personal and social conflict that are sometimes closed to rational examination. The closures may arise from community taboos or personal prejudice.

Two Kinds of Social Conflict

Large-scale conflict is a trait of any culture that has reached our stage of development. But compared with many other cultures, ours is particularly conflict-ridden, and with good reasons. Settled by peoples of diverse origins and outlooks, the United States has been, ever since its founding, the scene of competing political, economic, and social beliefs. Add to this diversity the factor of industrialization. The change from agrarian-rural to industrial-urban society has generated some of our greatest conflicts. Industrialization speeds change with a result that from generation to generation beliefs undergo marked alteration. Gulfs are created between children and parents, parents and grandparents. Industrialization also fragmentizes society into specialized occupational and other economic groupings, each with its own version of the general welfare. "What is good for business is good for the country" is met or countered by the cry, "Our nation's welfare depends upon the freedom of the working man." And finally, we must add to our list of causes of conflict the fact that industrialization is taking place at an ever more rapid rate generation by generation, and consequently we seem to be falling farther and farther behind in our adjustments. A nation that has not brought its beliefs into line with the first Industrial Revolution now finds itself confronted by a second.

Students of present-day social conflict have found two levels of conflict, *interpersonal* and *intrapersonal*. Interpersonal conflict is exemplified by individuals or groups with sharply opposed beliefs. Such conflicts are usually referred to as "controversial issues." Persons on each side of an interpersonal conflict may be quite consistent in their own outlooks, even though in sharp disagreement with an opposing position. When the advocates of school integration clash with the proponents of racial segregation, we witness interpersonal conflict. Interpersonal conflicts rage in our culture between capital and labor; among social classes; among racial, religious, and ethnic groups; between the sexes; among age groups; and most tragically of all, among nation states, each of which knows that today's advanced weaponry has the capacity to obliterate the human race.

It is not unusual for an interpersonal conflict to become internalized within individual personalities so that people are at war not only with one another but with themselves. Caught in a culture in which interpersonal conflict is always present, they often accept as true and good both sides of many issues, thus incorporating cultural conflicts into their own personalities. When individuals become aware of their own incompatibilities of outlook, the resulting internal struggle produces intrapersonal conflict. Although the content of an intrapersonal conflict may be no different from that of an interpersonal one, it is more difficult to handle and may exact a greater toll as it leads to disintegration of personality.

Although these two kinds of conflict are different, they are often present at one and the same time. Disputants on opposing sides of an issue may be possessed of intrapersonal conflict, making self-understanding and compromise difficult to achieve. The interrelationship of these two kinds of conflict and their bearing upon moral problems has been best expressed by Myrdal in his discussion of American race relations:

> The American Negro problem is in the heart of the American. It is there that the interracial tension has its focus. It is there that the decisive struggle goes on. This is the central viewpoint of this treatise. Though our study includes economic, social, and political race relations, at bottom our problem is the moral dilemma of the American—the conflict between his moral valuations on various levels of consciousness and generality. The "American Dilemma," referred to in the title of this book, is the ever-raging conflict between, on the one hand, the valuations preserved on the general plan which we call the "American Creed" where the American thinks, talks, and acts under the influence of high national and Christian precepts, and, on the other hand, the valuations on specific planes of individual and group living, where personal and local interests; economic, social, and sexual jealousies; considerations of community prestige and conformity; group prejudice against particular persons or types of people; and all sorts of miscellaneous wants, impulses, and habits dominate his outlook. . . .
>
> The Negro problem in America would be of a different nature, and, indeed, would be simpler to handle scientifically, if the moral conflict raged only between valuations held by different persons and groups of persons. The essence of the moral situation is, however, that the conflicting valuations are also held by the same person. *The moral struggle goes on within people and*

not only between them. As people's valuations are conflicting,
behavior normally becomes a moral compromise. There are no
homogeneous "attitudes" behind human behavior but a mesh of
struggling inclinations, interests, and ideals, some held conscious
and some suppressed for long intervals but all active in bending
behavior in their direction.[1]

Moral dilemmas are not restricted to the area of race relations.
They abound in all areas of cultural existence. Consider the following: We have a great number of norms, or standards, to which
individuals are expected to accede—success, friendliness, honesty,
sexual purity, and a certain degree of gentility. Under given conditions these norms may conflict, as in the case of one who perceives
honesty as a barrier to his economic success. Current efforts of the
television industry to balance the extravagance of sponsor claims
with serious and responsible treatment of news events represent
one kind of compromise between competing ideals. Another kind
of conflict is between ends and means. Culturally imposed barriers
of physical and social conditions make it difficult or impossible
for many to achieve the goals implied by their culturally learned
ideals—for example, the inability of those whose lot is poverty to
achieve economic success.

Closed Areas

Individuals in our culture who have acquired intrapersonal conflict
are increasingly uncertain as to what to believe or value. Individuals who are inconsistent or uncertain, cannot engage in morally
responsible behavior based upon intellectual understanding and
personal commitment. The continued existence of uncertainty and
inconsistency on a large scale can be explained only as one turns to
the factor of *closed areas*.

Certain areas of conflicting belief and behavior are largely
closed to thought. In these areas, people usually react to problems
blindly and emotionally. Closed areas are saturated with prejudices
and taboos. Inconsistency or mutual contradiction in beliefs and
values rule behavior in any closed area. There is usually a reluctance to examine certain ideas because it is believed that they are
"impractical, theoretical, or in violation of common sense." Those
areas of belief which are most important to individuals are likely to
be those in which rational thought is least valued. In our culture,

irrational responses commonly occur in such areas as power and the law; religion and morality; race and minority-group relations; social class; sex, courtship and marriage; nationalism and patriotism; and economics.

The pedagogical significance of those closed areas is not well understood by most teachers of social studies. If a teacher were intent upon a reduction of prejudice, it would be necessary for him to address his efforts at beliefs and values in closed areas. Any belief that has not been subjected to rational examination is by definition a prejudice no matter how correct or incorrect it may be. Yet teachers rarely invade any closed area, even though every closed area can be opened by skillful, tactful, fair, and objective teachers.

Allusion to the "common sense" of the American people usually refers to their dominant beliefs in one or more of the closed areas. Failure to examine these beliefs in a social-studies classroom has certain effects upon the learning and motivation of students. Students do not learn in any significant and relevant sense the subject matter of history, economics, sociology, anthropology, political science, and geography. These are the very subjects teachers of social studies are hired to teach; but since the knowledge in each of these subject fields conflicts at many points with beliefs that predominate in the closed areas, teachers who take their teaching seriously are placed in a quandary. Many search desperately for items of information that have no bearing upon what students regularly believe, and proceed to teach these rather than basic concepts that would awaken or disturb latent conflicts of students. Students commit to memory names of all state capitals along with other items of information readily available in the reference volumes of any good library. But concepts such as cultural lag, ethnocentrism, deficit financing, gross national product, judicial review, to mention only a few, the meaning of which throws light upon the common sense of students, are either omitted entirely from the curriculum, or given the kind of treatment that leaves their relevance to society and its problems unclear.

Students from this kind of classroom express their boredom by complaint against the necessity of taking courses in the social studies. It is not unusual to find students from a culturally disadvantaged environment attending a social-studies course in which no attention is given to problems of caste and class as root causes of poverty. These students are expected to solve their problems of poverty by learning a trade. Teachers frustrated by this kind of situation often turn to a search for new techniques rather than significant content in order to increase student motivation. Symposia on programmed instruction or team-teaching become popular in-service training. Students who retain genuine intellectual interests pursue them outside school, and pretty much on their own.[2] Unfortunately, very few students retain an intellectual interest in social-scientific content after having been drugged over the years by a safe and sane social-studies education that specializes in an avoidance of issues in closed areas.

Our closed areas change from one historical period to another. Sex is now much more open to reflective study than it was fifty years ago, whereas comparative socioeconomic ideologies (including the issue of Communism) is more nearly closed to rational examination than even twenty years ago. At any given time, some of the closed areas we have listed will be much more tightly closed to reflection than will others; and all have their open aspects, facets which are relatively free of prejudiced belief.

At the same time, certain ideas remain immune to rational consideration from generation to generation. The current view that criticism of American policy in Vietnam gives aid, comfort, and hope to Hanoi reminds one of past criticisms of any dissent expressed during time of war.

Our closed areas exist as sources of totalitarian belief and practice in a culture that strains in two directions, democratic and authoritarian. The term *totalitarian* is appropriate here because the behavior of the American people with respect to closed areas is akin to behavior of leaders of totalitarian states. Each closed area has a set of sanctioned (albeit often irrational and inconsistent) beliefs that everyone is expected to follow, and which we try to inculcate in the minds of the young through propaganda; no one is taught to rely upon independent thinking for his answers, but on tradition, the church, or political leaders. People who get out of line find themselves in deep trouble; and severe pressure, both social and legal, may be placed on persons who have original ideas in these areas.

CLOSED AREAS, SOCIAL ISSUES, AND MENTAL HEALTH

It is hardly surprising that our sharpest intrapersonal conflicts occur in closed areas. Conflicts in areas of belief such as sex, religion, and race are not only common but often sufficiently intense to cause severe emotional disturbance. Many newspaper readers have been impressed by the "madness" of individuals who oppose equal rights for Negroes. In areas open to free thought, conflicts are frankly faced and resolved—if not easily, at least without undue tension. But in closed areas, every problem is likely to be troublesome simply because of the barriers to examining it.

During recent decades it has come to be widely recognized among social scientists and mental hygienists that discrepancies in a culture may have an eroding effect on the mental health of its members. We are told that "A well-integrated culture will presumably not produce as many maladjusted personalities as a disintegrated one. Cultures that are full of glaring inconsistencies will produce more than their share of personality difficulties."[3] Therapists who would reach the root causes of the difficulties faced by their patients dare not ignore the data and concepts of social-science disciplines.

Horney in pointing to cultural conflict as the root of certain personality problems has said, "When we remember that in every neurosis there are contradictory tendencies which the neurotic is unable to reconcile, the question arises as to whether there are not likewise certain definite contradictions in our culture, which underlie the typical neurotic conflicts."[4]

Jung observed that "We always find in the patient a conflict which at a certain point is connected with the great problems of society."[5] Since Jung's day we have witnessed the emergence of an entirely new discipline called social psychiatry.

Some cultural conflicts are more basic than others and cut across all our closed areas. Horney perceives three conflicts at the heart of American culture. One is between "competition and success, on the one hand, and brotherly love and humility on the other." Another is to be found in the tendency of our culture to stimulate needs far beyond the point where they could possibly be fulfilled. A third is between the individual's alleged freedom of choice and all the limitations our culture places upon him.[6]

In the first case, the ideology of competition and success

pushes one to be aggressive and assertive, willing to shove others out of the way. Christian ideals, on the other hand, insist that one should be unselfish and humble, willing to turn the other cheek, and prepared to accept the legacies of the meek.

The second conflict mentioned by Horney depends partly for its life blood upon the advertising industry. Advertisements encourage conspicuous consumption and keeping up with the Joneses. But great numbers of Americans find it impossible to fulfill the needs created by the advertising industry, and in Horney's words experience "a constant discrepancy between their desires and their fulfillment." This conflict would, however, probably exist without any assistance from advertisements. Our general culture stimulates individuals to want what they are not supposed to have. Adolescents, for example, are submitted to a variety of influences all of which seem to have sexual arousal or titillation as their aim. These influences often originate with respectable, nonpornographic, and nonobscene sources. These same adolescents are told, on the one hand, that sex before marriage is immoral, and on the other, that 50 percent of teen-age marriages end in divorce and that they should complete their education before marriage. Movies that deal sensitively and maturely with sexual problems are labeled "adult" and therefore officially off limits to teen-agers. Another type of movie, designed especially for teen and subteen clientele, narrates crudely and without artistic merit stories that involve prurient and lascivious themes. Only a confused culture, or a mad one, would ban the first kind of movie, and actively promote the second. An objective measure of prurience would no doubt find that teen-age movies are among our "dirtiest" and least edifying.

The third major conflict in our culture concerns any individual who learns to believe that "he can get what he wants if he is efficient and energetic." The counterpart of this belief attributes failure in any endeavor to individual rather than societal deficiencies. Individuals who learn this belief also learn that even such basic choices as occupation and mate are hemmed in by a variety of social limitations. Very few Americans are free to decide what their life is to be. The occupations of sons are often limited by the opportunities of fathers. And marital choices continue to be functions of propinquity, social class, and proper religious faith. An individual who is caught somewhere between free will and determinism is likely to waver "between a feeling of boundless power in determining his own fate and a feeling of entire helplessness."

Lynd has elaborated upon Horney's list of conflicts and has mentioned such contradictions as those "between saving and spending; between playing safe and 'nothing ventured, nothing gained'; between 'you've got to look like money in order to make money' and spending your money for the things you really want; between (if you are a woman) having 'brains' and having 'charm'; between things that are 'right in theory' and 'wrong in practice'; between change and stability; between being loyal and 'looking out for Number One'; between being efficient and being human; between being democratic and 'getting to know the right people'."[7]

Not everyone who grows up in a culture of contradictions becomes mentally disturbed. It is true that some authorities feel that, since certain conflicts are central to our culture and tend to be reflected in most personalities, there is a common neurotic type expressive of the times. Whether this is the case or not, there is no doubt that a substantial proportion of Americans—including the most sensitive, responsive, and intelligent—find it very difficult to come to terms with the conflicting pressures put upon them. Hullfish and Smith have argued convincingly that the mental practices of rationalization and compartmentalization are absolutely necessary to thousands of Americans who otherwise would be unable to deny or avoid conflict, and its concomitant heavy load of guilt.[8]

A social-studies education that helped young people to openly and rationally examine their conflicts in beliefs and values within closed areas would probably reduce rather than increase the incidence of neurosis. An intellectually rigorous as well as permissive and non-threatening examination would enable young people to progress toward solution of their problems of self-esteem, identity, anomie, alienation, and self-actualization, while at the same time acquiring many of those cognitive understandings possessed by social scientists.[9] Although such study of social issues would be desirable at all grade levels, it probably is most feasible in junior and senior high school. By the time students reach junior high school many are capable of the kind of propositional thinking necessary to a certain kind of social understanding.

Capacity to examine ideas in the closed areas depends very much upon the character of early childhood experience. Some homes and elementary schools provide children with a largely emotional basis for believing that certain outlooks are the only proper views of man and society. Many children are crippled mentally by schools and homes which provide them with rigid attitudes that act as blocks to their reflective development. Elementary schools need to decide whether their pupils can understand the big social issues. If it is decided that most of them cannot, then these issues should be omitted from the curriculum. Indoctrination of "right" social attitudes is least justifiable with a clientele that is said to be incapable of understanding the issues. A lack of analysis plus indoctrination of fixed attitudes is almost certain to produce the kind of student who finds it impossible to entertain new ideas.

CONFLICT RESOLUTION IN DEMOCRATIC SOCIETIES

The method by which culture is transmitted from generation to generation differs from society to society. We can illustrate this generalization by examining how education functions in two contrasting types of societies.

Education in a Modern Totalitarian State. An educational system designed to serve the needs of dictatorship will differ fundamentally from an education system designed to serve the interests of a democracy. One of the most significant facts of dictatorship, from the standpoint of education, is the existence of a body of doctrine which functions as a national ideology. This group of beliefs may be fairly consistent internally and pervade all areas of the culture. Its central ideas could be relatively unchanging over long periods of time, whether they revolve around racial supremacy or around the beliefs of Marx and Lenin. If the ideology does undergo change, it must first change within the thinking of totalitarian leadership, after which the new ideology is purveyed to the masses through the educational system.

The function of education in a dictatorship is the uncritical transmission of an official belief structure. The subject matter of education is thus predetermined and essentially the same in every school. The method of instruction is likewise uniform; it is the method of prescription and indoctrination. The "correct" beliefs are taught by withholding or slanting evidence. Doubt and reflection are rigorously excluded from classrooms, because in a dictatorship these are the truly subversive influences. It is particularly the case that reflection will be discouraged in the social sciences and moral philosophy.

In any culture, schools must take some stand with respect to how conflict and doubt are to be treated in classrooms. In a dictatorship, schools try to minimize both interpersonal and intrapersonal conflict by teaching an official ideology and by allowing students, so far as possible, to perceive only one side of questions which in a democracy would be regarded as highly controversial. In short, school authorities hope that suppression of free intellectual inquiry will reduce conflict to an innocuous level. Even so, in a dictatorship some conflicts are bound to appear, for many of the same reasons that they appear in any culture. When interpersonal conflicts arise, attempts are made to remove them from sight through use of propaganda and terror. If either interpersonal or intrapersonal conflict appears in the classrooms of a dictatorship, teachers have no alternative but to tell students what to believe and to try to gain assent through use of rewards and punishments.

In summary, a foremost task of education in dictatorships is uncritical transmission of sanctioned features of the culture, achieved by suppressing intelligence and by dealing forcefully with controversy wherever it threatens to unsettle the social order.

Education in a Democratic State. Although a democratic culture does not have an official ideology in the sense that a dictatorship has, it is assumed that, if a democratic society is to survive, there will have to be general agreement among its members as to central values. While peripheral values may remain in flux, a democracy is in peril if its citizens cannot agree on the meaning of core values such as dignity and worth of the individual, freedom, liberty, and equality. If agreement is absent at this level, survival of the society is still possible provided there is agreement on a method of inquiry by which to explore differences in the meaning and truth of propositions and the justifiability of values. In a democratic society the preferred intellectual method, sometimes called the method of intelligence, consists of logic and scientific investigation. If there is failure to establish agreement on core values, conflicts among individuals and groups and disintegration of personalities are likely to reach unmanageable proportions.

Some students of American culture feel that it is approaching a state of possible breakdown and disintegration because of a growing inability to agree on central values. It is thought that in addition to conflict normally attached to dispute over peripheral values, conflict is developing over fundamental ends. We are ceasing to be a community, as this term is used by sociologists.[10]

A challenge now before American education is to help the American people find consensus on the meaning of democracy—but in ways consistent with the requirements of democratic society. To say that the schools of America should teach children the American heritage, or that, whatever is meant by the American heritage, it should be taught to the young as something absolutely true and good, is an oversimplification. Any school in the United States which tries to transmit the cultural heritage uncritically, in the same manner in which officially supported beliefs are transmitted to the young in a dictatorship, finds itself in a difficult position. *There is not one heritage in the United States; there are many heritages.* The competing traditions that to some extent have always characterized our history and culture have had their conflicts accentuated by an accelerated rate of change during the past century. Uncritical transmission of all of them can do little but compound confusion and intensify conflict.

Consensus building has become synonymous with resolution of conflict. The means used to achieve consensus determine whether our society shall move in authoritarian or democratic directions. The achievement of consensus through reflective thought should mean two things: general agreement among individuals and inner harmony of individual personalities. An apt term for describing the unique task of education in a democracy is "creative resolution of conflict." By this we mean achievement, by disputing persons and by individuals suffering inner turmoil, of "third alternatives," that is, new positions which, although perhaps to some degree compromise competing outlooks, also include genuinely new values which effectively erase conflict and place life on a level of deeper insight. It is assumed that creative resolution of conflict can occur only in an atmosphere which is reflective and in which ego defenses are reduced to a minimum.

In summary, we say that the chief role of education in a democracy is intelligent or critical transmission of cultural heritages, during the course of which disagreements among individuals and incompatibilities in personal outlook are exposed and resolved creatively. Social-studies education gets to the heart of the matter when it recognizes that our many heritages include a totalitarian or authoritarian one. The most troublesome of present issues are over the question of whether we are to become more democratic or more authoritarian in our core values. To become more democratic is to expose closed areas to rational study. To close down further on inquiry in these areas is to move away from our democratic heritage and toward the authoritarianism we delight in denouncing when practiced by foreign powers.

THE ISSUE DRAWN

The issue posed in this chapter may be sharpened by reviewing briefly what has been said. Two features of American culture should be understood by every teacher of the social studies: the widespread presence of conflict and the existence of areas largely closed to rational inquiry. These two aspects of the culture are closely related. In closed areas, conflicts are more intense and more difficult to resolve than in areas relatively open to scientific inquiry.

The decisive differences between modern totalitarian and democratic societies lie in the methods of handling conflict and in the relative number of areas closed to rational thought. Again, these two are related. A culture which is consistently democratic resolves conflict in all areas reflectively, whereas a totalitarian culture tries to suppress conflict and to preserve its many closed areas.

The present is a time of moral crisis in that large numbers of persons in some nominally democratic nations have come to question certain ideas traditionally associated with democracy. They are afraid of their own creed. This fear shows primarily in a tendency to reject the method of critical inquiry in the realm of social affairs. There seems instead to be a growing disposition to flee to some sort of authoritarian principle in areas of pressing conflict.

The schools are implicated in this crisis. In any society, the schools serve as an arena in which typical methods of handling conflict are perfected and demonstrated. In a democracy, the schools must remain a sanctuary for creative resolution of conflict, which in turn requires the practice of critical inquiry in a democratic environment.

A RECOMMENDED APPROACH TO SELECTION OF SUBJECT MATTER IN THE SOCIAL STUDIES

We are now ready to suggest a purpose for social-studies education which takes into account both method and content: *The foremost aim of instruction in high-school social studies is to help students reflectively examine issues in the problematic areas of American culture.*

According to this statement of purpose, teaching materials should be drawn from a selection of conflicting propositions in such controversial areas as race and minority-group relations, social class, economics, sex, courtship and marriage, religion and morality, and national and patriotic beliefs, plus a wide range of relevant data to be used in testing them. Many of these propositions will be derived from, or correspond to, the values, beliefs, and attitudes of high-school students. One might say, therefore, that in any given learning situation teaching materials should be drawn from (1) broadly social and highly controversial issues of the culture; (2) knowledges, values, and attitudes of students; and (3) relevant data of the social sciences.

One reason why social-studies education should focus on issues in problematic areas is that it is here that personally felt problems (particularly intrapersonal conflicts) tend to intersect with pervasive and troublesome cultural issues. To study such problems provides a way of meeting both individual and social needs, by reducing the amount and intensity of intrapersonal conflict and by making such conflict more manageable as it arises. It is to be hoped that society will thus gradually achieve a clearer sense of direction, more harmony and cohesiveness, and fuller realization of the democratic idea.

Many objections will be raised to the above statement of purpose, method, and content. Some persons will argue that, if a policy of reflective learning is to be pursued at all, it should be followed only in connection with problems unaffected by strong emotional blockings; that further attempts to study problematic areas in the schoolroom not only will inflict on teachers the wrath of organized interest groups in the community but, because the same taboos operate in the minds of students as in the minds of parents, will necessarily be unsuccessful. It is thought that students, like their parents, believe what they want to believe— particularly in the problematic areas—and that attempts to produce reflection will not overcome this habit.

The task of getting students themselves to reflect on highly controversial matters has at least been made easier by knowledge gained from experience in psychiatry and group dynamics. Our concern now is to examine whether a teacher may reasonably expect to succeed (i.e., to produce reflection and help students achieve more harmonious and adequate beliefs), if he focuses his instruction on problematic areas. Assuming that the proper emotional climate has been achieved, there are at least two reasons why a teacher can expect success.

First, it is impossible to induce serious reflection in students unless they can be made to *feel* a problem. Reflection is hard and often painful work. Unless a fairly pressing or enticing reason has emerged, very few persons will willingly engage upon it. It is in the problematic areas that the great controversies, perplexities, and doubts of adolescent youth occur. A skillful teacher should be able to produce a higher level of motivation through study of issues in problematic areas than through study of almost anything else. It is true that beliefs in these areas are deeply cherished and that this may produce a serious barrier to reflection; but, by the same token, a teacher can usually create a reason for reflection by showing how one cherished belief is incompatible with an equally prized one.

Second, young people are reputedly more flexible and open-minded than adults. There are no problematic areas at all in the outlook of a very small child. It is education, both formal and informal, which gradually closes certain areas of living to rational discussion. However, the high-school period is also a time when youth begin to wonder about many of the beliefs they have learned to take for granted. Intellectual interests of many young persons reach their peak at this time. Serious doubts develop as it is noted that adults do not always practice taboos which they have taught children to embrace. Faith in the omniscience of adults is shaken and one may note a general tendency to rebel against parental authority. Given the storm, the stress, the uncertainty, and the rebelliousness of this period, a serious threat to social stability results from any educational program which fails to take advantage of the motives for reflective study which develop during the high-school years.

Many adults fear that tender young minds will not be able to understand the more serious controversies of life. Actually, the so-called tender young minds are more likely than adult minds to profit from reflective study of deeply controversial issues. If it is postponed until adulthood, such study never is likely to occur.

The fear that youth will accept "wrong" beliefs if they open their minds to new ideas is actually only a fear that they will accept *different* beliefs. This is not necessarily the outcome. Reflection may fortify or it may undermine conventional beliefs. There are no prior guarantees as to what conclusions it will produce, but a great many conventional beliefs can emerge from reflective scrutiny more strongly accepted than before. The aim of reflection is never to destroy a belief, but to evaluate it in light of the best evidence and logic. Reflection can only guarantee the emergence of beliefs which are relatively more adequate and harmonious than the ones young persons normally hold.

CURRICULUM ORGANIZATION FOR A REFLECTIVE APPROACH TO LEARNING

Standard Subjects As Burdened with Irrelevant Content

Much of the subject matter of standard social studies is irrelevant to problem solving in areas of ideological controversy. Learning materials are relevant when they can set and clarify problems for students or move them toward conclusions, preferably in the form of generalizations which have predictive value. If materials are unrelated, or cannot be related, to any imaginable values, beliefs, or attitudes of students, it will be difficult and probably impossible for them to supply content for reflection. This does not mean that a student must have an attitude toward the tariff, for example, in order to learn reflectively about the tariff. He may have an attitude toward something else—say, the cost of living—which can be clarified by his introduction to scholarly studies of the tariff.

Inclusion in the standard subjects of irrelevant material is not in itself an argument against a curriculum of separately organized subjects. We might retain our history, geography, and civics courses and, by proper revision of the subject matter in each, create courses far more provocative and useful than anything we now have. There is another respect, however, in which a curriculum of separately organized courses is less than ideal.

Life Problems and Subject-matter Boundaries

The content of any act of thought is likely to cut across subject-matter boundaries. Life problems of students almost invariably extend across more than one field of inquiry, unlike textbook problems of history, political science, economics, or any other social-science subject. If any issue of broad social import is to be under-stood, probably it can best be done through study of data from several of the social sciences and perhaps a number of other fields as well. For example, problems of race cut across the fields of politics, economics, religion, biology, psychology, and probably others. In commenting on the curricular consequences of a separate-subject organization, Professor Harold C. Hand said:

> In consequence of this conflict of inner logic—i.e., the inner logic of real-life-problem-solving vs. the inner logic of standard subjects which at best admits of but incidental attention to such problems—efforts to functionalize the traditional high school subjects invariably and inevitably result in asking the teacher simultaneously to serve two contrarily-oriented masters. That this is frustrating in the extreme, there can be little doubt—as any number of intelligent and conscientious teachers will testify. What is more important, the traditional master almost invariably wins out in this unhappy and unequal struggle—to the educa-tional neglect of society and youth, as we have demonstrated. If the course is labeled "English" or "social studies" or any other name identified with a recognized body of more or less standard subject matter, the teacher is conscience-stricken unless he gets across at least a respectable minimum of whatever this subject matter may be. This he usually does regardless of the fate of the problems with which he is also supposed to be dealing. But this neglect of problems also induces feelings of guilt, it must be recognized. What this adds up to is scarcely a recipe for good mental health.[11]

The Logic and Plan of the Core Curriculum

The core curriculum, or course in "common learnings," has been proposed as a solution to this conflict. Although many of the standard school subjects are retained for purposes of specializa-tion, the most important offering of the curriculum focuses deliber-ately on problems of living. A block of time, two or more hours, is reserved for their study, and teachers responsible for this are freed from other subject-matter commitments. Experience to date sug-gests that teachers working with a core curriculum have not always understood the pedagogical implications of a reflective approach to learning. Teachers who are free to organize a core along lines most congenial to a reflective approach may be helped by the following suggestions: *A core should be problem centered, and organized on the basis of a series of apparent contradictions in belief in problematic areas of the culture which we might expect to be shared by most students.* Work should be organized in a sequence of blocks, one on the study of discrepancies in our racial ideology, another concerned with discrepancies in our beliefs about government and politics, another with discrepancies in our economic thinking, and so on. Ideally, all the major problematic areas would be covered in such a core, although probably not in any one year. In fact, it might be advisable to limit a single year to exploration of no more than two or three broad problem areas.

Although a core of this sort would inevitably "integrate" the social studies and embrace data from fields such as literature, psychology, philosophy, human biology, and perhaps other fields, it would not integrate simply for the sake of integration. The focus would always be *on a problem and what is needed to study it.* Irrelevant material would be rigorously excluded. The study of a particular issue might be regarded as a "unit of work," provided *unit* is defined broadly to refer to the experiences related to reflective study of an issue.

What Problematic Areas Should Be Studied?

How should a curriculum maker select which problematic areas to treat in the social studies? Answering this question is not as difficult, perhaps, as it seems. A teacher needs to ask questions such as, "Is this an area of wide social concern, an area generating problems for large numbers of Americans?" "Is this an area which, in addition to widespread concern, is also of concern to my own students?" "If it is not of concern to my students, am I likely to have reasonably good luck in getting them concerned?" "Is this an area which I am capable of handling competently?" "Will we have in this school and community, or in what we can secure from elsewhere, teaching materials containing sufficient relevant factual data so that beliefs may be tested reflectively?" And last, "Is this an area too touchy to treat openly in the classroom in this particular community?"

NOTES

1. Gunnar Myrdal, with the assistance of Richard Sterner and Arnold Rose, *An American Dilemma; The Negro Problem and Modern Democracy,* Harper & Row, 20th Anniversary Edition, 1962, pp. lxxi–lxxii. Italics in original.

2. By intellectually serious students we do not refer to those grade-grabbers and credit-chasers seeking entrance into a university who seem to abound in the habitat of suburbia.

3. Francis E. Merrill and H. Wentworth Eldredge, *Culture and Society*, Prentice-Hall, 1952, p. 180.

4. Karen Horney, *The Neurotic Personality of Our Time*, Norton, 1937, p. 287.

5. C. J. Jung, *Two Essays on Analytical Psychology*, Dodd, Mead, 1928, p. 23.

6. Horney, *op. cit.*, pp. 287–289.

7. Robert S. Lynd, *Knowledge For What?*, Princeton University Press, 1948, p. 103.

8. H. Gordon Hullfish and Philip G. Smith, *Reflective Thinking: The Method of Education*, Dodd, Mead, 1961, pp. 54–56.

9. Louis E. Raths, Merrill Harmin, and Sidney B. Simon, *Values and Teaching*, Merrill, 1966. See chaps. 1, 2, 3, and 4 for a significant theory of values.

10. See Joseph K. Hart, *Education in the Humane Community*, Harper & Row, 1951. Also W. O. Stanley, *Education and Social Integration*, Columbia University Press, 1953.

11. B. Othanel Smith, William O. Stanley, Kenneth D. Benne, Archibald W. Anderson (eds.), *Readings in the Social Aspects of Education*, Interstate Press, 1951, pp. 387–388.

CHAPTER 6

Decision Making

Shirley H. Engle
1960

My theme is a very simple one. It is that, in teaching the social studies, we should emphasize decision making as against mere remembering. We should emphasize decision making at two levels: at the level of deciding what a group of descriptive data means, how these data may be summarized or generalized, what principles they suggest; and also decision making at the level of policy determination, which requires a synthesis of facts, principles, and values usually not all found on one side of any question.

In order to make my case, it is useful to draw certain distinctions between the social sciences and the social studies. The social sciences include all of the scholarly, investigate work of historians, political scientists, economists, anthropologists, psychologists, and sociologists, together with such parts of the work of biologists and geographers as relate primarily to human behavior. Closely related fields include philosophy, literature, linguistics, logistics, and statistics. The social studies, including the content of the textbooks, courses of study, and whatever passes in the school for instruction in civic and social affairs, are based on the social sciences but they clearly involve always a selection of and distillation from the social sciences—they encompass only a minor portion of the social sciences.

From *Social Education,* 24 (November 1960). 301–306. © National Council for the Social Studies. Reprinted by permission.

Selectivity, therefore, is one of the features which distinguishes the social sciences from the social studies. To social science, knowledge is useful for its own sake; all knowledge is of equal worth; there is no concern for immediate usefulness. To the social studies, a central consideration must always be that of determining what knowledge is of most worth. If all of the knowledge of a field of study is to be boiled down into one textbook, what is to be emphasized? If all of the knowledge of the area is to be boiled down into one course of study, what is most important?

There is a more basic distinction to be drawn between the social sciences and the social studies than merely that of selectivity. The impelling purpose of the two is quite different. The orientation of the social scientist is that of research. The more scientific the social scientist, the more specialized becomes his interest, the more consuming becomes his desire to know more and more about less and less, the less concern he shows for broad social problems. He is far more inclined to analyze, dissect, and proliferate than to unite, synthesize, and apply. His absorbing interest is to push back the frontier of dependable knowledge in some limited sector of the social scene.

In marked contrast to the meticulous research orientation of the social sciences, the social studies are centrally concerned with the education of citizens. The mark of the good citizen is the quality of decisions which he reaches on public and private matters of social concern. The social sciences contribute to the process of decision making by supplying reliable facts and principles upon which to base decisions—they do not supply the decisions ready made. The facts are there for all to see but they do not tell us what to do. Decision making requires more than mere knowledge of facts and principles; it requires a weighing in the balance, a synthesizing of all available information and values. The problems about which citizens must reach decisions are never confronted piecemeal, the facts are seldom clearly all on one side, and values, too, must be taken into consideration. A social problem requires that the citizen put together, from many sources, information and values which the social sciences treat in relative isolation. Thus in the social studies the prevailing motive is synthesis rather than analysis. The social studies begin where the social sciences end. Facts and principles which are the ends in view in the social sciences are merely a means to a further end in the social studies. The goal of the social studies lies not merely in information but in the character of people. The goal is the good citizen.

A good citizen has many facts at his command, but more, he has arrived at some tenable conclusions about public and social affairs. He has achieved a store of sound and socially responsible beliefs and convictions. His beliefs and convictions are sound and responsible because he has had the opportunity to test them against facts and values. In the process of testing his ideas he has greatly increased his fund of factual information and he has become increasingly skillful at intelligent decision making. The development in the mind of students of such a synthesis of facts and values, together with the development of skill in making decisions in the light of numerous and sometimes contrary facts and values, is the special forte of the social studies.

If the purpose of the social studies is to be education for citizenship, if its primary concern is to be the quality of the beliefs and convictions which students come to hold on public questions, and if we are to be concerned with the development of skill at decision making, then there are some things which it becomes imperative that we do in teaching the social studies. I would like to develop briefly some of these imperatives.

We must abandon our use of what I shall call the ground-covering technique, and with it the wholly mistaken notion that to commit information to memory is the same as to gain knowledge. By ground covering I mean the all too familiar technique of learning and holding in memory, enforced by drill, large amounts of more or less isolated descriptive material without pausing in any way, at any time, to speculate as to the meaning or significance of the material, or to consider its relevance and bearing to any general idea, or to consider its applicability to any problem or issue past or present. Even when such material is interesting, and it sometimes is, merely to cover it in this uncritical, matter-of-fact fashion robs the material of its potential for accurate concept formation or generalization which will be useful to students in understanding events and conditions in other times and places in which like data appear. Simply reading and remembering the stories about Indians in our history, no matter how many times repeated, has never insured the development of accurate concepts about Indians or correct generalizations about the relationships between people of divergent cultures and histories. Or, if in our haste to cover ground, we refuse to deal contemplatively and critically with the material we are covering, the student may generalize haphazardly and may, without our help, arrive at totally erroneous conclusions. Thus, it may be said with good reason that the study of Indians frequently does more harm than good, teaching more untruth than truth.

The ground-covering fetish is based on the false notion that remembering is all there is to knowing or the equally false notion that one must be well drilled in the facts before he can begin to think. M. I. Finley, noted British historian, says about ground covering that "a mere telling of individual events in sequence, no matter how accurately done, is just that and nothing else. Such knowledge is meaningless, its mere accumulation a waste of time. Instead, knowledge must lead to understanding. In the field of history this means trying to grasp general ideas about human events. The problem is to move from particular events to the universal; from the concrete events to the underlying patterns and generalities."

Equally fallacious is the background theory of learning, or the notion that we must hold the facts in memory before we are ready to draw conclusions from them or to think about their meaning. This theory is at considerable variance with recognized scientific method and the ways in which careful thinkers approach an intellectual problem. The thinker or scientist frequently engages in speculation or theorizing about possible relationships, from which he deduces tests or possible facts which, if observable, verify his theory. (Some of the great break-throughs in knowledge have come about in this way.) To say that a thinker must know all that he needs to know, let alone hold all this in memory, before engaging in thought is to completely hog-tie his intellectual development. And there is no valid reason in this respect for differentiating between a student trying to understand Indians and an Einstein speculating about the meaning of space.

What happens in our classrooms from too strict an adherence to ground covering is that the number of facts committed to memory is reduced to a relatively small number. These are the so-called basic facts which we learn, and just as promptly forget, over and over again. Thus ground covering actually works to reduce and restrict the quantity of factual information treated in our classes. What is needed instead is a vast multiplication of the quantity of factual material with which students are asked to deal in the context of reaching a reasoned conclusion about some intellectual problem. Such an enrichment of factual background will come about when we turn from our preoccupation with remembering to a more fruitful concern for drawing conclusions from facts or for testing our speculations and ideas about human events with all of the relevant data we are able to collect.

For ground covering, or remembering, we should substitute decision making, which is reflective, speculative, thought provoking, and orientated to the process of reaching conclusions. My thesis is simply this, decision making should afford the structure around which social studies instruction should be organized. The central importance of decision making in the social studies has been cited earlier. The point here is that students are not likely to learn to reach better decisions, that is, grounded and reasoned decisions, except as they receive guided and critically oriented exercise in the decision-making process.

Decision-making opportunities in the social studies classroom may run the entire gamut of difficulty, from very simple situations which take the form merely of posing questions for class consideration which require some thought and a synthesis of information supplied in a single descriptive paragraph to very complex social problems involving questions of public policy or individual behavior. Thus, in studying the Plains Indians in the post-Civil-war period a low level decision could be required by asking which of the following sentences accurately, or most accurately, summarizes the difficulty continually experienced in Indian affairs: (1) The Indians were treated by the settlers as trespassers on land which they (the Indians) had inhabited and claimed as their own for centuries; (2) The Plains Indians were wanderers who knew no fixed abodes and recognized no exclusive right of anyone to own the land; (3) Renegade Indians nd white outlaws were at the seat of Indian trouble (this is the Hollywood version of Indian affairs); (4) The handling of Indian affairs by the United States government was characterized by wanton disregard of Indian rights, by treachery, and by broken promises; or (5) The different manner of using the land by the Indians and the whites made agreements between the two impossible. At a higher level of difficulty a decision would be required if one asked, "Do you think General George Crook dealt fairly with the Shoshone chief, Washakie, during the military campaigns to pacify the Plains Indians? What are your grounds?" Or at a still higher level of complexity, there is the question of what should be the policy of the United States toward Indians who contest the sovereignty of the United States.

Some decisions involve essentially matters of fact. For example, suppose we are reading about the building of the transcontinental railroads in the 1870's, 1880's, and 1890's and how the government gave large grants of land and money to the railroad companies to encourage them to build the railroads. We read further that subsequently the railroads, or most of them, went into bankruptcy but also that following their construction the country experienced a great expansion of agricultural and industrial wealth whereby our exports of wheat and corn multiplied tenfold in 20 years, and in the same period the value of our manufacturers' products increased 200 percent, 180 new factories were being built in Philadelphia alone. We have these and many other facts. But the decision rests in concluding what these facts mean. What do they all add up to? Which of the following generalizations accurately summarize these facts? Government subsidization of key industries brings a vast multiplication of other industries under private ownership; private investors will not take the extraordinary risk necessary to start a really new industrial development; one industrial development inevitably leads to other industrial developments; industry in which the government interferes is always inefficient and will fail in the end; private industry can never be expected to provide the transportation facilities needed for an expanding economy; government participation in industry tends to dry up the growth of private industry; industry resulting from government spending is uneconomical and is doomed to fail in the end; if the government had foregone the tax money used to aid the railroads, private individuals would have had money which they would have invested in the railroads. Clearly, the making of decisions among the alternatives listed above is essentially a matter of sorting out and applying facts until a conclusion is reached which honestly and accurately summarizes all facts that are relevant to the problem.

Other decisions, perhaps we should say most decisions, involve values as well as facts. Thus, in dealing with the issue of which of two proposed solutions to the problems of farm surpluses is best, one may conclude, factually, that government support of farm prices leads inevitably to inefficiency in agriculture and to unnecessarily high cost for food and fibre which the farm produces. This much is a factual conclusion. But this does not necessarily get us out of the woods, for one might still prefer government-supported agriculture to an unregulated agriculture because he feared the control of large agricultural corporations (which will almost inevitably follow the removal of governmental restrictions—another factual generalization) more than he fears governmental controls. The latter decision is a value judgment, though one fraught, as are all value decisions, with still further implications which could be grounded factually. For instance, in a hierarchy of values, the *greatest degree of individual freedom* may be the value sought or agreed upon by all involved in the decision. From this premise a factual investigation could be conducted of the relationship between government regulation and individual freedom on the one hand and between corporate control and individual freedom on the other. Thus, though the decision as to value is not in this way resolved, the exact issue over values is clarified by such a factual investigation of the alternatives.

If decision making is to be the focus of social studies instruction, we will need to introduce vastly larger quantities of factual information into our classrooms. Drill to the point of memory on a few basic facts will never suffice. The superficial coverage of one textbook will never be enough. The very moment that a conclusion, such as any of those suggested above, is reached tentatively, the natural demand is for more facts with which to test the conclusion. This means almost surely the introduction of large quantities of supplementary materials, with far too much content to be committed to memory. It means a reversal in the usual attitude on reading habits whereby students will be expected to read larger quantities of materials, to read them more rapidly, and to read them for purposes of getting general ideas or of locating relevant information rather than to read small quantities of material, slowly and laboriously, a few pages each day, for purposes of committing the material to memory. It may mean in the end the abandonment of textbooks and the substitution of numerous, more substantive, more informative, and more exciting books and other materials.

If the quality of decision making is to be the primary concern of social studies instruction, we must take steps to up-grade the quality of intellectual activity in the social studies classroom. Research is demonstrating the disquieting prevalence in many social studies classrooms of what is generously labeled shoddy thinking procedures. In fact, social studies classrooms seem to exhibit quality of logic far below that exhibited in classrooms in which science, mathematics, or even English is being taught. Admitting the greater difficulty of our content, this is still something about which we cannot be complacent. Among the common errors in logic easily observed in social studies instruction is the acceptance of an assertion as if it were a fact, the confusing of fact with opinion, the validation of the truth of something on authority, the acceptance of a merely plausible explanation for a sufficient explanation, the failure to agree on the meaning of key words (frequently value laden) before engaging in an argument in which the meaning of the word is essential as, for instance, to argue over whether the first Roosevelt was a good or a strong President without first agreeing on a common meaning for "good" and for "strong," and the confusing of questions which must be referred to facts for an answer and those which defer to values for an answer. The persistent practice in our classrooms of errors in logic of the kind mentioned can lead only to intellectual confusion and irresponsibility. If we are really concerned with effective citizenship, we must not only provide the opportunity for decision making but we must see to it that decisions are made in keeping with well known rules of science and logic and that students get practice in making such decisions.

Lastly, if responsible decision making is the end of social studies instruction, we must recognize values formation as a central concern of social studies instruction. Real life decisions are ultimately value decisions. To leave a student unaware of the value assumptions in his decision or to leave him untrained in dealing with value questions is literally to lead an innocent lamb to the slaughter. Such a student could, and he frequently does, return to our fold and say, "But you didn't tell me it was this way." Or he may quickly sink into cynicism or misbelief. The question of what values he should hold probably cannot be settled in the classroom, but values can be dealt with intelligently in the classroom. The nature of the values which people hold can be made explicit, the issues over values can be clarified, and the ends to which holding to a particular value will lead can be established factually to some extent. For instance, it is possible to predict with some accuracy the factual results of valuing segregation over integration in the United States with respect to such matters as economic productivity of the American people, the respect with which America is held abroad, the effect on the efficiency of our educational system, the genetic mixing of the races, etc. Thus, it becomes possible to engage in some appraisal of the value in terms of other values held, as, for instance, world peace, Christian brotherhood, economic security and well being, national unity, the right to choose one's own friends, etc. We can compare and appraise value, to some extent, in an extended hierarchy of values from lower value, such as a preference for having one's hair cut in a segregated barber shop, to higher values, such as the belief that all men should be treated with equal respect.

To duck the question of values is to cut the heart out of decision making. The basic social problem of America today is a problem of value. In simple terms the problem may be stated as to whether we value more the survival of a free America which will require sacrifice for education, for materials of defense, etc., or whether we value more our right as individuals to spend our resources on extra fins for our cars and for all the other gadgets of conspicuous consumptions. It is not impossible to predict the outcome of hewing to either choice. It is not at all certain that our students are being prepared to make the right decision and to make it in time.

My thesis has been a very simple one. It is that quality decision making should be the central concern of social studies instruction. I could cite many renowned people as having essentially supported the position I have here tried to state. Among the ancients these would include Socrates, Plato, and Thucydides, the father of objective history. These would include the great modern philosopher Alfred North Whitehead and such modern critics as the economist Peter Drucker and President Robert F. Goheen of Princeton. But to quote these would continue the discussion overlong, as I suspect I may have done already. So may I quote instead a simple statement from the noted modern scientist Hans Selye, who has said that "facts from which no conclusions can be drawn are hardly worth knowing."

CHAPTER 7

Teaching Strategies and Thought Processes

Hilda Taba and Freeman F. Elzey
1964

The development of critical thinking has figured as an important objective of education for a long time. Yet, the implementation of this objective in curriculum construction and teaching has been sporadic and ineffective for a variety of reasons.

First, thinking has been treated as a global process. Consequently, the problem of defining thinking is still before us, as is the need to identify its specific elements, especially in terms which are helpful to planning effective teaching strategies. In a jungle of definitions, thinking has meant anything that goes on in the head, from daydreaming to creating a concept of relativity. Neither has knowledge of the development of thinking been too adequate. While Piaget has spent his lifetime in studying the development of thinking and has produced a quantity of reports, until recently, his work received scant attention in the United States.

Implementation of thinking as an educational objective has also been handicapped by several questionable assumptions. One rather widely accepted assumption is that reflective thinking cannot take place until a sufficient body of factual information is accumulated. Teaching which follows this assumption stresses factual coverage and burdens the memory with unorganized and, therefore, rather perishable information.

An opposite, but equally unproductive, assumption is that

From *Teachers College Record*, 65(6), 1964, 524–534. Reprinted by permission.

thought is an automatic by-product of studying certain subjects and of assimilating the end-products of disciplined thought. Some subjects are assumed to have this power independently of how they are taught or learned. Inherently, memorizing mathematical for-mulae or the steps in mathematical processes is assumed to be better training than memorizing cake recipes, even though both may be learned in the same manner and call for the same mental process—rote memory.

The combination of these factors has prevented the focusing of attention on the development of teaching strategies designed to stimulate productive and creative thought. The curriculum is sel-dom organized to focus on active discovery and the use of abstract ideas. Classroom learning experiences are not usually designed to provide a cumulative sequence in the maturation of thought which is at once psychologically sound and logically valid.

All this has contributed to considerable underachievement in the mastery of autonomous and disciplined thought processes. Hence, a rather frequent criticism of current teaching-learning pro-cedures is that they tend to cultivate passive mastery instead of an active discovery of ideas—a tendency to follow "recipes" in solving problems instead of analyzing them and searching for generaliza-tions with which to organize the needed facts and to plan an attack on them (1, 3).

COGNITION REVISITED

Recently, there has been a renewed interest in the study of cognitive processes in general and thinking in particular. For example, Bart-lett (1) and Rokeach (15) have been concerned with open and closed thought. Getzels and Jackson's study (8) of creativity and Gallagher's study (7) of productive thinking employed the classifi-cation of divergent and convergent styles of thought. Sigel (16) has been interested in the relationship of the styles of organizing and labelling to personality dynamics.

The difficulty with such studies is that the findings about gen-eral cognitive styles fail to shed light on the processes by which these styles are acquired. Consequently, the data cannot be trans-lated into guidelines for more effective teaching.

The study of thinking in elementary school children, on which this paper is based, set out to examine the processes of thought in the classroom in terms which are capable of shedding a light on the learning and teaching of certain cognitive skills in the school setting. The fundamental assumption was that thought consists of specific, describable processes which are subject to training, not in some category of powers which are inherent in the individual. Therefore, the study sought to create categories for analyzing thought which described learnable, and therefore also teachable, processes of thought. Specific processes in three cognitive tasks were identified: (1) concept formation, (2) the making of inferences and the induction of generalizations from interpretations of specific data, and (3) the application of generalizations to explain new phenomena and to predict the consequences of certain events and conditions. Critical thinking *per se* was excluded because the curriculum offered meager opportunities for its development.

The study was also conducted under conditions which presumably offered optimal conditions for the training of thought processes. First, the 20 elementary classrooms involved followed a social studies curriculum which centered on a series of basic ideas and was organized for an inductive discovery and development of these ideas. In addition, the curriculum outline also included a planned sequence of learning experiences designed to enhance the development of generalizations and their application to solving pro'·lems (4).

Finally, the design for the study provided for special training of the teachers in the analysis of thought processes and in devising effective teaching strategies for their development. In other words, the study proposed to explore thinking under conditions which included the twin impact of the curriculum and of specified teaching methods.

THE THEORETICAL FRAMEWORK

The study, as well as the curriculum which provided the context for it, and the training of teachers were based on several concepts regarding the nature of thought and its development. First among these was the idea that the maturation of thought follows an evolutionary sequence in which the simpler mental operations form a basis for the creation of the increasingly more complex and abstract mental structures. For example, the learning experiences in the curriculum outlines were arranged so that each preceding step developed skills and cognitive operations which constituted a pre-requisite for the next more complex or more abstract mental operations. The cycle of these operations usually began with the analysis of a concrete instance of the general idea on which the unit was centered and ended with the formulation of the idea and its application to new problems and situations (4, 18).

The exploration of the logical structure of the three cognitive tasks with which the study was concerned revealed another, more specific series of hierarchically ordered sequences of thought processes. For example, the sequence in concept formation begins with enumeration of concrete items, such as listing the differences one would expect to encounter when traveling in Latin America. The next step is that of grouping these items on some conscious basis, such as deciding the basis on which to group together "climate," "weather," and "altitude." The process ends with labeling or classifications, such as deciding to subsume a group of items under "standards of living." These steps constitute a necessary sequence in the sense that each preceding step is a prerequisite for mastering the next one. Underlying the steps are still other cognitive processes, such as differentiation of certain properties of phenomena or events with some degree of precision and an ability to abstract common elements and to determine the basis on which to group and label them.

In a similar manner, the logic of interpreting information and making inferences involves the assimilation of specific points of information, followed by relating several points to each other and making inferences or generalizations which go beyond that which is explicitly given.

The process involved in applying known facts and principles is a bit more complex, involving as it does divergent lines of prediction as well as the hierarchies of leaps in each according to the distance, ranging from the most immediate consequences to the most remote—such as predicting that water will bring grass, in comparison to predicting that the presence of water will cause nomads to cease to be nomads and turn to building cities.

The logic of the sequential steps in this process is not entirely clear. This unclarity is reflected in the rating scheme used. Obviously, the individual must draw upon his memory for the relevant information to form any predictions at all. But he must also relate this information to the requirements of the situation and to construct the parameters of conditions necessary for the predicted consequences to occur. This process entails both the construction of chains of consequences, such as water → growing crops → settling down → building cities, and the perception of the logical relationships between the conditions and consequences.

The chief point about the sequences in the development of thinking is that a deficiency in mastering the first step, such as the analysis of concrete instances, leads to incapacity to function on the level of the final step, such as the formulation of generalizations. The chief task of teaching, then, is to determine the order of learning tasks and to pace each step appropriately. This is a crucial point in the formulation of teaching strategies, and one against which current teaching methods commit the greatest errors.

COGNITIVE COMMERCE

The concept that the cognitive operations are an active transaction between the individual and his environment or the material was another idea which influenced the design both of the curriculum and of the study. Children inevitably build mental schemes with which to organize the information they encounter. The quality of the learning experiences determines the degree of productivity of these schemes. All learning experiences teach what Harlow (10) calls "sets to learn." Depending on the teaching strategies employed, children may learn to look for the structure of the problems set by the learning tasks or for arbitrary procedures. They may acquire a disposition to search for relationships and patterns among ideas and facts, or to look for single "right answers."

When the teaching strategies pay little attention to creating models for thinking, children tend to acquire faulty or unproductive conceptual schemes with which to organize information or to solve problems. For example, procedures such as asking students to name the important cities in the Balkans, without revealing the criterion for importance or without developing such a criterion with the class, leave students no alternative but to guess what the teacher wants or to recollect what the book said about the matter. Repeated experiences of this sort cause students to adopt irrational, unproductive, and arbitrary models of thinking and a dependence on memory rather than on judgment or inference.

Burton (2) cites an extreme example of an irrational or mechanical model or schema. He describes an elementary school child who made good grades in arithmetic because she "came up" with the right answers. When asked how she decided when to use which process, she explained her method as follows: "I know what to do by looking at the examples. If there are only two numbers I subtract. If there are lots of numbers, I add. If there are just two numbers and one is smaller than the other, then it is a hard problem. I divide to see if it comes out even, but if it doesn't, I multiply." Evidently this child had built a scheme to fit the manner of presentation of problems in the arithmetic book. By applying the scheme, she was also learning an unproductive model of thinking or a "set" which excluded understanding the structure of the problems.

The idea of thought as an active organization of mental processes underscores the importance of addressing teaching strategies to the development of autonomy and productivity. Effective teaching is seen as consisting primarily of what we get out of the children instead of what we put into them (16). In other words, helping students to develop a basis for and a method by which to judge the importance of cities may be of greater value than their simply knowing which cities are important.

Of special relevance is the idea that thought matures through a progressive and active organization and reorganization of conceptual structures. The individual fits the information he receives at any moment into the conceptual scheme he already possesses. When the requirements of the situation do not fit his current scheme, however, the individual is forced to alter it or to extend it to accommodate new information. Piaget (14) calls this fitting process "assimilation" and the process of alteration "accommodation."

This process suggests a teaching strategy which includes a rotation of learning tasks, calling for the assimilation of new information into the existing conceptual scheme with information that requires an extension and reorganization of the scheme (12). Prolonged assimilation of facts without a corresponding reshaping of the conceptual schemes with which to organize them is bound to retard the maturation of thought. On the other hand, a premature leap into a more complex or a higher level of thought is likely to immobilize mental activity and cause reversion to rote learning or, at any rate, to a lower level of thought. Students need a sufficient amount of assimilation to have the "stuff" to think with. But they need equally a challenge to stretch their modes of thinking and their conceptual schemes. An appropriate transition from one to the other demands a proper match between the current level and that which is required. Determining the proper match is perhaps one of the most difficult tasks in teaching and constitutes, in effect, a new concept of readiness and pacing. This task is complicated by the fact that the mastery of abstract communications, such as language and number, often masks the actual level of thinking. Verbalization may deceive the teacher and lead him to assume that thinking is more advanced than it is and, hence, to pushing the child's verbal habits of learning beyond his level of thinking (*13*).

REASONABLE HOPES

It seems reasonable to assume that, given an adequate analysis of the learning processes involved in certain important cognitive tasks, and teaching strategies which effectively implemented the principles of sequence, of active mental organization, and of adequate rotation of assimilation and accommodation, it should be possible for all students to achieve higher levels of cognitive operation than seems possible under current teaching. Furthermore, it is not beyond possibility that by far the most important individual differences may be found in the amount of concrete thinking an individual needs before formal thought can emerge. This difference may distinguish the slow but capable learner from one who is incapable of abstract thought. It is not beyond possibility, therefore, that many slow learners can achieve a high level of abstract thought, provided that they have the opportunity to examine a greater number of concrete instances than the teaching process typically allows. The employment of teaching strategies which are scientifically designed for the development of cognitive skills may make it possible to develop cognitive processes at a much higher level and in a greater number of students.

This rationale set certain requirements for the methodology of studying the development of thought processes in the classroom. It required, first, securing records of classroom transactions. Second, it required a multidimensional analysis of these transactions in terms of what the teacher does, of what the responses of the students are, and of the products of the interaction.

Four discussions were taped in each of the 20 classrooms. Because the curriculum outline projected learning activities, it was possible to place each taping at a point in a sequence at which a specified cognitive task of concern to the study occurred. The first taping was made during the very first class session in which enumeration, grouping, and classification was the chief task. The next two tapings recorded discussions involving interpreting data and formulating inferences from them: one an interpretation of a film, and another at a point at which students reported information from preceding research, compared and contrasted their data, and attempted to express their findings in generalizations. These tapings were taken at the midyear. The final taping, at the end of the year, was of discussions involving application of previously learned knowledge to predicting consequences from described hypothetical conditions.

UNITS AND SCORES

One problem in analyzing classroom transactions for the purpose of describing thought processes is to decide on units of analysis which are at once capable of being scored accurately and which express sensible units of thought. In this study, the time sampling was discarded in favor of a "thought unit." "Thought unit" was defined as a remark or series of remarks expressing a more or less complete idea, serving a specified function, and classifiable according to a level of thought. It is, therefore, possible for one word or an entire paragraph to be designated as a "thought unit." For example, the word "cement," when it occurs in the process of enumerating materials for building houses, is considered a thought unit. So is a paragraph, such as "The people in the other country do not have electric saws and things that the men in this country use to build houses. The children help chop the wood and can do a lot of things to help build the houses. But the children over here cannot do very many things because of the danger."

In order to describe simultaneously the teaching acts and the levels of thinking of students, the verbal transactions were "scored" by three different "ratings." The first is that of *designation*. It describes the source of the thought unit—whether it emanated from the teacher or from the student and whether the person is giving or seeking information. The code symbols for designation are *child gives* (CG), *child seeks* (CS), *teacher gives* (TG), and *teacher seeks* (TS).

The rating of *function* describes how a thought unit functions in the context of discussion. When applied to remarks or questions by teachers, these ratings may be used to describe teaching strategies which affect the subsequent thought of children.

Two large groups of function ratings may be distinguished: (1) questions or statements made by the teacher or the students which are psychological or managerial in their function and unrelated to the logic of the content. Statements of this type include those that express agreement (A), approval (AP), disagreement (D), disapproval (Dp), management (M), and reiteration (R). (2) The second group includes teacher or student statements which function to give direction to discussions, but which at the same time can be rated according to the logic of content. Such ratings include focusing (F), refocusing (F2), change of focus (FC), deviating from focus (Fd), controlling thought (C), extending thought on the same level (X), and lifting thought to a higher level (L).

The third rating, called *levels of thought,* describes both the student's and the teacher's verbal behavior by specifying the logical quality and the level of thought expressed. A separate rating scheme was developed for each of three cognitive tasks. For each of these tasks, categories were established which represent the hierarchical levels of thought, according to their level of abstraction and complexity. These categories refer to the specific thought processes which need to be mastered in a sequential order, because performing on the preceding level is a prerequisite to being able to perform on the next. Thus, the rating scheme represents the developmental sequence for each cognitive task. In addition, within each category, distinctions were made between the irrelevant, the disconnected, and the related information or content.

The rating scheme used for designating the levels of thought for each of the cognitive tasks is as follows:

Cognitive task: Grouping and labeling[1] (giving or seeking)

- 10 specific or general information outside of focus
- 11 specific or general information within focus
- 12 specific or general information with qualifications
- 30 grouping information without basis

31 grouping information with implicit basis
32 grouping information with explicit basis
40 categorizing information without basis
41 categorizing information with implicit relationships between items
42 categorizing information with explicit relationships between items

Cognitive task: interpreting information and making inferences: (giving or seeking)

10 specific or general information outside of focus
11 specific or general information within focus
12 specific or general information with qualifications and relationships
50 specific reason or explanation that does not relate to the information
51 specific reason or explanation that relates or organizes the information
52 specific reason or explanation that states how it relates or organizes the information
60 irrelevant or incorrect inference which is derived from information
61 relevant inference which is derived from information
62 relevant inference which is derived from information and expresses a cause and effect relationship, explanation, consequence, or contrast
70 relationship between information which implies an irrelevant or incorrect principle or generalization
71 relationship between information which implies a principle or generalization
72 principle or generalization which is derived from information

Cognitive task: predicting consequences (giving and seeking)

90 correcting the cause or condition
Establishing parameter information
100 relevant information
101 relevant information for establishing the total parameter (if-then) or for a particular hypothesis or prediction

102 relevant information for the total parameter or any
particular prediction with appropriate explanation

Establishing parameters of conditions

110 irrelevant or untenable condition for the total parameter
or for the particular prediction or hypothesis

111 relevant condition without connecting it with relevant
information

112 relevant condition and information and establishing
logical connection between them

Prediction: Level one, immediate consequences
Level two, remote consequences

120–220 incorrect or out of focus prediction

121–221 prediction with no elaboration

122–222 prediction accompanied by explanation,
qualification, differentiation, comparison, or contrast

123–223 prediction accompanied by a stated or implied
principle

In determining the level at which to rate a particular thought unit, it was necessary to consider the context in which the thought unit occurs. For example, the statement, "a hammer, because you can drive large nails with it," may be rated as "specific information with qualifying statement" if it is offered in response to the task of naming tools used in building a house; it merely gives additional information about the hammer and does not constitute a reason for naming "hammer." If the focus is on identification of tools most useful to primitive people, however, the same response would be rated as "relevant inference derived from information," because the phrase is an explicit reason for naming "hammer."

FUNCTION AND LEVEL

In describing the effect of teaching strategy on thought levels, four groups of function rating are especially important: focusing (F), extending the thought on the same level (X), lifting thought to a higher level (L), and controlling thought (C). Focusing establishes both the topic and the particular angle for its treatment. It sets the cognitive task. For example, the statement by the teacher, "If the desert had all the water it needed, what would happen?" establishes the central focus for discussion and calls for prediction of consequences.

The coding system also specifies the shifts in subject matter (change of focus), the degree to which the teacher finds it necessary to bring the discussion back to the original topic (refocus), and the number of times that the discussion wanders from the subject (deviation from focus).

A statement of the teacher or a child is coded as extension of thought (X) when it gives or seeks additional information or provides elaboration and clarification on an already established level. The following example illustrates a series of extensions on the level of providing specific information:

(1)	C Malobi took the money home with her.	CG 11
(2)	T What did Malobi do with the money?	TS 11
(3)	C She saved it.	CG 11X
(4)	C She put it underground.	CG 11X
(5)	C She put sticks and tin over it.	CG 11X
(6)	C Before she did that, she put it in a little pot.	CG 11X

A thought unit is functioning to lift the level of thought whenever the teacher or child seeks or gives information that shifts thought to a higher level than had previously been established. In the following example, the teacher attempts to lift the level of thought from giving information to explanation:

(1)	C They carried things in baskets on their heads.	CG 11
(2)	T Explain why.	TS 61L
(3)	C I suppose they can carry more things that way.	CG 61L

A question may function to extend the thought in one context and to lift it in another, as illustrated in the following example:

(1)	C They were working fast on the house.	CG 11
(2)	T Why?	TS 51L
(3)	C They wanted to get the house done before the rain came.	CG 51L
(4)	T Why?	TS 51X
(5)	C Because unless it is finished, the rain will destroy it.	CG 52X

The inquiry on line two is rated as teacher seeking to lift the level of thought from the established level of giving specific information to the level of inference. The child's response provides the reason on the level sought by the teacher. The same inquiry on line four and the child's response on line five function to extend the thought because the level at which the question is asked has already been established.

Controlling of thought occurs when the teacher performs a cognitive task that students should be induced to do. This is the case when the teacher gives a category for classification, an inference in interpretation, or a prediction in the task of applying principles.

STRATEGIC PATTERNS

As elements of teaching strategy, the frequencies of these functions may represent either effective or ineffective teaching strategies. For example, frequent shifts in focus may be needed at some points in the discussion to introduce sufficient information to form a basis for comparison and generalization. Other tasks may require that the discussion remain on one focus long enough to provide full treatment of the subject before proceeding to another, higher level of thought process. Frequent refocusing may indicate a faulty handling of the sequence in thought processes, which results in the necessity for constantly having to bring the children back to the focus.

This multiple coding scheme makes it possible to depict the flow of the classroom discussion by charting the sequences of transactions between the teacher and the children, the changes in the level of thought during the discussion, and the effect of these strategies upon the level and the direction of thought. The flow of thought can be reconstructed even though the specific content of the discussion is not given.[2] For example, an empirical sequence of thought may, when translated from the code, be read as *child gives specific information, teacher seeks an extension of that information, child provides the requested extension, teacher seeks to lift the level of thought from the "information" level to the "reason" level, child provides a reason as requested by the teacher,* and *teacher gives approval to the child.* In a similar manner, any sequence of ratings can be reconstructed from the observationally developed flow charts.

When the flow charts identify individual children, then one can describe the characteristic modes and levels of thought of particu-

lar pupils, such as a tendency to operate only on the level of concrete information or on the level of inference and generalization,
the tendency to remain focused or to stray from the focus, to give
relevant or irrelevant information, etc. It also permits the accounting of the frequencies of the various thought patterns which prevail
in the classroom group and the discrepancies between what the
teacher seeks and how the children respond.

Data of this sort depict the various strategies which teachers
may employ and their consequences. For example, when the teacher attempts to raise the level of thought very early in the discussion,
this typically results in the children's returning to a lower level and
in their inability to sustain discussion at the higher levels of
thought. On the other hand, a strategy representing an effective
pacing of shifting the thought onto higher levels seems to follow a
characteristic course. The level of seeking information is sustained
for a considerable time during the first portion of the discussion.
Grouping is requested only after a large amount of information has
been accumulated. The result is that in a fairly brief period, children transcend from grouping to labeling and then to providing
reasons for labeling and to inferences.

Other strategic patterns that have been empirically identified
include the teacher's repeated attempts to steer discussion to the
inferential level without permitting the development of a body of
needed information; in such a case, the children repeatedly return
to the information level. Or when there is a constant change of
focus, the children's thought alternates between several levels, is
not sustained at the higher level, and gradually stabilizes on the
most primitive one.

SOME IMPLICATIONS

This multidimensional analysis of classroom transactions has several advantages. First, by combining the description of the teacher's
acts in terms of their explicit functions with the assessment of the
logical quality of student responses, it is possible to evaluate the
impact of the teacher's behavior in terms of its productivity. This
addition of the dimension of the logical quality of the content of
thought carries the analysis of classroom transactions a step beyond
what has been available to date. Most current studies of classroom
transactions concentrate more or less exclusively on the analysis of

the psychological functions of teaching acts (*5, 11*). This emphasis has evoked the criticism that teaching is explained and controlled exclusively in terms of psychological principles and that the logic of teaching and of its product in learning is overlooked (*17*).

A further advantage lies in the fact that, in addition to describing the impact of teaching exclusively in terms of the frequencies of specific acts, this scheme permits studying the cumulative impact of certain patterns or combinations of acts, including their pacing. It is at this point that a transfer is made from the study of teaching acts to the study of teaching strategies. Flanders (*6*) has taken a step in this direction by describing the points of shift in the nature of teaching acts.

Finally, the scheme permits the examination of the effect of teaching strategies in terms of a measurable change in a specified outcome—levels of thinking in this case—and thus frees the study of teaching from the necessity of inferring the effect from the assumed consequences of the frequencies of certain types of teacher behavior.

A preliminary analysis of the typescripts of classroom discussion reveals an enormous influence of teacher behavior on the thinking of students. This impact is exercised in a variety of ways: by the nature of the questions asked, what the teacher gives to the students or seeks from them, the timing of these acts in the total sequence, which ideas are picked up for elaboration and which are passed over, points at which approval and disapproval are given, etc. For example, the focus which the teacher sets determines which points students can explore and establishes the models for thought they can practice. Of great importance is the sequence of mental operations called for and the appropriateness of this sequence to developing productive thought models.

It seems clear, further, that the level of thinking attained is influenced not only by the nature of the single act by a teacher just preceding a given response. The level of thought attained seems to be determined by the whole pattern of transactions: the particular combination of focusing, extending, and lifting; the timing of these acts; the length of time spent on a particular focus, such as exploring specific descriptive information before examining causes or attempting explanation; the distance between the mental operations of the students at the moment from the level required by the teacher, and the points at which the teacher seeks information from students and gives it. These combinations, not merely the frequencies alone, constitute a teaching strategy.

Only a casual identification of these strategies is available at the moment of writing this article. The variations in the patterns are too numerous to permit analysis by ordinary means. The staff, in cooperation with experts in computer programing, has developed a high-speed computer program designed to aid in accounting for these patterns. Such a computer program should permit the identification of the elements and the cumulative patterns of strategies associated with high and low performance.[3]

The findings so far suggest that if the acquisition of skills in autonomous thinking is to be a realistic objective, a much more thorough study of and experimentation with the appropriate teaching strategies and their impact on the development of thinking is called for. As Flanders (6) suggests, any step in the direction of specifying productive teaching strategies should lead to a more adequate understanding of the connection between teachers' behavior and student response. A scientific mapping of such strategies should also add considerably to the developing theory of instruction, and especially to our understanding of the conditions which maximize the development of higher mental processes on the part of all students, not only the intellectual elite.

NOTES

1.   Categories in the 20 series were originally reserved for "general information" but were later combined with the 10 series.

2.   Charts based on empirical observation will be published later as a part of the report to the US Office of Education of a study of "Thinking in Elementary School Children" (Project No. 1574).

3.   Such a computer program has been devised by P. J. Stone and M. S. Smith as a general sequence analyzer, planned to identify recurrent patterns in a list of events.

REFERENCES

1. Bartlett, F. E. *Thinking: an experimental and social study.* New York: Basic Books, 1958.

2. Burton, W. N. *The guidance of learning activities.* New York: Appleton-Century, 1952.

3. Buswell, G. T., & Hersch, B. Y. *Patterns of solving problems*. Berkeley, California: Univer. California Press, 1956.

4. *Contra Costa County Social Studies Units, Grades 1–6*. Pleasant Hill, California: Contra Costa County Schools, 1959.

5. Flanders, N. A. *Teacher influence, pupil attitudes, and achievement*. Pre-publication manuscript of a proposed research monograph for the U. S. Office of Education, Cooperative Research Branch, Washington, DC, 1960.

6. Flanders, N. A. Some relationships between teacher influence, pupil attitudes, and achievement. Ditto MS of a chapter submitted to the AASA, the NTBA, and the NEA Classroom Teachers Division. No date.

7. Gallagher, J. J. , Aschner, Mary Jane, Perry, Joyce M., & Afaar, S. S. A system for classifying thought processes in the content of classroom verbal interaction. Ditto MS. Urbana, Ill.: Institute for Research on Exceptional Children, Univer. Illinois, 1961.

8. Getzels, J. W., & Jackson, P. *Creativity and intelligence*. New York: Wiley, 1962.

9. Guilford, J. P. Basic conceptual problems in the psychology of thinking. *Annals NY Acad. Sci.*, 1961, *91*, 9–19.

10. Harlow, H. F. The formation of learning sets. *Psychol. Rev.*, 1949, *56*, 51–60.

11. Hughes, Marie, *et al. Development of the means for the assessment of the quality of teaching in elementary s ʹool.* (Mimeo.) Salt Lake City: Univer. Utah, 1959.

12. Hunt, J. McV. *Experience and Intelligence*. New York: Ronald Press, 1961.

13. Peel, E. A. *The pupil's thinking*. London: Oldbourne, 1960.

14. Piaget, J. *The psychology of intelligence*. L ndon: Routledge, Kegan Paul, 1947.

15. Rokeach, M. *The open and closed mind*. New York: Basic Books, 1960.

16. Sigel, I. Cognitive style and personality dynamics. Interim report, Merrill-Palmer Institute, 1961.

17. Smith, B. O. Concept of teaching. *Teach. Coll. Rec.*, 1950, *61*, 229–241.

18. Taba, Hilda. *Curriculum development: theory and practice*. New York: Harcourt, Brace & World, 1962.

CHAPTER 8

Using a Jurisprudential Framework in the Teaching of Public Issues

Donald W. Oliver and James P. Shaver
1966

We have attempted to develop some concepts that can be used in relating moral imperatives, principles of government, and standards of proof. These can be fitted together into a framework which allows the teacher—and the student—to focus on a limited number of important questions whenever issues of public policy arise. A curricular approach needs a "handle" for easy reference. We have called our model simply a "legal-ethical," or "jurisprudential," framework. It has been difficult to label because of its complexity; it combines several ingredients not commonly put together in the social studies curriculum. Beginning with a type of contemporary issue commonly mentioned in the problems of democracy course, but initially stating the issue in terms of a concrete setting most often included in "current events" discussions, it then relates the contemporary case to cases which range widely in time and space, appealing especially to historical analogies to broaden the context of discussion. The initial questions raised by this material tend to be "should"-type ethical questions, but the class is inevitably thrust into legal, factual, and definitional questions when the students' own views of the "good" solution are com-

Chapter 7 in *Teaching Public Issues in the High School* (Logan: Utah State University Press, 1974; originally published by Houghton Mifflin, 1966). Reprinted by permission.

pared with other "legitimate" social solutions. It is this amalgamation of law-government, ethics, contemporary, and historical factual questions developed around perennial issues of public policy that we refer to as *jurisprudential teaching.*

It is important to distinguish between jurisprudential teaching and what is commonly called "critical thinking." Critical thinking in this context refers to the ability to differentiate factual statements from opinion statements, the ability to identify logical fallacies, etc. While there is clearly a relationship between such a notion of "critical thinking" and the approach described here, there are major differences. Our approach emphasizes the clarification of two or more legitimately held points of view as they bear on a public policy question. In general there is much less concern with rhetorical devices or the logic of deductive reasoning than with the anatomy of legitimate communication and persuasion.

The distinction between the conventional teaching of "critical thinking" or applied logic and the approach suggested here can, perhaps, best be understood by thinking about the pedagogical strategies employed in each. The direct teaching of "critical thinking" usually involves the analysis of the persuasive message (sometimes referred to as propaganda) or the analysis of different accounts of the same events to illustrate the problem of interpreting information and drawing conclusions. In the jurisprudential framework, the teacher is likely to begin the discussion by reading a provocative message presenting a controversial situation and quickly move to a dialogue about the substance of the issue or problem described in the message. What he seeks to analyze is less the controversy-provoking message than the disputative discussion about the controversy that ensues. Our focus, then, is on the dialogue, either between teacher and student or among students.

The role of the teacher in such a dialogue is complex, requiring that he think on two levels at the same time. He must first know how to handle himself as he challenges the student's position and as his own position is challenged by the student. This is the socratic role. Second, he must be sensitive to and aware of the general processes of clarification or obscuration that take place as the dialogue unfolds. He must, that is, be able to identify and analyze complicated strategies being employed by various protagonists to persuade others that a particular stand is "reasonable" or "correct." Nor is it sufficient for the teacher simply to teach a process of questioning evidence, questioning assumptions, or pointing out "loaded words." In matters of public policy, factual issues are generally handmaids to ethical or legal stands, which cannot be sloughed off as "only matters of opinion." Clarification of evaluative and legal issues, then, becomes a central concern. At this point in the curriculum the student is not taught to believe or accept certain values but rather to clarify his evaluative commitments and to understand the relationships among the justification of a value position, the clarification of a definitional issue, and the proof process involved in a factual issue.

It should be stressed again that teaching oneself to be sensitive to strategies of justification, clarification, and proof requires the teacher to "double think" or think at two levels simultaneously. He must be aware of the substantive issues on which the controversy has focused *and* the intellectual process by which these issues might be clarified, if not resolved. Moreover, it is our contention that the intellectual processes or strategies are much more complex than have conventionally been described in "critical thinking" or "how to think" educational literature. Below we suggest a few such strategies by way of illustration. The context is obviously *not* one in which the teacher simply describes these strategies to students. The student must, in fact, engage in a controversial discussion before the definition of a strategy becomes relevant or meaningful. Such engagement may be between the teacher and the student or between students. Again we would affirm that such discussions are not *simply* to teach the student intellectual process, nor are they only to teach about the topic under discussion. There is a dual purpose requiring a dual intellectual process by the teacher, and eventually by the student: the student must learn the legal, ethical, and factual substance of the issues under discussion, the way this information relates to his own personal knowledge and values, *and* sensitivity to the general processes by which the issues might be clarified.

The second or analytic level, moreover, involves not only *identifying* definitional, evaluative, or factual problems that are embedded within broader public issues but also awareness of the more complex relationships among these different kinds of problems. In a controversial discussion there are undoubtedly an infinite number of patterns by which these problems can be usefully related. At this point we will suggest only a few such patterns which commonly arise in political controversy, and show how the three dimensions of political conflict play a part. We do *not* think it useful or desirable for students to "memorize" something called "patterns of intellectual clarification." The point is that the teacher, and in turn the students, hopefully will develop a general rhetoric for describing strategies involved in political arguments. At best, the patterns described below can only suggest that it is possible to talk about strategies of persuasion in a useful way; they do not constitute a "handbook for public debate."

Pattern 1. Establishing the Point at Which a Value is Violated: The Factual Emphasis

The problem of determining *when* a social situation violates an important social value is both definitional—does the value term apply?—and evaluative. Arguments along these lines, however, often center on a descriptive controversy over the nature of the situation under discussion, emphasizing factual disagreement.

In school segregation, for example, the argument often has focused on the issue of whether or not the separate schools provided for the Negro were in fact equal to those provided for whites in terms of objective criteria like quality of buildings, teaching load, teacher salary, and physical equipment. Both antagonists in such an argument may assume that separate-but-equal could be a legitimate answer to the problem of race relations in the schools, but they disagree on whether or not Negro schools will ever be brought up to white standards under segregated conditions. The 1954 desegregation decision of the Supreme Court was finally argued on such factual grounds. Both segregationists and integrationists agreed on the value of an equal education for the Negro. The question was: Does the situation that exists (segregation) prevent the Negro from getting an equal education?

A second point in the segregation problem which may begin with a value statement but soon reverts to a factual controversy is the "self-determination" issue: the right of each state to deal with its own race relations problems as it sees fit—the states' rights doctrine. The southerner argues this position because he believes that most southerners are violently opposed to desegregation. Some integrationists have questioned this assumption, asserting that in fact many southern moderates would prefer integration to breaking the law but are intimidated and forced to remain silent by more vocal extremists. Whether or not the majority of southerners would prefer to comply with the Supreme Court's decision of 1954 or the Civil Rights Act of 1964 is, or course, an empirical, or factual, question.

It is on the basis of factual questions such as these that political disputes can perhaps best be initiated. Unless solid evidence exists that the description of the situation by an "injured" party is to some extent accurate, there is little sound basis for extended debate.

We are not suggesting, however, that once the problem situation is accurately described the factual issues are resolved. More probably the argument will proceed through *alternating cycles* among the various issues. For example, the controversy may well begin with an "atrocity story" describing a situation in which an individual or group is allegedly being treated unjustly. Implicit but obvious is the assumption that an important value is violated. The argument may turn from emphasis on the violation of the value to the question of whether or not the atrocity story is true or representative of a larger class of situations. (Are the poor educational facilities provided for Negroes in rural Mississippi representative of all segregated Negro facilities?) The factual discussion will often reveal a wide spectrum of degrees of justice and injustice.

The alternating-cycle concept in argument analysis has direct implications for teaching. Teachers commonly comment that students must know the "facts" before they can get into issues of public policy, which inevitably involve "opinions" or values. This is a somewhat simplistic way of stating the problem. A critical pedagogical objective is teaching the student to select those factual claims (not facts) which, if their validity were known, would have an important bearing on the controversy. To teach the student the "relevant background information" before the argument begins short-circuits the opportunity for the student to evaluate the relevance of facts needed to argue policy questions intelligently. This is not to say that the student should start discussing an issue with no background whatsoever. It does contend that the student should learn to accumulate information as he sees its bearing on the central legal and ethical issues surrounding a public question.

Pattern 2. Establishing the Point at Which a Value Is Violated: The Emphasis Upon Evaluative Clarification

We may now look at the problem of clarifying the hypothetical point at which a value is violated, e.g., when liberty becomes license; when equal opportunity becomes enforced mediocrity. Extreme violations of American social and political values are generally obvious to the large majority of citizens. Such violations create special problems for political decision-making when they are suppressed or ignored by an uninterested majority or when they can be justified by facts indicating that other equally important values are thereby maintained, e.g., censorship in wartime. In the center of the value continuum, however, is that vague area in which the citizen may not know whether an abuse being perpetrated is sufficiently important to require governmental action or governmental coercion.

For example, to what extent would the policy of separate-but-equal, actually enforced, be a violation of "equal protection under the law"? The history of the separate-but-equal doctrine is itself a study of conflicting interpretations of the point at which justice or dignity is sufficiently violated so that the Supreme Court feels obligated to interfere with the rights of the states. This kind of conflict cannot immediately be resolved or clarified with facts. There is often agreement on the facts. One person describes segregation as a badge of slavery and therefore a violation of equal protection. The other person describes segregation as protecting the cultural integrity of two distinct racial groups and sees no violation of constitutional rights.

The Use of Analogy in the Process of Ethical Clarification. One approach to the clarification of this type of conflict is the use of comparative cases or analogies. The case in question is analyzed by comparing and contrasting it with an array of real or hypothetical situations in which are embedded the same value conflict. We then ask ourselves which of the comparative cases are violations of an important value and how similar these cases are to the one in question.

Let us again take the example of racial segregation in the public schools. Suppose we compare and contrast this with segregation by sex in the public schools in areas such as the practical arts or physical education. Boys and girls are normally given separate facilities and training for physical education. If each group has equally good instruction and equipment, is our idea of equality violated? Probably not. We might rationalize our position by saying that there are good reasons for segregating the sexes in physical education. It is commonly assumed that girls are not physically equal to boys. They have different interests. Boys and girls are somewhat self-conscious and modest in the presence of one another, especially in gym suits. But would these arguments not apply as well to racial segregation? Perhaps girls could achieve the same physical prowess as boys if they did not have a negative self-image concerning their ability to perform athletic feats.

Now let us take a second comparative situation. Would segregation by social class be a violation of equal protection? Suppose the population were divided into thirds according to income, and three separate school systems for these groups were established. Most Americans, including racial segregationists, would probably oppose this kind of segregation (although many schools in fact condone and promote it). But wouldn't the protection of the cultural integrity of various social classes apply as an argument for this kind of segregation, as well as for racial segregation? (One might even say that the lower classes provide a kind of uninhibited response to life which invigorates the culture; efforts should therefore be made to preserve its integrity.)

We thus have three situations, each violating with increasing intensity the common use of the equal protection concept. Americans in general appear to have no great stake in the inequalities brought about by sexual segregation or discrimination in physical education. Racial segregation is subject to much controversy: Is it or is it not a violation of equal protection? Undoubtedly, most Americans would be horrified if social class segregation were legalized and enforced in the public schools.

The use of analogous cases allows us to broaden the context of discussion by developing a series of points along the continuum of equality-inequality, and thus to clarify the depth of our own commitment to a particular value. It does not, however, solve the problem of how to determine which particular case provides the critical point at which equality must have priority over cultural self-determination. This point is determined by each individual, although all may agree that a common legal standard should exist.[1]

The use of analogous cases not only clarifies the range of situations we might consider as violations and non-violations of a particular value but also impels us to seek criteria which will distinguish one situation from another. For example, the person who sees sexual segregation as legitimate but racial and social class segregation as wrong may say that the basic difference is that men and women, boys and girls, are really considered social equals in the society, whereas Negroes and members of lower-class families are not. (This, of course, may be subject to question.) On the other hand, the person who sees sexual segregation and racial segregation as similar but who sees social class segregation as the violation might assert that, while many lower-class people want to be like middle-class people and live near them, girls do not want to participate in sports with boys and the great majority of Negroes do not want to live among or go to school with whites.

The Return to Factual Problems.   Once we begin to categorize one group of cases as a "violation of equality" and another group as a "non-violation," we again move from our intuitive judgment of "rights" in the controversial situation to questions of fact. In this situation we might ask: Do women and girls really feel equal to men and boys, or do they envy them as social superiors? Do most Negroes really want to move from a segregated way of life to closer association with whites? The analogy thus leads us to identify characteristics in several similar situations which differentiate those that violate a value from those that apparently do not. Analogy thus becomes a powerful instrument of rational ethical clarification.

The use of analogy in *teaching* issues of public controversy deserves comment on two counts. In logical terms, teachers tend to be suspicious of the analogy as a method of "false reasoning," or at least one of questionable validity. We would point out, first, that proving a factual point by the use of analogy is quite different from presenting an array of analogous situations to clarify and rationalize decisions on public policy. Attempting to differentiate among seemingly similar cases is, in fact, a fundamental element of legal reasoning.

Second, the use of analogy is probably the most effective way to test the consistency of a student's policy stand and to show him that the major problem of justification is rationalizing inconsistency rather than learning how to be consistent. (Americans do believe in segregation under certain circumstances.) Moreover, "good" analogies, i.e., analogies which require more than a trivial rebuttal, are often difficult to come by. They may be hypothetical situations or real cases. In the planning of a controversial discussion, therefore, it is usually important to anticipate what issues will come up, what inconsistencies should be illustrated, and what analogies can serve this purpose.

Pattern 3. The Clarification of Value Conflicts

In dealing with public controversy probably the most important type of issue revolves around a value conflict or political dilemma. A political dilemma occurs when we are faced with a choice in which any of the available alternatives will enhance one value at the expense or violation of another. Dilemmas are commonly handled in two ways: We either deny, distort, or repress the negative consequences which attend our actions so that the value violation remains below the level of consciousness; or we maintain that the value we are preserving is more important than the value we are violating—we assign static priorities to values. The latter strategy deserves more extensive comment.

The usual static value priority approach asserts that the value given the higher priority is more important because it more closely approximates our conception of human freedom and dignity or the conditions necessary to preserve dignity. The school desegregation situation, for example, has been characterized by assertions from both sides that the values each upholds are more closely associated with "human freedom." The southern white generally selects two values to support his position: local control or states' rights and the individual freedom of the parent to protect his child's cultural integrity. The first argument, of course, has a constitutional basis. The northern liberal bases his argument on the value of equal opportunity, which enjoys constitutional support in the equal protection clause of the Fourteenth Amendment. Within the framework of a value priority position, it is possible to argue that the "higher" value is inviolable and then refuse to consider the "facts" of the case. The "conservative" stand on desegregation illustrates such a position: Constitutionally guaranteed states' rights and local control must be supported, although we know that the races are given unequal educational opportunity within certain states;

the federal government has simply never been delegated constitutional power to deal with the problem of education, including racial inequality in the public schools. Constitutionalism must be upheld because it is the basis of freedom and justice, even to the point of tolerating temporary injustice.

When the initial statement of such a position appears irrefutable, the persuasiveness of the argument depends partly on the extent to which there is in fact a gross violation of the value which is given second priority—in this case equal educational opportunity. If one can demonstrate that the Negroes in a particular southern state have been getting few or no educational privileges compared to white children, the states' rights argument becomes somewhat hollow. And if the dogmatic states' rights advocate maintains that extreme violation of equal educational opportunity is irrelevant to the argument, he is forced to ignore or deny a fundamental value of the Creed. As Myrdal pointed out, since most Americans have internalized the whole Creed, this becomes a difficult position to maintain.

In general, appeal to one value as "more basic" than another operates effectively in political controversy only when the "less basic" value is not under extreme violation. This is why the separate-but-equal position, assuming that it has been fairly implemented, is so persuasive. While imposing a system of race relations on the majority of people within a state is clearly an extreme violation of the concept of local control and states' rights (especially when no such powers have been expressly delegated to the federal government), separate-but-equal does not appear to be so extreme a violation of the value of equality.[2] Only when we see overwhelming factual evidence indicating that although separate-but-equal is a legal fact it is, in reality, a myth, or that it is inherently impossible because of its damaging psychological effects on young Negro children, does the integrationist's argument gain force.

So while initially simply giving one value permanent priority over another appears to be a secure political position in the face of conflicting values, the position loses force when there is a major violation of the "secondary" value. The basic values of the Creed are usually so important to people that they cannot simply be ignored.

As we have already indicated in Pattern 2, analogies are particularly useful to clarify value issues and especially to underline the fact that there is a real *conflict* over values which cannot be obscured by the rhetoric of a static value priority argument. Situations analogous to an initial problem case can be suggested from which one can abstract the same values as those in the problem case. In each of two situations—the problem case and the analogy—one value is being supported at the expense of another. Yet one situation may be judged "good" and the other "bad," although both involve the support of one value and the violation of another. The problem is to clarify the reasons and accept the inconsistency. The following example illustrates this process:

Between 1763 and 1776 the British became increasingly restrictive on the rights of self-government which American colonists had come to assume were theirs. Finally, some colonists considered the restrictions an unbearable loss of freedom. In pursuit of greater freedom they struck out at the British by holding the "Boston Tea Party" and storing arms and ammunition in Concord. Committees of Correspondence were set up to increase agitation against the British. For some the purpose of this agitation was to gain concessions from the British. For others it was to gain independence through violent revolution, if necessary.

How do most Americans feel about these efforts to gain independence? We celebrate the men who worked toward independence; we celebrate the day on which it occurred as a national holiday.

Now let us look at a similar hypothetical case or analogy:

Some states in the South have traditionally refused to give the Negroes voting privileges and equal educational and job opportunities and have excluded them from the full privileges of citizenship. Suppose Negroes were able to accumulate stores of arms and ammunition and plot a general uprising against such states as Mississippi and Alabama, as well as the United States. The Negro claims he is fighting for some territory in the South which is now largely occupied by Negroes. Should the United States put down such a revolt? Should Mississippi and Alabama put down such a revolt?

It is quite possible that many Americans would admit that the Negro might have some justification for revolting, but probably few would support the revolt. Both situations could be extended by the suggestion that Russia might give arms to the Negroes in their fight for independence just as France gave military aid to the English colonies in America.

Does it not seem as though we have contradicted our stand from the first situation to the second? More precisely, what is the nature of the contradiction? We can begin to answer this question by asking ourselves what values were being defended in the American Revolution. The interests of the American colonies were not represented in the decisions of the King and the English Parliament, the colonists felt; nor were the colonists being given the rights that Englishmen of comparable social class were accorded in England. In order to gain their rights they had to achieve independence, which finally meant fighting a revolution, violating English law, and committing acts of subversion and violence. The hypothetical Negro revolution in America has obvious similarities. The Negro is denied basic rights of citizenship: representation and equal treatment under the law. The American colonist was denied similar rights. The Negro is (in our hypothetical example) resorting to lawlessness and violence to gain his rights. This is what the American actually did in the American Revolution.

The analysis of these two cases illustrates a number of points. A political problem often begins when a specific decision violates an important social value. The problem becomes more complicated when we recognize that the social value given to support our decision in one situation may well be ignored by a second decision we make in a comparable situation. We are thus faced with inconsistent decisions.

It is possible, of course, to give some values such high priority that few value conflicts or inconsistencies are faced. Many Quakers, for example, place so much importance on the values of peace and non-violence that when situations involve the choice of violence or non-violence they usually behave consistently. Most of us, however, are not in this position. We value many of our personal freedoms so much that if we felt they were being taken away unjustly or illegally we would physically injure others to protect them. We would violate one value to protect another when in a particular situation the first value seemed more important for the protection of human dignity. For example, Negroes claim the protection of the law and also the right to ignore and violate laws that they do not approve. And the more important point is that we do *not consistently* violate one value and *consistently* protect another.

We often deal with similar situations in different ways because each has its own unique characteristics which must be taken into account if we wish to protect the basic value of human dignity as each of us may define it.

While inconsistency on the general value level may well be justified in terms of the specifics of the two cases we are comparing, it is often disconcerting to the person who considers consistency an essential criterion of rationality. As the inconsistency begins to impinge upon our consciousness, we may find it easier to pretend that the salient value, the value that is obviously supported in one particular situation, surely leads to the most reasonable decision. In thinking about the American Revolution, for example, we focus our attention upon the values of political independence and self-government (and the fact that these values were violated by the English) rather than upon the value of remaining within the legal boundaries of English law to effect an orderly, peaceful settlement of disputes. One of the major difficulties in discussing a controversial political situation, then, is forcing antagonists to recognize that they share *both* of the conflicting values involved in it. (This fact is precisely what provides the basis for a controversial dialogue.) The American patriot has so often been conditioned to associate the American Revolution with "fighting for freedom," for example, that he cannot see that the phrase upholds one value but violates another important value. The analogy is an effective device by which to expose values "in the shadow of consciousness," as Myrdal puts it, and force an antagonist to admit that a dilemma does, in fact, exist. It serves the function of pointing up a latent value which the person would just as soon play down or ignore.

There is no implication here that by casting the Revolution in an unfavorable light through the use of analogy we can or should teach students to reject the total situation. The point is simply that a political decision and its consequent actions often involve conflicts in value, and by understanding this fact we are in a better position to rationalize our position and consider alternative positions that we might otherwise ignore. In most cases, however, we are forced to accept the fact that the final decision will have some negative consequences. It is better to admit this with honesty and candor and deal with it than to conceal it with euphemistic phrases or a turning of the head.

Pattern 4: Translating a Value Conflict into an Issue of Fact

This strategy for dealing with value conflicts is, of course, commonly associated with pragmatism. As White says, "The important point is that Dewey thinks that judgments of *desirability* are simply judgments that something is desired under conditions which have been thoroughly investigated in the way that a scientist checks his test conditions."[3] Commonly the strategy involves initially asking the question "What are the consequences of my value or policy position?" If it turns out that individuals or groups holding differing policy positions based on different values ask this question and arrive at the same consequences, or vice versa, the difference in policy position (and value) theoretically may be resolved by empirically testing whether the assumed relationship between policy and social consequence does in fact hold up. For example, the segregationist often argues that he wants to maintain the cultural integrity of the two races, because it will lead to the greatest *mutual respect* and *harmony* in race relations. The integrationist will argue that this violates the "brotherhood of man" doctrine. He believes that all races, creeds, and colors should mingle freely with each other because such interaction fosters mutual respect and harmony. One supports the value of cultural integrity and "freedom of association" by legal safeguards, if necessary; the other supports the value of sharing common experiences and closer association. Both justify their conflicting value positions on the basis of their common concern for peaceful and harmonious relations between the races.

From the pragmatic point of view, the approach to this controversy is, in the broad sense, experimental. We look at particular situations in which one or the other method has been tried and evaluate the extent to which each has contributed to racial peace within the community. Often, however, when either assumption is contradicted by substantial factual evidence, the antagonist on the "wrong" side of the issue reverses the priority of his values and places the instrumental value above the final value. If the evidence indicates that segregation produces more violence and ill will between races, for example, this consequence is justified as a necessary evil to maintain a greater good, cultural integrity. If the evidence indicates that close association between the races produces racial strife, this is looked upon as perhaps a temporary evil that must be endured for the sake of the greater good, practicing brotherhood. But when the controversy is genuinely approached as an experimental problem, it is potentially "solvable."

Obtaining firm and non-controversial data bearing on such problems is, of course, difficult. While broad sociological, historical, and journalistic studies provide the most appropriate kind of data, they are also the most sensitive to contamination by the author's personal biases. And although the behavioral sciences offer a more objective methodology, they usually lack the depth and scope for dealing with complex political issues.[4] Obviously there is no recourse but to use whatever data are available, however variable their quality and relevance. Unfortunately, many factual questions in politics begin as controversial issues and after exhaustive historical or scientific research end up being just as controversial.[5]

A GENERAL STRATEGY FOR TEACHING THE ANALYSIS OF POLITICAL CONTROVERSY

In all of this discussion our orientation has been toward the analysis of controversy and the general process of inquiry that might be applied to it. But we have specifically tried to avoid formularizing an approach to political-ethical problems. The reason is simple: We believe that the process of argumentative inquiry into such problems is too complex to be comprehended by a single approach.

From the point of view of pedagogy, however, the analytic formulation presented thus far is unwieldy, complicated, and difficult to translate into a teaching strategy. It is relatively easy, for example, to teach the analytic concepts; the difficult question is: How does one teach the student to select and focus the appropriate concepts on a particular problem? In attempting to answer this question, we have tried to steer a middle course between "a problem-solving formula" on the one hand and the general mandate "Take our analytic formulations and face the problem in any way you see fit" on the other. We have attempted (1) to *summarize* the major intellectual operations which can be made explicit in the analysis of political controversy and (2) to place the operations in some rough logical order. The following description of the intellectual operations, therefore, not only is a restatement of certain analytic concepts already described in greater detail but also implies a strategy or order of consideration.

Summary of Major Operations in the Analysis of Public Controversy

1. Abstracting General Values from Concrete Situations.   In order to use the patterns of analysis suggested above, the student must understand selected ethical and legal concepts and be able to construe concrete problem situations in these terms. If the problem is whether or not Congress should pass an antitrust act, for example, the student must be able to see that the decision can be construed in terms of such general values as property and contract rights, protection of equal rights for large and small businessmen alike, and protection of the interests of the community at large.

2. Using General Value Concepts as Dimensional Constructs. People commonly interpret general values as categorical concepts, as ideals or "goods." When we abstract two or more conflicting values from a single situation and reflect about how the situation may be changed to lessen the conflict, it is difficult to use values as all-or-none categories. In the segregation issue, the northern liberal asserts that the Negro's rights are violated; the southern conservative asserts that school integration violates his right to freedom of association. Under these circumstances the concept of compromise is simply not possible. One must give up his whole value position or none of it. Our approach to this problem is to deal with social values as dimensional constructs. For example:

> Freedom of speech————————Censorship
> Equal opportunity————————Caste system
> Christian brotherhood————————Self-interest

Dealing with values as constructs allows us to conceptualize the higher value, human dignity, as a "blend" or amalgamation of values attained through compromise. In a particular value conflict we seek such a compromise, recognizing that everyone cannot be satisfied. Moreover, the resolution of a problem usually does not dissolve the value conflict; it rather adjusts a situation to the interests of the debating parties. But adjustment does not necessarily mean that the basic value of human dignity has been diluted or violated; it may, in fact mean that we have come closer to it.

3. Identifying Conflicts Between Value Constructs.   Once the student can abstract general values from concrete situations, and see them as dimensional constructs which can be violated to a greater or lesser degree, he must be able to see that two or more values can be abstracted from the same situation, and that often these values conflict. That is, a decision which enhances one value may work to the detriment of one or more other values.

4. Identifying a Class of Value Conflict Situations.   In order to compare one situation in which a value conflict occurs with others similar to it, the student has to see a particular situation as an instance of a general type of value conflict. For example, he might see that violations of state segregation laws by Negroes in the South are similar to violations of English law by the colonists before the American Revolution. The problem is one of violation of the "rights of man" by the legally constituted government versus violation of the law in the protection of these rights.

5. Discovering or Creating Value Conflict Situations Which Are Analogous to the Problem Under Consideration.   The purpose of constructing analogies is to force an antagonist to compare a number of similar situations to which he reacts inconsistently. If the comparison is to be useful, the situations must embrace conflicting values both of which are likely to be favored. For example, while most of us support the actions of the English colonists in America during the American Revolution, probably few of us would support a comparable action by the Negroes in Mississippi, although the issue is similar. As we have indicated in our pattern analysis, the purpose of analogy is to expose the inconsistency between positions. The person is then forced to change one position or to rationalize the apparent inconsistency by seeking criteria which differentiate the two seemingly similar cases.

6. Working Toward a General Qualified Position.   The quest for criteria by which to differentiate two situations characterized by the same conflicting values should lead to a qualified decision stating under what circumstances priority will be given to one value or the other. For example, a person who approved of the 1776 revolt of the English colonists in America but disapproved of a current revolt by Negroes in Mississippi might rationalize his position in the following way: Negroes are citizens not only of Mississippi but also of the United States. The national government is sympathetic to their cause and is in the process of ameliorating their condition. However, the colonists were citizens of one government, and it was actually responsible for the "abuses" they were suffering. He might then generalize that whenever a major governmental force is working successfully to reduce inequalities among citizens, and whenever there is a realistic chance that they will eventually be removed, it is better to stay within the legal framework of government. As Jefferson said, ". . . governments long established should not be changed for light and transient causes. . . ." When hope of reform is finally gone, however, this person may conclude that one can justifiably resort to violence and revolt.

One is thus "driven" to the process of qualification by a series of antecedent intellectual operations. The person states a general policy with respect to a given case. He then encounters a similar case in which his decision is reversed; opposite values are supported in the two cases. He then tries to find some general characteristics about one situation which make him judge it to be "good," while at the same time rejecting the other situation as "bad." Finally, he arrives at a general policy statement, including the qualification, which will anticipate future cases and how he will deal with them, e.g., "I will support a violent revolution only when and if it can be shown that all reasonable hope of governmental reform is gone."

Perhaps another example will further clarify this process. Americans of Japanese ancestry on the west coast were forcibly relocated shortly after the attack on Pearl Harbor in 1941. Let us assume that we support the relocation, seeing in the situation a value conflict between certain freedoms guaranteed to all citizens, in this case the right to due process under law, as against the security of the community or nation. We then think of an analogy which reverses our position. Suppose there are five Americans of Japanese ancestry in a community. One is seen committing a murder. The witnesses who observe the crime from a distance know only that the murderer had Oriental physical characteristics. Should all five men who have Oriental physical characteristics be locked up to protect the security of the community? Most of us would answer "no." It is the same dilemma, however; the security of the community versus denial of due process. How do we explain our inconsistency? We might say that "security" of the nation or community has two different meanings. In the Japanese relocation case, the legal framework of government which guarantees our basic rights was threatened; in the murder case, while perhaps some citizens' lives were jeopardized by allowing all suspects to go free for lack of evidence, the government itself was not threatened. We then arrive at a general position: The government can justifiably deny citizens basic rights only when that government itself, which is committed to protect those rights, is threatened with destruction; otherwise the action is wrong. This is not to say that one cannot argue convincingly the opposite position, and qualify it in another way.

7. Testing the Factual Assumptions Behind a Qualified Value Position.   Stating a qualified value position will, to some extent, "explain" our inconsistency or clarify our reasoning in a controversy, but it does not necessarily resolve the differences with someone who takes an opposite position, even though both of us have similar ethical commitments. Our position depends not only upon the weight we give conflicting values in two situations but also upon a number of factual assumptions. In the Negro revolt in Mississippi, we are assuming that the Negro's position will be ameliorated by the federal government. There may be little evidence to support the assumption. In the Japanese relocation situation, we assume that there was an immediate danger to the security of the American government which could be partially removed by relocating citizens of "doubtful" allegiance. Today this assumption is generally rejected as false.

As stated before, the analogy exposes inconsistency, the inconsistency forces one to state the factual differences between the situations about which he makes inconsistent judgments, and the argument can then shift from a controversy over the priority or relative importance of values to a test of the factual differences which each antagonist claims support his qualified position. The concepts describing the appropriate strategy for attacking factual disagreements include the identification of conflicting claims; the search for evidence bearing upon the claims; the evaluation of types of evidence; the evaluation of the quality of evidence, especially that coming from authorities with various kinds of qualifications and biases; and the evaluation of the quantity of evidence (e.g., a consideration of how many sources are sampled, the basis of each source, and the extent to which the sources are representative).

8. Testing the Relevance of Statements.   The various patterns of analysis and intellectual operations described above presumably apply to a wide variety of controversial political situations. A valid pattern of analysis, however, is not necessarily useful in the context of a *particular* discussion. The pattern must not only be valid but relevant to the issue. In an argument over segregation in housing, for example, the southerner will often charge that there is more segregation in New York City than in southern cities. One is prone to ask, "So what if this is true?" The claim has no bearing on whether segregated housing is good or bad. It would be relevant only if one defended segregation in one place and not in the other, or if one were trying to demonstrate that there is some "natural" or "normal" tendency toward segregation.

Relevance is difficult to define and teach. It has both a *specific factor,* which applies to the particular points being made in a discussion, and a *general factor,* which applies to the total issue under consideration. That is, a statement can be relevant to the general discussion but irrelevant at a particular point in a discussion. It is important that both types of relevance be kept in mind in evaluating statements or strategies. Fruitful argumentative progression is often sidetracked by issues relevant to the total issue but not to the point under discussion.

Conclusion

We have now described some major concepts and analytic processes we would select as a basis for a social studies curriculum whose major topical focus is political controversy. The justification for selecting these analytic concepts depends upon a number of assumptions, some of the more important of which are:

1. It is useful to distinguish facts from values.
2. It is useful to describe political controversy in terms of general values rather than simply in terms of specific controversial cases.
3. It is useful to differentiate the general values of the Creed from the ultimate concern of a democratic society, the dignity of man.
4. The process of using comparative cases or analogies has the

value of clarifying one's value position and leading one toward
an empirical statement of a political disagreement.

5. The methods of history, journalism, and the social sciences are
appropriate ways of dealing with empirical disagreements.

It is difficult to justify any particular selection of analytical
processes by which one might approach political controversy because so little is known about how to release man's creative
problem-solving energies, especially in the direction of clarifying
and resolving political and ethical disagreement. The basic reason
for choosing these particular concepts and operations, aside from
their presence in the literature on logic and ethics, is simply that
they have proved useful to us in discussing ethical issues; they
appear to help clarify and resolve political disagreement. What else
can one say? Nor can we describe or finally justify the intellectual
operations we went through ourselves in arriving at these patterns
and processes of analysis.

A second question, of course, is whether or not a student
should be taught directly or indirectly any explicit analytical
framework. Our own position on this issue is clear. It is necessary
to have *some* framework from which to approach political conflict
in order to feel any sense of adequacy or competence in handling it.
The framework we have described, however skeletal and inadequate, gives the student an orientation from which to begin analysis. This is especially important from a pedagogical standpoint.
Without a framework the student is likely to view social controversy as a maze of facts, opinions, and conflicting claims. When his
own opinions are challenged, he approaches the controversy by
simply embracing unreflected judgments. And because he cannot
distinguish different kinds of conflict, different kinds of disagreements, he strikes in several directions at once in an effort to regain
a comfortable equilibrium of contradictory beliefs and values.
Myrdal has described one aspect of this tortuous process:

> We have already hinted at the fact that valuations are seldom
> overtly expressed except when they emerge in the course of a
> person's attempts to formulate his beliefs concerning the facts
> and their implication in relation to some section of social reality.
> Beliefs concerning the facts are the very building stones for the
> logical hierarchies of valuations into which a person tries to
> shape his opinions. When the valuations are conflicting, as they

normally are, beliefs serve the rationalization function of bridging illogicalities. The beliefs are thus not only determined by available scientific knowledge in society and the efficacy of the means of its communication to various population groups but are regularly "biased," by which we mean that they are systematically twisted in the one direction which fits them best for purposes of rationalization.[6]

One cannot hope adequately to understand and control either his natural or social universe unless he has some analytic elements in his frame of reference, no matter how crude and inadequate they may be. Without such a framework he is a creature of impulse, wasting his energies by rationalizing his failures rather than focusing his reason upon the challenges to his existence.

It is crucial, however, that the student be taught at some point to question the framework we have presented, to identify shortcomings in it, and to reject it if, from his point of view, it fails to deal with important issues adequately. (The framework herein presented is obviously not the first version of our own analytic construction of political controversy.) Many of the concepts presented above should certainly be changed, discarded, or forgotten, depending upon how useful they turn out to be. This is as it should be. The most useful tools of analysis for each of us are often the ones we invent ourselves. Good arguments are complex, subtle, and intricate. They defy explicit rules of analysis. They are the creation of an original mind. So our hope is not just that people can be taught to use *our* analytic scheme. It is that concepts such as these will be useful enough to make each person recognize their shortcomings and inadequacies, and that, as necessary, each person can discard them in favor of more appropriate ones.

PATTERN ANALYSIS AND THE TEACHING OF THE SOCIAL STUDIES

The implications of pattern analysis for teaching the social studies should be quite clear. First, the patterns illustrate the inadequacy of the simple dichotomy made between "facts" and "opinions." The social studies teacher who assumes that his job is to teach the "facts" and then let the student form his own "opinions" is simply ignoring the complex problem of teaching the student *to relate* fact to "opinion" or value. Second, to assume that it is efficient pedagogically to teach a "fund" or "storehouse" of facts or abstract skills which will, at some later time, be used by the student is to ignore the very obvious point that the facts surrounding a political controversy are both useless and meaningless unless they are related in the student's mind to broader questions of public policy. Third, the process of teaching suggested here means that a central objective is to relate the way social problems are framed *publicly* to the way the student construes them in his own mind. This inevitably means that students must take "personal" positions and attempt to justify them. It is the only way complex patterns of justification can, in fact, be made manifest in the classroom.

Allowing (and in fact encouraging) the student to take an active role in judging the rightness of public decisions, moreover, is likely to affect not only the intellectual climate of the classroom but the student's attitude toward the responsibility and role of the teacher as well. If the teacher is well informed on public issues and intellectually facile, there is little problem. If, on the other hand, the teacher depends on the symbols of adult authority to maintain the respect of the student, obviously the student will reveal personal attitudes which may contradict those of the teacher. For "truth" and "goodness" now become open classroom issues to be determined by a process of public intellectual justification. They are no longer in the hands of the teacher. Static facts or generalizations that happen to appear on a printed page or are uttered by an authority figure are no longer adequate.

Finally a word should be said about the relationship between jurisprudential teaching and self-instruction. When a student "joins an issue" or engages in controversy, he is often relating fundamental components of his own personality (e.g., beliefs, attitud to a public decision-making situation. It is, therefore, more th u likely that different students will construe a controversy in ve different terms. Different questions become important to individual students. Part of the process of teaching involves defining these questions so that they have some common meaning and relevance for all students. Probably just as important, however, is teaching the student the research skills to deal with his own individual questions.

Obviously there is nothing new in teaching high school students the process of social or historical research. What might be stressed is the source of questions researched. Students are perennially asked to write themes on such questions as "Did FDR abuse Presidential power?" or "Was the American 'Revolution' really a revolution?" The questions usually are either found at the end of the chapter or invented by the teacher. More important, they are as a rule the questions of the "academic mind" rather than those of the politician. It is our experience that students are more likely to ask specific factual questions that bear on general legal or value questions, e.g.: What were the living conditions like, in personal terms, for an unemployed worker in 1933? In a jurisprudential approach to the teaching of public issues, individual student research becomes a much more substantial part of the curriculum, and, more important, this research evolves from the *student's efforts* to define and grapple with issues.

NOTES

1.   While the use of analogous cases may not resolve the issue, it is sometimes an effective device in causing people to change their position which, in fact, does resolve the issue. For example, although a person may have first been against racial segregation, through the use of our analogy he may come to see it as no different from sexual segregation, with which he finds nothing wrong. Or initially he may have seen nothing wrong with racial segregation, but after seeing its similarity to social class segregation he may change his mind and be firmly against both.

2.   Such segregation on religious grounds exists, for example, in Montreal with little apparent sense of "atrocity" by either party.

3.   Morton White, *Social Thought in America: The Revolt Against Formalism* (Boston: Beacon Press, 1957), p. 213.

4.   Some exceptions to this statement might be noted: the work of Myrdal on the American Negro, the work of Allport on prejudice, the work of Riesman on mass culture, and the general work of Lewin, which has influenced many social psychologists, as evidenced, for example, by Ralph White and Ronald Lippitt, *Autocracy and Democracy* (New York: Harper & Row, Publishers, 1960).

5.   See e.g., Alfred Kelly's address to the American Historical Association, 1961, parts of which are reprinted in *U.S. News and World Report*, February 5, 1962. Kelly makes the point that the litigants of the segregation cases of 1953 were commissioned by the Supreme Court to determine whether or not the framers of the Fourteenth Amendment intended it to apply to such areas as public education. The Court reached the conclusion after hearing exhaustive testimony on both sides that a

clear conclusion could not be arrived at, and finally made its decision on sociological rather than historical grounds. The incident well illustrates our point. One must make political decisions, which in some cases should be based on empirical considerations, using whatever data seem relevant and appropriate, although they may be clearly inadequate.

6. Gunnar Myrdal, *An American Dilemma* (New York: Harper & Row, Publishers, 1944), p. 1030.

PART 3

Recent Years The 1970s and 1980s

. . . in which Michael Apple argued that the typical avoidance of conflict in the school curriculum cultivates passive spectators, Lawrence Kohlberg proposed that justice can be taught when the subject is a moral dilemma and the group discussing it is diverse, Fred Newmann and his colleagues developed a curriculum for citizen action, and Paul Gagnon turned educators' attention back again to history, arguing that "democracy can be seriously explored only by historical study."

QUESTIONS FOR DISCUSSION

1. What problems are emphasized? Neglected?
2. What was happening in North America and the world that might have shaped how these problems were articulated?
3. How is democracy defined? How are diversity and mutuality (difference and unity) treated?
4. What are similarities and differences across the chapters?

CHAPTER 9

The Hidden Curriculum and the Nature of Conflict

Michael W. Apple
1975

There has been, so far, little examination of how the treatment of conflict in the school curriculum can lead to political quiescence and the acceptance by students of a perspective on social and intellectual conflict that acts to maintain the existing distribution of power and rationality in a society. This paper examines two areas— social studies and science—to indicate how an unrealistic and basically consensus-oriented perspective is taught through a "hidden curriculum" in schools. The argument centers around the fundamental place that forms of conflict have had in science and the social world and on the necessity of such conflict. The paper suggests that a greater emphasis in the school curriculum upon the ideal norms of science, e.g., organized skepticism, and on the uses of conflict could counterbalance the tacit assumptions being taught.

CONFLICT AND THE HIDDEN CURRICULUM

The fact that schools are usually *overtly* insulated from political processes and ideological argumentation has both positive and negative qualities. The insulation has served to defend the school

From William Pinar, *Curriculum Theorizing: The Reconceptualists*, 95–119. © 1975 by McCutchan Publishing Corporation, Berkeley, CA 94702. Permission granted by the publisher.

against whims and fads that can often have a destructive effect upon educational practice. It also, however, can make the school rather unresponsive to the needs of local communities and a changing social order. The pros and cons of the school as a "conservative" institution have been argued fervently for the last ten years or so, at least. Among the most articulate of the spokesmen have been Edgar Z. Friedenberg and the late Jules Henry. The covert teaching of an achievement and marketplace ethic and the probable substitution of a "middle-class" and often "schizophrenic" value system for a student's own biographical meanings are the topics most usually subject to analysis. A good deal of the focus has been on what Jackson (1968) has so felicitously labeled the "hidden curriculum"—that is, on the norms and values that are implicitly, but effectively, taught in schools and that are not usually talked about in teachers' statements of ends or goals. Jackson (pp. 3–37), for instance, deals extensively with the way students learn to cope with the systems of crowds, praise, and power in classrooms: with the large amount of waiting children are called upon to experience, with the teacher as a child's first "boss," and how children learn to falsify certain aspects of their behavior to conform to the reward system extant in most classrooms.

These critiques of the world view being legitimated in the schools have been incisive, yet they have failed to focus on a prevailing characteristic of current schooling that significantly contributes to the maintenance of the same dominant world view. There has been, so far, little examination of how the treatment of *conflict* in the school curriculum can lead to political quiescence and the acceptance by students of a perspective on social and intellectual conflict that acts to maintain the existing distribution of power and rationality in a society. The topic of conflict is crucial for two reasons. How it is dealt with helps to posit a student's sense of the legitimate means of gaining recourse within industrial societies. This is particularly important, and will become more so, in urban areas. It may be rather imperative that urban students develop positive perspectives toward conflict and change, ones that will enable them to deal with the complex and often repressive political realities and dynamics of power of their society in a manner less apt to preserve current institutional modes of interaction a (cf. Eisinger 1970). Also, there may well be specific programmatic suggestions that can be made and instituted fairly readily in ongoing school programs that may alleviate some of the problems.

We can learn a bit about the importance of tacit or hidden teaching from the literature on political socialization. It is beginning to be clear that "incidental learning" contributes more to the political socialization of a student than do, say, civics classes or other forms of deliberate teaching of specific value orientations (Sigel 1970, p. xiii). Children are taught how to deal with and relate to the structures of authority of the collectivity to which they belong by the patterns of interaction they are exposed to to a certain extent in schools.

Obviously, it is not only the school that contributes to a student's "adjustment to authority." For instance, peer groups and especially the family, through its child-rearing practices and its style of interpersonal interaction, can profoundly affect a child's general orientation to authority (Sigel, p. 105). However, there is a strong suggestion in recent research that schools are rather close rivals to the family as significant agents of political socialization. As Sigel (p. 316) puts it:

> [There] is probably little doubt that the public schools are a choice transmission belt for the traditional rather than the innovative, much less the radical. As a result, they facilitate the political socialization of the mainstream young and tend to equip them with the tools necessary for the particular roles they are expected to play in a given society. One may wish to quarrel with the differential roles the government and the schools assign to students, but it would probably be considerably more difficult to deny the school's effectiveness.[1]

It should be stated that the negative treatment given to the uses of conflict goes far beyond the way with which it is overtly dealt in any one subject, say, social studies, the area in which one usually finds material on and teaching about conflict situations. Rather, the negative and quite unrealistic approach seems endemic to many areas, and especially to science, the area usually associated with objectivity and noninterpersonal conflict.

It has become increasingly evident that history books and social studies texts and materials have, over the years, presented a somewhat biased view of the true nature of the amount and possible use of internecine strife in which groups in this country and others have engaged. Our side is good; their side is bad. "We" are peace loving and want an end to strife; "they" are warlike and aim to dominate. The list could be extended considerably, especially in racial matters (Gibson 1969; Willhelm 1970). Yet, we must go beyond this type of analysis, often even beyond the work of the revisionist historians, political scientists, students of political socialization, and educators to get at many of the roots of the teaching of this dominant orientation. We examine here two specific areas—social studies and science. In so doing, we point out that the presentation of these two areas (among others) in schools both mirrors and fosters an ideology that is oriented to a static perspective: in the social studies, on the positive and even essential functions of social conflict; and in science, on the nature of scientific work and argumentation and on what has been called "revolutionary" science. The view presented of science, especially, in the schools is particularly interesting since it is essentially an archetype of the ideological position on conflict we wish to illuminate.

The tacit assumptions seem to be prominent in teaching and in curricular materials. The first centers around a negative position on the nature and uses of conflict. The second focuses on man as a recipient of values and institutions, not on man as a creator and recreator of values and institutions. These assumptions act as basic guidelines that order experiences.

BASIC RULES AND TACIT ASSUMPTIONS

Fundamental patterns in society are held together by tacit assumptions, rules if you will, which are not usually conscious. These rules serve to organize and legitimate the activity of the many individuals whose interaction makes up a social order. Analytically it is helpful to distinguish two types of rules—constitutive or basic rules and preference rules (McClure and Fischer 1969). Basic rules are like the rules of a game; they are broad parameters in which action takes place. Preference rules, as the name suggests, are the choices one has within the rules of the game. Take chess, for instance. There are basic ground rules (which are not usually brought to a level of awareness) that make chess different from, say, checkers or other board games or even nonboard games. And, within the game of chess, one has choices of the moves to make within this constitutive framework. Pawns' choices involve moving forward (except in "taking" an opponent), rooks move forward or side to side, and so forth. If an opponent's pawn were to jump over three men to put you in check, then he obviously would not be following the "rules of the game"; nor would he be following the tacitly accepted rules if he, say, swept all your men from the board and shouted "I win!"

On the very broadest level, one of the constitutive rules most predominant in our society involves the notion of trust. When we drive down the street, we trust that the car approaching from the opposite direction will stay in its lane. Unless there is some outward manifestation of deviance from this rule, we never even bring to a level of conscious awareness how this basic rule activity organizes our lives.[2] A similar rule is the one that posits the legitimate bounds of conflict. The rules of the game implicitly set out the boundaries of the activities people are to engage or not to engage in, the types of questions to ask, and the acceptance or rejection of other people's activities.[3] Within these boundaries, there are choices among a range of activities. We can use the courts, but not bomb; we can argue, but not duel; and so forth. A basic assumption seems to be that conflict among groups of people is inherently and fundamentally bad and we should strive to eliminate it within the established framework of institutions.

Clearly, my critique is not an attempt to impugn the motives or integrity of schools. Some of the better schools and classrooms are alive with issues and controversy. However, the controversies usually exhibited in schools concern choices *within* the parameters of implicitly held rules of activity. Little attempt is made to focus on the parameters themselves.

The hidden curriculum in schools serves to reinforce basic rules surrounding the nature of conflict and its uses. It posits a network of assumptions that, when internalized by students, establishes the boundaries of legitimacy. This process is accomplished not so much by explicit instances showing the negative value of conflict, but by nearly the total absence of instances showing the importance of intellectual and normative conflict in subject areas. The fact is that these assumptions are *obligatory* for the students, since at no time are the assumptions articulated or questioned. By the very fact that they are tacit, their potency is enlarged.[4]

The potent relationship between basic assumptions dominant in a collectivity and the hidden curriculum of school is examined by Dreeben (1968). He argues that students tacitly learn certain identifiable social norms mainly by coping with the day-to-day encounters and tasks of classroom life. The fact that these norms that students learn penetrate many areas of later life is critical since it helps document how schooling contributes to individual adjustment to an ongoing social, economic, and political order. Schooling, occupation, and politics in the United States are well integrated for Dreeben (pp. 144–45). The former acts as a distributor of a form of rationality that, when internalized by the student, enables him to function in and, often, accept "the occupational and political institutions which contribute to the stability of an industrial society."

Social studies and science as they are taught in the large majority of schools provide some of the most explicit instances of the hidden teaching. We have chosen these areas for two reasons. First, there has been built up a rather extensive and important literature concerned with the sociology of the disciplines of scientific endeavor. This literature deals rather insightfully with the "logic in use" of scientists (that is, what scientists seem actually to do) as opposed to the "reconstructed logic" of scientists (that is, what philosophers of science and other observers say scientists do) that is normally taught in schools (Apple 1972). Second, in social studies the problems we discuss can be illuminated rather clearly by drawing upon selected Marxian notions (ideas, not necessarily dogma) to show that the commonsense views of social life often found in the teaching of social studies are not inevitable. Let us examine science initially. In so doing, we propose an alternate or, rather, a broader view of scientific endeavor that should be considered by educators and, especially, curriculum workers, if they are, at the very least, to focus on the assumptions inherent in much that is taught in our educational institutions.

CONFLICT IN SCIENTIFIC COMMUNITIES

One of our basic theses is that science, as it is presented in most elementary and a large proportion of secondary classrooms, contributes to the learning by students of a basically unrealistic and essentially conservative perspective on the usefulness of conflict. Scientific domains are presented as bodies of knowledge ("thats" and "hows"), at best organized around certain fundamental regularities as in the many discipline- and inquiry-centered curricula that evolved after the "Brunerian revolution," at worst as fairly isolated data one masters for tests. Almost never is it seriously examined as a personal construction of human beings. Let us examine this situation rather closely.

A science is not "just" a domain of knowledge or techniques of discovery and formulating justifications; it is a *group* (or rather, groups) of individuals, a *community* of scholars in Polanyi's (1964) terms, pursuing projects in the world. Like all communities, it is governed by norms, values, and principles that are both overtly seen and covertly felt. By being made up of individuals and groups of scholars, it also has had a significant history of both intellectual and interpersonal struggle. Often the conflict is generated by the introduction of a new and usually quite revolutionary paradigm that challenges the basic meaning structures that were previously accepted by the particular body of scientists, often, thereby, effectively dividing the scholarly community. These struggles have been concerned with the modes of gaining warranted knowledge, with what is to be considered properly scientific, with the very basic foundations upon which science is based. They have also been concerned with such situations as conflicting interpretations of data, with who discovered what first, and many more.

What can be found in schools, however, is a perspective that is akin to what has been called the "positivist ideal" (Hagstrom 1965, p. 256). In our schools, scientific work is tacitly always linked with accepted standards of validity and is seen (and taught) as always subject to empirical verification with no outside influences, either personal or political. "Schools of thought" in science do not exist, or, if they do, "objective" criteria are used to persuade scientists that one side is correct and the other wrong. Just as is evident in our discussion of social studies instruction, children are presented with a *consensus theory of science*, one that underemphasizes the serious disagreements over methodology, goals, and other elements that make up the paradigms of activity of scientists. By the fact that scientific consensus is continually exhibited, students are not permitted to see that without disagreement and controversy science would not progress or would progress at a much slower pace. Not only does controversy stimulate discovery by drawing the attention of scientists to critical problems (Hagstrom, p. 264), but it serves to clarify conflicting intellectual positions. More is mentioned about this point later in our discussion.

A point that is also quite potent is that it is very possible that the standards of "objectivity" (one is tempted to say "vulgar objectivity") being exhibited and taught in school may often lead to a detachment from political commitment. That is, it may not be neutrality as it is overtly expressed, but it may mirror a rather deep fear of intellectual, moral, and political conflict (Gouldner 1970, pp. 102–3) and the personally intense commitment that coheres with the positions taken (Polanyi 1964). The focus in educational institutions on the student scientist (who is often a passive observer in many classrooms despite the emphasis being placed on inquiry by theorists and curriculum specialists) as an individual who objectively and rationally tests or deduces warranted assumptions or makes and checks hypotheses or what have you critically misrepresents the nature of the conflicts so often found between proponents of alternative solutions, interpretations, or modes of procedure in scientific communities. It cannot enable students to see the political dimension of the process by which one alternative theory's proponents win out over their competitors. Nor can such a presentation of science do more than systematically neglect the power dimension involved in scientific argumentation.

Not only is the historical and continuing conflict between competing theories in scientific domains ignored, but little or no thought has evidently been given to the fact that hypothesis testing and the application of *existing* scientific criteria are *not sufficient* to explain how and why a choice is made between competing theories. There have been too many conterinstances that belie this view of science (Kuhn 1962).[5] It is much more perceptive to note that science itself is not necessarily cumulative, nor does it proceed according to a basic criterion of consensus, but that it is riven by conceptual revolutions that cause groups of scientists to reorganize and reconceptualize the models by which they attempt to understand and manipulate the world. "The history of science has been and should be [seen] as a history of competing research programs (or, if you wish 'paradigms'), but it has not been and must not become a succession of periods of normal science: the sooner competition starts the better for progress" (Lakatos 1970, p. 155).[6]

We are not trying to make a case here for a view of science that states that "objectivity" and "neutrality," hypothesis-testing and inquiry procedures are not of paramount importance. What we are saying is that scientific argumentation and counterargumentation are a major part of the scientific enterprise and that the theories and modes of procedure ("structures of disciplines," if you will) act as norms or psychological commitments that lead to intense controversy between groups of scientists (Apple 1972; Mulkay 1969). This controversy is central to progress in science, and it is this continuing conflict that is hidden from students.

Perhaps this point can be made clearer by delving a bit more deeply into some of the realistic characteristics of scientific disciplines often hidden from public view and almost never taught in schools. We have been discussing conflict in scientific domains, yet it is difficult to separate conflict from competition.[7] One of the more important oversights in schools is the lack of treatment whatsoever of the "problem" of competition in science. Competition over priority and recognition in new discoveries is a characteristic of *all* established sciences (Hagstrom 1965, p. 81). One need only read Watson's (1968) lively account of his race with Linus Pauling for the Nobel Prize for the discovery of the structure of DNA to realize how intense the competitiveness can be and how very human are scientists as individuals and in groups.

Competition also can be seen quite clearly between specialties in a discipline (Hagstrom 1965, p. 130), not necessarily on the "frontiers" of knowledge as in Watson's case. Here, as in football, the "commodity" (if I may speak metaphorically) is top-notch students who can be recruited to expand the power and prestige of an merging specialty. There is continuous, but usually covert, competition among subdisciplines in science for what seem to be limited amounts of prestige available. The conflict here is crucial. Areas whose prestige is relatively high tend to recruit members with the most talent. Relatively lower prestige areas can have quite a difficult time gaining adherents to their particular interests. Realistically a prime factor, if not the most important factor, in high quality scientific research is the quality of student and scientific "labor" a specialty can recruit. Prestige has a strong influence in enticing students and the competition over relative prestige can be intense, therefore, because of these consequences (Hagstrom, p. 173).

My point here is decidedly not to denigrate competition in science, nor is it to present a demonic view of the scientific enterprise in all its ramifications. Rather it is to espouse a more realistic perspective on this enterprise and the *uses of conflict among its practitioners*. Conflict and competition themselves are quite functional. They induce scientists in each area to try to establish a domain of competence in their subjects that is specifically theirs. Competitive pressures also help to assure that less popular research areas are not neglected. Furthermore, the strong competitive element in the scientific community encourages members to take risks, to outdistance their competitors, in effect, thereby increasing the possibility of new and exciting discoveries (Hagstrom 1965, pp. 82–83).

Conflict is also heightened by the very normative structure of the scientific community itself. In fact, it may be a significant contributing agent in both conflict and competition. Among the many norms that guide the behavior of scientists, perhaps the most important for our discussion here is that of organized skepticism. Storer (1966, pp. 78–79) defines it as follows:

> This norm is directive, embodying the principle that each scientist should be held individually responsible for making sure that previous research by others on which he bases his work is valid. He cannot be excused if he has accepted a false idea and then pleads innocence "because Dr. X told me it was true," even if privately we cannot accuse him of willfully substituting error for truth; he should have been properly sceptical of Dr. X's work in the first place. . . .
>
> The scientist is obligated also by this norm to make public his criticisms of the work of others when he believes it to be in error. . . . It follows that no scientist's contribution to knowledge can be accepted without careful scrutiny, and the scientist must doubt his own findings as well as those of others.

It is not difficult to see how the norm of organized skepticism has contributed to the controversies within scientific communities.

Other examples of conflict abound. Perhaps the one most important for our own topic is the existence of "rebellious" subgroups in scientific communities. Specialties that revolt against the goals and/or means of a larger discipline are quite common within the scientific tradition. These rebellious groups of researchers are alienated from the main body of current scientific discourse in their particular areas and sparks may very well fly because of the argumentation between the rebels and the traditionalists. Here, often added to this situation, even the usual arguments that we associate with science—that is, arguments among groups and individuals over substantive issues such as warranted knowledge and the like—blend with arguments over goals and policies (Hagstrom 1965, pp. 193–94).[8] Even more importantly today, it is becoming quite common (and in my view, happily so) for there to be heated discussion and dissension over the political stance a discipline should take and over the social uses of its knowledge.

So far we have been documenting the rather important dimension of conflict in scientific communities. We have been making the point that scientific knowledge as it is taught in schools has, in effect, been divorced from the structure of the community from which it evolved and which acts to criticize it. Students are "forced," because of the very absence of a realistic picture of how communities in science apportion power and economic resources, to internalize a view that has little potency for questioning the legitimacy of the tacit assumptions about interpersonal conflict that govern their lives and their own educational, economic, and political situations. Not only are they presented with a view of science that is patently unrealistic, but, what is more important for our own position, they are not shown how critical interpersonal and intergroup argumentation and conflict have been for the progress of science. When this situation is generalized into a basic perspective on one's relation to the economic and political paradigms of activity in a society, it is not difficult to see how it can serve to reinforce the quiescence of students or lead them into "proper channels" for changing these structures.

CONFLICT IN SOCIETY

The second area of schooling in which one finds hidden curricular encounters with and tacit teaching of constitutive assumptions about conflict, and that we have chosen to explicitly focus upon, is that of social studies. As in our discussion of science, in delving into this area we propose an alternative or broader view on conflict in society. We also document some of the social uses of intellectual and normative conflict, uses that are ignored in most of the curricular encounters found in schools.

An examination of much of the literature in social studies points to an acceptance of society as basically a cooperative system. Observations in classrooms over an extended period of time reveal a similar perspective. The orientation stems in large part from the (perhaps necessarily unconscious) basic assumption that conflict, and especially social conflict, is not an essential feature of the network of social relations we call society (Dahrendorf 1959, p. 112). More often than not, a social reality is pictured that tacitly accepts "happy cooperation" as the normal if not the best way of life. Now it must be made clear that the truth value of the statement that society is a cooperative system (if only everyone would cooperate) *cannot* be determined empirically. It is essentially a value orientation that helps determine the questions that one asks or the educational experiences one designs for students. And the educational experiences seem to emphasize what is fundamentally a conservative perspective.

The perspective found in schools leans heavily upon how all elements of a society, from the postman and fireman in first grade to the partial institutions in civics courses in high school, are linked to each other in a functional relationship, each contributing to the ongoing *maintenance* of society. Internal dissension and conflict in a society are viewed as inherently antithetical to the smooth functioning of the social order. *Consensus* is once more a pronounced feature. This orientation is also evident in the implicit emphasis upon students (and man in general) as value-transmitting and value-receiving persons rather than as value-creating persons in much of their school experience (Gouldner 1970, p. 193).

The fact that there are a number of paradigmatic ways one can perceive the social world has long been noted. However, it is also important to note that each posits a certain logic of organization upon social activity and each has certain, often strikingly different, valuative assumptions that underlie it. The differences between the Durkheimian and the more subjectivistic Weberian perspectives offer a case in point. The recent analysis of structural-functional social theories, especially those of Parsons, by Gouldner offers a more current example. His examination, one that has a long intellectual history in the sociology of knowledge, raises intriguing questions about the social and political consequences of contemporary social thought—that much of its background of assumptions is determined by the personal and class existence of the thinker, that it presents a "very selective, one-sided picture of American society," one geared to "the avoidance of political tensions" and aimed at a notion that political stability, say, "would be achieved if efforts at social change prudently stopped short of changing established ways of allocating and justifying power" (Gouldner 1970, p. 48). In short the underlying basis of such a social "paradigm" used to order and guide our perceptions is fundamentally oriented to the legitimation of the existing social order. By the very fact that it seeks to treat such topics as social equilibrium and system maintenance, for example, there is a strong tendency toward conformity and a denial that there need be conflict (pp. 210–18).

Opposed to the structural-functional type of reasoning, Gouldner advocates a different "paradigm," one that is rooted in the individual's search to transform himself and his activity, and one that sets not existing society as measure but rather the possibility of basic structural change through an individual's passionate commitment and social involvement. The question of legitimation, hence, becomes less a process of studying how institutional tensions evolve and can be "settled," and more an attempt to link institutions with their historical development and their need for transformation according to explicitly chosen principles based on political and moral argumentation. The perspective on conflict of the latter position is quite different from that of the school of thought Gouldner criticizes.

In its analysis of the background assumptions of Parsonian social thought, for example, Gouldner's examination documents the place of moral argumentation and value conflict, which are at the heart of the human sciences and their understanding of society. He thereby considerably expands the boundaries of possible conflict. This situation is perhaps most evident in his criticism of the inordinate place Parsons gives to a socialization process that implicitly defines man as primarily a recipient of values (Gouldner 1970, p. 206). He censures functionalist social theories for being incapable of dealing with "those who oppose social establishments actively and who struggle to change its rules and membership requirements." Gouldner opposes this view with a focus upon human beings as engaged in a dialectical process of receiving, creating, and recreating values and institutions (p. 427; Berger and Luckmann 1966). The continual recreation of values in a society is a difficult process and often involves conflict among those of disparate valuative frameworks. It is this type of conflict, among others, to which Gouldner attempts to give a place.

By their very nature, social "paradigms" themselves are constantly changing. In fact, Gouldner's recent work can be seen to mirror and be a part of this change. However, they leave behind reifications of themselves found in both elementary and high school curricula. This may be particularly true in the case of the models of understanding of social life we find in schools today.

There is, perhaps, no better example of the emphasis upon consensus, order, and the absence of any conflict in social studies curricula than that found in one of the more popular sets of educational materials, Science Research Associates' economics "kit," *Our Working World*. It is designed to teach basic concepts of disciplined economics to elementary school students. The primary grade course of study subtitled "Families at Work" is organized around everyday social interaction, the likes of which children would be familiar with. Statements such as the following pervade the materials. "When we follow the rules, we are rewarded; but if we break the rules, we will be punished. So you see, dear, that is why everyone does care. That is why we *learn* customs and rules, and why we *follow* them. Because if we do, we are all rewarded by a nicer and more orderly world" (Senesh 1964, p. 22).

The attitude exhibited toward the *creation* of new values and customs and the value placed on an orderly, nonconflicting world seem to be indicative of a more constitutive set of assumptions concerning consensus and social life. When one realizes that students are inundated with examples of this type throughout the day, ones in which it is rather difficult to find any value placed upon disorder of any significant sort, it makes one pause.

Even most of the inquiry-oriented curricula, though fruitful in other ways to be sure, show a signal neglect of the efficacy of conflict and the rather long and deep-seated history it has held in social relationships. For examples, the basic assumptions that conflicts are to be "resolved" within accepted boundaries and that continuing change in the framework and texture of institutional arrangements is less than desirable can be seen in the relatively sophisticated discipline-centered social science curricula that are being developed currently. One of these curricula (Center for the Study of Instruction 1970) overtly offers a "conceptual schemes" approach that puts forward a hierarchy of generalizations that, ideally, are going to be internalized by the student through his active participation in role playing and inquiry. These levels of generalizations range from rather simple to fairly complex and are subsumed under a broad "descriptive" generalization or "cognitive scheme." For example, subsumed under the organizing generalization "Political organization (government) resolves conflicts and makes interactions easier among people" are the following subgeneralizations. They are listed in ascending complexity.

1. The behavior of individuals is governed by commonly accepted rules.
2. Members of family groups are governed by rules and law.
3. Community groups are governed through leadership and authority.
4. Man's peaceful interaction depends on social controls.
5. The pattern of government depends upon control by participation in the political system.
6. Stable political organization improves the quality of life shared by its citizens. (p. T-17).[9]

Coupled with these "descriptive" generalizations, which the students are to be led up to, are such "supporting concepts" as "Rules help to maintain order" and "Rules help protect health and safety" (p. T-26). Now, few will quarrel with these statements. After all, rules do help. But, like the assumptions prevalent in the economics material, children are confronted with a tacit emphasis once again on a stable set of structures and on the maintenance of order.

What is intriguing is the nearly complete lack of treatment of or even reference to conflict as a social concern or as a category of thought in most available social studies curricula or in most classrooms observed. Of the more popular materials, only those developed under the aegis of the late Hilda Taba refer to it as a key concept. However, while the Taba Social Studies Curriculum overtly focuses on conflict, and while this focus in itself is a welcome sight, its orientation is on the serious consequences of sustained conflict rather than on the many positive aspects also associated with conflict itself. Conflict again is viewed as "dysfunctional," even though it is pictured as being ever present (Durkin, Duvall, and McMaster 1969, p. v).

As we noted previously, to a large extent society as it exists, in *both* its positive and negative aspects, is held together by implicit commonsense rules and paradigms of thought. Social studies materials such as this (and there are many others to which we have not referred) can contribute to the reinforcing and tacit teaching of certain dominant basic assumptions and, hence, a proconsensus and antidissension belief structure.

This view is being countered somewhat by a portion of the content now being taught under the rubric of Black Studies. Here, struggle and conflict on a communal basis are often explicitly and positively focused upon (Hare 1969; Wilcox 1969, pp. 20–21). While many curriculists may find such overt espousal of community goals somewhat antithetical to their own inclinations, the fact that there has been an attempt to present a comparatively realistic outlook on the significant history and uses of conflict in the progress of social groups, through the civil rights and black power movements for instance, must be recognized. Even those who would not applaud or would applaud only a rather safe or conservative view on this subject should realize the potency and positive value of just such a perspective for developing a group consciousness and a cohesiveness not heretofore possible. This point is made again in our more general discussion of the uses of conflict in social groups.

To say, however, that most Black Studies curricula exhibit this same perspective would be less than accurate. One could also point to the by now apparent presentation of black historical material where those blacks are presented who stayed within what were considered to be the legitimate boundaries (constitutive rules) of protest or progressed in accepted economic, athletic, scholarly, or artistic fields. Usually, one does not find reference to Malcolm X, Marcus Garvey, or others who offered a potent critique of existing modes of activity. However, it is the *massiveness* of the tacit presentation of the consensus perspective that must be stressed, as well as its occurrence in the two areas examined in this paper.

It is not sufficient, though, for our purposes to "merely" illuminate how the hidden curriculum obligates students to experience certain encounters with basic rules. It is essential that an alternative view be posited and that the uses of social conflict that we have been mentioning be documented.

It is possible to counter the consensus orientation with a somewhat less consensus-bound set of assumptions, assumptions that seem to be as empirically warranted, if not more so, as those to which we have raised objections. For instance, some social theorists have taken the position that "society is not primarily a smoothly functioning order of the form of a social organism, a social system, or a static social fabric." Rather, continuous change in the elements *and* basic structural form of society is a dominant characteristic. Conflicts are the systematic products of the changing structure of a society and by their very nature tend to lead to progress. The "order" of society, hence, becomes the regularity of change. The "reality" of society is conflict and flux, not a "closed functional system" (Dahrendorf 1959, p. 27). It has been stated that the most significant contribution to the understanding of society made by Marx was his insight that a major source of change and innovation is internal conflict. This crucial insight can be appreciated without the necessity of accepting his metaphysical assumptions (Walker 1967, pp. 217–218). In essence, therefore, conflicts must be looked at as a basic and often beneficial dimension of the dialectic of activity we label society.

An examination of positions within and closely allied with this general orientation can help to illuminate the importance of conflict. One of the more interesting perspectives points to its utility in preventing the reification of existing social institutions by exerting pressure upon individuals and groups to be innovative and creative in bringing about changes in institutional activities. Coser (Dahrendorf 1959, p. 207) puts it well:

> Conflict within and between groups in a society can prevent accommodations and habitual relations from progressively impoverishing creativity. The clash of values and interest, the tension between what is and what some groups feel ought to be, the conflict between vested interests and new strata and groups demanding their share of power, have been productive of vitality.

Yet one is hard pressed to find anything akin to this orientation in most of the materials and teaching exhibited in schools. The basic rules of activity that govern our perception tend to cause us to picture conflict as primarily a negative quality in a collectivity. However, "happy cooperation" and conflict are the two sides of the societal coin, neither of which is wholly positive or negative. This outlook is forcefully put by Coser (1956, p. 31):

> No group can be entirely harmonious for it would then be devoid of process and structure. Groups require disharmony as well as harmony, dissociation as well as association; and conflicts within them are by no means altogether disruptive factors. Group formation is the result of both types of processes. The belief that one process tears down what the other builds up, so that what finally remains is the result of subtracting the one from the other, is based on a misconception. On the contrary, both "positive" and "negative" factors build group relations. Conflict as well as cooperation has social functions. Far from being necessarily dysfunctional, a certain degree of conflict is an essential element in group formation and the persistence of group life.

The basic rule of activity that constitutes the unconscious negative value associated with conflict tends to lead to the designing of experiences that focus on the "law or rule breaking" dimension of conflict, yet it should be made clear that conflict leads not "merely" to law breaking but, in effect, law *creating* as well (Coser 1956, p. 126).[10] It performs the considerable task of pointing to areas of needed redress. Furthermore, it brings into conscious awareness the more basic rules that govern the particular activity over which there is conflict but that were hidden from view. That is, it performs the unique function of enabling individuals to see the hidden imperatives built into situations that act to structure their actions, thereby partially freeing individuals to create relevant patterns of actions to an extent not usually possible. These law-creating and expanding-awareness properties of conflict situations offer, in combination, a rather positive effect. Since conflict brings about inherently new situations that to a large degree are undefined by previous assumptions, it acts as a stimulus for the establishment of new and possibly more flexible or situationally pertinent norms of activity. By literally forcing conscious attention, issues are defined and new dimensions can be explored and made clear (Coser, pp. 124–215).

Documentation of the positive effects of conflict would not be even nearly adequate if a major use were to go unmentioned, especially given our own commitment to making urban education, in particular, more responsive to the needs of the community it serves. Here we are speaking of the importance of conflict for both creating and legitimating a conscious and specifically ethnic experience. It is now well known that one of the primary ways groups define themselves is by perceiving themselves as struggling with other groups and that such struggle both increases members' participation in group activities and makes them more conscious of the bonds that tie them together (Coser 1956, p. 90). That the black and other ethnic communities have, to a significant extent, defined themselves along these in-group/out-group lines is of no small moment since it enables a greater cohesiveness among the various elements within their respective communities. By drawing upon "primordial sentiments" such as race a communal meaning structure is created that makes plausible an individual's and a group's continued and separate existence (Berger 1967, pp. 24–25; Geertz 1963, p. 118). Just as conflict seems to be a primary means for the establishment of individual autonomy and for the full differentiation of personality from the outside world (Coser, p. 33),[11] so too it is effective for the full differentiation of community autonomy. Respect for pluralistic societies may require a greater acceptance of this perspective.

We have been proposing an alternative outlook on the presence and uses of conflict in social groups. It is feasible for it to be used as a more objective foundation for designing curricula and guiding teaching so that the more static hidden curriculum students encounter can be counterbalanced to some extent. The explicit focusing on conflict as a legitimate category of conceptualization and as a valid and essential dimension of collective life could enable the development by students of a more viable and potent political and intellectual perspective from which to perceive their relation to existing economic and political institutions. At the least, such a perspective gives them a better understanding of the tacit assumptions that act to structure their own activity.

PROGRAMMATIC CONSIDERATIONS

There are a number of programmatic suggestions that can be made that could at least partially serve to counterbalance the hidden curriculum most evident in science and social studies. While these are by their very nature still rather tentative and only partial, they may prove important.

A more balanced presentation of some of the espoused values of science is essential, especially that relating to organized skepticism. The historical importance to the scientific communities of the overriding skeptical outlook needs to be recognized and focused upon.

The history of science can be seen as a continuing dialectic of controversy and conflict between advocates of competing research programs and paradigms, between accepted answers and challenges to these "truths." As such, science itself could be presented with a greater historical orientation documenting the conceptual revolutions necessary for significant breakthroughs to occur.

Rather than adhering to a view of science as truth, the balanced presentation of science as "truth until further notice," a process of continual change, could prevent the crystallization of attitudes (Apple and Popkewitz 1971). In this connection also, the study of how conceptual revolutions in science have proceeded would contribute to a less positive perspective on consensus as the only mode of progress.

To this point can be added a focus upon the moral uses and dilemmas of science. For example, personalizing the history of science through cases such as Oppenheimer, Watson, and, intriguingly, the controversy surrounding the Velikovsky case (cf. Mulkay 1969), would indeed be helpful. When taken together, these suggestions would help to eliminate the bias of present curricula by introducing the idea of personal and interpersonal controversy and conflict.

In the social studies, a number of suggestions can be made. The comparative study of revolution, say the American, French, Russian, and Chinese, would serve to focus upon the properties of the human condition that cause and are ameliorated by interpersonal conflict. This suggestion is made more appropriate when coupled with the fact that in many countries revolution is the legitimate (in a quite real sense of the word) mode of procedure for redressing grievances.

A more realistic appraisal and presentation of the uses of conflict in the civil rights movement of blacks, Indians, and others would no doubt assist in the formation of a perspective that perceives these and similar activities as legitimate models of action. The fact that laws *had* to be broken and were then struck down by the courts later is not usually focused upon in social studies curricula. Yet, it was through these types of activities that a good deal of progress was and is made. Here community and "movement" studies by urban students of how changes have been effected is an interesting process, one that should prove of considerable moment.

Finally, the comparison of different paradigmatic views on social life and the differing value assumptions of each would be helpful. While the normative implication of many paradigms of social thought may serve to limit their usefulness as models of action, and in fact may make them totally unacceptable on occasion, the presentation and analysis of alternative conceptions to those now dominant could still be effective.

Beyond these suggestions for specific programmatic changes, one further area should be noted. Sociological "paradigms" also attempt to account for the commonsense reality in which students and teachers dwell. Schools are integrally involved in this reality and its internalization. It might be wise to consider engaging students in the articulation and development of paradigms of activity within their everyday lives at school. Such involvement could enable students to come to grips with and amplify crucial insights into their own conditionedness and freedom. Such insights could potentially alter the original paradigm and the commonsense reality itself. It would also make possible to a greater degree a concrete and meaningful educational encounter for students with the process of value and institutional recreation.

CONCLUSIONS

Research on political socialization of children seems to indicate the importance of the president and policeman as points of contact between children and the structures of authority and legitimacy in a society (Easton and Dennis 1969, p. 162). For instance, there is a strongly personal initial bond between the child and these representatives of the structures of authority. As the child matures, these very personal ties are transferred to more anonymous institutions such as a congress or to political activities such as voting. The tendency to lift impersonal institutions to high esteem may be quite an important source of the relative stability and durability of the structures of authority in industrial societies (pp. 271–76).

Yet it is not quite certain that this formulation really answers the questions one could raise concerning political and social stability. The foundation of political (broadly conceived) leanings and relations to political and social structures is in a belief system that itself rests upon basic patterns of assumptions. Such rules for activity (and thought as a fundamental form of this activity) are probably more important to a person's relation to his life-world than we realize. We have been examining one of these constitutive assumptions.

It is our contention that the schools systematically distort the functions of social conflict in collectivities. The social, intellectual, and political manifestations of this distortion are manifold. They may contribute significantly to the ideological underpinnings that serve to fundamentally orient individuals.

Students in most schools and in urban centers in particular are presented with a view that serves to legitimate the existing social order since change, conflict, and man as creator as well as receiver of values and institutions are systematically neglected. We have pointed to the massiveness of the presentation. Now something else must be stressed once again—the fact that these meaning structures are obligatory. Students receive them from persons who are "significant others" in their lives, through their teachers, other role models in books and elsewhere. To change this situation, students' perceptions of to whom they are to look as holders of "expert knowledge" must be radically altered. In ghetto areas, a partial answer is, perhaps, instituting a more radical perspective in the schools. This change can be carried out only by political activity. It may very well be that to divorce an educator's educational existence from his political existence is to forget that as an act of influence, education is also an inherently political act.

One of the primary tasks of this analysis has been to present lenses that are alternatives to those that normally legitimate many of the activities and encounters curricularists design for students. The curriculum field has limited its own forms of consciousness so that the political and ideological assumptions that undergird a good deal of its normal patterns of activity are as hidden as those that students encounter in schools (Huebner 1962, p. 88). We have pointed to the possibilities inherent in a more theoretically realistic approach to the nature of conflict as one alternative "form of consciousness." Yet when all has been said, it is still possible to raise the question of whether such theoretical investigations are either heuristically, politically, or programmatically helpful.

One of the difficulties in seeking to develop new perspectives is the obvious and oft-pointed-to distinction between theory and practice or, to put it in common-sense language, between "merely" understanding the world and changing it. This distinction is rooted in our very language. Yet it is crucial to remind ourselves that while, say, Marx felt that the ultimate task of philosophy and theory was not merely to "comprehend reality" but to change it, it is also true that according to Marx revolutionizing the world has as its very foundation an adequate understanding of it. (After all, Marx spent most of his lifetime writing *Das Kapital*—Avineri 1968, p. 137.)

The significant danger is not that theoretical thought offers no mode of critiquing and changing reality, but that it can lead to quietism or a perspective that, like Hamlet, necessitates a continuing monologue on the complexity of it all, while the world tumbles down around us. It would seem important to note that not only is an understanding of existing reality a necessary condition for changing it (Avineri 1968, p. 148), but it is a major (and perhaps the major) step in actually effecting this reconstruction. However, with this understanding of the social milieu in which curriculists operate, there must also be a continual attempt to bring to a conscious level those hidden epistemological and ideological assumptions that help to structure the decisions they make and the environments they design (Huebner 1962).[12] These fundamental assumptions can have a significant impact on the hidden curriculum in which students tacitly dwell.

Without an analysis and greater understanding of these latent assumptions, educators run the very real risk of continuing to let values work through them. A conscious advocacy of a more realistic outlook on and teaching of the dialectic of social change would, no doubt, contribute to preparing students with the political and conceptual tools necessary to deal with the dense reality they must face. I do not think it is necessary to enumerate the possible consequences if this self-evaluation should not occur.

NOTES

1. Such a statement is both realistic and rather critical. In a way, critics of the schools (and the present author to a large extent) are caught in a bind. It is rather easy to denigrate existing "educational" structures

(after all, everyone seems to do it); yet, it is not quite as easy to offer alternative structures. The individual who attempts to ameliorate some of the more debilitating conditions runs the risk of actually helping to shore up and perpetuate what may very well be an outmoded set of institutional arrangements. Yet, not to try to better conditions in what are often small and stumbling ways is to neglect those real human beings who now inhabit the schools for most of their preadult lives. Therefore, one tries to play both sides of the battle often. One criticizes the fundamental assumptions that undergird schools as they exist today and, at the same time, paradoxically attempts to make these same institutions a bit more humane, a bit more educative. It is an ambiguous position, but, after all, so is one's total situation. Our discussion of the fundamental glossing over of the nature and necessity of conflict and the tacit teaching that accompanies it shows this ambiguity. However, if urban education in particular is to make a difference (and here we should read politically and economically), then concrete changes must be effected now *while* the more basic criticisms are themselves being articulated. One is not an excuse for the other.

2.   The language of "rules of activity" is less analytically troublesome than the distinction often made between thought and action, since it implies that the distinction is somewhat naive and enables action, perceptual, conceptual, and bodily, to be the fundamental category of an individual's response to his situation. While we often use rules of activity and assumptions interchangeably, the point should be made that assumptions usually connote a less inclusive category of phenomena and are actually indicative of the existence of these socially sedimented rules and boundaries that seem to affect even our very perceptions. Further work on such rules can be found in the ethnomethodological literature (Garfinkel 1967) and, of course, in the later Wittgenstein (1958).

3.   In essence, the "system" that many individuals decry is *not* an ordered interrelationship of institutions, but a framework of fundamental assumptions that are prior to and act in a dialectical relationship with these institutions.

4.   The questions we are posing can obviously lead to a circular type of controversy. Do the children learn, say, political quiescence and acceptance in school and then transfer these to life in general, or do the schools "merely" reinforce constitutive rules learned elsewhere? This is not the point (though it is, no doubt, quite important). What is more important is to at least begin to ask *how* the schools may function, through the hidden curriculum, to obligate and reinforce the learning by children of a certain perspective.

5.   Kuhn's seminal work is subjected to rather acute analysis, and

discussed with rebuttal and counterrebuttal in Lakatos and Musgrave (1970). The entire volume is devoted to the issues, epistemological and sociological, raised by Kuhn's book.

6.   Normal science refers to that science that has agreement (consensus) on the basic paradigms of activity to be used by scientists to interpret and act on their respective fields. See Kuhn (1962; 1970) for an intensive analysis of normal and revolutionary science.

7.   It is important to distinguish between conflict and competition, however. While conflict seems to stem from a number of the conditions we have examined or will examine—new paradigms, disagreements over goals, methodology, etc.—competition seems to have its basis in the exchange system of science. See, for example, Storer's (1966) interesting examination of the place of professional recognition and commodity exchange in the scientific community.

8.   Statistics is an interesting example.

9.   It is questionable whether many blacks in the ghettos of the United States would support this "description."

10.   Perhaps the best illustration of material on the law-breaking dimension of conflict is a primary grade course of study, "Respect for Rules and Law" (New York State Bureau of Elementary Curriculum Development 1969). One set of curricular materials does take some interesting and helpful steps in allowing for a more honest appraisal of conflict. See Oliver and Newmann (1968).

11.   This is perhaps one of Piaget's most fruitful insights.

12.   The commonsense assumptions that seem to posit a rather static logic upon curriculum design also seem to cohere with a type of bureaucratic rationality that has had a long tradition in curriculum thought. For an excellent analysis of this tradition, see Kliebard (1971).

REFERENCES

Apple, M. W. "Community, Knowledge, and the Structure of Disciplines." *The Educational Forum* 37, no. 1 (1972): 75–82.

_____, and Popkewitz, T. S. "Knowledge, Perspective and Commitment: An Essay Review of Thomas Kuhn and Alvin Gouldner." *Social Education* 35 (1971): 935–37.

Avineri, S. *The Social and Political Thought of Karl Marx*. New York: Cambridge University Press, 1968.

Berger, P. L. *The Sacred Canopy.* New York: Doubleday, 1967.

_____, and Luckmann, T. *The Social Construction of Reality.* New York: Doubleday, 1966.

Center for the Study of Instruction. *Principles and Practices in the Teaching of the Social Sciences: Teacher's Edition.* New York: Harcourt, Brace and World, 1970.

Coser, L. *The Functions of Social Conflict.* New York: Free Press, 1956.

Dahrendorf, R. *Class and Class Conflict in Industrial Society.* Stanford, Calif.: Stanford University Press, 1959.

———, *Essays in the Theory of Society.* London: Routledge & Kegan Paul, 1968.

Dreeben, R. *On What Is Learned in School.* Reading, Mass.: Addison-Wesley, 1968.

Durkin, M. C., Duvall, A., and McMaster, A. *The Taba Social Studies Curriculum: Communities around Us.* Reading, Mass.: Addison-Wesley, 1969.

Easton, D., and Dennis, J. *Children in the Political System.* New York: McGraw-Hill, 1969.

Eisinger, P. K. "Protest Behavior and the Integration of Urban Political Systems." Unpublished paper, Madison, Wis.: Institute for Research on Poverty, University of Wisconsin, 1970.

Garfinkel, H. *Studies in Ethnomethodology.* Englewood Cliffs, N.J.: Prentice-Hall, 1967.

Geertz, C. "The Integrative Revolution: Primordial Sentiments and Civil Politics in the New States." In *Old societies and New States,* edited by C. Geertz, pp. 105–57. New York: Free Press, 1963.

Gibson, E. F. "The Three D's: Distortion, Deletion, Denial." *Social Education* 33 (1969): 405–9.

Gouldner, A. W. *The Coming Crisis of Western Sociology.* New York: Basic Books, 1970.

Hagstrom, W. O. *The Scientific Community.* New York: Basic Books, 1965.

Hare, N. "The Teaching of Black History and Culture in the Secondary Schools." *Social Education* 33 (1969): 385–88.

Huebner, D. "Politics and the Curriculum." In *Curriculum Crossroads,* edited by A. H. Passow, pp. 87–95. New York: Teachers College Press, 1962.

Jackson, P. *Life in Classrooms.* New York: Holt, Rinehart & Winston, 1968.

Kliebard, H. M. "Bureaucracy and Curriculum Theory." In *Freedom, Bureaucracy and Schooling,* edited by V. Haubrick, pp. 74–93. Washington, D.C.: ASCD, 1971.

Kuhn, T. S. *The Structure of Scientific Revolutions.* Chicago: University of Chicago Press, 1962.

_____. *The Structure of Scientific Revolutions,* 2d ed. Chicago: University of Chicago Press, 1970.

Lakatos, I. "Falsification and the Methodology of Scientific Research Programmes." In *Criticism and the Growth of Knowledge,* edited by I. Lakatos and A. Musgrave, pp. 91–195. New York: Oxford University Press, 1970.

_____, and Musgrave A., eds. *Criticism and the Growth of Knowledge.* New York: Oxford University Press, 1970.

McClure, H., and Fischer, G. "Ideology and Opinion Making: General Problems of Analysis." Unpublished paper. New York: Bureau of Applied Social Research, Columbia University, July 1969.

Mulkay, M. "Some Aspects of Cultural Growth in the Natural Sciences." *Social Research* 36 (1969): 22–52.

New York State, Bureau of Elementary Curriculum Development. *Respect for Rules and Law.* Albany: New York State Dept. of Education, 1969.

Oliver, D., and Newmann, F. *Harvard Social Studies Project: Public Issues Series.* Columbus, Ohio: American Education Publications, 1968.

Polanyi, M. *Personal Knowledge.* New York: Harper & Row, 1964.

Senesh, L. "Recorded Lessons." In *Our Working World: Families at Work,* edited by L. Senesh. Chicago: Science Research Associates, 1964.

Sigel, R., *Learning about Politics.* New York: Random House, 1970.

Storer, N. W. *The Social System of Science.* New York: Holt, Rinehart & Winston, 1966.

Walker, J. L. "A Critique of the Elitist Theory of Democracy." In *Apolitical Politics,* edited by C. A. McCoy and J. Playford, pp. 199–219. New York: Cromwell, 1967.

Watson, J. D. *The Double Helix.* New York: Atheneum, 1968.

Wilcox, P. "Education for Black Liberation." *New Generation* 51 (1969): 17–21.

Wilhelm, S. M. *Who Needs the Negro?* Cambridge, Mass.: Schenkman, 1970.

Wittgenstein, L. *Philosophical Investigations.* New York: Macmillan, 1958.

CHAPTER 10

Moral Reasoning

Lawrence Kohlberg
1976

In this article, I present an overview of the cognitive-developmental approach to moral education and its research foundations, compare it with other approaches, and report the experimental work my colleagues and I are doing to apply the approach.

MORAL STAGES

The cognitive-developmental approach was fully stated for the first time by John Dewey. The approach is called *cognitive* because it recognizes that moral education, like intellectual education, has its basis in stimulating the *active thinking* of the child about moral issues and decisions. It is called developmental because it sees the aims of moral education as movement through moral stages. According to Dewey (1964):

> The aim of education is growth or *development* both intellectual and moral. Ethical and psychological principles can aid the school in the *greatest of all constructions—the building of a free and powerful character*. Only knowledge of the *order and connection of the stages in psychological development* can insure this. Education is the work of *supplying the conditions* which will enable the psychological functions to mature in the freest and fullest manner.

From David Purpel and Kevin Ryan, *Moral Education . . . It Comes with the Territory*, 176–195. © 1976 by McCutchan Publishing Corporation, Berkeley, CA 94702. Permission granted by the publisher.

Dewey postulated three levels of moral development: (1) the *premoral* or *preconventional* level "of behavior motivated by biological and social impulses with results for morals," (2) the *conventional* level of behavior "in which the individual accepts with little critical reflection the standards of his group," (3) the *autonomous* level of behavior in which "conduct is guided by the individual thinking and judging for himself whether a purpose is good, and does not accept the standard of his group without reflection."[1]

Dewey's thinking about moral stages was theoretical. Building upon his prior studies of cognitive stages, Jean Piaget (1948) made the first effort to define stages of moral reasoning in children through actual interviews and through observations of children (in games with rules). Using this interview material, Piaget defined the premoral, the conventional, and the autonomous levels as follows: (1) the *premoral stage,* where there was no sense of obligation to rules; (2) the *heteronomous stage,* where the right was literal obedience to rules and an equation of obligation with submission to power and punishment (roughly ages four–eight); and (3) the *autonomous stage,* where the purpose and consequences of following rules are considered and obligation is based on reciprocity and exchange (roughly ages eight–twelve).[2]

In 1955 I started to redefine and validate (through longitudinal and cross-cultural study) the Dewey-Piaget levels and stages. The notion that stages can be *validated* by longitudinal study implies that stages have definite empirical characteristics (Kohlberg, 1975). The concept of stages (as used by Piaget and myself) implies the following characteristics:

1. Stages are "structured wholes," or organized systems of thought. Individuals are *consistent* in level of moral judgment.

2. Stages form an *invariant sequence.* Under all conditions except extreme trauma, movement is always forward, never backward. Individuals never skip stages; movement is always to the next stage up.

3. Stages are "hierarchical integrations." Thinking at a higher stage includes or comprehends within it lower-stage thinking. There is a tendency to function at or prefer the highest stage available.

Each of these characteristics has been demonstrated for moral stages. Stages are defined by responses to a set of verbal moral dilemmas classified according to an elaborate scoring scheme. Validating studies include:

1. A twenty-year study of fifty Chicago-area boys, middle- and working-class. Initially interviewed at ages ten–sixteen, they have been reinterviewed at three-year intervals thereafter.
2. A small, six-year longitudinal study of Turkish village and city boys of the same age.
3. A variety of other cross-sectional studies in Canada, Britain, Israel, Taiwan, Yucatan, Honduras, and India.

With regard to the structured whole or consistency criterion, we have found that more than 50 percent of an individual's thinking is always at one stage, with the remainder at the next adjacent stage (which he is leaving or which he is moving into).

With regard to invariant sequence, our longitudinal results have been presented in the *American Journal of Orthopsychiatry* (Kohlberg and Elfenbein 1975), and indicate that on every retest individuals were either at the same stage as three years earlier or had moved up. This was true in Turkey as well as in the United States.

With regard to the hierarchical integration criterion, it has been demonstrated that adolescents exposed to written statements at each of the six stages comprehend or correctly put in their own words all statements at or below their own stage but fail to comprehend any statements more than one stage above their own (Rest, Turiel, and Kohlberg 1969). Some individuals comprehend the next stage above their own; some do not. Adolescents prefer (or rank as best) the highest stage they can comprehend.

To understand moral stages, it is important to clarify their relations to stage of logic or intelligence, on the one hand, and to moral behavior on the other. Maturity of moral judgment is not highly correlated with IQ or verbal intelligence (correlations are only in the 30s, accounting for 10 percent of the variance). Cognitive development, in the stage sense, however, is more important for moral development than such correlations suggest. Piaget has found that after the child learns to speak there are three major stages of reasoning: the intuitive, the concrete operational, and the formal operational. At around age seven, the child enters the stage of concrete logical thought: He can make logical inferences, classify, and handle quantitative relations about concrete things. In adolescence individuals usually enter the stage of formal operations. At this stage they can reason abstractly, i.e., consider all possibilities, form hypotheses, deduce implications from hypotheses, and test them against reality.[3]

Since moral reasoning clearly is reasoning, advanced moral reasoning depends upon advanced logical reasoning; a person's logical stage puts a certain ceiling on the moral stage he can attain. A person whose logical stage is only concrete operational is limited to the preconventional moral stages (Stages 1 and 2). A person whose logical stage is only partially formal operational is limited to the conventional moral stages (Stages 3 and 4). While logical development is necessary for moral development and sets limits to it, most individuals are higher in logical stage than they are in moral stage. As an example, over 50 percent of late adolescents and adults are capable of full formal reasoning, but only 10 percent of these adults (all formal operational) displays principled (Stages 5 and 6) moral reasoning.

The moral stages are *structures of moral judgment* or *moral reasoning*. *Structures* of moral judgment must be distinguished from the *content* of moral judgment. As an example, we cite responses to a dilemma used in our various studies to identify moral stage. The dilemma raises the issue of stealing a drug to save a dying woman. The inventor of the drug is selling it for ten times what it costs him to make it. The woman's husband cannot raise the money, and the seller refuses to lower the price or wait for payment. What should the husband do?

The choice endorsed by a subject (steal, don't steal) is called the *content* of his moral judgment in the situation. His reasoning about the choice defines the structure of his moral judgment. This reasoning centers on the following ten universal moral values or issues of concern to persons in these moral dilemmas:

1. Punishment
2. Property
3. Roles and concerns of affection
4. Roles and concerns of authority

5. Law
6. Life
7. Liberty
8. Distributive justice
9. Truth
10. Sex

A moral choice involves choosing between two (or more) of these values as they *conflict* in concrete situations of choice.

The stage or structure of a person's moral judgment defines: (1) *what* he finds valuable in each of these moral issues (life, law), i.e., how he defines the value, and (2) *why* he finds it valuable, i.e., the reasons he gives for valuing it. As an example, at Stage 1 life is valued in terms of the power or possessions of the person involved; at Stage 2, for its usefulness in satisfying the needs of the individual in question or others; at Stage 3, in terms of the individual's relations with others and their valuation of him; at Stage 4, in terms of social or religious law. Only at Stages 5 and 6 is each life seen as inherently worthwhile, aside from other considerations.

MORAL JUDGMENT VS. MORAL ACTION

Having clarified the nature of stages of moral *judgment,* we must consider the relation of moral judgment to moral *action.* If logical reasoning is a necessary but not sufficient condition for mature moral judgment, mature moral judgment is a necessary but not sufficient condition for mature moral action. One cannot follow moral principles if one does not understand (or believe in) moral principles. However, one can reason in terms of principles and not live up to these principles. As an example, Richard Krebs and I found that only 15 percent of students showing some principled thinking cheated as compared to 55 percent of conventional subjects and 70 percent of preconventional subjects. Nevertheless, 15 percent of the principled subjects did cheat, suggesting that factors additional to moral judgment are necessary for principled moral reasoning to be translated into "moral action." Partly, these factors include the situation and its pressures. Partly, what happens depends upon the individual's motives and emotions. Partly, what the individual does depends upon a general sense of will, purpose, or "ego strength." As an example of the role of will or ego strength in moral behavior, we may cite the study by Krebs: Slightly more than half of his conventional subjects cheated. These subjects were also divided by a measure of attention/will. Only 26 percent of the "strong-willed" conventional subjects cheated; however, 74 percent of the "weak-willed" subjects cheated.

If maturity of moral reasoning is only one factor in moral behavior, why does the cognitive-developmental approach to moral education focus so heavily upon moral reasoning? For the following reasons:

1. Moral judgment, while only one factor in moral behavior, is the single most important or influential factor yet discovered in moral behavior.

2. While other factors influence moral behavior, moral judgment is the only distinctively *moral* factor in moral behavior. To illustrate, we noted that the Krebs study indicated that "strong-willed" conventional stage subjects resisted cheating more than "weak-willed" subjects. For those at a preconventional level of moral reasoning, however, "will" has an opposite effect. "Strong-willed" Stages 1 and 2 subjects cheated more, not less, than "weak-willed" subjects, i.e., they had the "courage of their (amoral) convictions" that it was worthwhile to cheat. "Will," then, is an important factor in moral behavior, but it is not distinctively moral; it becomes moral only when informed by mature moral judgment.

3. Moral judgment change is long-range or irreversible; a higher stage is never lost. Moral behavior as such is largely situational and reversible or "loseable" in new situations.

AIMS OF MORAL AND CIVIC EDUCATION

Moral psychology describes what moral development is, as studied empirically. Moral education must also consider moral philosophy, which strives to tell us what moral development ideally *ought to be*. Psychology finds an invariant sequence of moral stages; moral philosophy must be invoked to answer whether a later stage is a better stage. The "stage" of senescence and death follows the "stage" of adulthood, but that does not mean that senescence and death are better. Our claim that the latest or principled stages of moral reasoning are morally better stages, then, must rest on considerations of moral philosophy.

The tradition of moral philosophy to which we appeal is the liberal or rational tradition, in particular the "formalistic" or "deontological" tradition running from Immanuel Kant to John Rawls (1971). Central to this tradition is the claim that an adequate morality is *principled,* i.e., that it makes judgments in terms of *universal* principles applicable to all mankind. *Principles* are to be distinguished from *rules.* Conventional morality is grounded on rules, primarily "thou shalt nots" such as are represented by the Ten Commandments, prescriptions of kinds of actions. Principles are, rather, universal guides to making a moral decision. An example is Kant's "categorical imperative," formulated in two ways. The first is the maxim of respect for human personality, "Act always toward the other as an end, not as a means." The second is the maxim of universalization, "Choose only as you would be willing to have everyone choose in your situation." Principles like that of Kant's state the formal conditions of a moral choice or action. In the dilemma in which a woman is dying because a druggist refuses to release his drug for less than the stated price, the druggest is not acting morally, though he is not violating the ordinary moral rules (he is not actually stealing or murdering). But he is violating principles: He is treating the woman simply as a means to his ends of profit, and he is not choosing as he would wish anyone to choose (if the druggist were in the dying woman's place, he would not want a druggist to choose as he is choosing). Under most circumstances, choice in terms of conventional moral rules and choice in terms of principles coincide. Ordinarily, principles dictate not stealing (avoiding stealing is implied by acting in terms of a regard for others as ends and in terms of what one would want everyone to do). In a situation where stealing is the only means to save a life, however, principles contradict the ordinary rules and would dictate stealing. Unlike rules which are supported by social authority, principles are freely chosen by the individual because of their intrinsic moral validity.[4]

The conception that a moral choice is a choice made in terms of moral principles is related to the claim of liberal moral philosophy that moral principles are ultimately principles of justice. In essence, moral conflicts are conflicts between the claims of persons, and principles for resolving these claims are principles of justice, "for giving each his due." Central to justice are the demands of *liberty, equality,* and *reciprocity.* At every moral stage, there is a concern for justice. The most damning statement a school child can make about a teacher is that "he's not fair." At each higher stage, however, the conception of justice is reorganized. At Stage 1, justice is punishing the bad in terms of "an eye for an eye and a tooth for a tooth." At Stage 2, it is exchanging favors and goods in an equal manner. At Stages 3 and 4, it is treating people as they desire in terms of the conventional rules. At Stage 5, it is recognized that all rules and laws flow from justice, from a social contract between the governors and the governed designed to protect the equal rights of all. At Stage 6, personally chosen moral principles are also principles of justice, the principles any member of a society would choose for that society if he did not know what his position was to be in the society and in which he might be the least advantaged (Rawls 1971). Principles chosen from this point of view are, first, the maximum liberty compatible with the like liberty of others and, second, no inequalities of goods and respect which are not to the benefit of all, including the least advantaged.

As an example of stage progression in the orientation to justice, we may take judgments about capital punishment (Kohlberg and Elfenbein 1975). Capital punishment is only firmly rejected at the two principled stages, when the notion of justice as vengeance or retribution is abandoned. At the sixth stage, capital punishment is not condoned even if it may have some useful deterrent effect in promoting law and order. This is because it is not a punishment we would choose for a society if we assumed we had as much chance of being born into the position of a criminal or murderer as being born into the position of a law abider.

Why are decisions based on universal principles of justice better decisions? Because they are decisions on which all moral men could agree. When decisions are based on conventional moral rules, men will disagree, since they adhere to conflicting systems of rules dependent on culture and social position. Throughout history men have killed one another in the name of conflicting moral rules and values, most recently in Vietnam and the Middle East. Truly moral or just resolutions of conflicts require principles which are, or can be, universalizable.

Alternative Approaches

We have given a philosophic rationale for stage advance as the aim of moral education. Given this rationale, the developmental approach to moral education can avoid the problems inherent in the other two major approaches to moral education. The first alternative approach is that of indoctrinative moral education, the preaching and imposition of the rules and values of the teacher and his culture on the child. In America, when this indoctrinative approach has been developed in a systematic manner, it has usually been termed "character education."

Moral values, in the character approach, are preached or taught in terms of what may be called the "bag of virtues." In the classic studies of character by Hugh Hartshorne and Mark May (1928–1930), the virtues chosen were honesty, service, and self-control. It is easy to get superficial consensus on such a bag of virtues—until one examines in detail the list of virtues involved and the details of their definition. Is the Hartshorne and May bag more adequate than the Boy Scout bag (a Scout should be honest, loyal, reverent, clean, brave, etc.)? When one turns to the details of defining each virtue, one finds equal uncertainty or difficulty in reaching consensus. Does honesty mean one should not steal to save a life? Does it mean that a student should not help another student with his homework?

Character education and other forms of indoctrinative moral education have aimed at teaching universal values (it is assumed that honesty or service are desirable traits for all men in all societies), but the detailed definitions used are relative; they are defined by the opinions of the teacher and the conventional culture and rest on the authority of the teacher for their justification. In this sense character education is close to the unreflective valuings by teachers which constitute the hidden curriculum of the school.[5] Because of the current unpopularity of indoctrinative approaches to moral education, a family of approaches called "values clarification" has become appealing to teachers. Values clarification takes the first step implied by a rational approach to moral education: the eliciting of the child's own judgment or opinion about issues or situations in which values conflict, rather than imposing the teacher's opinion on him. Values clarification, however, does not attempt to go further than eliciting awareness of values; it is assumed that becoming more self-aware about one's values is an end in itself. Fundamentally, the definition of the end of values education as self-awareness derives from a belief in ethical relativity held by many value-clarifiers. As stated by Peter Engel, "One must contrast value clarification and value inculcation. Value clarification implies the principle that in the consideration of values there is no single correct answer." Within these premises of "no correct answer," children are to discuss moral dilemmas in such a way as to reveal different values and discuss their value differences with each other. The teacher is to stress that "our values are different," not that one value is more adequate than others. If this program is systematically followed, students will themselves become relativists, believing there is no "right" moral answer. For instance, a student caught cheating might argue that he did nothing wrong, since his own hierarchy of values, which may be different from that of the teacher, made it right for him to cheat.

Like values clarification, the cognitive-developmental approach to moral education stresses open or Socratic peer discussion of value dilemmas. Such discussion, however, has an aim: stimulation of movement to the next stage of moral reasoning. Like values clarification, the developmental approach opposes indoctrination. Stimulation of movement to the next stage of reasoning is not indoctrinative, for the following reasons:

1. Change is in the way of reasoning rather than in the particular beliefs involved.

2. Students in a class are at different stages; the aim is to aid movement of each to the next stage, not convergence on a common pattern.

3. The teacher's own opinion is neither stressed nor invoked as authoritative. It enters in only as one of many opinions, hopefully one of those at a next higher stage.

4. The notion that some judgments are more adequate than others is communicated. Fundamentally, however, this means that the student is encouraged to articulate a position which seems most adequate to him and to judge the adequacy of the reasoning of others.

In addition to having more definite aims than values clarification, the moral development approach restricts value education to that which is moral or, more specifically, to justice. This is for two reasons. First, it is not clear that the whole realm of personal, political, and religious values is a realm which is nonrelative, i.e., in which there are universals and a direction of development. Second, it is not clear that the public school has a right or mandate to develop values in general.[6] In our view, value education in the public schools should be restricted to that which the school has the right and mandate to develop: an awareness of justice, or of the rights of others in our Constitutional system. While the Bill of Rights prohibits the teaching of religious beliefs, or of specific value systems, it does not prohibit the teaching of the awareness of rights and principles of justice fundamental to the Constitution itself.

When moral education is recognized as centered in justice and differentiated from value education or affective education, it becomes apparent that moral and civic education are much the same thing. This equation, taken for granted by the classic philosophers of education from Plato and Aristotle to Dewey, is basic to our claim that a concern for moral education is central to the educational objectives of social studies.

The term *civic education* is used to refer to social studies as more than the study of the facts and concepts of social science, history, and civics. It is education for the analytic understanding, value principles, and motivation necessary for a citizen in a democracy if democracy is to be an effective process. It is political education. Civic or political education means the stimulation of development of more advanced patterns of reasoning about political and social decisions and their implementation in action. These patterns are patterns of moral reasoning. Our studies show that reasoning and decision making about political decisions are directly derivative of broader patterns of moral reasoning and decision making. We have interviewed high school and college students about concrete political situations involving laws to govern open housing, civil disobedience for peace in Vietnam, free press rights to publish what might disturb national order, and distribution of income through taxation. We find that reasoning on these political decisions can be classified according to moral stage and that an individual's stage on political dilemmas is at the same level as on nonpolitical moral dilemmas (euthanasia, violating authority to maintain trust in a family, stealing a drug to save one's dying wife). Turning from reasoning to action, similar findings are obtained. In

1964 a study was made of those who sat in at the University of California, Berkeley, administration building and those who did not in the Free Speech Movement crisis. Of those at Stage 6, 80 percent sat in, believing that principles of free speech were being compromised, and that all efforts to compromise and negotiate with the administration had failed. In contrast, only 15 percent of the conventional (Stage 3 or Stage 4) subjects sat in. (Stage 5 subjects were in between.)[7]

From a psychological side, then, political development is part of moral development. The same is true from the philosophic side. In the *Republic,* Plato sees political education as part of a broader education for moral justice and finds a rationale for such education in terms of universal philosophic principles rather than the demands of a particular society. More recently, Dewey claims the same.

In historical perspective, America was the first nation whose government was publicly founded on postconventional principles of justice, rather than upon the authority central to conventional moral reasoning. At the time of our founding, postconventional or principled moral and political reasoning was the possession of the minority, as it still is. Today, as in the time of our founding, the majority of our adults are at the conventional level, particularly the "law and order" (fourth) moral stage. (Every few years the Gallup Poll circulates the Bill of Rights unidentified, and every year it is turned down.) The Founding Fathers intuitively understood this without benefit of our elaborate social science research; they constructed a document designing a government which would maintain principles of justice and the rights of man even though principled men were not the men in power. The machinery included checks and balances, the independent judiciary, and freedom of the press. Most recently, this machinery found its use at Watergate. The tragedy of Richard Nixon, as Harry Truman said long ago, was that he never understood the Constitution (a Stage 5 document), but the Constitution understood Richard Nixon.[8]

Watergate, then, is not some sign of moral decay of the nation, but rather of the fact that understanding and action in support of justice principles are still the possession of a minority of our society. Insofar as there is moral decay, it represents the weakening of conventional morality in the face of social and value conflict today. This can lead the less fortunate adolescent to fixation at the preconventional level, the more fortunate to movement to principles. We find a larger proportion of youths at the principled level today than was the case in their fathers' day, but also a larger proportion at the preconventional level.

Given this state, moral and civic education in the schools becomes a more urgent task. In the high school today, one often hears both preconventional adolescents and those beginning to move beyond convention sounding the same note of disaffection for the school. While our political institutions are in principle Stage 5 (i.e., vehicles for maintaining universal rights through the democratic process), our schools have traditionally been Stage 4 institutions of convention and authority. Today more than ever, democratic schools systematically engaged in civic education are required.

Our approach to moral and civic education relates the study of law and government to the actual creation of a democratic school in which moral dilemmas are discussed and resolved in a manner which will stimulate moral development.

Planned Moral Education

For many years, moral development was held by psychologists to be primarily a result of family upbringing and family conditions. In particular, conditions of affection and authority in the home were believed to be critical, some balance of warmth and firmness being optimal for moral development. This view arises if morality is conceived as an internalization of the arbitrary rules of parents and culture, since such acceptance must be based on affection and respect for parents as authorities rather than on the rational nature of the rules involved.

Studies of family correlates of moral stage development do not support this internalization view of the conditions for moral development. Instead, they suggest that the conditions for moral development in homes and schools are similar and that the conditions are consistent with cognitive-developmental theory. In the cognitive-developmental view, morality is a natural product of a universal human tendency toward empathy or role taking, toward putting oneself in the shoes of other conscious beings. It is also a product of a universal human concern for justice, for reciprocity or equality in the relation of one person to another. As an example, when my son was four, he became a morally principled vegetarian and refused to eat meat, resisting all parental persuasion to increase his protein intake. His reason was, "It's bad to kill animals." His moral commitment to vegetarianism was not taught or acquired from parental authority; it was the result of the universal tendency of the young self to project its consciousness and values into other living things, other selves. My son's vegetarianism also involved a sense of justice, revealed when I read him a book about Eskimos in which a real hunting expedition was described. His response was to say, "Daddy, there is one kind of meat I would eat—Eskimo meat. It's all right to eat Eskimos because they eat animals." This natural sense of justice or reciprocity was Stage 1—an eye for an eye, a tooth for a tooth. My son's sense of the value of life was also Stage 1 and involved no differentiation between human personality and physical life. His morality, though Stage 1, was, however, natural and internal. Moral development past Stage 1, then, is not an internalization but the reconstruction of role taking and conceptions of justice toward greater adequacy. These reconstructions occur in order to achieve a better match between the child's own moral structures and the structures of the social and moral situations he confronts. We divide these conditions of match into two kinds: those dealing with moral discussions and communication and those dealing with the total moral environment or atmosphere in which the child lives.

In terms of moral discussion, the important conditions appear to be:

1. Exposure to the next higher stage of reasoning.

2. Exposure to situations posing problems and contradictions for the child's current moral structure, leading to dissatisfaction with his current level.

3. An atmosphere of interchange and dialogue combining the first two conditions, in which conflicting moral views are compared in an open manner.

Studies of families in India and America suggest that morally advanced children have parents at higher stages. Parents expose children to the next higher stage, raising moral issues and engaging in open dialogue or interchange about such issues (Parilch 1975).

Drawing on this notion of the discussion conditions stimulating advance, Moshe Blatt conducted classroom discussions of conflict-laden hypothetical moral dilemmas with four classes of junior high and high school students for a semester. In each of these classes, students were to be found at three stages. Since the children were not all responding at the same stage, the arguments they used with each other were at different levels. In the course of these discussions among the students, the teacher first supported and clarified those arguments that were one stage above the lowest stage among the children; for example, the teacher supported Stage 3 rather than Stage 2. When it seemed that these arguments were understood by the students, the teacher then challenged that stage, using new situations and clarified the arguments one stage above the previous one; Stage 4 rather than Stage 3. At the end of the semester, all the students were retested; they showed significant upward change when compared to the controls, and they maintained the change one year later. In the experimental classrooms, from one-fourth to one-half of the students moved up a stage, while there was essentially no change during the course of the experiment in the control group.

Given the Blatt studies showing that moral discussion could raise moral stage, we undertook the next step: to see if teachers could conduct moral discussions in the course of teaching high school social studies with the same results. This step we took in cooperation with Edwin Fenton, who introduced moral dilemmas in his ninth- and eleventh-grade social studies texts. Twenty-four teachers in the Boston and Pittsburgh areas were given some instruction in conducting moral discussions around the dilemmas in the text. About half of the teachers stimulated significant developmental change in their classrooms—upward stage movement of one-quarter to one-half a stage. In control classes using the text but no moral dilemma discussions, the same teachers failed to stimulate any moral change in the students. Moral discussion, then, can be a usable and effective part of the curriculum at any grade level. Working with filmstrip dilemmas produced in cooperation with Guidance Associates, second-grade teachers conducted moral discussions yielding a similar amount of moral stage movement.

Moral discussion and curriculum, however, constitute only one portion of the conditions stimulating moral growth. When we turn

to analyzing the broader life environment, we turn to a consideration of the *moral atmosphere* of the home, the school, and the
broader society. The first basic dimension of social atmosphere is
the role-taking opportunities it provides, the extent to which it
encourages the child to take the point of view of others. Role
taking is related to the amount of social interaction and social
communication in which the child engages, as well as to his sense
of efficacy in influencing attitudes of others. The second dimension
of social atmosphere, more strictly moral, is the level of justice of
the environment or institution. The justice structure of an institution refers to the perceived rules or principles for distributing rewards, punishments, responsibilities, and privileges among institutional members. This structure may exist or be perceived at any of
our moral stages. As an example, a study of a traditional prison
revealed that inmates perceived it as Stage 1, regardless of their
own level (Kohlberg, Scharf, and Hickey 1972). Obedience to arbitrary command by power figures and punishment for disobedience
were seen as the governing justice norms of the prison. A behavior-
modification prison using point rewards for conformity was perceived as a Stage 2 system of instrumental exchange. Inmates at
Stage 3 or 4 perceived this institution as more fair than the traditional prison, but not as fair in their own terms.

These and other studies suggest that a higher level of institutional justice is a condition for individual development of a higher
sense of justice. Working on these premises, Joseph Hickey, Peter
Scharf and I (1973) worked with guards and inmates in a women's
prison to create a more just community. A social contract was set
up in which guards and inmates each had a vote of one and in
which rules were made and conflicts resolved through discussions
of fairness and a democratic vote in a community meeting. The
program has been operating four years and has stimulated moral
stage advance in inmates, though it is still too early to draw conclusions as to its overall long-range effectiveness for rehabilitation.

One year ago, Fenton, Ralph Mosher, and I received a grant
from the Danforth Foundation (with additional support from the
Kennedy Foundation) to make moral education a living matter in
two high schools in the Boston area (Cambridge and Brookline)
and two in Pittsburgh. The plan had two components. The first
was training counselors and social studies and English teachers in

conducting moral discussions and making moral discussion an integral part of the curriculum. The second was establishing a just community school within a public high school.

We have stated the theory of the just community high school, postulating that discussing real-life moral situations and actions as issues of fairness and as matters for democratic decision would stimulate advance in both moral reasoning and moral action. A participatory democracy provides more extensive opportunities for role taking and a higher level of perceived institutional justice than does any other social arrangement. Most alternative schools strive to establish a democratic governance, but none we have observed has achieved a vital or viable participatory democracy. Our theory suggested reasons why we might succeed where others failed. First, we felt that democracy had to be a central commitment of a school, rather than a humanitarian frill. Democracy as moral education provides that commitment. Second, democracy in alternative schools often fails because it bores the students. Students prefer to let teachers make decisions about staff, courses, and schedules, rather than to attend lengthy, complicated meetings. Our theory said that the issues a democracy should focus on are issues of morality and fairness. Real issues concerning drugs, stealing, disruptions, and grading are never boring if handled as issues of fairness. Third, our theory told us that if large democratic community meetings were preceded by small-group moral discussion, higher-stage thinking by students would win out in later decisions, avoiding the disasters of mob rule.[9]

Currently, we can report that the school based on our theory makes democracy work or function where other schools have failed. It is too early to make any claims for its effectiveness in causing moral development, however.

Our Cambridge just community school within the public high school was started after a small summer planning session of volunteer teachers, students, and parents. At the time the school opened in the fall, only a commitment to democracy and a skeleton program of English and social studies had been decided on. The school started with six teachers from the regular school and sixty students, twenty from academic professional homes and twenty from working-class homes. The other twenty were dropouts and troublemakers or petty delinquents in terms of previous record.

The usual mistakes and usual chaos of a beginning alternative school ensued. Within a few weeks, however, a successful democratic community process had been established. Rules were made around pressing issues: disturbances, drugs, hooking. A student discipline committee or jury was formed. The resulting rules and enforcement have been relatively effective and reasonable. We do not see reasonable rules as ends in themselves, however, but as vehicles for moral discussion and an emerging sense of community. This sense of community and a resulting morale are perhaps the most immediate signs of success. This sense of community seems to lead to behavior change of a positive sort. An example is a fifteen-year-old student who started as one of the greatest combinations of humor, aggression, light-fingeredness, and hyperactivity I have ever known. From being the principal disturber of all community meetings, he has become an excellent community meeting participant and occasional chairman. He is still more ready to enforce rules for others than to observe them himself, yet his commitment to the school has led to a steady decrease in exotic behavior. In addition, he has become more involved in classes and projects and has begun to listen and ask questions in order to pursue a line of interest.

We attribute such behavior change not only to peer pressure and moral discussion but to the sense of community which has emerged from the democratic process in which angry conflicts are resolved through fairness and community decision. This sense of community is reflected in statements of the students to us that there are no cliques—that the blacks and whites, the professors' sons and the project students, are friends. These statements are supported by observation. Such a sense of community is needed where students in a given classroom range in reading level from fifth-grade to college.

Fenton, Mosher, the Cambridge and Brookline teachers, and I are now planning a four-year curriculum in English and social studies centering on moral discussion, on role-taking and communication, and on relating the government, laws, and justice system of the school to that of the American society and other world societies. This will integrate an intellectual curriculum for a higher level of understanding of society with the experiential components of school democracy and moral decision.

There is very little new in this—or in anything else we are doing. Dewey wanted democratic experimental schools for moral and intellectual development seventy years ago. Perhaps Dewey's time has come.

NOTES

1.   These levels correspond roughly to our three major levels: the preconventional, the conventional, and the principled. Similar levels were propounded by William McDougall, Leonard Hobhouse, and James Mark Baldwin.

2.   Piaget's stages correspond to our first three stages: Stage 0 (premoral), Stage 1 (heteronomous), and Stage 2 (instrumental reciprocity).

3.   Many adolescents and adults only partially attain the stage of formal operations. They do consider all the actual relations of one thing to another at the same time, but they do not consider all possibilities and form abstract hypotheses. A few do not advance this far, remaining "concrete operational."

4.   Not all freely chosen values or rules are principles, however. Hitler chose the "rule," "exterminate the enemies of the Aryan race," but such a rule is not a universalizable principle.

5.   As an example of the "hidden curriculum," we may cite a second-grade classroom. My son came home from this classroom one day saying he did not want to be "one of the bad boys." Asked "Who are the bad boys?" he replied, "The ones who don't put their books back and get yelled at."

6.   Restriction of deliberate value education to the moral may be clarified by our example of the second-grade teacher who made tidying up of books a matter of moral indoctrination. Tidiness is a value, but it is not a moral value. Cheating is a moral issue, intrinsically one of fairness. It involves issues of violation of trust and taking advantage. Failing to tidy the room may under certain conditions be an issue of fairness, when it puts an undue burden on others. If it is handled by the teacher as a matter of cooperation among the group in this sense, it is a legitimate focus of deliberate moral education. If it is not, it simply represents the arbitrary imposition of the teacher's values on the child.

7.   The differential action of the principled subjects was determined by two things. First, they were more likely to judge it right to violate authority by sitting in. But second, they were also in general more consistent in engaging in political action according to their judgment. Ninety percent of all Stage 6 subjects thought it right to sit in, and all 90 percent

lived up to this belief. Among the Stage 4 subjects, 45 percent thought it right to sit in, but only 33 percent lived up to this belief by acting.

8.   No public or private word or deed of Nixon ever rose above Stage 4, the "law and order" stage. His last comments in the White House were of wonderment that the Republican Congress could turn on him after so many Stage 2 exchanges of favors in getting them elected.

9.   An example of the need for small-group discussion comes from an alternative school community meeting called because a pair of the students had stolen the school's video-recorder. The resulting majority decision was that the school should buy back the recorder from the culprits through a fence. The teachers could not accept this decision and returned to a more authoritative approach. I believe if the moral reasoning of students urging this solution had been confronted by students at a higher stage, a different decision would have emerged.

REFERENCES

Blatt, Moshe, and Kohlberg, Lawrence. "Effects of Classroom Discussions upon Children's Level of Moral Judgment." *Recent Research in Moral Development,* edited by Lawrence Kohlberg. New York: Holt, Rinehart & Winston, in preparation.

Dewey, John. "What Psychology Can Do for the Teacher." *John Dewey on Education: Selected Writings,* edited by Reginald Archambault. New York: Random House, 1964.

Hartshorne, Hugh, and May, Mark. *Studies in the Nature of Character* (3 vols.). New York: Macmillan, 1928–1930.

Kohlberg, Lawrence. "Moral Stages and Moralization: The Cognitive-Developmental Approach." *Man, Morality, and Society,* edited by Thomas Lickona. New York: Holt, Rinehart & Winston, 1976.

Kohlberg, Lawrence; Scharf, Peter; and Hickey, Joseph. "The Justice Structure of the Prison: A Theory and an Intervention." *The Prison Journal* (autumn-winter 1972).

Kohlberg, Lawrence; Kauffman, Kelsey; Scharf, Peter; and Hickey, Joseph. *The Just Community Approach to Corrections: A Manual, Part I.* Cambridge, Mass.: Education Research Foundation, 1973.

Kohlberg, Lawrence, and Elfenbein, Donald. "Development of Moral Reasoning and Attitudes Toward Capital Punishment." *American Journal of Orthopsychiatry* (summer 1975).

Krebs, Richard, and Kohlberg, Lawrence. "Moral Judgment and Ego Controls as Determinants of Resistance to Cheating." *Recent Research in Moral Development,* edited by Lawrence Kohlberg. New York: Holt, Rinehart & Winston, in preparation.

Parilch, Bindu. "A Cross-Cultural Study of Parent-Child Moral Judgment." Ph.D. dissertation, Harvard University, 1975.

Piaget, Jean. *The Moral Judgment of the Child* (2nd ed.). Glencoe, Ill.: Free Press, 1948.

Rawls, John A. *Theory of Justice*. Cambridge, Mass.: Harvard University Press, 1971.

Rest, James, Turiel, Elliott, and Kohlberg, Lawrence. "Relations Between Level of Moral Judgment and Preference and Comprehension of the Moral Judgment of Others." *Journal of Personality* 37 (1969): 225–52.

CHAPTER 11

Skills in Citizen Action

Fred M. Newmann, Thomas A. Bertocci, and Ruthanne M. Landsness
1977

In spite of incessant rhetoric about the need to educate youth for responsible citizenship, civic education in the United States receives low priority, is approached unsystematically, and is fraught with crippling contradictions. Our troubles are due in part to an intellectual problem, the lack of a coherent conception of education for civic competence. In part we also face *institutional* obstacles—particular structures, programs, and requirements in public education that make it difficult to place central priority upon civic education. Here we speak to each problem.

Conceptual Difficulties

What is the difference between a competent, responsible, well-educated citizen and an incompetent, irresponsible, or poorly-educated one? What do those adjectives mean in a society such as ours? We are innundated with diverse conceptions of civic education, some of which are logically contradictory, and others, while not necessarily inconsistent, reflect different priorities. Some conceptions stress obedience to the law, respect for and allegiance to existing institutions, while others stress critical questioning of the existing social order and independent moral reasoning. Some approaches see knowledge of history and social science as the intellec-

Chapter 1 in *Skills in Citizen Action* (Madison: Citizen Participation Curriculum Project, University of Wisconsin, 1977), 1–15. Reprinted by permission of the authors.

tual foundation of citizenship, others stress knowledge of particular social problems (e.g., racism, environmental issues, global interdependence). Still others stress specific knowledge of the functioning of the political-legal system. Some approaches seem less concerned with content or substantive knowledge, more concerned with intellectual skills such as critical thinking, problem-solving, or communication skills in reading, writing, speaking, and listening. Some stress the importance of participation skills over academic preparation, but the "participation" position itself divides on different points of emphasis; for example, student governance and decision-making in school vs. volunteer service to help others in the community vs. social-political action for institutional change.

Different philosophies manifest themselves in several curriculum movements; the academic disciplines, social problems, law-related education, values clarification, moral development, critical thinking, community involvement. In a sense these approaches compete with each other for a place in the school curriculum as teachers and administrators are bombarded with requests to give all of these top priority. A particular approach is not usually derived from an explicit conception of civic competence, or when it is, the conception is woefully incomplete.[1] Thus, the approaches are not usually proposed with reference to civic competence, but on other grounds (e.g., "academic disciplines are important for college and have inherent value as well," or "community involvement is good, because it facilitates the transition to adulthood.") As proponents argue for specific curricula, the "cause" in question becomes values clarification, moral development, law-related education, etc. rather than civic competence. When educators are continually preoccupied with accepting or rejecting particular proposals, they can be seduced into defining the problem in terms that the proposals initiate, before they have worked out a coherent answer to the more basic question, what is civic competence? It would make more sense to *begin* with a conception of civic competence and to derive from that the kind of curriculum which might teach it.

Institutional Difficulties

Once a conception of civic competence is articulated, certain factors make it difficult to launch comprehensive civic education programs in schools as they now exist.

1. It is generally accepted that public education should serve *several* legitimate purposes (vocational preparation, general literacy, management of certain aspects of personal life: health, consumption, use of leisure time), and that civic education—dealing primarily with the relationship of the person to the state—should, therefore, consume only a small part of the total effort. The assumption that students should have the opportunity to study and grow in a variety of areas, rather than paying exclusive attention to any single one, results in a supermarket conception of curriculum, a fragmented school schedule that divides the student's instructional life into many subjects (and extra-curricular activities), rather than concentrating on a few. One consequence of the multiple-purpose assumption is a set of requirements for graduation from secondary school and admission to higher education. Students must earn particular credits and learn certain proficiencies in such subjects as English, math, science, social studies, foreign language, and vocational areas in order to proceed to the next step in the societal reward system. Regardless of the relevance of such subjects to civic education, students must have time to pursue them, for civic education cannot dominate the curriculum.

2. So that education is offered efficiently, systematically, in an organized fashion, it has come under the exclusive control of professionals, who, presumably, have special competence to teach. Many professionals assume that learning must occur in specially designed places (schools) that must be insulated from interruption or interference by incidental, non-instructional activity or "normal life." Thus schools are segregated, allowing little contact (for teachers or students) with adults in their daily occupational work, with persons caring for others in families or other relationships, or with persons active in trying to influence the political-legal system. This protective, almost possessive, attitude makes it difficult to send students to learn in places other than schools or from people who are not credentialed educators.

3. As publicly supported institutions, schools must be "accountable" to the tax-paying public. This creates pressure to demonstrate "school effectiveness," which in turn generates pressure to conceptualize curriculum and learning only in those terms that lead to immediately quantifiable, objective measurement of student achievement. By restricting ways in which educational goals can be conceived and phrased, the pressure for accountability

poses additional constraints, especially when criteria stress goals other than civic competence.

These problems might be seen as symptoms of more fundamental obstacles to social change: the undemocratic nature of bureaucracies and their tendency to centralize and expand into structures unresponsive to purposeful action; systemic forces in the economy, especially profit motives for publishers and others economically dependent upon school expenditures from teamsters to teachers; the political conservatism of adults who control socialization. All are formidable roadblocks to meaningful curriculum change. In offering a curriculum proposal we imply the belief that the power of such obstacles has not been sufficiently demonstrated to warrant surrender. But our main task here is not to verify this, not to give a social analysis on how to bring curriculum change in schools. Rather, our purpose is to offer a curriculum that is at least minimally responsive to institutional constraints. The structure we suggest attempts to address the three institutional difficulties first mentioned.

I. A CONCEPTION OF CIVIC COMPETENCE

A. Ability to Exert Influence in Public Affairs

We begin with a few assumptions. First, that the purpose of civic education, as opposed, for example, to aesthetic, economic, or psychological education, is to teach students to function in a particular relationship with the state. Second, that the most desirable type of relationship between the citizen and the state is outlined in the structure of constitutional representative democracy. Third, that the major way in which this political arrangement differs from others is that the state "belongs" to the citizens, and the citizens have certain unalienable rights to influence what the state shall do. The primary educational mission, therefore, is to teach citizens to exert influence in public affairs, for without the competence to influence the state, the unalienable right to do so (that is, the key feature of representative democracy) cannot be exercised.

According to these assumptions the most fundamental civic competence is the ability to exert influence in public affairs. The phrase needs clarification. Public affairs are those issues of concern to groups of people to which, it is generally agreed, institutions of government should respond—through legislation, administrative action, judicial opinion, selection of officeholders, and other activities. There may be a tendency to recognize as public affairs only those issues with widespread impact, reported in the mass media (wars, elections, inflation, pollution). Our definition, however, also calls attention to countless issues at the local level and less publicized: cyclists trying to establish or regulate bike trails; volunteers trying to influence visitation policies in a mental hospital; students trying to increase the budget for women's sports in their school; black students trying to gain official school recognition of their "union." These are all "public affairs," and the citizens' ability to exert influence on such matters is as important to the functioning of democracy as a sense of involvement in issues with more global consequences.

The attempt to exert influence can be viewed as a process, diagrammed in figure 11.1, in which the individual develops goals or desired outcomes (e.g., closing a juvenile detention center, electing a candidate). One then works for support of the goals through organizing, bargaining—various methods of persuasion. In building support it is often necessary to modify goals (e.g., hiring a new director instead of closing the center, or publicizing crucial issues instead of actually winning the election). Revised goals serve as a

FIGURE 11.1
Exerting Influence in Public Affairs

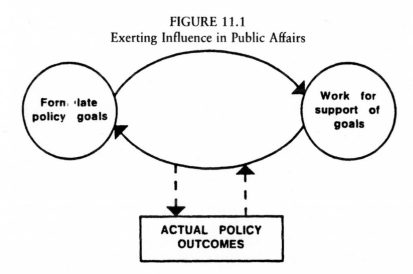

new basis for action that might eventually call for even further revision as an action effort evolves. According to this dynamic, ability to exert influence should not be equated with the ability always to "win," but rather the ability to produce outcomes in public affairs in directions consistent with one's goals.

This view of civic competence may imply that each student should learn how to impose all his or her views on the world, but that would be both unethical and logically impossible. It would be ethically irresponsible to endorse unconditionally any view on public affairs that a student might profess. If a student wishes to provoke violence to protest racism, the teacher is not obligated to help, even though the student may believe this will increase his or her ability to win support. In some cases the teacher may, instead, be obligated to make it impossible for the student to succeed. Rather than assuming that students have a blank check to exercise their will as they see fit, students and staff have a moral responsibility to study and discuss the ethics of proposed policies and actions. While it is certainly possible to exert influence without offering moral justification, our definition assumes that attempts to exert influence in a constitutional representative democracy must be ethically justified. In this sense the ability to exert influence requires ability in moral reasoning (discussed below).

No social system could function on the premise that each person has a right to implement all preferences, for this would require the logical impossibility that persons with contradictory views could each have their way. Genuine controversy over public affairs inevitably spawns "winners," "losers," and people who see themselves as somewhere in between; it is impossible to have only winners. Thus, a conception of ability to exercise influence should recognize (a) the impossibility of all citizens winning all of the time, but the desirability of all having the competence to win some of the time; (b) the fact that, in the process of "losing," even "losers" can exert influence on policy (for example, by demonstrating a power base that will have to be contended with in the future); and (c) that the decision to modify one's ideals in order to exert influence in a particular situation is not necessarily an indication of one's lack of ability to exert influence. Having one's way is surely implied in the concept of influence, but it cannot be taken to the extreme. The goal is to assist students in having some impact in public affairs, consistent with intentions which they develop through a process of rational moral deliberation.

As another point of clarification, note that the objective is not to make all students into adults obsessed with public affairs who participate intensively and continuously on every conceivable issue. Rather than prescribing for all students a standard style or expected frequency of actual involvement, the objective is concerned mainly with increasing the ability to exert influence. Each individual must retain choice as to where, when, and how he or she wishes to use competence, and some may choose to use it only sparingly. Without appropriate skills, however, the individual does not have the option to exert influence. An incompetent person has only two options: not to participate or to participate without effect. The school should create for all students a third option: to participate in a way that makes an impact. Even if this objective were achieved for most citizens, however, we would expect wide variation in rates and types of actual participation.

B. *Specific Competencies*

If people are to formulate goals, win support for them and thereby exert influence, we suggest they must have the more specific competencies to

1) communicate effectively in spoken and written language;
2) collect and logically interpret information on problems of public concern;
3) describe political-legal decision-making processes;
4) rationally justify personal decisions on controversial public issues and strategies for action with reference to principles of justice and constitutional democracy;
5) work cooperatively with others;
6) discuss concrete personal experiences of self and others in ways that contribute to resolution of personal dilemmas encountered in civic action and that relate these experiences to more general human issues;
7) use selected technical skills as they are required for exercise of influence on specific issues.

As we elaborate on each, we shall see how the competencies suggest some concrete directions for curriculum.

1. Communicate effectively in spoken and written language. Skills in reading, writing, speaking and listening are obviously required in order to learn about issues, to develop one's views, and to win support. To receive and send messages effectively one needs technical skills of literacy, sensitivity and analytic ability to identify what one "really" wants to say, what others may be "trying to say," what kinds of messages may be most effective, given some knowledge of one's audience. This view of communication acknowledges the significance of both verbal and nonverbal cues, of personal dynamics within groups, of ways in which the medium affects the message.

2. Collect and logically interpret information on problems of public concern. To have impact, citizens must defend their views with persuasive evidence. They will need information on the history surrounding specific people and events, on social trends, on existing law. Relevant data is often difficult to find and to interpret. The skills needed might be considered analogous to investigative skills of the journalist or private detective, the disciplined skills of the social scientist, the research skills of a legislative assistant. In short this refers to digging for the facts and making warranted inferences from them.

3. Describe political-legal decision-making processes. To formulate goals and to work for their support, one must know something about the formal and informal structures through which public decisions are made, and about strategies that seem appropriate for affecting different people and agencies. This calls for knowledge of realities in the dynamics of power wherever it relates to public affairs. Only a portion of this knowledge comes from formal descriptions of the political-legal system (such as the Constitution or a chart on how a bill becomes a law). In addition students need to view the system from the perspectives of actual participants and analysts who try to "tell it like it is." The intent here is to overcome myths or political naivete, to look closely at ways in which political-legal decision-making is and is not susceptible to deliberate citizen action efforts.

4. Rationally justify personal decisions on controversial public issues (including justifications of strategies for action) with reference to principles of justice and constitutional democracy. In recommending courses of action, the citizen expresses value prefer-

ences that affect the lives of others. To develop support for value claims, students need instruction both in the format or style of argument and on the substantive values on which to defend their positions. In matters of style, this calls for a sincere attempt to be "rational" in the sense of providing reasons for one's preferences, grounding the reasons in some underlying principles, striving for consistency among the principles, and modifying one's views to eliminate serious logical contradictions. These can be seen as criteria for "rational" argument.

In the realm of substantive values, citizens must show that proposed actions help to advance, or at least do not violate, unalienable rights which the community is entrusted to protect. These rights are grounded in the principle of human dignity, or equal respect for every human life. From this basic premise a number of other values or principles can be derived; the right to certain liberties, to due process of law, to participation in the consent process, and more generally the value of organizing society according to principles of representative constitutional democracy. There are two general reasons why value judgments ought to be defended rationally and with reference to these particular principles. First, an ethical, philosophical argument can be made that this is required in order to have any reasonable moral system.[2] Second is the pragmatic argument that those persons skilled in such discourse will actually be more persuasive and act with more influence than those unskilled.

The commitment to rationality and the values of constitutional representative democracy, however, cannot justify moralistic preaching or blind faith in particular regimes, law, values or the USA as a nation. Now, as in the past, legitimate controversy rages over what the "best" values may be, the extent to which representative democracy might serve them, and the extent to which representative democracy actually exists or can conceivably ever exist. Students should not be insulated from such controversy but encouraged to pursue it in a studious uncensored fashion. The essential educational task is not to indoctrinate, but to remain intellectually honest and at the same time to help students justify the belief that principles of representative constitutional democracy offer the most promise for organizing community to serve the value of human dignity.

5. Work cooperatively with others. A prevailing image of the responsible citizen is the "intelligent voter" or the person who writes a letter to a Congressional representative. Most individuals, however, can exert influence only to the extent that they are backed by united group effort, and this requires far greater attention to collective process as the foundation for citizen action. Individuals need to learn to work within groups in selecting and attacking issues. Groups must develop internal mechanisms for governance and division of labor, along with approaches for eliciting cooperative alliance with other groups. Solidarity and commitment to a group must be generated, but it must also remain receptive to criticism and fulfill genuine individual needs of group members. All of this suggests the need to teach skills in group work and community organization.

6. Discuss concrete experiences of self and others in ways that contribute to resolution of personal dilemmas encountered in civic action and that relate these experiences to more general human issues. The effective citizen must be able to see relationships between specific happenings and issues phrased in general terms. If one feels frustrated at being apparently ignored by a public official, one should be able to talk about the incident in ways that help to explain why it occured and what might be done in the future to avoid it. If students observe a leader trying to justify dishonesty on the grounds that it was necessary to gain enough power to "do good," they should be able to discuss this as the more general problem of means and ends. The point here is to try to transcend the immediacy, specificity, or concreteness of personal incidents to search for meanings that have some generalizability, and can therefore, make personal action more informed in the future.

7. Use selected technical skills as required for exercise of influence on specific issues. Here we refer to the "nuts and bolts" of civic action, "tricks of the trade," or skills in such areas as political canvassing, fund-raising, record-keeping, bargaining and negotiating, preparing public testimony, gaining endorsements, use of the mass media, or parliamentary procedure. Such skills should not be taught to all students as general preparation, but learned as needed with regard to students' pursuit of specific issues. This last competence differs from the first six by calling attention to specific technical training in an ad hoc or issue-related fashion.

II. CURRICULUM OVERVIEW

To teach the civic competencies, we propose a voluntary year-long program in the 11th or 12th grade, where students would spend almost full time in the citizen action program (e.g., 9:30 a.m. to 2:00 p.m.). They would earn the equivalent of two academic credits in English and two in social studies, would have time to take one additional course such as math, science, or foreign language, and could participate as time permits in music, athletics, or other activities. Initially we recommend a pilot program of sixty student volunteers and a teaching team with the equivalent of two full time teachers, one in English, one in social studies. Aiming toward a balance among systematic classroom instruction, field observation, and active student participation, the program includes six main components:

1. *Political-Legal Process Course,* three mornings per week for 14 weeks, first semester, including one morning per week of first-hand observation in the field. This course would teach the "realities" of influence and power in the political-legal system. In addition to information on the formal structure of the system, including constitutional rights, emphasis would be placed on informal and "behind the scene" processes, especially at local levels of decision-making. Classroom instruction would relate to field assignments in which students conduct interviews, attend meetings, observe aspects of the political-legal process in the community at large. Skills in gathering data and drawing valid conclusions would be emphasized. Empirical observation and conceptual teaching would provide background for ethical analysis and moral deliberation on problems of justice. Students would develop positions on controversial aspects of public policy and political-legal process.

2. *Communication Course,* four afternoons per week for 16 weeks, first semester. The course would focus on the use of written, spoken and nonverbal language in four contexts: intrapersonal, interpersonal, group, and public. Listening, speaking, reading and writing would be emphasized in receiving and sending messages accurately and effectively. Students would have extensive practice in different communication styles and techniques appropriate for interpersonal helping, problem-solving in groups, developing rational justifications, building group cohesion, and addressing public audiences. To improve skills in such areas, students would learn

to analyze the dynamics of communication in different settings according to communication and group theory.

3. *Community Service Internship,* two full mornings per week for 14 weeks, first semester. Students would be placed in volunteer service positions in social agencies, governmental bodies, public interest groups, etc. They would have responsibility for working for the host organization and would be supervised by agency and school personnel. As they become involved in public service work, they would analyze aspects of institutional process in the political-legal process course, and in the communication course they would work on language skills relevant to the internship. One afternoon per week, students would share their volunteer experiences, discuss common problems, and begin to explore issues that might develop into the citizen action project for the second semester.

4. *Citizen Action Project,* four mornings per week for 10 weeks, second semester. Students would work in small groups in attempts to influence public policy. Projects could involve working for political candidates, establishment of special youth institutions, revision of administrative regulations, lobbying for legislation, etc. The issues could concern national, state, or local agencies, including the schools; for example, student rights within a school, zoning provisions to protect the environment, consumer protection, interracial cooperation, improved social services for youth in trouble. The projects would hopefully grow out of the first semester internship and field studies in the political-legal process course. During the project students would take selected "skill clinics" on such matters as techniques of canvassing, bargaining and negotiation skills, fund-raising, how to run a meeting, press releases. They would also participate in "project counseling sessions" where peers and faculty discuss issues arising from the action work. The counseling sessions would give psychological support and deal with confusion, stress, uncertainty likely to arise in active participation.

5. *Action in Literature Course,* two afternoons per week for 10 weeks, second semester. The aim would be to examine persisting issues of citizenship, rather than to focus on specific problems of students' projects, and to pursue this through diverse literature: fiction, biography, poetry, drama, and non-fiction social analysis. Students might read a biography of Ghandi, Thoreau on civil disobedience, a novel such as All the King's Men, the work of James Baldwin. They might study such questions as, "What is meaningful social change?" "Can an individual make a difference?" "How should humans

govern themselves?" The course would offer a special opportunity for the teacher to introduce the work of previous thinkers whose distinguished writing illuminates universal problems of citizenship.

6. *Public Message,* periodically through second semester. Each citizen action group would develop a final "message" which communicated the meaning of its work to peers and the public at large. The message could take the form of a written report, a radio or TV program, a play, a film or photo essay. The point would be to tell the public what has been accomplished and to interpret the students' experience. A unit on critical analysis of the mass media would precede the creation of student messages. Producing the message would further refine communication skills, and offer a creative opportunity for students to synthesize previous coursework.

The program is not advocated as a verified model. To our knowledge no such program has ever been tried, although many schools seem to offer in some form one or more of its parts. We propose it only as a suggestion for how schools which take citizen participation seriously might create an alternative program at the 11th or 12th grade. The design is responsive, we think, to certain institutional givens; for example, the need to assign formal credit based on disciplinary categories (English and social studies), the fact that schools have other missions besides civic education, and the conventional workloads of teachers.

Note that no component is aimed exclusively at any one of the seven competencies. Communication skills, for example, would not be restricted to the communication course; they would be taught in all parts of the program. The nature of political-legal decision-making would be taught most directly in the political-legal process course, but to function successfully in the program, students would have to develop political knowledge continuously beyond that, especially in the internship, action project and public message. While some components would stress certain competencies more than others, our intent is that all competencies would be reinforced in all components. The decision not to develop a specialized instructional module for each competency reflects our assumption that educational programs must aim toward more than expedient individual mastery. Students have a right not only to become individually competent, but also to a sense of personal dignity in the learning process. That dignity can often be violated by curricula that increasingly separate and dissect human compe-

FIGURE 11.2
Sample Program Schedule

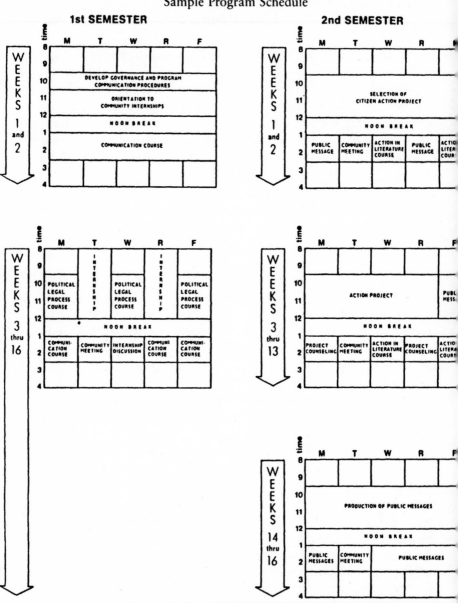

tence. Instead, the instructional environment must encourage a holistic, interactive view of learning. Its own activities must nourish interpersonal sharing and a just system of governance, as well as individual achievement. (See figure 11.2.)

III. RELATIONSHIP TO OTHER INNOVATIVE PROGRAMS

The program integrates a variety of innovative themes currently advocated in secondary education: communication skills, media analysis, moral development, values clarification, volunteerism, law-related education, psychological awareness. The program can be considered an alternative "school-within-a-school," where, for a full year, students take major responsibility for their actions and can develop a sense of community among themselves. By providing intensive opportunities for learning with adults in the community at large and integrating this experience with school-based instruction, it implements recommendations from reports of recent commissions on youth and secondary education (e.g., National Association of Secondary School Principals, 1972; National Commission on the Reform of Secondary Education, 1972; Report of the Panel on Youth, 1974). As will become apparent later, the program also incorporates much of the experience of the alternative school movement (e.g., use of out of school resources, combined role of teacher and counselor, project and advocacy-oriented coursework).

While it synthesizes many efforts, the citizen action curriculum in no sense tries to offer all things to all people, nor does it pursue objectives precisely as intended by other programs. To illustrate consistencies and differences between the citizen action (CA) program and other approaches, consider table 11.1. Our entries give an incomplete picture of related movements, for we identify only those aspects that seem particularly pertinent to the citizen action

TABLE 11.1
Educational Movements Related to the Citizen Action Curriculum

Related Program	*CA Consistency*	*CA Difference*
Kohlberg Moral Development	Systematic discussion of moral issues, aiming toward ethical justification through principled reasoning.	Focus on moral issues related to public affairs. Not aimed primarily at stage development in individual students, but more at general participation skills.

(Continued)

TABLE 11.1
(*Continued*)

Related Program	CA Consistency	CA Difference
Values Clarification	Emphasizes clarification of personal values related to public issues in non-threatening atmosphere.	Preparation to face challenges and strong opposition to one's values.
Communication Skills	Major emphasis on use of spoken and written language to receive and send messages.	Focus on use of language in the role of citizen. Add to technical literacy skills the role of interpersonal dynamics and mass media.
Law-related Education	Major emphasis on dynamics of political-legal system.	Focus on problems related to citizens exerting influence, rather than abstract understanding of topics in political science or law.
Media Education	Emphasis on analysis of and production of media.	Orientation to how the citizen is influenced by and can use the media to exert influence, rather than only aesthetic dimensions.
Psychological Awareness	Examines students' sense of self and emotional stress.	Focus on sense of efficacy and anxiety related especially to citizen participation.
Volunteerism	Students placed in responsible roles of participation in the community beyond the school.	An integrated set of courses surrounds the experience. Volunteer service is seen as a first step toward action for some institutional change.

programs. We do not pretend to list all differences between our program and theirs, but highlight only one or a few of the most significant.

When each of the related approaches is considered in isolation, we may quibble with aspects of its philosophy, yet each has something to offer civic education. We have tried to structure a program that builds on strengths that these otherwise disparate movements might contribute toward enhancing student ability to exert influence in public affairs.

NOTES

1. Newmann (1977) discusses criteria for a comprehensive rationale for civic education.

2. For elaboration on this point see Kohlberg (1971) and Rawls (1971).

REFERENCES

Kohlberg, Lawrence, "From is to Ought: How to Commit the Naturalistic Fallacy and Get Away with it in the Study of Moral Development," in T. Mischel (Ed.), *Cognitive and Developmental Epistemology,* Academic Press, 1971.

National Association of Secondary School Principals, National Committee on Secondary Education, *American Youth in the Mid-Seventies,* The Association, 1972.

National Commission on the Reform of Secondary Education, *The Reform of Secondary Education: A Report to the Public and the Profession,* McGraw Hill, 1972.

Newmann, Fred M., "Building a Rationale for Civic Education," Bulletin of the National Council for the Social Studies, publication expected September, 1977.

Newmann, Fred M., *Education for Citizen Action: Challenge for Secondary Curriculum,* McCutchan, 1975.

Rawls, John, *A Theory of Justice,* Harvard University Press, 1971.

Report of the Panel on Youth of the President's Science Advisory Committee, *Youth: Transition to Adulthood,* University of Chicago Press, 1974.

CHAPTER 12

History's Role in Civic Education: The Precondition for Political Intelligence

Paul Gagnon
1989

Why do students need to know the past? What does it have to do with citizenship, or anything else in their lives? Why is the civics course not enough, or the American government course? Why claim that in most schools the 11th grade course in American history is the only place where the meaning and requirements of democracy can be seriously explored? What are students expected to learn and why do we want them to learn it?

Like most history textbooks for schools and colleges, these five books on United States[1] history begin badly by failing to hear or to respond to these good questions. None provides an introductory discussion. None says what history is, or suggests the many forms it may take, or tells how it relates to students' lives and to their other studies. On history as part of civic education, only one text, Davidson, has a single line: "As you study the nation's past, you will begin to better understand the challenges of the present and the major issues of the future."

The absence of ideas is evident from the start. Presumably, the authors do believe that what appears in their 800 or more pages will make some imprint on the readers' intellect, and perhaps on emotions too. But what it may be, and why students should bother,

Chapter 1 and Appendix in *Democracy's Half-Told Story* (Washington, D.C.: Education for Democracy Project, American Federation of Teachers, 1989), 15–22, 160–172. Reprinted by permission of the publisher.

they do not say. It is disappointing to find the historian-teachers who write these books so insensitive to pedagogical questions and to the case for history as the best source of political sophistication. Why not leap at Jefferson's argument that the "general education" of citizens should be "chiefly historical"?

> History, by apprising them of the past, will enable them to judge of the future; it will avail them of the experience of other times and other nations; it will qualify them as judges of the actions and designs of men; it will enable them to know ambition under every disguise it may assume; and knowing it, to defeat its views.

Why is it that democracy can be seriously explored only by historical study? The first answer must be that no system, religious, political, economic or educational, can be understood without knowing its adventures—its origins and their circumstances, the ideas and forces that propelled or obstructed it, its successes and failures, its changing role in the larger world of other systems.

Civics and government courses are undeniably useful, but only when added to the student's confrontation of reality: What has happened to people, how and why? Historical knowledge is the precondition for political intelligence. In a proper curriculum, as described in "Education for Democracy" (Appendix), such knowledge would proceed not only from the American history course, but from required courses in the history of Western civilization and of the world.

These three courses, or three blocks of time however tailored into courses, are needed to project the three kinds of reality a modern civic education requires: United States history, to learn who we are, how we got this way, and who we are becoming; the history of Western civilization, to learn the origins and evolution of democracy and its moral bases—our common political heritage as Americans, however diverse our cultural heritages may be; and third, world history, to learn about the other nations and peoples with whom we share, like it or not, a common global destiny.

To leave out or minimize any of these realities is to leave citizens civically ill-educated, unfree to make informed choices about public life, no matter how well-drilled they may be in the principles, the written law, or inner workings of American political institutions. In most American schools the curriculum in history—and in its sister subjects, geography, biography and literature—is plainly inadequate for the preparation of free citizens. The 11th grade American history course is no longer universally required, the 8th grade American history is optional in many districts, and more than half of all American high school students take no world or Western history whatsoever.

In response to this situation, the Bradley Commission on History in Schools, made up of seventeen distinguished historians and classroom teachers, has recently published a powerful argument for history as essential to civic education. It argues that history and geography should be restored as the continuing core of social studies, from kindergarten through the 12th grade:

> History belongs in the school programs of all students, regardless of their academic standing and preparation, of their curricular track, or of their plans for the future. It is vital for all citizens in a democracy, because it provides the only avenue we have to reach an understanding of ourselves and of our society, in relation to the human condition over time.

This plea that history be universally required because of its unique power to educate citizens has an honorable ancestry. Nearly a century ago an illustrious group of scholars and teachers, Woodrow Wilson among them, was charged with reviewing the American high school curriculum. The 1892 report of the Committee of Ten declared that democratic schooling called for common, substantial requirements in historical and political studies for all students, whether or not they were college-bound (and especially if they were not). The Committee argued that such studies prepared the student to exert a "salutary influence" on the affairs of his country:

> History and its allied branches are better adapted than any other studies to promote the invaluable mental power which we call judgment.

To ensure that students would have enough chance to develop such power of judgment, the Committee of Ten prescribed eight years of history, starting with mythology and biography for the 5th and 6th grades, American history and government for the 7th grade, Greek and Roman history for the 8th, European history in the 9th, English history in the 10th, American history in the 11th, and a selected historical topic, studied in depth, in the 12th grade. In 1899, the Committee of Seven, appointed by the American

Historical Association, prescribed a similar four year curricular pattern for high schools: ancient history in the first year, medieval and modern Europe in the second, English history in the third, and American history and government in the senior year. These demanding, egalitarian versions of civic education did not survive the 1920s except in certain preparatory schools and college-preparatory tracks, where they were, of course, no longer egalitarian. As time passed, even those courses were watered-down, and today, even college preparatory programs seldom require half the time for history or geography that the Ten and Seven believed to be necessary. This, despite the fact that we must now recognize a whole new dimension: the entire non-European world that the Committees of Ten and Seven had left largely to geography.

What happened to history? In the name of "social efficiency" professional educators, who had steadily gained influence over the schools since the turn of the century, played down those studies they regarded as lacking immediate utility, or interest, for the mass of students not going on to college. History (what use is it? what job can it get you?) was a casualty. A differentiated, tracked curriculum called "progressive" soon became segregated by class, race, ethnic background—and by the self-fulfilling prophecies of economic occupation and social destiny. On the one hand, academic substance, including history (though less and less of it), was taught to the few college-bound students. On the other hand, vocational subjects and a social studies program aiming at socialization (later to be called "Life Adjustment") were taught to the many, substituting for history an array of courses, deemed to be practical, in applied social sciences.

The good intentions behind the progressive education movement —including an understandable concern for the "holding power" of the schools—did not make up for its undemocratic consequences in regard to civic education. Certain progressives were not in fact democrats themselves but believed in a top-down social engineering of the good society by the enlightened few, who would remain few. Nor should the progressives be given too much credit for advocating innovative teaching methods and "active learning." The Committee of Ten was much concerned with both the 1892, urging that students be encouraged to exercise independent judgment: They should read at least two differing accounts of events; they should study by asking questions, by discriminating among authorities and between original sources and secondary works; they should debate in "mock legislatures, parliaments and congresses"; they should be given responsibility for teaching classes themselves.

> [We] have to suggest only the use of the methods which, in good schools, are now accustoming pupils to think for themselves, to put together their own materials, to state their results, to compare one series of events with another series and the history of one country with that of another.

Now, a century later, our concern about education for democracy leads us back to the ideas of the Committees of Ten and Seven, those "elite" few with faith in the ability of all students to profit from an education both substantial and universal, both "elitist" and egalitarian. The Bradley Commission urges state and local school districts to adopt a history and geography-centered social studies program for the early grades, full of lively, engaging readings from history, mythology, biography, legend and literature, and a commonly required program of no fewer than two full years of American history and two years of world (or Western and world) history, in the span from grade 7 through grade 12. It urges the closest possible attention to imaginative materials and methods, and it argues for the teacher's authority to decide on when and how to present materials.

Just as the Committee of Ten spoke of "the invaluable mental power which we call judgment," the Bradley report says that the aim of historical study is to promote certain "habits of the mind." Students, as future citizens, should develop a sense of "shared humanity." They need to understand themselves and others by learning how they resemble and how they differ from other people, over time and space; to question stereotypes of others (and of themselves); to discern the difference between fact and conjecture, between evidence and mere assertion; to grasp the complexity of historical cause; to distrust the simple answer and dismissive explanation; to respect particularity and avoid false analogy; to recognize the abuse of historical "lessons" for partisan advantage; to consider that ignorance of the past may make us prisoners of it; to realize that not all problems have solutions, but that amelioration has been won by patient effort; to be prepared for the irrational and the accidental in human affairs; to grasp the power of ideas, values, and individual character in history. In such qualities of mind, well beyond the usual meaning of "critical thinking," lies true civic education, and only the study of history can develop them.

Why, then have educators decided that civic education can do without history, or with only a small portion here and there? One reason relevant here is that some social studies specialists have believed that good citizenship can be taught in the abstract, that proper values and right attitudes can be inculcated through object lessons or case studies out of the social sciences. They assume "morals" can be drawn out of historical vignettes cut away from the long and messy chronological narrative and nicely trimmed to make a point.

Moreover, and to their credit, educators want very much to believe that civics can attract and engage all students, but they find that history is difficult to teach well. Indeed, one reason for its decline was that it was, and is, so often taught badly, failing to attract and engage even the most willing students. But instead of working to teach history more effectively, as the Committee of Ten had urged, the schools turned to what seemed to be easier, more enticing ways to develop the power called "judgment."

The solution has not worked. Student polls repeatedly place social studies last in interest and relevance among their high school subjects and tests reveal wide ignorance of facts, ideas and institutions central to the workings of a democratic system. It is time to admit that there is no painless remedy. Genuine civic education is neither easier nor more attractive than other fields of study. It cannot be easy because it deals with politics—the most difficult of all the human arts. Nor is it automatically attractive to students, particularly when it is well and seriously taught with the historical detail necessary for genuine understanding of concepts, issues, and choices.

Seasoned history and social studies teachers have known all along that teaching the art of democratic politics is extraordinarily difficult, demanding more of learners than other subjects do, not only as they study, but as they conduct their lives afterward. One reason is that the aims of education for democratic citizenship are by their nature contradictory, or at least sharply different in style and in the modes of teaching they require. We seek to develop at one and the same time a taste for teamwork and a taste for critical, thorny individualism, at once the readiness to serve and the readiness to resist, for no one can foretell which way the "good" citizen ought to turn in future crises. Classroom work must range from systematic, disciplined study of history, politics and ideas all the way to skeptical, free-swinging debate on public issues past and present. Neither socialization nor consciousness-raising will do. Both are, or seem, too easy. Each alone is wretched preparation for the subtleties of judgment free citizens must exercise.

Another reason for the difficulty of civic education, as Alexis de Tocqueville explained in *Democracy in America,* is that most of the important problems for democratic politics are not solvable in any neat or final way. To take his foremost example, democratic people cherish both liberty and equality, both personal freedom and social justice. There is no recipe for just the right blend in any given situation of liberty and equality. The two impulses inevitably collide, yet each is indispensable to the preservation of a bearable level of the other. Civic education teaches the young why this is so not by some "concept" to be memorized but by the memorable, sometimes deeply disturbing historical experiences that have convinced us of it. Students need to see that such conflict is natural and to be expected, not some "failure" of a system that should run itself and leave them alone.

Civic education asks people to accept the burdens of living with tentative answers and with unfinished and often dangerous business. It asks them to accept costs and compromises, to take on responsibilities as eagerly as they claim their rights, to honor the interests of others while pursuing their own, to respect the needs of future generations, and to speak the truth and to do the right thing when lying and doing the wrong thing would be more profitable. Generally it asks them to restrain their appetites and expectations. Civic education asks all this, and that citizens inform themselves on the multiple problems and choices their elected servants confront.

It is easy enough to lay out these "values" and wholesome attitudes in classroom lessons, followed by quizzes and papers wherein the students repeat the phrases and swear devotion to them. And it is not so hard even to practice them on the playground and in the school, provided a certain level of morale exists. There is no trick to virtuous behavior when things are going well. Most people will hold right attitudes, without much formal instruction, when they feel themselves free, secure, and justly treated.

The tough part of civic education is to prepare people for bad times. The question is not whether they will remember the right phrases, but whether they will put them into practice when they feel wrongly treated, in fear for their freedom and security. Or when authorities and the well-placed, public or private, appear to flout every value and priority taught in school. The chances for democratic principles to surmount crises depend upon the number of citizens who know how free societies, their own and others, have responded to crises of the past, how they acted to defend themselves, and how they survived. Why did some societies fall and others stand? Citizens need to tell each other, before it is too late, what struggles had to be accepted, what sacrifices borne and comforts given up, to preserve freedom and justice.

It would be unreasonable to expect all students to thrill to history and civic education, any more than all thrill to geometry or physics. The deep, discriminating historical knowledge required to ward off panic, self-pity, and resignation is not always fun to acquire. We would not think of dumbing-down math or science for the professions requiring them; we would end with incompetent bridge-builders and physicians. However vexing they may find it, students accept the need to master facts and concepts necessary in such professions. But what of the profession of citizen, which nobody can escape? We can be sure that by dumbing-down civic education, we shall end with incompetent citizens, because democratic values must be rooted in the kind of political and historical wisdom that nourishes them no matter how bad the weather.

When students ask why they need to know the past, and what it has to do with citizenship, they are entitled to some such answer as this. They have the right to be told about our purposes, why we ask so much of them, and why we have no choice but to do so, in all fairness to them and to the larger society.

APPENDIX: EDUCATION FOR DEMOCRACY: A STATEMENT OF PRINCIPLES

As the bicentennial for our Constitution approaches, we call for a special effort to raise the level of education for democratic citizenship. Given the complexities of our own society, of the rest of the world, and of the choices we confront, the need is self-evident and improvement is long past due.

As the years pass, we become an increasingly diverse people, drawn from many racial, national, linguistic, and religious origins. Our cultural heritage as Americans is as diverse as we are, with multiple sources of vitality and pride. But our political heritage is one—the vision of a common life in liberty, justice, and equality as expressed in the Declaration of Independence and the Constitution two centuries ago.

To protect that vision, Thomas Jefferson prescribed a general education not just for the few but for all citizens, "to enable every man to judge for himself what will secure or endanger his freedom." A generation later, Alexis de Tocqueville reminded us that our duty was to "educate democracy." He believed that all politics were but the playing out of the "notions and sentiments dominant in people." These, he said, are the "real causes of all the rest." Ideas—good and bad—have their consequences in every sphere of a nation's life.

We cite Tocqueville's appeal with a sense of urgency, for we fear that many young Americans are growing up without the education needed to develop a solid commitment to those "notions and sentiments" essential to a democratic form of government. Although all the institutions that shape our private and public lives—family, church, school, government, media—share the responsibility for encouraging democratic values in our children, our focus here is on the nation's schools and their teaching of the social studies and humanities.

In singling out the schools, we do not suggest that there was ever a golden age of education for citizenship, somehow lost in recent years. It is reported that in 1943—that patriotic era—fewer than half of surveyed college freshmen could name four points in the Bill of Rights. Our purpose here is not to argue over the past, but only to ask that everyone with a role in schooling now join to work for decisive improvement.

Our call for schools to purposely impart to their students the learning necessary for an informed, reasoned allegiance to the ideals of a free society rests on three convictions:

First, that democracy is the worthiest form of human governance ever conceived.

Second, that we cannot take its survival or its spread—or its perfection in practice—for granted. Indeed, we believe that the great central drama of modern history has been and continues to be the struggle to establish, preserve, and extend democracy—at home and abroad. We know that very much still needs doing to achieve justice and civility in our own society. Abroad, we note that, according to the Freedom House survey of political rights and civil liberties, only one-third of the world's people live under conditions that can be described as free.

Third, we are convinced that democracy's survival depends upon our transmitting to each new generation the political vision of liberty and equality that unites us as Americans—and a deep loyalty to the political institutions our Founders put together to fulfill that vision. As Jack Beatty reminded us in a *New Republic* article one Fourth of July, ours is a patriotism "not of blood and soil but of values, and those values are liberal and humane."[2]

Such values are neither revealed truths nor natural habits. There is no evidence that we are born with them. Devotion to human dignity and freedom, to equal rights, to social and economic justice, to the rule of law, to civility and truth, to tolerance of diversity, to mutual assistance, to personal and civic responsibility, to self-restraint and self-respect—all these must be taught and learned and practiced. They cannot be taken for granted or regarded as merely one set of options against which any other may be accepted as equally worthy.

Why We Are Concerned

Are the ideas and institutions—and above all the worth—of democracy adequately conveyed in American schools? Do our graduates come out of school possessing the mature political judgment Jefferson hoped for, an ability to decide for themselves "what will secure or endanger" their freedom? Do they know of democracy's short and troubled tenure in human history? Do they comprehend its vulnerabilities? Do they recognize and accept their responsibility for preserving and extending their political inheritance?

No systematic study exists to answer these questions. We lack adequate information on students' knowledge, beliefs, and enthusiasms. There has been little examination of school textbooks and supplementary materials, of state and district requirements in history and social sciences, or of what it takes in everyday school practice. A study of how high school history and government textbooks convey the principles of democracy is underway, and we hope that several other studies will be launched soon.

Meanwhile, the evidence we do have—although fragmentary and often anecdotal—is not encouraging. We know, for instance, of the significant decline over several decades in the amount of time devoted to historical studies in American schools, even in the college preparatory track; fewer than twenty states require students to take more than a year of history in order to graduate. We know that, as a result, many students are unaware of prominent people and seminal ideas and events that have shaped our past and created our present. A recent study shows that a majority of high school seniors do not know what the 1954 *Brown v. Board of Education* decision was about.[3] Nor could majorities identify Winston Churchill or Joseph Stalin. Without knowledge of our own struggle for civil rights, how much can students understand of democracy's needs at home—what it has taken and will still take to extend it. And what can they know of democracy's capacity to respond to problems and reform? In ignorance of the Second World War and its aftermath, how much can they grasp of the cost and necessity of defending democracy in the world? Having never debated and discussed how the world came to be as it is, the democratic citizen will not know what is worth defending, what should be changed, and which imposed orthodoxies must be resisted.

We are concerned also that among some educators (as among some in the country at large), there appears a certain lack of confidence in our own liberal, democratic values, an unwillingness to draw normative distinctions between them and the ideas of non-democratic regimes. Any number of popular curriculum materials deprecate the open preference for liberal democratic values as "ethnocentric." One widely distributed teaching guide on human rights accords equal significance to freedom of speech, the right to vote, and the guarantee of due process on the one hand, with the "right" to take vacations on the other.[4] In the rush to present all cultures in a positive light, the unpleasant realities of some regimes are ignored, as when the guide talks of the high value accorded the right to strike by governments in Eastern Europe (a notion that would surely be disputed by the supporters of Solidarnosc). Or as when another guide—financed by the U.S. Department of Education—lauds the Cuban government's commitment to women's rights, noting with approval that men who refuse to share equally in household responsibilities can be penalized with "re-education or assignment to farm work."[5]

This insistence upon maintaining neutrality among competing values, this tendency to present political systems as not better or worse but only different, is illustrated by this test question designed by the National Assessment of Educational Progress and administered in the 1981–1982 school year to students aged nine, thirteen, and seventeen:

> Maria and Ming are friends. Ming's parents were born in China and have lived in the United States for twenty years.
>
> "People have no freedom in China," Maria insists. "There is only one party in the election and the newspapers are run by the government."
>
> "People in China do have freedom," Ming insists. "No one goes hungry. Everyone has an opportunity to work and medical care is free. Can there be greater freedom than that?"
>
> What is the best conclusion to draw from this debate?
>
> A. Ming does not understand the meaning of freedom.
> B. Maria and Ming differ in their opinions of the meaning of freedom.
> C. There is freedom in the U.S. but not in China.
> D. People have greater freedom in China than in the U.S.

According to NAEP, choice B—"Maria and Ming differ in their opinions of the meaning of freedom"—is correct. The test's framers explained in a 1983 report summarizing the survey's findings that students choosing answer B "correctly indicated that the concept of freedom can mean different things to different people in different circumstances." And, of course, in the most narrow, literal sense, B is correct.

Around the world, people and governments do apply different meanings to the word "freedom." Some states that deny freedom of religion, speech, and conscience nonetheless define themselves as free. But we need not accept their Orwellian self-definitions as if words had no meaning. Were we to use Ming's definition of freedom—a job, medical care, and ample food—many of history's slaves and today's prisoners would have to be called "free"! To offer such a definition, and to leave it at that, without elaboration—as NAEP has done—is grossly to mislead students about history, about politics, and above all, about human rights. In fact, the "rights" to food and work and medical care, when separated from the rights to free speech, a free press, and free elections, are not rights at all. They are rewards from the government that are easily bestowed and just as easily betrayed.

We are rightly accustomed to honest scrutiny of our own faults, and so it is all the more inexplicable when educational materials sidestep or whitewash violations of human rights and pervasive injustice in other lands. Students need an honest, rigorous education that allows them to penetrate Orwellian rhetoric and accurately compare the claims and realities of our own society and those of others. Such a goal is compromised when the drawing of normative distinctions and values is frowned upon as a failure of objectivity, on the premise that all values are arbitrary, arising from personal taste or conditioning, without cognitive or rational bases. They are not to be ranked or ordered, the argument runs, only "clarified"; so the teacher must strive to neutrality. It is hardly necessary to be neutral in regard to freedom over bondage, or the rule of law over the rule of the mob, or fair wages over exploitation, in order to describe objectively the differences among them, or among their human consequences.

What of Nazi values and their consequences? To grasp the human condition in the twentieth century objectively, we need to understand the problems of German society that pushed so many to join the Nazis and to acquiesce in their crimes. But to "understand" is not to forgive, or to trivialize, those crimes. Or to teach, in Richard Hunt's phrase, "no-fault, guilt-free history" where nobody is to blame for anything and fixing responsibility is disallowed.

Finally, no discussion of the discomfort that some feel in teaching children to cherish democracy can fail to mention that some may be indifferent, or even alienated from American democracy, out of disillusion over its failings in practice. The postwar confidence in the American way of life was undermined by the political upheavals of the 1960s and early 1970s. First, America had its long-overdue reckoning with the historic national shame of racial discrimination. Then the country found itself mired in the Vietnam War, and was further shocked and disheartened by assassinations and the events of Watergate. As we struggled to confront our failings and correct our flaws, legitimate self-criticism turned at times into an industry of blame. The United States and its democratic

allies were often presented as though we alone had failed, and as
though our faults invalidated the very ideals that taught us how to
recognize failure when we met it.

While the realities of our own society are daily evident, many
students remain ignorant of other, quite different, worlds. How can
they be expected to value or defend freedom unless they have a
clear grasp of the alternatives against which to measure it? The
systematic presentation of reality abroad must be an integral part
of the curriculum. What are the political systems in competition
with our own, and what is life like for the people who live under
them? If students know only half the world, they will not know
nearly enough. We cannot afford what one young writer recalled as
a "gaping hole" in his prestigious, private high school's curriculum.[6] He and his classmates, he says, were "wonderfully instructed
in America's problems . . ."

> but we were at the same time being educated in splendid isolation
> from the notion that democratic societies have committed ene-
> mies; we learned next to nothing of the sorts of alternatives to
> bourgeois liberalism that the twentieth century had to offer . . .
> [We] learned nothing of what it meant to be a small farmer in
> Stalin's Russia or Ho Chi Minh's Vietnam. That it had been part
> of Communist policy to "liquidate as a class" the "kulaks" was
> something we had never heard spoken of. It was perfectly pos-
> sible to graduate from the Academy with honors and be alto-
> gether incapable of writing three factual paragraphs on the histo-
> ry of any Communist regime (or for that matter of any
> totalitarian regime whether of the Right or Left).

What the Citizen Needs to Know

What was, and is, lacking is a fullness of knowledge, an objective
and balanced picture of world realities, historical and contemporary. We do not ask for propaganda, for crash courses in the right
attitudes, or for knee-jerk patriotic drill. We do not want to capsu-
lize democracy's argument into slogans, or pious texts, or bright
debaters' points. The history and nature and needs of democracy
are much too serious and subtle for that.

Education for democracy is not indoctrination, which is the
deliberate exclusion or distortion of studies in order to induce
belief by irrational means. We do not propose to exclude the hon-

est study of doctrines and systems of others. Or to censor history—our own or others'—as closed societies do, or to hide our flaws or explain them away. We do not need a bodyguard of lies. We can afford to present ourselves in the totality of our acts. And we can afford to tell the truth about others, even when it favors them, and complicates that which indoctrination would keep simple and comforting.

And then we leave it to our students to apply their knowledge, values, and experiences to the world they must create. We do not propose a "right" position on, say, American involvement in the Vietnam War; or on the type of nuclear weapons, if any, we should have; or on what our policy in Central America should be; or on whether the E.R.A. should be passed or hiring quotas supported. Good democrats can and do differ on these matters. On these and a host of other policy issues, there is no one "truth." Our task is more limited, and yet in its way much greater; to teach our children to cherish freedom and to accept responsibility for preserving and extending it, confident that they will find their own best ways of doing so, on the basis of free, uncoerced thought.

The kind of critical thinking we wish to encourage must rest on a solid base of factual knowledge. In this regard, we reject educational theory that considers any kind of curricular content to be as good as any other, claiming that all students need to know is "how to learn," that no particular body of knowledge is more worth noting than any other, that in an age of rapid change, all knowledge necessarily becomes "obsolete." We insist, on the contrary, that the central ideas, events, people, and works that have shaped our world, for good and ill, are not at all obsolete. Instead, the quicker the pace of change, the more critical it will be for us to remember them and understand them well. We insist that absent this knowledge, citizens remain helpless to make the wise judgments hoped for by Jefferson.

First, citizens must know the fundamental ideas central to the political vision of the eighteenth-century founders—the vision that holds us together as one people of many diverse origins and cultures. Not only the words—never only the words—but the sources, the meanings, and the implications of the Declaration of Independence, the Constitution, the Federalist Papers, the Bill of Rights.

To go deeper than the words, and truly to understand the

ideas, students must know where and how they arose, in whose minds, stirred by what ideas. What historical circumstances were hospitable, and encouraged people to think such things? What circumstances were hostile? What were the prevailing assumptions about human nature? About the relationship of God and themselves? About origins of human society and the meaning and direction of human history? To understand our ideas requires a knowledge of the whole sweep of Western civilization, from the ancient Jews and Christians—whose ethical beliefs gave rise to democratic thought—to the Greeks and Romans, through the Middle Ages, the Renaissance and the Reformation, the English Revolution—so important to America—the eighteenth century Enlightenment, and the French Revolution, a violent cousin to our own. Such a curriculum is indispensable. Without it, our principles of government—and the debates over them ever since—are not fully comprehensible. They are mere words, floating in air without source, life, drama, or meaning.

Second, citizens must know how democratic ideas have been turned into institutions and practices—the history of the origins and growth and adventures of democratic societies on earth, past and present. How have these societies fared? Who has defended them and why? Who has sought their undoing and why? What conditions—economic, social, cultural, religious, military—have helped to shape democratic practice? What conditions have made it difficult—sometimes even impossible—for such societies to take root? Again, it is indispensable to know the facts of modern history, dating back at least to the English Revolution, and forward to our own century's total wars; to the failure of the nascent liberal regimes of Russia, Italy, Germany, Spain, and Japan; to the totalitarianism, oppressions, and mass exterminations of our time. How has it all happened?

Third, citizens in our society need to understand the current condition of the world and how it got that way, and to be prepared to act upon the challenges to democracy in our own day. What are the roots of our present dangers and of the choices before us? For intelligent citizenship, we need a thorough grasp of the daily workings of our own society, as well as the societies of our friends, of our adversaries, and of the Third World, where so many live amid poverty and violence, with little freedom and little hope.

This is no small order. It requires systematic study of American government and society; of comparative ideologies and political, economic, and social systems; of the religious beliefs that have shaped our values and our cultures and those that have shaped others; and of physical and human geography. How can we avoid making all of this into nothing more than just another, and perhaps longer, parade of facts, smothering the desire to learn? Apart from needed changes in materials and methods, in the structure of curricula and of the school day itself, we believe that one answer is to focus upon the fateful drama of the historical struggle for democracy. The fate of real men and women, here and abroad, who have worked to bring to life the ideas we began with deserves our whole attention and that of our students. It is a suspenseful, often tragic, drama that continues today, often amid poverty and social turmoil; advocates of democracy remain, as before, prey to extremists of Left and Right well-armed with force and simple answers. The ongoing, worldwide struggle for a free center of "broad, sunlit uplands," in Churchill's phrase, is the best hope of the earth, and we would make it the heart of a reordered curriculum for history and social studies.

History and the Humanities As the Core of Democratic Education

We regard the study of history as the chief subject in education for democracy, much as Jefferson and other founders of the United States did two centuries ago. In revamping the social studies curriculum, we should start with the obvious: History is not the enemy of the social sciences, but is instead their indispensable source of nourishment, order, and perspective. We aim at nothing less than helping the student to comprehend what is important, not merely to memorize fact and formula. But it is clearly impossible to reach genuine comprehension of economic, political, social, and cultural questions without examining them in their historic context. To pull "case studies" and "concepts" out of historical narrative, as so many social studies programs do, not only confuses students but is likely to distort the truth of the human condition.

Of all the subjects in the curriculum, history alone affords the perspective that students need to compare themselves realistically with others—in the past and elsewhere on earth—and to think critically, to look behind assertions and appearances, to ask for the "whole story," to judge meaning and value for themselves. History is also the integrative subject, upon which the coherence and usefulness of other subjects depend, especially the social sciences but also much of literature and the arts. Taught in historical context, the formulations and insights of the social sciences take on life, blood, drama, and significance. And, in turn, their organizing concepts and questions can help rescue history from the dry recital of dates and acts so many students have rightly complained about.

We are pleased that several major reform proposals agree on the centrality of history. Theodore Sizer, in *Horace's Compromise*, makes the joint study of history and ideas one of the four required areas of learning throughout the secondary years. *The Paideia Proposal* puts narrative history and geography at the center of the social studies curriculum, during every grade beyond the elementary. Ernest Boyer's Carnegie Report, *High School*, asks for a year of the history of Western Civilization, a year of American History, another of American government, and a term's study of non-Western society. The Council for Basic Education sets an "irreducible minimum" of two years of American history, one year of European, and the study of at least one non-Western society in depth. The state of California now calls for at least two years of high school history.[7]

We also ask for wider reading and study in the humanities. For we are concerned, again, with values, with every citizen's capacity for judging the moral worth of things. In this, courses in "values clarification" do not get us very far. They either feign neutrality or descend to preachiness. Values and moral integrity are better discovered by students in their reading of history, of literature, of philosophy, and of biography. Values are not "taught," they are encountered, in school and life.

The humanities in our schools must not be limited, as they so often are now, to a few brief samples of Good Things, but should embrace as much as possible of the whole range of the best that has been thought and said and created, from the ancient to the most recent. Otherwise, students have little chance to confront the many varied attempts to answer the great questions of life—or even to be aware that such questions exist. The quest for worth and meaning is indispensable to the democratic citizen. The essence of democracy, its reason for being, is constant choice. We choose what the good life is, and how our society—including its schools—may order its priorities so that the good life is possible, according to what we ourselves value most. That is what Tocqueville meant by the "notions and sentiments" of a people.

Education for democracy, then, must extend to education in moral issues, which our eighteenth century founders took very seriously indeed. This is hardly surprising. The basic ideas of liberty, equality, and justice, of civil, political, and economic rights and obligations are all assertions of right and wrong, of moral values. Such principles impel the citizen to make moral choices, repeatedly to decide between right and wrong or, just as often, between one right and another. The authors of the American testament had no trouble distinguishing moral education from religious instruction, and neither should we. The democratic state can take no part in deciding which, if any, church forms its citizens' consciences. But it is absurd to argue that the state, or its schools, cannot be concerned with citizens' ability to tell right from wrong, and to prefer one over the other in all matters that bear upon the common public life. This would be utterly to misunderstand the democratic vision, and the moral seriousness of the choices it demands of us.

Conclusions

In calling for a decisive improvement of education for democracy, we are well aware that this will require a sea-change in the typical curriculum. Specifically, we call for the following:

1. A more substantial, engaging, and demanding social studies curriculum for all of our children—one that helps students to comprehend what is important, not merely to memorize names, dates, and places. The required curriculum should include the history of the United States and of democratic civilization, the study of American government and world geography, and of at least one non-Western society in depth.

2. A reordering of the curriculum around a core of history and geography—with history providing the perspective for considered judgment and geography confronting students with the hard realities that shape so many political, economic, and social decisions. Around this core of history and geography, students should be introduced to the added perspectives offered by economics, psychology, sociology, anthropology, and political science.

3. More history, chronologically taught and taught in ways

that capture the imagination of students. Historical biography, colorful historical narrative, and debate over the central ideas that have brought us here are all appealing to students. And we recommend that a central theme in the study of history be the dramatic struggles of people around the globe and across the centuries to win, preserve, and extend their freedom.

4. More attention to world studies, especially to the realistic and unsentimental study of other nations—both democratic and non-democratic. Comparative study of politics, ideology, economics, and culture, and especially the efforts of citizens to improve their lot through protest and reform, offers students a healthy perspective on our own problems and a needed window on problems elsewhere.

5. A broader, deeper learning in the humanities, particularly in literature, ideas, and biography, so that students may encounter and comprehend the values upon which democracy depends. Through such study, moral education—not religious education and not neutral values clarification—can be restored to high standing in our schools.

We understand that such a major reform of the curriculum will require more effective textbooks and auxiliary materials, aimed less at "coverage" than at comprehension of what is most worth learning. It will require continuing collaboration between faculty members from the schools and universities, where both work together as equals to clarify what is most worth teaching in their subjects and to devise ways to convey the material to diverse clienteles. And it requires new approaches to teacher education, both pre-service and in-service, to help teachers present the revamped and strengthened curriculum.

Our proposal asks for great intensity of teaching effort. Students will not reach genuine understanding of ideas, events, and institutions through rote learning from texts, classroom lecture, and recitation followed by short-answer quizzes. We ask for active learning on the part of students—ample time for class discussions, for coaching, for frequent seminars to explore ideas, and for regular writing assignments.

We know that teachers would like nothing better than to work in this way. We also know that they cannot be expected to do so when they are responsible for 150 or more students, coming at them in a kaleidoscopic, five-times-fifty minute daily lockstep, frequently requiring three or four different preparations. We thus ally ourselves with recent calls to dramatically restructure education. Over time, we must sharply alter the management, the schedules, and the staffing patterns of our schools to afford teachers more authority, a wider latitude of methods and materials, more time to devote to the intellectual lives of fewer students, and more time to devote to their own intellectual growth.

We understand that the dramatic changes we call for—in curriculum and structure—will not come easily. We know also that these changes can be made, and must be.

As citizens of a democratic republic, we are part of the noblest political effort in history. Our children must learn, and we must teach them, the knowledge, values, and habits that will best protect and extend this precious inheritance. Today we ask our schools to make a greater contribution to that effort and we ask all Americans to help them do it.

NOTES

1. Ed. note: The author is referring to his review of five high school United States history textbooks, which prompted this essay. They are: Boorstin, Daniel J., and Brooks M. Kelley, *A History of the United States,* (Boston: Ginn, 1986); Bragdon, Henry W., and Samuel P. McCutchen, *History of a Free People* (New York: Macmillan, 1981); Davidson, James West, and Mark H. Lytle, *The United States: A History of the Republic* (Englewood Cliffs, N.J.: Prentice-Hall, 1981); Risjord, Norman K., and Terry L. Haywoode, *People and Our Coutry* (New York: Holt, Rinehart and Winston, 1982); and Todd, Lewis Paul, and Merle Curti, *Triumph of the American Nation* (New York: Harcourt Brace Jovanovich, 1986).

2. Jack Beatty, "The Patriotism of Values." *The New Republic,* July 4 and 11, 1981.

3. National Assessment of Educational Progress, *Foundations of Literacy,* 1986.

4. National Council for the Social Studies, *International Human Rights,* Society and the Schools, 1982.

5. Women's Educational Equity Act Program, "In Search of Our Past," in *World History Teacher Guide.* Funded by a grant from the U.S. Department of Education.

6. Scott McConnell, "Vietnam and the '60s Generation: A Memoir." *Commentary,* June 1985.

7. Theodore Sizer, *Horace's Compromise*. Boston: Houghton-Mifflin Company, 1984.

Mortimer J. Adler, et al., *The Paideia Proposal*. New York: McMillan Publishing Company, 1984.

Ernest Boyer, *High School*. New York: Harper & Row Company, 1983.

Thomas C. Mendenhall and James Howard, *Making History Come Alive*. Council for Basic Education, 1984.

California State Board of Education, *Model Curriculum Standards, Grades 9–12: History–Social Studies*.

PART 4

Reflections and Possibilities
New Works

. . . in which David Mathews points to the unique role of
deliberation in the education of democrats; Jane Bernard-Powers
points to the transforming power of *inclusion;* James Anthony
Whitson and William Stanley redefine *mind* and, with it, the place
of values in democratic reasoning; and a cross-cultural perspective
on citizenship education in the United Kingdom, Denmark and
Japan is provided by Ann Angell and Carole Hahn.

QUESTIONS FOR DISCUSSION

1. What problems are emphasized? Neglected?
2. What was happening in North America and the world that
   might have shaped how these problems were articulated?
3. How is democracy defined? How are diversity and mutuality
   (difference and unity) treated?
4. What are similarities and differences across the chapters?

CHAPTER 13

Reviewing and Previewing Civics

David Mathews

The Ballad of Civic Studies
by Lu Xun

General He Jian, the well-armed educator,
Has told us what in schools he'd like to see.
First comes a course that's known as "civic studies":
Perhaps you wonder what that course might be.

Good people all, I beg you to be patient
While I compile a textbook just for you.
It's not an easy thing to be a subject:
You must be very careful what you do.

Start by accepting all that they hand out:
Sweat like a pig, toil like a buffalo,
Work while you live, be eaten when you're dead,
Or if diseased be rendered down to tallow.

Next you must grasp the art of the kowtow,
First to the mighty general, our great head,
Next to that old fellow called Confucius.
Or else you're surely bound to end up dead.

Thirdly, no love: free marriage is just crap.
Better to be the nineteenth concubine,
Uphold morality, be sold for thousands,
And be to your poor parents a gold-mine.

Fourthly, do always just what you are told,
And carry out the great man's least commands,
For many are the duties of the subject:
None but the great man really understands.

But there is one more warning I must give you:
Don't cling too closely to this text of mine
In case the great man changes his ideas
And labels my "reactionary swine."[1]

He Jian, warlord of Hunan from 1929 to 1936, proposed a course of civic studies in the values he felt appropriate for China. To Lu Xun, poet with a very different conception of what China should be, He Jian's civics prompted bitter satire. Lu's ballad reminds us that questions about civic education are really answered by our responses to a prior and very political question: What kind of country do we want to live in? As answers to that question and political environments change over time, so do concepts of civic education.

CHANGING TIMES: CHANGING CIVICS

The political history of our country parades through this book's essays on civic education. To read them is to be reminded of how much political circumstances in America have influenced the way we have understood civic education.

In the beginning, our political objectives as a new nation led us to see all education as education for civic purposes. America's public schools were created to serve public or, in the broadest sense, civic rather than narrow pedagogical purposes. They were to complete the great work of the Revolution: to educate people to be citizens capable of making the dream of a New Republic into a reality.

Questions of what is good education and good schooling continued to be answered by responses to prior questions: What is the good life for individuals, what is a good community, what is a good country?[2] After the Revolution, in an era of national growth, education took on new civic purposes. Popular schooling was responsible for creating one nation out of many groups with long histories of destructive conflicts in Europe. While many other institutions have served the public interest, the schools have been charged with doing more: they were established by the public to create a continually responsible public.[3]

So civic education serves political purposes. Which ones? That issue has kept civic education at the center of a continuing debate—a debate not only about political purposes but, more fundamentally, about the nature of politics itself.

What follows is not a review of all the previous chapters in this book nor is it a complete history of civic education. Reflecting on these essays on civic education does, however, show how much changing circumstances have affected the way we have understood civic education. And that demonstration sets the stage for what this chapter will do, which is to propose a civic education appropriate to what is happening to politics today.

Dewey's essay recalls the original understanding that all of education, not just a course called "civics," should prepare citizens capable of directing a democratic society. For most of the nineteenth century the content for civic education was democratic culture in all of its forms: Fourth of July oratory, patriotic poems, songs, parades, works of art, biographies of the Founding Fathers, histories of the new nation. Civic education was a public enterprise, not just a matter of schooling. And it was largely about citizens.

By the early twentieth century our political circumstances were changing again—and so was our concept of civic education. Our early courtship with the science of Franklin and Jefferson had changed into a full-blown romance with modern, experimental science—science writ large, science with facts that had to be mastered, science with universal principles that had to be understood. As America became a scientific republic, political education took on the cast of scientific education. Gradually the notion that all education was for civic purposes was replaced by the idea that we had to have specific courses in the science of politics.

The Second World War, in which we fought against the best scientifically educated country in the world, forced us to rethink this notion of civics a bit. Why had our well-educated friends become our enemies? One persuasive answer was that they had been overcome by the mysterious powers of propaganda. We discovered that knowledge did not correlate with political attitudes. Consequently, political education was given the mission of "immunizing" Americans against the tricks of the propagandist. We put our faith in such things as "critical thinking," meaning the ability to see through the manipulative arguments of our oppressors. Because we were forced to deal with the highly subjective realities of politics—beliefs and opinions—we also used political education to impress upon students the Values of a democratic society, which were clearly distinguishable from the Values or beliefs of totalitarian societies. (Note that I always capitalize *Values* when I am referring to democratic Values or any norms or belief systems that are held in high esteem in a society. My reasons will become apparent later in this chapter when I describe other "values.")

The cold War rekindled our fear of the "wrong" Values; although at the same time—in the 1960s—we were becoming sensitive to our own diversity in opinions and cultures. As internal conflicts over race and other "closed" subjects grew, we had to find a way to recognize the importance of a core of democratic Values, but without indoctrination. The solution: teach students *how to agree* on core Values.

How did we think we could teach students this "consensus building"? We continued to have great faith in knowledge. Teachers were advised that instructional techniques for consensus building worked best when "large amounts of information had been accumulated." Yet we weren't sure. Sometimes we argued for more knowledge, meaning more information; at other times we touted the processes for acquiring knowledge—ways of knowing, like critical thinking or reflective reasoning. More articles began to appear examining the process of thinking as it was developed in group discussions. We toyed with the notion that the objective of civic instruction was not just to "know about," but rather to solve, common problems. Advocates of this approach to civic education argued that common decision making was the key to common problem solving. For example, Dean Shirley Engle at Indiana University urged that decision making by citizens be the main objective of social studies instruction.

Engle's contemporaries took the next step in the refinement of what had earlier been called critical thinking (learning how to see through propagandists' tricks). In 1966, Oliver and Shaver distinguished "critical thinking" of the World War II era from making "political judgments." Judgment was not merely judging what others said; it was making shared decisions when values on policy questions clashed. Facts had to be put into a public context in order for them to have meaning in a political dialogue. Political questions, they said, had to be "framed publicly," that is, framed in the terms in which people saw political issues "in their own minds." What did these two writers mean by the values that were important in making political judgments? Whatever they might have meant, everyone assumed they meant Values—the sacred norms of our country. And that assumption brought the house down.

Proposals to teach students how to deal with controversies by clarifying the values at work in political disputes created their own controversy. There was an adverse popular reaction to the innocent phrase "values clarification."[4] While the phrase only meant to suggest that students should recognize the role values played in political controversies, the phrase soon became a code word for the belief that the cherished Values of a democratic society were all relative. If conflicts could be resolved by deciding which Values to give priority to, then there were no enduring Values. Fearing that educators might *not* give priority to the Values they held dear, many people were outraged. And they said so—loudly. After that, a speaker could stampede an audience of teachers just by suggesting that they should try to clarify someone's Values.

Thus, by the 1970s, with the country disillusioned with the political establishment, many Americans were not as interested in agreeing on a core of common Values as in celebrating diversity and teaching the creative uses of conflict. Controversy became a positive good. Science was reinterpreted as "organized skepticism" and critical thinking was returned to its World War II definition, figuring out the oppressors. Articles suggested that we shouldn't be teaching so much conflict resolution; it was too dominant a subject in the hidden curriculum of the schools already. Schools, said revisionist historians, had done too much to perpetuate the status quo, the dominating culture, and too little to change it.[5] Schools had too long been under the influence of conservative forces.

By the 1980s we were criticizing and "deconstructing" everything, challenging established verities, including the idea that there was any such thing as established verities. Objectivity became a vulgar word for a consensus of some people that deliberately excluded others—like women and minorities. If what passed for knowledge was only someone's construct, then students should know who did the constructing and why. They should be able to assess for themselves the justice of the political consequences that followed from these constructs. New standards of political correctness challenged old standards of political correctness, most obviously on college campuses.

The writings of this new generation of political educators saw the purpose of civic education more as expanding individual freedom and expression than preserving social order or the common good. Perhaps better said, social good was redefined in terms of social justice for marginalized groups in society.

By the lights of those who worried that education would make all Values relative and in the process push their beliefs to the bottom of the priority order, their worst fears were confirmed. Higher education, for example, appeared to be in the grasp of thought police with their own standards of political correctness. Other levels of education were sure to follow.

While what is usually described as the "political correctness movement" generated a widespread reaction and a spate of articles and books, most notable Allen Bloom's best-selling *The Closing of the American Mind,* others' writings on civic education in the late 1980s turned to "new" issues. Political reasoning was not discussed, but moral reasoning was. Teaching moral reasoning was about changing ways of reasoning, not changing beliefs or Values, as articles on this subject were quick to point out. The ethical behavior of individuals also received a fair amount of attention. Under these influences, civic education becomes the moral or ethical education of individuals. Perhaps the justification was that democracies depend on citizens and leaders of good moral character.

Service education is another recent contender for reshaping civic education. Student volunteerism is up as we try to restore what many worry is an eroded sense of community. Service programs, although filled with political implications that bright students are likely to recognize, tend to be kept carefully distanced from political education. So it is difficult to say what effect, if any, these service programs will have on civic education.

Preparing students for citizenship through historical knowledge or knowledge of how governments work also continues to be very popular. One of the more recent and most comprehensive reports on civic education, the *CIVITAS* report, published in 1991 by the Council for the Advancement of Citizenship and the Center for Civic Education, devoted 500 of its 652 pages to what Harry Boyte (1994), who reviewed the report for *Teachers College Record,* called "mainstream civics." The concept of politics that informs this type of civic education often equates politics with what governments and politicians do. The role of citizens is limited to voting or to advocating for some particular interest or cause.

Citizenship is depicted as a special, though not very active, part of life. Texts sometimes claim that most Americans are too busy or too apathetic to care much about politics. While some materials urge a more active citizenship, other literature interprets disinterest as a sign of widespread satisfaction with the political system. In fact, in some cases, the political system is described as being rather independent of what citizens do, as this textbook explains:

> If the survival of the American system depended upon an active, informed, and enlightened citizenry, then democracy in America would have disappeared long ago; for the masses of America are apathetic and ill-informed about politics and public policy, and they have a surprisingly weak commitment to democratic values . . . fortunately for these values and for American democracy, the American masses do not lead, they follow. (Dye and Zeigler, 1978, p. 2)

THE POLITICS OF THE 1990s: IMPLICATIONS FOR CIVIC EDUCATION

Shortly after the *CIVITAS* report was issued, public dissatisfaction with the state of American politics hit the political establishment with the force of a pent-up volcano. The citizens of the 1990s present a new challenge for civic education, and the remainder of this chapter deals with the implications of this revolt.

A 1991 report *Citizens and Politics* (Harwood Group, 1991), which was based on a study of public attitudes about politics, provided some of the first evidence that Americans were not apathetic at all. They were "mad as the devil" about a political system they saw pushing them out of their rightful place in governing the nation.

According to the study, no interpretation of the public was less accurate than the often-repeated contention that people were apathetic or too consumed with private matters to care about politics.[6] Certainly the people who participated in the study weren't apathetic. They were just the opposite; they had a clear sense of their civic duty. And they cared so deeply that their frustration ran to anger and cynicism—a cynicism they worried about passing on to their children. Americans felt pushed out of the political system by a professional political class of powerful lobbyists, incumbent politicians, campaign managers—and a media elite. They saw a system in which votes no longer made any difference because money ruled. They saw a system with its doors closed to the average citizen.

Symptoms of this public anger had been evident for some time but not acknowledged. Low voter turnouts were almost expected, but we rationalized away the absence of this simplest form of participation. Perhaps people were asked to vote too often, or perhaps the small numbers at the ballot box meant citizens were just casting an unwritten ballot for the status quo. However, as participation at the polls dropped lower and lower, these rationalizations lost their power to placate. By the 1992 presidential election, voter anger was palpable. People voted incumbents out of office—just because they were incumbents. New laws to limit terms passed by large margins.

People talked as though American democracy had been taken over by alien beings. Lincoln's words—"government of the people, by the people, for the people"—seemed like hollow rhetoric. Even after the Clinton victory, his staff acknowledged, "Most Americans still hate politics" (Nagourney, 1992).

The citizens' revolution isn't over yet. And we are just beginning to learn its implications for civic education. Some of our insights are coming from what students tell us about the way they understand their place in the political world.

Students and Politics

In 1993 The Harwood Group completed another study, this one on how college students—America's next generation of civic leaders—felt about politics. Although students voiced many of the same criticisms that other Americans did, there were important differences between the feelings of younger and older Americans. While adults showed anger and frustration, the next generation battled far more dangerous feelings of pessimism and alienation. After all, anger can be put to constructive use and frustration is filled with political energy that can be redirected. Pessimism and alienation do not have such constructive possibilities. The difference in these feelings is profound, not merely semantic.

This is not to say that students don't care about the day-to-day issues that confront the country—about poverty or injustice or threats to the environment. Despite charges that the younger generation is preoccupied with personal self-interest, the study found that the younger generation is no more uncaring than the older generation is apathetic. *The good news is that students care a great deal.* The bad news is that the younger generation is even more cynical than the present generation about the way the political system operates and far more pessimistic about their ability to change the situation for the better.

College students who care about issues are often at a loss about how to act on their concerns in an effective way. Many don't think the political system addresses the problems they care about. And they are particularly turned off by the tone of politics today—by the extremes and negative tenor of what appears to be a grossly adversarial system with no regard for fair play. Some say the political system is "a system I'd never want to be a part of." Most alarming of all, the study found students saying, "Politics has nothing to do with my life." The older generation seldom says politics has no effect on their lives; they are angry about the kinds of effects it does have. Young people who believe that politics has no effect have crossed the line from alienation to disengagement.

These attitudes are informed by what students see on the news, by their experiences on campus, and—most of all—by the examples set by their elders.

Americans on Main Street worry that they are passing their cynicism on to the next generation. They *should* worry, because they are. Their attitudes are having a devastating effect on younger people. Americans now on Main Street are angry because they have a historic memory of a citizen's place in a democracy. They know that citizens should not be displaced by a professional political class. They remember what it means to be a citizen. So even when their anger causes them to walk away from voting in protest, they feel guilty. They have a sense of duty; they know they are supposed to vote. Students may not have such a democratic memory. Today's cynicism runs the danger of erasing more than two centuries of democratic consciousness.

Students see citizenship through a glass darkly. They often talk more about their rights, more about what government should do *for* them, than they do about their own responsibilities as citizens. They see citizenship, at best, as a deferred responsibility, something they'll think about after graduation. Even when they talk about citizenship, they say things such as "Being a citizen is your God-given right. *Politics doesn't have anything to do with being a citizen*" (emphasis added). That is an astounding and seemingly confused statement. What students mean is that being a good person is enough. They don't seem to "remember" that a citizen, by definition, is someone active in the public life of community and country—that citizens are more than individuals living responsible private lives.

Students may have to reeducate themselves *after* college in order to take their place in the democratic revolutions going on all about them. They may have to acquire what a democratic memory should have provided. For example, students' imagination of what they might do in politics is largely confined to what they might do as individuals. That is one of the reasons they often feel powerless. As an Oklahoma State student confessed, "We . . . still tend to do things that are more individualistic." A democratic memory would remind students that very little success in politics has come from individuals acting alone.

Even though students in the study were adamant in their views of politics, it would be a mistake to conclude that they will never change their minds. Attitudes aren't yet set in concrete; students are open to thinking about a different kind of politics. While they may not normally spend much time thinking about politics, when pressed on the subject, they say things such as, "There needs to be a better way." What they see happening in politics is different from what they would like to see. When given an opportunity in the focus group discussions that The Harwood Group conducted, students eagerly seized the chance to imagine what politics could be. Watching students talk about democracy was not, as someone said about watching the collapse of democratic government in Europe a generation ago, like seeing the lights go out all over the world. Sometimes the lights go on. The study found that students have retained a remarkable "instinct" for democratic practice; there is a buried civic consciousness in students.

As part of the study, researchers asked students what they thought *should* happen in politics. The question took students a while to answer because they lacked a common language to name what was on their minds. In time, however, the conversation centered on the most basic element of politics, the political debate. The debates students hear often appall them. A Wake Forest student complained, "People are very opinionated in my classes. There is no moderation at all and [the discussion] gets totally out of bounds." On or off campus, political debates seem to be dominated by extremes. These diatribes don't strike students as being capable of resolving the country's major problems. As one Morgan State student observed, "There are no solutions discussed; it is all rhetoric."

Students knew what was missing in the political discussions they criticized—a diversity of perspectives, listening, and the careful weighing of trade-offs. They could even identify what they would need to practice a different kind of politics—the ability to keep an open mind, to stand in another person's shoes, to change, and to make decisions with others. There was no indication that any of these students had studied the theory of deliberative democracy; yet they could describe the essential characteristics of a more deliberative kind of politics, a politics in which people talk and think together in order to be able to act together. What the students said points us toward a reformulation of civic education.

EDUCATION FOR PUBLIC DECISION MAKING

What students find missing in their political education and in politics itself is somewhat like what Shirley Engle and his colleagues were advocating, *but with some very important clarifications.* Students sense that constructive, problem-solving politics begins in learning the skills of making the common decisions Engle wrote about. That requires dealing with differing estimates of the worth of various proposals for common action. It requires skill in moving from first impressions to more reflective and shared judgments. But it does not require changing anyone's beliefs (which is impossible anyhow, at least in the short run). It does not require ranking Values or believing in a hierarchy of Values. While it is true that certain values inform our political actions, it does not follow that a political discussion is about understanding values of any description. The process of making political decisions is not an analytic process of values clarification. It is a messy process of making hard, practical choices about policy and action. While clarity may result, it is a by-product. Politics is not about understanding others better or having deeper personal insights, or even developing better attitudes. *Politics is about solving problems that affect, in common, people who may have little else in common*—people with all the "imperfections" in beliefs, attitudes, and ethics to which humankind is prone.

Values and "values"

One critical distinction that doesn't seem to have been made at the time of the values-clarification controversy is a critical distinction between Values as belief systems or norms (Values such as a belief in justice and freedom) and the everyday "values" or concerns that come to play in making common decisions about solving immediate political problems. Values with a capital V are things we are taught and which are no doubt valuable in politics. If people didn't believe in the Value of democracy, they wouldn't think making common decisions was important in the first place. But the "values" people consult first when making decisions about policies are no more than those things people consider valuable in everyday life. They are basic human motivations rather than ideological constructs or personal beliefs. They are the "value" we place on being secure or the "value" we place on being treated fairly in our dealings with one another. These kinds of values are somewhat the public equivalents of our private need for food and love; they have a claim on everyone to one degree or another. Milton Rokeach and Sandra J. Ball-Rokeach (1989), after studying what prompted people to respond as they did to a variety of policy questions, were able to identify most of these values, which they found to be both terminal and instrumental.

Conflict and values

When people have to make a decision, they think about how various options for action are likely to affect what is valuable to them. In specific situations, these values conflict and pull us in different directions. Yet the conflict is as much within us (since we all value many things) as it is among us. And we don't resolve such conflicts by clarifying these values or discarding some of what is valuable to us. We don't give up our basic civic motivations any more than we give up our basic personal needs.

For instance, on national defense policy, the issue really revolves around the values associated with national security. What drives the debate goes deeper than the relative merits of weapons systems. We are influenced by different notions of security. For example, we value the security that comes from being stronger than our enemies. We also value the security that comes from being far away from sources of danger. And we value the security that comes from being on good terms with those who might harm us. Security is not a general or abstract value; it has specific meanings in specific contexts. Most people are motivated, at least to some degree, by all three of these notions of security. There are few people who don't feel secure if they are stronger than what endangers them. There are few who don't feel secure when danger is far away. There are few of us who don't value being on relatively friendly terms with someone who is a potential threat.

In matters of defense, although we value all the various kinds of security, each would take us in a different policy direction. One would cause us to build a strong army; another would cause us to isolate ourselves more, and still another would cause us to rely more on our diplomatic skills. That is where the conflict arises: not over the values per se, but over which values should inform our behavior in a specific situation. Having to decide what to do when there is no certainty, when our values pull us in different directions, is what makes policy choices so hard. Real choice reflects the difficulty of having to decide among policy options, each of which has both positive and negative implications for what we find valuable.

We usually think that differences among individuals or among interest groups are the main source of conflict: environmentalists oppose developers, conservatives oppose liberals. People in one ʼmp are not likely to be in the other. When it comes to values, ⸜wever, we are often in the same camp. That is, we have similar notions about what it means to be secure. Yet despite sharing political ⸝otivations, different people order and apply their values in differe t ways. What is more, no one of us is entirely consistent in the v ⸝y we order and apply our own values. So conflict in politics is ⸝ot as simple as conflict between just two opposing sides or points of view.

Because the values in policy issues are often hidden and, when obvious, difficult to deal with, Engle and his contemporaries were on solid ground in pointing out that there is a real temptation to let facts stand in for values. Facts often mask the values at issue. Even though people try to fortify their position with all the "right facts," issues can never be resolved merely by getting the facts right. The real source of the conflict is not the facts but the values.

Still, just knowing what values are at issue is not enough. That is only good for political analysis. In political decision making we have to know the *consequences* of the choices we are considering for what we consider valuable. If, for example, a policy protecting the environment means that we would have to make certain sacrifices, such as curtailing the production of particular consumer goods, would we be willing to accept those consequences? If protection meant even greater sacrifices, perhaps the loss of jobs, would we still support the policy? Our discretion is not fully informed until we have searched out the possible consequences of the options we are considering.

When it comes to knowing the consequences of possible courses of action, we are obviously not just considering the facts, such as the capability of a new piece of medical equipment or the reactive properties of an agricultural chemical. We are not just concerned with something's physical or chemical properties; we are estimating something's worth.

Estimating the worth of actions and making a judgment is hardly an exact science. We can't use the same standard we use for deciding whether the facts are correct. Yet, there is a standard for assessing political judgment and holding one another accountable for our opinions. We aren't just left with relativism, having to throw up our hands and say that one person's opinions are as good as another's. The standard we can use is *soundness*. Soundness means that the public knows and accepts the consequences of the actions it favors. Obviously, we can't be certain about what the consequences of our choices will be until we act. Still, we can use our history and our imagination to anticipate the likely effects of what is proposed. For a public to reach sound judgments about how it should act, citizens have to do what judges do in court. That is, they have to reach judgments with due regard for both what they hold valuable and what they know of the situations before them.

Surely one of the critical functions of civic education in a democracy is to prepare us to make sound decisions with others when the consequences are great and there is no authority to tell us exactly what we should do. Civic education has to prepare us for making public judgments. How, then, are we to go about making shared judgments? How can we increase the chances that our public decisions will be sound decisions?

THE PROCESS OF DECIDING: DELIBERATION

How can we avoid the violent upheavals that have occurred throughout history when countries have been unable to answer questions of what should be or reach shared judgments?

Making hard choices requires a certain kind of public discussion—a dialogue in which people engage one another face-to-face and eye-to-eye. Communities or countries that cannot talk together in this way cannot work together democratically. Not any kind of talk will do. The talk we need to make sound choices has one overriding characteristic—it must be deliberative.

A deliberative dialogue is not the same as other forms of political discourse. Usually when we talk politically we talk to express or persuade. People voice their needs and desires. They try to persuade one another that their cause or candidate is the right one. Yet, as important as expression and persuasion are, democratic politics requires more.

Deliberation is open, exploratory dialogue, the kind of dialogue college students in the Harwood study said they often found missing on campus. Deliberation is not taking positions and scoring points to win. Deliberation is the act of weighing carefully; it implies stepping back in reflection, so we can really see what is before us. When we deliberate, we evaluate the consequences of various options and, most of all, the views of others. In deliberating, we do publicly what we do personally when we are genuinely uncertain about what we should do—we try to keep our minds open to all alternatives so that we are not locked in by past positions.

DEALING WITH CONFLICTS: FINDING COMMON GROUND FOR ACTION

Even when people deliberate, making sound choices is very difficult. For every course of action we like, we discover there are serious costs and constraints that we don't like. Imagine it is Friday night. You come home from work late; you are tired. But your spouse, who has also had a difficult week, wants to go out to dinner. Your children want you to take them to the movies. Your mother-in-law calls and invites you over for dinner. And no sooner have you put down the phone than your boss calls and asks if you would come back to work for two more hours. You value your marriage, your children, your job, and your mother-in-law, but you have to decide what you should do as a family on this particular evening. You can't resolve the problem by doing away with one of the things you value. Neither can you do everything everyone wants you to do. and there is no authority who can give you the "right" answer.

That is very much like the dilemma we face in public life when we make a choice. There is no escaping the contradicting pulls and tugs on our time, no escaping the constraints on what we can do— and no escaping the frustrations that go with these dilemmas. How then can we resolve conflicts that are rooted so deeply in what is valuable to us? Agreement or consensus may be unlikely, compromise hard to achieve.

In politics, we react to constraints and inconsistencies between what we value and the way we want to behave much as we do in other facets of our lives. First we have to "work through" those reactions to constraint and loss so that we are again in control and able to make sound choices about our future.

"Working through" is an apt phrase for describing what we do in dealing with difficult choices because as people begin to face up to political costs and conflicts in their own views, they often react with a sense of shock that they have to overcome. People can be immobilized politically in somewhat the way they are personally immobilized when confronted with a crisis or loss in their family. Daniel Yankelovich (1981, pp. 190–91), noted survey analyst, tells the story of a man in his mid-fifties who learns that he will not receive the pension he had been counting on for his retirement. At first he is angry, incredulous, suspicious, and depressed. But over time he may regain his composure, if he has "worked through" the loss of his pension. He might have found an alternative source of income or accepted the inevitability of a lower standard of living. In any event, he will have reoriented his thinking and emerged from the emotional storms that made it impossible to act in his best interest.

As people begin to work their way through a political issue, they look for a "way" to navigate through the conflicts, or they find a series of actions that are as consonant as possible with all that is valuable to them.

Recall the example of the conflict about what to do on Friday night, when there were more demands on our time than we could handle. In that kind of situation, we don't devalue our family or our job. We find the best way we can to chart a general direction and try to integrate all the demands on our time. We may go to dinner with our spouse first, take the children to a matinee the next day, reschedule dinner with our mother-in-law for the next week, and spend a few hours at the office on Sunday afternoon. These aren't exactly compromises nor exercises in setting priorities. Even together, they certainly aren't a course of action that everyone agrees is just right. These are just a series of actions that all point in the same direction; they were put together in the way we put a puzzle together. That is what also happens in politics when it works as it should. We don't necessarily agree, we just find practical ways to move ahead.

Deliberative forums assist in the search for ways to move ahead by helping locate *common ground for action*. Common ground for action is not total agreement. It is usually a range of diverse actions that point in the same direction and, in the best of all worlds, are mutually reinforcing. One community leader summed up the results of one deliberative forum this way: "Here are five statements about what might be done on the issue we have discussed. Not everyone agreed with all of them, but there is nothing in them that we couldn't live with." While there was no unanimous agreement, the five statements pointed to a range of complementary actions that seemed reasonable—actions that were politically permissible.

TEACHING A DELIBERATIVE PUBLIC POLITICS

Like all skills, deliberation is best taught by practice—we teach students to play a piano by having them practice on a keyboard. We teach students art by having them paint and sculpt. We teach students deliberative politics by having them deliberate. Only deliberation will teach deliberation.

The implications for classrooms are obvious. They have to become forums where students engage one another directly in an exchange that is not always mediated by a teacher playing the role of Socrates. Classrooms have to allow for a dialogue rather than demand a debate. Students have to be free to explore to be tentative, to test ideas. The classroom forum, like all deliber ive forums, has to work toward a choice. Just airing views and ga iering information isn't enough. Students have to learn that choice work is real work—and *their* work.

Classrooms have to be forums because learning democratic politics—like learning science and music—requires laboratories and practice rooms. One educator who promotes this practical approach to civic learning is Mary McFarland, instructional coordinator of K–12 studies for the Parkway School District of St. Louis. She works with teachers, at all levels and throughout the district, who hold classroom deliberations, using National Issues Forums (NIF) study guides.[7] These issue books are also used by thousands of civic and educational groups around the country; the NIF books are specifically designed to stimulate deliberation.

McFarland (1993) describes these classroom forums as "the closest thing students do to real citizen activity." She says, "In fact it *is* citizen activity. It's not fabricated or contrived. It is education linked to the real world, so it's the best form of civic learning. This kind of real world education should be the focus of the social studies curriculum.

Deliberation not only teaches a practical political skill; it teaches a way of thinking and knowing that depends on public dialogue. Deliberation allows us to know those things we can know only when we are together—things we could never know if we are alone and unengaged. Deliberation is necessary for the development of civic intelligence and public thinking. This is not the same as critical thinking understood as a critique of what others are doing politically. Public thinking's job is to *create*, not *critique*. Political thinking has to find answers to quintessential political questions. What kind of community or country do we want to live in? What should we do in response to the problems that invade our lives and rob our future? Civic education must develop a student's capacity to think publicly!

THE ULTIMATE CHALLENGE: ENRICHING OUR CONCEPT OF POLITICS

Why isn't public deliberation more a part of public education? The major obstacle is probably not pedagogical; it is in the way we usually think about or define politics. As long as politics remains primarily what governments and politicians do, as long as there isn't much for citizens to do—there will be very little to teach in civics.

The conventional definition of politics is deeply entrenched. Children learn it from the dinner table and the television set long before they ever enter school. Everybody knows how our political system works. Talk to any community in the country, to any college group, to any assembly of high school students, to any collection of U. S. senators and you will get exactly the same story.

It's very simple. We're organized into interest groups which compete with one another in a political arena that is like a marketplace with all kinds of competition and transactions. Some of the interest groups are able to amass a majority and get legislation passed and candidates elected because of their skill in manipulating the public and the media. The function of government is to adjudicate this competition and distribute resources as dictated by the outcomes. Everybody knows this is how politics works. And it's true. That's the way *part* of politics works.

Why so much of civic education is about the procedures of government—or the way a law is passed—is obvious. If politics is nothing but self-interest, how could anyone teach you your own self-interest? And if the activities of politics are really the down-in-the-trenches, friction of factions—transactions, deals, manipulations—who would ever think of going to school to learn such matters? So why do we teach politics as though it were a spectator sport? Because with politics understood as self-interested transactions, about all that is left to teach is how to keep score on government.

While few doubt that this is the way the system works, there is a widespread feeling that something is missing in this kind of politics. And what is missing is the public and its deliberations. Public deliberation gives democratic direction to government and common purpose to citizen action. It is the process by which the public defines the public's interest, a definition that is essential if representative governments are to operate effectively. Public deliberation is the way the public creates enough common ground so that people can act together to solve their problems. It is the essential preliminary to the creation of public responsibility and will. (People feel most responsible for what they have decided.) And deliberation is the gateway that brings private individuals into the public realm.

Interest-group competition can't substitute for public deliberation, the thoughtful interaction of a body politic holding counsel
with itself. And neither can governments.

There are some things that governments—even if they are
working perfectly and run by angels—can never do. No government can create its own legitimacy. No government can create
commonality. That is, governments can build common highways,
but they cannot build common ground. Neither can governments
create public will. Finally, no government, not even the very best
government, can create citizens.

Can anybody imagine a democratic system operating without
publicly defined interests, common ground, political will, and citizens? Certainly not. Unless we are willing to accept an anemic
democracy, we can't leave the public out of politics or relegate it to
the sidelines by treating citizens as no more than critical consumers
or clients of the states. We can't respond effectively to the rising
tide of public cynicism about the political system just by telling
people to vote. We have to tell them about the politics that comes
before voting—the politics that informs voting and continues after
the elections are over. We have to teach students the skills of deliberation, the essential skills for opening up politics to them as citizens.

We have to put the public and all that it does—good and bad—
back into our concept of politics. We have to broaden our concept
of politics to recognize the many roles citizens have to play before
we can write a distinctively new chapter in the history of civic
education.

NOTES

1.   *Lu Xun Selected Poems*, translated by W. J. F. Jenner. (Beijing:
Foreign Languages Press, 1982) pp. 113–15.

2.   See Cremin (1990).

3.   Lawrence Cremin was not the only person to see a connection
between education and America's larger political purposes. For another
account of this connection see Welter (1962).

4.   By "values clarification," I am referring to an approach suggested by Engle (1960) and chapter 6, this volume. As Engle writes, "The
question of what values he should hold probably cannot be settled in the
classroom, but values can be dealt with intelligently in the classroom.

The nature of the values which people hold can be made explicit, the issues over values can be clarified, and the ends to which holding to a particular value will lead can be established factually to some extent. . . . We can compare and appraise value, to some extent, in an extended hierarchy of values from lower value, such as a preference for having one's hair cut in a segregated barber shop, to higher values, such as the belief that all men should be treated with equal respect" (pp. 305–6).

5. For example, see Tyack and Hansot (1982, p. 8). Tyack and Hansot describe some of these revisionists' views of the educational past, citing the works of Merle Curti, George Counts, and Michael B. Katz.

6. This discussion of citizens' attitudes about politics is adapted from Mathews (1994).

7. National Issues Forums are a network of nonpartisan political discussions held in more than 5,000 communities nationwide. For twelve years NIF issue books have been prepared and published jointly by two nonpartisan research foundations, Kettering Foundation and Public Agenda Foundation. Regular and abridged editions of these issue books are copyrighted by the National Issues Forums Institute and, since 1988, printed by Kendall/Hunt Publishing Company, Dubuque, Iowa. College editions have been published since 1992 by McGraw-Hill, Inc., New York.

REFERENCES

Boyte, H. (1994). [Review of the book *Civitas: A framework for civic education*]. *Teachers College Record*, 95 (3):414–418.

Cremin, L. (1990). *Popular education and its discontents*. New York: Harper and Row.

Dye, T. R., & Zeigler, L. H. (1978). *The irony of democracy*. North Scituate, MA: Duxbury.

Engle, S. H. (1960). Decision making: The heart of social studies instruction. *Social Education*, 24(7): 305–306.

Harwood Group, The. (1991). *Citizens and politics: A view from main street America*. Dayton, OH: Kettering Foundation.

_____. (1993). *College students talk politics*. Dayton, OH: Kettering Foundation.

Mathews, D. (1994). *Politics for people*. Urbana: University of Illinois Press.

McFarland, M. (1993, December). Personal communication.

Nagourney, A. (1992, 5 November) Clinton faces "challenges we wanted." *USA Today*, p. 1A.

Rokeach, M., & Ball-Rokeach, S. J. (1989, May). Stability and change in American value priorities. *American Psychologist*, pp. 775–84.

Tyack, D., & Hansot, E. (1982). *Managers of virtue*. New York: Basic.

Welter, R. (1962). *Popular education and democratic thought in America*. New York: Columbia University Press.

Yankelovich, D. (1981). *New rules: Searching for self-fulfillment in a world turned upside down*. New York: Random House.

CHAPTER 14

The "Woman Question" in Citizenship Education

Jane Bernard-Powers

In a 1911 *Education Review* article Annie G. Porritt, a conservative American from Hartford, Connecticut, eschewed the common practice of allowing women to educate the future citizens of the United States and challenged the notion that women should be educated for citizenship. She wrote:

> [I]f the training for politics and for the larger life of the nation is necessary for boys, it is manifestly absurd to give such training for girls—training which would unfit them for their own sphere. (p. 448)

This narrow perspective on the political and civic roles of women reflects the ambivalence some Americans felt about women's growing influence and presence in public life. Yet the truth embedded in Porritt's perspective was that women were not really citizens in the full and literal sense of the word: they could not vote in national elections by virtue of law and they could not hold public office by virtue of ordinance and tradition. The "ladies" had not been remembered as Abigail Adams had cautioned her husband John Adams during the deliberations on the Constitution andas a result women were marginalized as citizens in

I gratefully acknowledge the contributions of Lynda Stone, Carole Hahn, and Wendy Saravasy to this paper.

the most literal interpretation of citizenship in a democracy. The definitive yardstick of citizen was man, and women were the Other.

In the fall of 1947, thirty-six years after Annie Porritt argued for limiting civic education for women, an exhibit of documents and memorabilia called "The Freedom Train" began a journey that would cover 322 cities for the purpose of reestablishing the common ground of all Americans, and "creat[ing] an ideal vision of America's past that would supersede contemporary partisan conflict and racial, class, and ethnic antagonisms." Embedded in the pictures and memorabilia of the exhibit was the clear message that women were still marginal citizens and that citizenship was still defined on the basis of normative male activities. According to American historian Stuart Little (1993), this reaffirmation of a media image of American citizenship was a response to post–World War II economics and social tensions. Race, class, regional differences, and gender were subsumed under a monolithic image of the ideal American citizen; a white, middle-class man who earned a good living, paid taxes, and upheld the American way of life.

If the essential American citizen characterized in the Freedom Train exhibit existed, he represented a minority. Yet the image of the ideal citizen—male and white—projected in the exhibit has prevailed in the public world of political and community life, and in media representations such as textbooks. Women and minorities and their (our) concerns continue to occupy marginal status in corridors and staterooms of public power.

Mirroring and echoing this marginalization is the wealth of literature on educating citizens for democratic life. The bulk of foundational and historical readings in this volume address dimensions of education for participation in a democracy without considering gender and minority concerns. Diversity in all its modern/postmodern complexity is invisible; hidden behind seamless and universal representations of the democratic man and democratic thought.

Some works could be characterized as more gender friendly than others. John Dewey validates the social aim of education in relation to the greater society; Rugg envisions a curriculum that would consider social and political problems; and Apple identifies the stultifying effect of implied consensus in texts which ignore conflict as a dynamic in schools and society. Newman suggests that learning how to influence public policy and public affairs is a critical focus for democratic education. Most of these perspectives can be construed to hold meaning for women and underrepresented minorities; none are direct in addressing the depth and scope of marginalization of diverse populations in society generally, and citizenship education specifically. Thus the issue of gendered multicultural perspectives is invisible in the text of democratic education writings included herein, with the possible exception of Gagnon, who seems openly hostile to gender concerns, eschewing what he sees as partisan perspectives and the deprecation of liberal democratic values evident in some women's history materials.

Given the relative invisibility of diverse voices and identities in the historical sample collected in this volume and the impenetrable authoritative voice of democratic education text generally, my own project in this chapter is to venture outside that text both to critique it and to provide a sense of the possibilities that arise from multicultural feminist scholarship. Alternative voices and critiques from women's studies have considered the relationship between historically marginalized (and invisible) citizens and education for participatory democracy.

This chapter raises multiple issues and perspectives germane to women and democratic education, but three should be noted. First, the silence of curriculum theorists and researchers in social studies regarding feminisms and multiculturalisms creates a clear need to explore issues of female identity and education for citizenship both historically and in a contemporary sense. This is "spade work" that preceeds "solutions" or prescriptions.

Second, women and minorities who were and are politically marginalized have constructed their own citizen identities from the margins. Community roles, work roles, and power relations in more intimate settings have served as a basis for citizen identity formation and action.

Third, the tension between equality and difference is particularly important for appreciating the complex relationship between women and the state. Engendering democratic education requires an understanding of the delicately balanced bridge between the need to acknowledge qualities that are distinctive to a group (e.g., women), and the need for equity based on universal rights and principles.

The chapter is based on ideas that have emerged in feminist studies over the past twenty years. The central focus is how women have creatively negotiated the boundaries and bridges between public and private, equality and difference. How have women identified themselves as citizens and what is the historical frame for women and citizenship education in schools and in the community? These questions are addressed in the first section of the chapter, which begins with a note about John Dewey. The second section turns to more contemporary considerations of engendering and diversifying the text and the goals of citizenship education in the interest of transformation. The third section, entitled "Meanings and Conclusions," weaves the story together. The reader is asked to be aware of the unevenness that attends this relatively unexplored terrain. It is a story in the making and is characterized by rough edges.

HISTORICAL PERSPECTIVES ON WOMEN, CITIZENSHIP, AND EDUCATION

In this section on historical perspectives I propose that historical sources provide information and perspectives on the development of ideas about women as citizens. Because their citizen roles were limited in a formal sense, women created networks and institutions in their communities and organizations. These were designed to meet the needs of citizens who didn't have access to formal power: women, children, senior citizens, and families. Moreover, developing networks, institutions, and leadership in the nineteenth century created intergenerational precedents on which twentieth-century feminists could build. Ultimately the early feminist movements resulted in the use of political power based on the differences between men and women, a blurring of distinctions between the private sphere of home and family and the public sphere of politics and power, and a sustaining historical precedent for contextualized, community-based, woman-citizen action.

John Dewey is an important source of ideas about women and democratic education because he was an influential Progressive Era curriculum theorist and philosopher. This historical discussion briefly considers John Dewey's feminism, and then turns to the broader context of the development of feminist/womanist citizen roles in the progressive era (Brown, 1990).

I pose this question: Was John Dewey, author of one of the readings in part 1 of this text, a closet Progressive Era feminist who really envisioned a sex-equitable social education for young people? The topic of John Dewey's feminism or lack thereof has been discussed in feminist philosophy and curriculum circles in recent years (Laird, 1988). I would argue that had John Dewey lived in a later time, he might have been a strong liberal feminist. But given the contest of his life, the Progressive Era and the hotly debated "Woman Question," he waffled on issues of feminism like most of his contemporaries.

John Dewey and his wife Alice Chipman Dewey established the Laboratory School at the University of Chicago in 1896, the same year that Hull House opened its doors in Chicago (Lagemann, 1989). Dewey was comfortable in his working relations with women, according to historians Lagemann and Laird and he collaborated with and worked alongside women in the Laboratory School as well as in Hull House. He seemed to appreciate the significance of intimacy created in work spaces, and in the Laboratory School he definitively established the practice of coeducation, arguing the virtues of boys and girls working together side-by-side to learn from each other. He even marched for women's suffrage in New York City (Laird, p. 117).

A contrasting position to what might be characterized as support for sex-equitable education is found in his article on coeducation, published in The Ladies Home Journal in 1911. In this article, entitled "is Co-Education Injurious to Girls," Dewey followed the lead of educators in his day by presenting domestically defined life experiences for women as normative. He supported education in home economics for young women and seemed to believe that their education should be differentiated from that of young men. Dewey was able to envision steps toward gender equality, but as was true for many of his contemporaries, the social traditions associated with separate spheres were not so easily moved—at least when he was writing for a women's magazine.

The kind of ambivalence evident in Dewey's statements about coeducation were typical of Progressive Era views about women and they are germane to this discussion of citizenship education. Citizenship and education have existed in an inadequately articulated relationship with domestic or family roles for wom n: it was in the Progressive Era that the discussion was explicit an unapologetic.

The Progressive Era is a particularly significant period to focus on because it was a time of change in the scope of women's participation in community affairs and it was a time when women's various societal roles and dispositions were being debated—both in the United States and in other parts of the world. "The Woman Question" was the expression that referred to this lively debate over women's psychological, intellectual, and physical capabilities; a debate which influenced educational decisions. John Dewey contributed to this discussion over women's education and their biologic and social destiny along with a vast number of citizens who read popular periodicals such as the *Ladies Home Journal* and the *Popular Science Monthly* (Laird, 1988; Newman, 1985).

Educational, work, and political roles for women were changing in that period and the changes were a source of great concern. Many women were knocking at the doors of higher education and secondary schools, having found that either the knowledge of clerical skills and English grammar or the credential would lead to higher paying or higher status jobs. In 1893, 19,154 young women graduated from high school, compared with 10,256 young men in the United States. The growing numbers of young women in school prompted a steady stream of articles published in the late nineteenth and early twentieth century about the deleterious or uplifting effects of education on women.

Women were also entering the paid work force in unprecedented numbers. Writing in her well-known book on women's education, Wyllistine Goodsell noted that "the steady and increasing influx of women into gainful occupations is . . . one of the most striking phenomena of the twentieth century" (Goodsell, 1924, p. 105). Department of Labor statistics cited by Goodsell show that the 17.4 percent of all females 10 years and over who worked in 1880 grew to 18.8 percent in 1900, and then 23.4 percent in 1910. Women's increasing presence in the workplace precipitated conservative responses among some segments of the population much as education had. Belief in the fragile feminine constitution influenced decisions such as the *Muller v. Oregon* Supreme Court case which limited the hours that women could work based on the apparent belief that "the prevailing ten-hour workday was likely to leave a woman exhausted, her high instincts dulled, craving only excitement and sensual pleasure" (Smuts, 1976).

This conservative attitude extended to the kinds of work and decision making women were engaged in. For example, a judge in Wisconsin prevented women from becoming justices of the court because the issues considered would be unsuitable for women's ears and sensibilities: "It would be shocking to man's reverence for womanhood and faith in woman that women should be permitted to mix professionally in all the nastiness of the world . . . sodomy, incest, rape, seduction, fornication, adultery, pregnancy, bastardy, legitimacy, prostitution, . . . divorce" (Newman, 1985, p. 247).

There were, of course, women who were outspoken and well-spoken defenders of women's rights in the work place, in voting booths, and in social institutions such as families. Writing in defense of universal suffrage and in answer to the exhortations of an antisuffrage man in *Popular Science Monthly,* Alice Tweedy observed that "thousands of women work in the mines of Belgium, England and Cornwall." She argued that they are not unsexed by it, they carry their weight in the world's work, they are not privileged by virtue of their femininity, and they deserve the right to represent themselves through the ballot (Newman, 1985, p. 233).

The parameters of women's idealized "traditional sphere"—hearth and children—were challenged in the Progressive Era by these indicators of change, much as in the 1960s and 1970s. The reality of women's visible presence in fields, halls, and shops of industry; in schools; and in organizations such as unions, suffrage groups, and women's clubs was both a reflection and precipitator of change. Thus conflicts and differences in belief over women's place in the social, economic, and political orders resulted in an expanded conception of women's roles and responsibilities as citizens. Embedded in the contextual issues were considerations of the connections between public and private spaces and domains, expectations of women's impact on political institutions and communities, equality and difference issues, and activism and a potentially transformed idea of democratic participation.

Ideas about women's role in society and their contributions to the state evolved over time, as Linda Kerber notes in her writing about rethinking the Progressive Era (Kerber, 1982). The Progressive Era is historically connected to events in the early nineteenth century, when in the early years of the nation state (1800–1840), white middle-class women were idealized as mothers of future citizens. "Republican Motherhood" is how Linda Kerber characterizes the role of women in the new country. Women—mainly white women, because African Americans were not highly visible in relation to the formal state—moved into academies and seminaries to learn how to be excellent housekeepers and to gain competencies for keeping a school. The perception of the role of women in relation to citizenship changed in this period from private citizen in male-headed households to citizen engaged in an activity of the state: educating future citizens (Kerber, 1982). The freedom and independence that came from education stirred many young women to pursue education for teaching, and the seedbeds of feminism were thus quietly sown in the common schools of the nineteenth century.

The nineteenth century provided the context for dramatic changes in the way women related as citizens to their communities. For African American women, working for "the race" began during slavery. Within the slave community, women not only played key roles in the development of family, education, and religion, but also developed a women's network that was a source of strength, leaders, and mutual aid (Gilkes, 1994). The creation of schools, churches, and networks of community support expanded during the nineteenth century and into the first decades of the twentieth century.

Middle-class Anglo-European and African American women of the late nineteenth and early twentieth century established a substantially expanded citizen role for themselves by virtue of both the limitations placed on them as well as the inherent opportunities of the period (Kerber, 1982). Even before suffrage, or perhaps especially before suffrage, women wanted a voice in the running of affairs of government and they marshaled their community-based power to organize and lobby for "women's issues," usually within the protection of women's organizations.

The National Women's Trade Union League was typical of these Progressive Era feminist organizations. It was an organization of several hundred women—mainly, but not exclusively, middle-class and white—who lobbied for, among other things, equal access to the trades for women. They were active proponents of equal educational opportunities for young women in the trades, and they networked with suffrage groups and other labor groups to advance their causes. Their motto was "A Working Wage to Guard the Home," and they worked to advance the position of all women connected to industrial occupations. They were well connected to Progressive Era politicians, by virtue of their leadership, and when they needed to rally behind a cause—the Federal Commission on Vocational Education, for example, or a suffrage demonstration—they were able to call on women from their various urban branches to lobby, write letters, or demonstrate (Bernard-Powers, 1992).

The General Federation of Women's Clubs, another prominent Progressive Era organization, had close to a million members, and they were joined in their activism for community issues by organizations such as the National Federation of Business and Professional Women's Clubs, the National Consumer's League, and the Women's Christian Temperance Union. The Urban League, the National Association of Colored Women, and the Association for the Study of Afro-American Life were among the organizations that, along with churches and missionary societies, worked for African American community interests such as maintaining children's homes, antilynching crusades, and organizing household workers (Gilkes, 1994). The women who supported progressive causes through organization building shared a common belief that women's interests—family health, children's welfare, family economies—had to be moved to the front of the public agenda and that women were best equipped to understand those needs and to address them.

Modern industrial society, according to feminists such as Jane Addams, had forced women to follow traditionally home-based concerns out into the community and the marketplace (Addams, 1914). "The home going forth into the world," as Frances Willard characterized it, meant that domestic feminists' interests would include environmental concerns such as pure air, water, and food; social issues such as protective labor legislation for women and children; education issues such as home economics and industrial training for working-class children; and political issues such as suffrage, because the vote was critical to protecting women's interests.

Progressive Era organizations served as a training ground for women leaders and there was an impressive group of women who championed Progressive Era women's causes and mediated the complexities of poverty and class and race oppression. Jane Addams, Grace Abbott, Mary Dreier, Margaret Dreier Robins, Agnes

Nestor, Sophonisba Breckenridge, Florence Kelly, and a young Eleanor Roosevelt were eastern and midwestern women who lead organizations. They worked alongside, (and only occasionally with) gifted African American women such as Lucy Laney, Mary McLeod Bethune, Ida Wells, Mary Jackson McCrorey, and Josephine St. Pierre Ruffin (James and James, 1985).

Lucy Craft Laney is a particularly good example of a civic leader whose community organizing could inspire generations of young women. President Carter named her as one of the three most important African Americans in Georgia's history, and her portrait hangs in the state house. Her prominence as a citizen was based on a number of contributions to African American social welfare, including the establishment and maintenance of a school in Augusta, Georgia, named Haines Normal and Industrial School, and her mentoring of young women such as Mary McLeod Bethune, Janie Porter Barett, and Charlotte Brown Hawkins, who went on to establish their own schools. She was a nationally recognized spokesperson for African American welfare issues and she was a leader in welfare activism in her own community. She was instrumental in establishing kindergartens for African American children in Augusta, she set up a nursing program at Haines, and she recruited artists such as Marion Anderson and Frederick Douglass's nephew, a violinist, to perform on the campus for the community in general (Bernard-Powers, 1994).

African American women defined their citizen roles to include both racial issues and women's issues. For example, Lucy Laney objected to racist governance and operations policies in the Phyllis Wheatley branch of the YWCA in Georgia. She lobbied the National YWCA office, along with other prominent African American women, to change racist policy, which stipulated that decisions made by African American women had to be approved by white women. The African American women went as a group to present their objections to the national board but they met with limited success (Neverdon-Morton, 1989). The point of this example is to suggest that the tactics and many of the concerns of women's civic organizations were the same, but there were also important differences created by race relations and racism.

A final chapter in this historical case-study of gender and citizenship is found in the postsuffrage period, when the needs of communities writ broad became the formal civic agenda of women's organizations and networks. As characterized by Lemons (1975) in his book about social feminism, "women saw the link between suffrage and temperance and other crusades such as civil service reform, conservation, child-labor laws, mothers' pensions, municipal improvements, educational reform, pure food and drug laws, industrial commissions, social justice, and peace" (p. ix). Individual women's organizations such as the National Consumer's League, directed by Florence Kelly, lobbied for legislation such as child labor laws, but they also joined forces under the umbrella of a mother organization called the Women's Joint Congressional Caucus. The genesis of this organization came "at the invitation of the League of Women Voters," which invited ten organizations whose membership totaled ten thousand to form an umbrella organization to push for "women's issues." This organization was called by friends "the most powerful lobby in Washington," and for a brief period following the winning of suffrage, legislators took women's concerns seriously. In particular, the Sheppard-Towner Maternity and Infancy Protection Act in 1921 was supported by a lobby that was described in the *American Medical Association Journal* as "the most powerful and persistent that had ever invaded Washington." It was, of course, the WJCC (Lemons, 1975). Without actually raising the issue of women's candidacy for public office, women seized power by leveraging their potential votes and by knocking on the doors of legislators and media people.

CITIZENSHIP EDUCATION AND SCHOOLING

The Progressive Era was marked by change in the lives of women. It was not abrupt change, as Linda Kerber (1982) so ably demonstrates: the history of women's evolution toward full participation as citizens—however we define that—spans the nineteenth and the twentieth centuries. As the late-twentieth-century women's movement is an extension of the Progressive Era women's movement, so are current conversations about gender and citizenship in schooling connected to Progressive Era ideas and issues. The legacy of family concerns, community welfare, and the economic, social, and political status of women is an unfinished agenda in public schools and a work-in-progress. These issues are also the basis for discussion in this second section, which considers contemporary feminist perspectives and research on the needs of young women.

Carol Gilligan's research on adolescent women, developed over the last decade, is particularly relevant for a discussion of social studies and [en]gendered citizenship. Beginning with the research for her book *In a Different Voice* (1982), Gilligan has written, coauthored, and edited a number of works that have taught readers about the relational worlds of young adolescent women and the loss of voice they seem to experience. In a brief overview of the work that she has done with Lynn Mikel Brown, Annie Rogers, Deborah Tolman, and other women associated with the Harvard Project on the Psychology of Girls and Women, Gilligan found that at about age eleven and twelve young women who were coming out of girlhood experienced a significant shift in their ability to articulate their feelings. They seemed to lose their voice or their power to speak with passion and conviction. The significance of the loss of voice is linked to issues of self-esteem and the needs of young women for sustained connection with others. Gilligan characterizes it as a "time when girls' desire for relationships and knowledge comes up against the wall of Western Culture" (Gilligan, 1993, p. 165). The need to know about the really important things, such as how relationships work and what motivates humans, gets subverted by other coded versions of important knowledge imposed by authoritarian voices. Gilligan quotes Ann Frank's diary in a passage that questions gender relations and justice:

> A question that has been raised more than once and that gives me no inner peace is why did so many nations in the past, and often still now treat women as inferior to men? Everyone can agree on just how unjust this is, but that is not enough for me. I would like to know the cause of the great injustice. (Frank, quoted in Gilligan, 1993, p. 145)

Young women, as Gilligan and her colleagues are finding, need to find and to exercise the voice that asks questions of relations, motivation, and moral dilemmas.

Young women need to find and see themselves in the school community and in the formal and informal curricula of citizenship education: "Humans desire to know, to be known, and to find their locations as members of communities (Pagano, 1991, p. 260). Citizenship education should constitute an imaginative field where "we acknowledge our identifications and claim our places as members of our communities" (p. 260). Yet for a young woman in our society, it is a dilemma of how to listen both to herself and to the tradition. Buss (1991) characterizes this connected and disconnected political and emotional terrain as "double discourses." The encouragement to do that—to connect the emotional and political terrain—needs to be acknowledged and understood in sites of citizenship education in schools, especially social studies classrooms.

Myra and David Sadker have recently organized research on the gender effects in schools. Their work *Failing at Fairness* (1994) and the American Association of University Women study *Short Changing Girls, Short Changing America* (1992) identify patterns in elementary and secondary schools that contribute to the silencing of girls and young women:

> Then girls and women learn to speak softly or not at all; to submerge honest feelings, withhold opinions, and defer to boys; to avoid math and science as male domains; to value neatness and quiet more than assertiveness and creativity; to emphasize appearance and hide intelligence. Through this curriculum in sexism they are turned into educational spectators instead of players. (Sadker and Sadker, p. 13)

As the Sadkers point out, many girls representing different ethnic and racial groups leave school disadvantaged in ways that were not present when they entered.

Learning to be silent in schools is one result of the ongoing sexual harassment that many students experience in school hallways, classrooms, and cafeterias. A 1993 American Association of University Women survey conducted by Louis Harris and Associates reported a high incidence of sexual harassment of both boys and girls in schools. "Sixty-five percent of girls and 42 percent of boys say they have been grabbed, touched, or pinched in a sexual way," and yet sexual harassment was not considered a legitimate problem in high schools and elementary schools until recently. "When a student is harassed by peers in public, observers as well as the victim feel threatened and intimidated" (Sadker and Sadker, 1994, p. 115). The students lose faith in the adults around them and in schools to protect them. The climate stays "chilly" and the silence that develops is profound, as Gilligan and her colleagues have found.

It is significant that many of the same issues that feminist theorists and educators are grappling with are being discussed in legal education and justice systems. As the report of the Ninth Circuit Task Force on Gender Bias notes, gender matters "inside and outside of the classroom, for judges, for lawyers, and litigants, in myriad ways that are inconsistent with our ideal of equal justice" (1993). Sexual harassment, innuendoes, differential treatment, and knowledge of gender issues are problems in the legal system, just as they are in public school classrooms. In the legal system and in schools, females show up with the expectation that their needs and interests will be considered fairly alongside those of their male counterparts. What they find is that gender bias leads to their needs being ignored—and this is a cross-racial and cross-ethnic issue.

The curriculum writ broad of the Progressive Era, which concerned families, health, the environment, the needs of elderly, the special needs of children, infant mortality, and a host of other issues that shape the quality of life, needs to be reintroduced into the schools (Bernard-Powers, 1992). Just as the Ninth Circuit Gender Bias Report comments, the problems that may have special significance to women—for example family life, domestic violence, and sexual harassment—need to be acknowledged as a formal part of the agenda.

The goal for schools and their communities is both to acknowledge these experiences and to use them to transform the agenda as a whole. Everyone needs to be concerned about classrooms being humane places; everyone has to be concerned about the elderly, the homeless, community structures, racism, racial pride; and everyone needs to be concerned about establishing curricula in schools that will acknowledge the injustices that visit students' lives in schools and in their communities. As Jane Radin (1993) expresses this idea in the Stanford Law Review, we have to "cross the gender divide" and the other divides which separate and silence our students.

One tactic to accomplish this is the development of leaders who can articulate and act on the significant and complex gender issues in education and social justice. Equal access to leadership and to the practice of leadership skills in schools is fundamental; the demographics of our polity should represented in legislative bodies; and the subject should be in the school curriculum.

The difference gender balancing makes is evident. As Hillary Clinton points out in an introduction to *Strangers in the Senate,* "the presence of women in the political arena has led to an increase in legislation affecting children, the elderly, education, health care, and the environment" (p. 19). Sexual violence, harassment, and other "forms of exploitation of women and children" have also been added to the legislative agenda (p. 19). Both the development of leadership potential in our students, through pedagogy that is sensitive to gender behaviors, along with the inclusion of stories of leadership among women [and men] who are changing the face of their communities is solid education for democratic citizenship. Social justice is still a critical piece of the agenda of schools. The first order of citizenship education is to take gender seriously. The covert curriculum of injustice needs to be uncovered, invalidated, and eliminated from schools so that students can believe in democracy and democratic institutions. Moreover, as so many educators and scholars argue, the curriculum of citizenship needs to be reformed so that it is reflective and inclusive of all citizens and our contemporary world.

MEANINGS AND CONCLUSIONS

This historical case-study of Progressive Era feminist civic action vis-à-vis women's organization building and citizenship education illuminates the elusive relationship between private and public spheres of influence and definitions of citizenship. The notion of "public" and "private" as separate domains of male and female experience was accepted as a matter of nature in the nineteenth century. This expression of nature in human activity was problematized during the Progressive Era, when the seeds and roots of modern feminism were laid down. Women's interests and concerns were part of a broader discussion—alluded to earlier—about what women should be and do. What were the domains of female citizenship and how do those relate to ideas and practice of democracy and, hence, justice? The myth of separate spheres which seemed to pull women into private realms and push men into public realms was challenged first by the reality of women's lives in the nineteenth century and then by the organized and audible voices of women who were influencing public policy and law in the twentieth century. The remarkable accomplishments of organized women citizens of this period in pushing the boundaries and definitions of public and private are relevant to a discussion of gender and citizenship in relation to education.

One of the central concerns of "social feminism" or "domestic housekeeping" was the welfare of families. The welfare of families also seemed to be the site of resistance in government. For example, the Sheppard-Towner Maternity and Infancy Protection Act encountered great resistance from the American Medical Association and was passed by "a reluctant Congress" (Lemons, 1975). Child Labor laws, minimum wages to help women support families, compulsory school attendance, and quality controls in the meat and dairy industries were among the issues taken up in defense of the family and opposed or ignored by Congress. Contemporary feminist analyses of the issues and methods of different groups reveal class, race, and ethnic considerations; however, the centrality of family concerns in Progressive Era citizen action is compelling. The privateness of family concerns has been one of the lines of demarcation between formal government structures and policies and the private domestic sphere.

This Western political tradition can be traced to Aristotle, who developed an idea of "household justice" where the household is governed by people who are not equal to free men because free men are participants in the broader domain of political justice. Women and children were conceptualized in political terms as less than full citizens, because household justice was inferior to political justice (Olkin, 1989). This political tradition subordinates both women and their interest in the family to grander issues of the state and the relationship between nation states. Feminist theorists such as Barrie Thorne, Susan Olkin, Nel Noddings, and Lynda Stone have wrestled with issues embedded in understanding the relationships among the family, society, and the state. Tradition, as I have noted, dictates that families are "private institutions" and outside the purview of society's legitimate interest. A compelling example of this tradition is found in the way that local law enforcement has dealt with domestic disputes and domestic violence. Until very recently, police officers called to the site of domestic violence would restore calm, admonish the perpetrator of violence, and then leave. The intrusion into a male-headed household's private space can be daunting.

Progressive Era women were actively engaged in redefining the relationship of the family to the state and of women in the family to the state. They were arguing, through action, that society has a compelling interest in the welfare of the family, an interest that had been ignored. Without actually attacking the hierarchical arrangement of family structure, they also assumed the expertise of women in speaking for family needs. By virtue of this argument they shifted the hierarchy, putting themselves along side the male "head of household" in relationship to the community and the state. Thus they were influencing or attempting to influence the content of societal interests, community interests, and the interests of governmental bodies, along with the status of women in relation to family and government. Rather than standing in the background, they pushed themselves to the foreground, along with the interests of children, families, and community.

A critical dimension of this issue was the relationship between the family and the state. Suffrage—only one of the Progressive Era issues—was the seat of controversy in part because it challenged the idea of representation. A republican government means that the voting polity voices its preferences for issues and candidates through the ballot. Men represented their family's interest in casting a vote for a representative. As the editor of *The Popular Science Monthly* expressed it in 1896: "When . . . a man gives a vote for one side or the other . . . he thinks, not solely of his own interest as a male individual, but of all the interests, domestic and social, which he represents. In that sense the average elector's vote is meant to be, and is, representative." (Newman, 1985, p. 239). Progressive Era women were challenging this idea through their arguments for suffrage. Through their organizing they were attempting to represent the ideas that local, state, and federal government had not seen fit to consider. There was both an explicit and an implicit challenge to the idea that women's needs are taken care of in the family by heads of household.

Another critical challenge to traditional notions that was implicit during the Progressive Era came from the organization of women. The women's club movement was a fixture in communities by the first decade of the new century. Women had been organizing to help the needy, effect reform in women's prisons, lobby for the ballot, and discuss books. As the number of organizations mushroomed along with the causes, Progressive Era women created public visibility and connections with government structures. In so doing they were supporting the idea that sororal organizations and community organizations were appropriate sites where women could gather together to conduct the affairs of government. They created another level of government where the needs of women, children, and families would be met—while not excluding the welfare interests of men, it should be noted.

In articulating the grand project and current debate over how a democracy can function effectively, especially in representing and addressing the needs and participation of all citizens, Wendy Sarvasy (1992) proposes potentially useful terms. Sarvasy, a political theorist and historian, makes the distinction between political citizenship in a liberal democracy undergirded by principles of equality, where female citizens use their access to political rights, voting, and representation; and social citizenship where social reform and the everyday activities of citizens in their local neighborhoods is the central concern. In fact, Sarvasy, who has written about women's citizenship in the Progressive and Postsuffrage Era, argues that we were left with a new conception of citizenship. Feminists argued for recognition of gender inequality, and they "argued for the elevation of women's traditional activities into publicly supported service, the overturning of male-biased conceptions of citizen knowledge, and the creation of women-run spaces outside the home. These women-run spaces included settlement houses and boardrooms for organizations.

Families, neighborhoods, child care, and mothering (professional and otherwise) became domains for research, study and policy formulation in Progressive Era feminine and feminist agendas. This represented a departure from what was considered important knowledge for the survival of a democracy. For example, lobbies for the creation of a children's bureau and a women's bureau in the federal government resulted in research on working conditions, infant mortality, and diet and the use of these findings to create legislation and policy on family welfare. Both the reality of the problems represented by the domains as well as the influence to create and validate new areas of knowledge were added dimensions of the Progressive Era legacy.

Susan Olkin, a contemporary political theorist, has grappled with the distinction between justice as an abstract universal notion and as an ethic of care that is contextual and relational. In her book *Justice, Gender, and the Family* (1989), she argues persuasively that ideas about justice originate in the family and that the site of change and hence gender justice is found in the study and reform of the family relation. As she characterizes it, the family is the place where we can learn to be just. It is especially important for the development of a sense of justice that grows from sharing the experiences of others and becoming aware of the points of view of others who are different in some respects from ourselves but with whom we clearly have interests in common. She goes on to argue that teaching about justice in the family, the politics of gender, and the likely consequences of making choices based on assumptions of gender is an important mandate for schools that want to prepare students for full participation as citizens.

One important consideration of the Progressive Era feminist/feminine milieu was the difference between African American women's organizations and Anglo-European women's organizations, a difference which grew out of different family organizations and history. As Gilkes (1994) points out in her article on African American women, community work, and social change, African American women were not economically dependent on African American men because of their role in slavery and in the aftermath of slavery. Gender equality was normative in family relations and thus negotiating the bounds of gender relations vis-à-vis the state and government was not the major focus of African American women's Progressive Era reform. Instead it was focused on negotiating and lobbying for full citizen rights, opposing racism and the white power structure (including their Anglo-European sisters), and looking out for the welfare of the community. Sarvasy (in press) suggests that African American women may have been masking their politics of resistance under the mantle of "mothering." It seems clear that while "racial uplift" was the theme of the National Association for Colored Women, a significant dimension of their work included ensuring the welfare of future generations by providing role models for younger women.

Whereas racial equality, not gender, was a major concern of African American women, Anglo-European women were lobbying for equality based on (*their*) gender-distinct characteristics. Anglo-European women characterized themselves as the conveyors of culture and morality, whose nurturing dispositions distinguished them from their masculine partners. They were uniquely fit to do the work of home and community building, and from that vantage point they argued for an equality based on difference: they wanted equal status (eventually including the ballot and political power) based on their gender differences.

The concern over how women define their gendered selves politically became a major issue in feminist circles of the eighties and it is still a topic of conversation in the nineties. It is clear in this chapter that women have a rich history of experience in participatory democracy, and that part of that history comes out of a history of discrimination. The processes and understandings necessary for citizenship in a representative democracy cannot be taught or learned effectively using teaching methods and historical texts that are exclusive or ignorant of gender, race, and class. Citizenship education has been and is now vulnerable to the criticism that while professing to represent and value social justice and diversity, it has turned a blind eye to injustice and exclusion. Moreover, students have been miseducated and their own experiences ignored in the interest of teaching the text and the canon. Like many of my colleagues in social studies education, I believe it is high time that we get on with our transformative work that dignifies the students, their histories and their eventual legacies. (En)gendering citizenship education is fundamental in this transformative work.

REFERENCES

Addams, J. (1914). The larger aspects of the woman's movement, *Annals of the American Academy of Political and Social Science, 56* (November): 1–8.

Bernard-Powers, J. (1992). *The girl question in education: Vocational education for young women in the Progressive Era.* Bristol: Falmer Press.

———. (1994). Lucy Laney. In M. Seller (Ed.), *Women educators in the United States: A biographical bibliographic sourcebook.* Westport, CT: Greenwood Press.

Brown, E. B. (1990). Womanist consciousness: Maggie Lena Walker and the Independent Order of St. Luke. In E. Dubois & V. Ruiz (Eds.), *Unequal Sisters: A multicultural reader in U. S. history* (pp. 208–223). New York: Routledge.

Buss, H. (1991). Reading for the doubled visioned discourse of American women's autobiography. *a/b Autobiography Studies, 5*(1):95–108.

Clinton, H. (1993). Foreword. In B. Boxer, *Strangers in the Senate: Politics and the new revolution of women in America.* Washington, D. C.: National Press Books.

Dewey, J. (1911, June). Is co-education injurious to girls? *Ladies Home Journal*, p. 2

Gilkes, C. T. (1994). If it wasn't for the women: African American women, community work, and social change. In M. B. Zinn & B. T. Dill (Eds.), *Women of Color in U. S. Society* (pp. 229–246). Philadelphia: Temple University Press

Gilligan, C. (1982). *In a difference voice: Psychological theory and women's development*. Cambridge: Harvard University Press.

_____. (1993). Joining the resistance: Psychology, politics, girls and women. In L. Weis, & M. Fine, (Eds.), *Beyond silenced voices: Class, race and gender in United States schools*. Albany: State University of New York Press.

Goodsell, W. (1924). *The education of women*. New York: Macmillan.

James, E. T. & James, J. (1985). *Notable American women* (3 vols.). Cambridge: Belknap Press.

Kerber, L. & Dehart-Matthews, J. (1982). *Women's America: Refocusing the past*. New York: Oxford University Press.

Lagemann, E. (1989). The plural worlds of educational research. *History of Education Quarterly*, 29 (2): 185–214.

Laird, S. (1988). Women and gender in John Dewey's philosophy of education. *Educational Theory*, 38 (1): 111–129.

Lemons, S. (1975). *The woman citizen: Social feminism in the 20's*. Urbana: University of Illinois Press.

Little, S. (1993). The Freedom Train: Citizenship and postwar political culture, 1946–1949. *American Studies*, 34 (1): 35–65.

Neverdon-Morton, C. (1989). *Afro-American women of the south and the advancement of the race, 1895–1925*. Knoxville: University of Tennessee Press.

Newman, M. (1985), *Men's ideas/women's realities*. New York: Pergamon Press.

Ninth Circuit Task Force on Gender Bias. (1993). Executive summary of the preliminary report. *Stanford Law Review*, 45 (6): 2153–2178.

Olkin, S. M. (1989). *Justice, gender and the family*. New York: Basic Books.

Pagano, J. (1991). Relating to students. *Journal of Moral Education, 20* (3): 257–266.

Porritt, A. G. (1911). The feminization of our schools and its political consequences. *Educational Review, 41*: 441–448.

Radin, M. J. (1993). Reply: Please be careful with cultural feminism. *Stanford Law Review, 45* (6): 1567–1569.

Sadker, M. & Sadker, D. (1994). *Failing at fairness: How America's schools cheat girls*. New York: Charles Scribner's Sons.

Sarvasy, W. (in press). From man and philanthropic service to social citizenship. *Social Politics*

———. (1992). Beyond the difference versus equality policy debate: Post-suffrage feminism, citizenship, and the quest for a feminist welfare state. *Signs, 17* (2): 329–362.

Smuts, R. (1976). *Women and work in America.* New York: Schocken.

CHAPTER 15

"Re-Minding" Education for Democracy

James Anthony Whitson and William B. Stanley

I. INTRODUCTION

Several essays in this volume represent the broad span of *progressive* discourses on educating citizens for democracy. Unsurprisingly, progressive proposals have generated opposition from a wide range of critics. Such critics often frame their arguments as an attack on public school programs that, they allege, have been taken over by politically motivated progressive followers of Dewey, to the detriment of real learning by the students.

This is especially ironic, considering the extent to which the programs advocated by critics such as E. D. Hirsch are often just the kind of teaching—giving first and almost exclusive priority to "covering" volumes of factual information—which in reality has constituted the established curriculum of public schools for decades, and which more informed critics, such as Theodore Sizer and John Goodlad, see as a cause of failure in American schools as they are. Not only are Hirsch and others wrong about the efficacy of their facts-driven approach, but they have their own facts wrong as well: The pedagogy advocated by adherents of "Progressive Education" never has been dominant—or even very influential—in the U. S. public schools (Zilversmit, 1993; Cuban, 1993). Moreover, critics such as Hirsch (1987) are dead wrong in identifying the range of ideas within the "Progressive Education" movement with Dewey's own thinking on education (Hertzberg, 1989).

Some of the differences between Dewey and other progressive critics of social education, in particular, are especially relevant to what we see as an important but relatively neglected dimension of discourse on the educational formation of a "democratic mind." As illustrated in the other chapters of this volume, the discussion of how to prepare children for their roles as members of a democratic society has generally begun with critical discussions of the true nature of democracy (or of the nature of a true democracy, or of the right choice among rival conceptions of democracy), and then proceeded to derive conceptions of the nature and requirements of democratic citizenship—from which could be derived, in turn, a formulation of how schooling should contribute to the formation of robustly qualified citizens within such democratic societies.

Such discussions have provided us with persuasive, well-developed arguments and visions of the qualities of social and political life to which we might aspire, and to which we, as educators, may have some especially crucial contributions to make. Yet, in focussing on the nature and requirements of *democracy*, we believe that these discussions have neglected another aspect of the question of how to understand formation of the democratic *mind*. While a broad range of approaches in social theory and political philosophy have been represented in the discussions of how to understand *democracy*, and the implications of such understanding for the educational requirements of democratic citizenship, we will argue that these discussions have remained within the limits of a peculiar view of the nature of the human *mind*, and of the mental capabilities involved in educated social practice.

While rival conceptions of democracy have been contested, a disputable but uncontested view of mind presides over these discussions. In one sense, this might not be so surprising, given the almost total monopoly of the prevailing view in academic and popular culture alike. The uncontested pervasiveness of this view of mind is quite peculiar in the specific context of the legacy reflected in this book, however, since Dewey spoke from a dissident tradition with a view of mind clearly at odds with the prevailing view inherited from Kant, Hume, Locke, and Descartes.

We expect that most teachers and students would be surprised, amused, or indifferent to the suggestion that their classroom activity is decisively affected by a peculiar view of mind expounded by those dead white males. And, surely, critical social educators would almost universally claim some degree of affinity with Dewey—his "pragmatic" philosophy and/or his "progressive" pedagogy—as against the intellectual legacy from Descartes to Kant. Despite such incidents, however, we will argue that even the more critical and progressive positions on social education for democracy have been articulated within a framework that presupposes fundamental aspects of Descartes' dichotomy between the realms of mind and world; of Hume's dichotomy between subjective values and objective facts; and of Kant's dichotomy between the known world of mental constructs and the unknowable world of things as they are "in themselves."

It is not so surprising that the pervasive view of mind would be presupposed in Benjamin Bloom's "taxonomic" differentiation between cognitive and affective "domains," or in retrogressive curriculum proposals such as Hirsch's "cultural literacy" program. It is more surprising to find fundamental aspects of the same framework presupposed in more progressive calls for reflective critical inquiry, or even "countersocialization," as touchstones for social education. The tenacity of that framework is all the more surprising given that its overt philosophical expression (as Cartesian dualism, or in other derivative manifestations, such as the variety of positivisms) is now so widely discredited. We believe that the persistence of this framework, despite its apparent ill-repute, is partly due to the simple fact that it has not been supplanted in our understanding or our practices by any other, more adequate, view of mind.

The framework for a more valid view of mind is, however, provided in the work of Dewey and in the pragmatic tradition that includes Dewey along with C. S. Peirce and G. H. Mead. This chapter will not be concerned with the philosophical history of this approach, but will attempt to present its basic principles, with speculation on the implications for educating democratic citizens. We begin with a brief critical review of conflicting approaches to social education, with special attention to issues that are relevant to the conflicting views of mind. Next, we critically analyze the presuppositions about mind that are implicit in contemporary discussions and practices in social education, and we present basic principles of an alternative view. After that, we will attempt to illustrate the significance of the nondualistic view of mind by suggesting some specific implications for curriculum and instruction in social education.

II. ISSUES AND APPROACHES

The very idea of democratic citizenship as the goal of social studies has been challenged recently by Leming (1989, 1992) on the grounds that, first, it hasn't worked (e.g., that decades of such efforts have had no demonstrable effects on even such weak indicia of democracy as voting rates), and, second, that progressive efforts to promote stronger forms of democratic participation are paradoxically *un*democratic, insofar as they attempt to enlist the schools in strategies to promote substantive political objectives that are *not* supported by the public whose wishes, in our democracy, should be served by the public schools. Leming's challenge is only a recent example of criticism that sees "citizenship" as a cloak for smuggling social objectives into the curriculum, objectives which distract the schools from serving their more proper and legitimate educational objectives.

As an alternative to citizenship, Leming proposes that the legitimate and potentially effective goal of social studies education is, "in a word, knowledge. The development of an accurate knowledge of our American history, our traditions and the social world, should be the superordinate goal of social studies instruction" (1992, p. 310). At this point, he is close to critics such as Hirsch (1987) and Bestor (1953/1985) in suggesting that properly defined *educational* objectives need to be restored in place of competing social objectives that have been proposed or imposed by the progressives.

We see this supposed dichotomy—between *information* as being truly educational, and other aspects of citizenship formation as being diversions from really educational objectives—as arising from the false but well-entrenched positivist dichotomy between facts and values. This dichotomy, in turn, arises from the Cartesian dualism that treats mind and world as fundamentally different realms of being and, in education, leads to the pervasive dichotomy between "cognition" and "affect" as discrete "domains" of learning and development. Such dichotomies are now so deeply entrenched in the received conceptual and linguistic framework for thinking and talking about education that to challenge them is to defy basic common sense. Yet, as we attempt to show in this chapter, the mind and its education are better understood without those false dichotomies, which have long been discredited in the light of nonpositivist philosophical traditions such as pragmatism and hermeneutical phenomenology.

Unfortunately, however, much of the progressive advocacy promoting social education for democratic citizenship has couched its defense of noninformational objectives in discourse that remains trapped within this pervasive dualistic framework. We believe that this confinement has constrained and distorted both the educational programs advocated by progressives for the preparation of more strongly democratic citizens, and the rationales articulated in support of those programs.

We have argued elsewhere (e.g., Stanley and Whitson, 1992; Stanley, 1992) for a conception of practical social competence that is informed by a nondualistic view of mind which does not observe the positivistic dichotomy between cognition and affect. This view of mind is not original with us, but is continuous with the tradition of pragmatic philosophy represented by Peirce and Dewey, and with the broader variety of nonpositivist traditions from Aristotle to Arendt. We begin with Dewey, therefore, in our review of issues in social studies education, after which we shall return to questions of the nature of mind, in relation to mental development and education for a democratic social world.

Dewey and his Critics

By the end of the nineteenth century in the United States the schools mainly functioned to transmit the dominant culture. While the rhetoric of democracy was evident, educational practice was largely focused on getting students, especially immigrants, to fit into society. Dewey's approach to progressive education appeared as a radical challenge to the educational establishment. Dewey understood education as an essential component of democratic society. The purpose of the schools was the cultivation of what Dewey called the "method of intelligence," which involved the development of the students' competence for what he called reflective inquiry, such as the competence to make reasoned judgments and solve social problems. Dewey had no blueprint for the "new social order" (beyond an open-ended conception of democracy), but he did assume that cultivation of the method of intelligence would gradually lead to the creation of a better society.

Not surprisingly, Dewey's ideas were attacked by more traditional educators who believed he neglected subject matter and the needs of society by overemphasizing student interests. Dewey was also criticized or ignored by other educational reformers (e.g., Bobbit, Charters, Snedden) who supported what has been called the "social efficiency" movement and wanted to apply the new technology of psychological testing and research to make schools more efficient and help students fit into the dominant society (Kliebard, 1986; Callahan, 1962). Most of Dewey's traditional critics have badly underestimated his commitment to teaching traditional subject matter (Westbrook, 1991). Dewey also argued that since the contemporary social order was seriously flawed, education aimed primarily at fitting students into society was both ill-conceived and antithetical to a democratic culture.

Ironically, some of the most significant criticisms of Dewey's ideas were provoked by those who claimed to be following his approach to education. The child-centered wing of the progressive education movement (e.g., William H. Kilpatrick) argued that the curriculum should be built around student needs and what the students themselves felt to be interesting. Dewey spent a great deal of time trying to disassociate himself from this position. He realized that student interest was important for education to be effective, but it was never a sufficient basis for building a curriculum. Both the scholarly disciplines and the method of intelligence provided a stronger foundation for selecting curriculum content and practice.

The social reconstructionists (e.g., George Counts, Theodore Brameld) offered yet another critique of Dewey's approach. The reconstructionists agreed with Dewey's emphasis on reflective inquiry but felt he did not go far enough. Dewey's approach was criticized for being instrumentalist and neutral. Lacking a theory of social welfare, reflective inquiry was criticized as merely a method for problem solving. According to the reconstructionists, such a method lacked both the critical stance required to challenge the dominant social order as well as a vision of a preferred social order to orient curriculum. As we shall see, Dewey had good reason for resisting this sort of critique.

Reflective Inquiry and Critical Pedagogy

Over the past fifty years, a number of social educators have proposed approaches to social education that are linked, explicitly or
implicitly, to Dewey's influence. In fact, the reflective inquiry tradition has been described as one of the major schools of thought in
social education (e.g., Barr, Barth, and Shermis, 1977; Brubaker,
1967; Haas, 1979; Hunt and Metcalf, 1968; Massialas and Cox,
1966; Stanley, 1985). The reflective inquiry tradition also formed a
major part of what was called the "new social studies" during the
1960s and early 1970s. But a careful examination of particular
representatives of this tradition reveals a number of conflicts with
or shifts away from Dewey's approach, and we will explore some of
these differences in a moment.

One other development should be noted before we turn to a
more detailed analysis of our critique of the reflective inquiry tradition. In the 1970s a new approach to social education emerged
that we will refer to as "critical pedagogy."[1] While critical pedagogy has much in common with the social reconstructionist position discussed above, it is also different in several important ways.
In particular, critical pedagogy has been more strongly influenced
by European theoretical perspectives, including the "new sociology" movement in Great Britian, "critical theory" (especially the
Frankfurt School), neo-Marxism (especially Gramsci and Al-
thusser), and structuralism. Nevertheless, in the United States, critical pedagogy also retains a strong neopragmatic orientation,
mainly rooted in the work of Dewey (e.g., Giroux, 1988). A second
major difference between critical pedagogy and social reconstructionism is the strong influence of feminist thought on the former.
Finally, critical pedagogy has developed in what some have called
the "postmodern era" (Lyotard, 1984), while social reconstructionism was largely part of the earlier modernist discourse.

Among the three traditional rationales for social studies that
were broadly identified by Barr, Barth, and Shermis[2], the "reflective inquiry" tradition would seem to be the most congenial to
both reconstructionism and critical pedagogy; and it is also the
rationale closest to our own approach to social education based on
practical competence. In practice, there is no unified reflective inquiry rationale, as different social educators stress different themes.

We can, however, point to some commonalities, such as (1) an emphasis on developing certain student competencies (e.g., critical thinking, decision making, problem solving, values analysis, the analysis of social issues); (2) the assumption that student interest is a prerequisite to successful learning; (3) an explicit link to the progressive education tradition derived from Dewey; and (4) an assumption that such rationales are an essential component of education in a democratic society. While we would agree with each of these positions, there are still some serious problems with the major reflective inquiry rationales developed since Dewey. We will consider some important examples to help illustrate our argument.

Student Interests and the Social Science Disciplines.   One difficulty is the assertion by some that what students identify as problems should form the basis for constructing the curriculum[3]. As noted above, student interest is certainly relevant for effective instruction; but students' preconceptions of their own needs and interests are never in themselves an adequate basis for building a curriculum. The central importance of subject matter to the construction of curriculum was a point frequently made by Dewey (e.g., 1899, 1902) in his critique of child-centered approaches to curriculum. Hunt and Metcalf (1968) would deal with this issue by having students study closed areas of our culture (e.g., power, poverty, religion, sexuality, etc.). Such closed areas are seen as major sources for conformist, authoritarian thought, as well as being controversial and likely to provoke student interest. Thus, while this approach does recognize the importance of having teachers determine how the curriculum should be constructed for purposes that transcend the already salient interests of their students, the nature of those purposes remains to be articulated. What is lacking in such approaches is the sort of sensitivity Dewey showed for the importance of the social science disciplines within education for reflective inquiry.

Countersocialization.   A second problem is the tendency by some social educators to combine reflective inquiry with countersocialization. This approach to reflective inquiry is particularly true of the major social reconstructionists (e.g., George Counts, Harold Rugg, Theodore Brameld). But countersocialization is also a goal of contemporary critical pedagogues (e.g., Apple, Aronowitz, Giroux) and social studies educators like Engle and Ochoa (1989).

Engle and Ochoa argue that the social studies program in schools should serve both the functions of socialization and countersocialization. While socialization is necessary to ensure cultural transmission, countersocialization is required to develop the student's competence for critical thinking and decision making necessary for effective citizenship in a democratic society. Giroux (1988) takes a similar position when he argues for a form of critical pedagogy whereby students are taught to critique and challenge dominant forms of socialization and to work for social transformation. The countersocialization approach to reflective inquiry assumes we have a choice in education between a set of "good" democratic values and a set of lesser values promoted by the dominant groups in society (i.e., power, efficiency, self-interest, individual choice, etc.).

The question of supporting or opposing countersocialization is a false issue that has been constructed on a misconception of socialization as some kind of debilitating imposition of conformity. As we argue below, socialization is actually better understood as the development in individuals of the *competence* for *praxis* as members of their society, including the practical competence for critical thinking that is capable of fundamentally challenging and transcending the practices and understandings that may currently be dominant within their society.

Core Values.   Other social educators supporting a reflective inquiry approach (e.g., Fraenkel, 1973; Hunt and Metcalf, 1968; Nelson and Michaelis, 1980; Newmann, 1975; Newmann and Oliver, 1970; Oliver and Shaver, 1966; Shaver and Strong, 1982) do not stress countersocialization per se, but do pose other related problems. Most if not all of these educators cast social problem solving in terms of an a priori commitment to a core set of democratic values (Stanley, 1992, pp. 71–73, 81–83). As Newmann (1975) puts it, his position is based on a commitment to "the general notion of human dignity which rests upon the more specific values of equality, freedom of choice, and rationality" (p. 71). Shaver and Strong (1982) agree and argue that "basic societal values are so fundamental to the reason for the existence of public schools that they are not only to be supported but even inculcated, with increasing attention to their rational bases as students gain intellectual ability" (p. 143).

The core values supported by Oliver and Shaver (1966), Newmann (1975) and Shaver and Strong (1982) are the basis for what Gunnar Myrdal referred to as the "American Creed" (Oliver and Shaver, 1966, pp. 11–12). Schools should both inculcate a fundamental commitment to these values and use them as fundamental standards for the analysis of social issues. These educators assume that the survival of a democratic culture requires a consensus among its citizens regarding central values. In Shaver and Strong's (1982) view, a social educator who is not committed to the ethos of the American Creed should not agree to work in public schools (p. 79).

Hunt and Metcalf (1968) argue that even if agreement on core democratic values is absent, "survival of the society is still possible provided there is agreement on a method of inquiry by which to explore differences in the meaning and truth of propositions and the justifiability of values" (p. 34). But in the end, they hope teachers "can help tip the scales" toward democracy over authoritarianism by having students focus on higher thought processes (p. 42): "Our position advocates reflective reconstruction of beliefs as a means of clarifying and preserving the central ideals of democracy." (p. 58).

Some (e.g., Giroux, 1988; Hunt and Metcalf, 1968; Nelson and Michaelis, 1980) begin to recognize the false fact-value dichotomy inherent in positivist thought. Rather than opposing facts and values as distinct entities, Hunt and Metcalf (1968) see both as existing on a continuum wherein facts are those things about which there is consensus on a common meaning. Values, in contract, do not have clear and common meanings. In this sense, all statements are evaluative; no statement is merely true or false (pp. 130–132).

As in the countersocialization argument discussed earlier, however, values are treated as dispositions that preexist human action, with differences arising only on the question of which values should actually orient programs for social education. In this way, the arguments of these progressive social educators do not challenge the familiar positivistic framework within which they can easily be understood: the framework in which students are taught *knowledge* and *skills* which they can use instrumentally in action oriented by their *values*. This framework provides conceptual and verbal resources for understanding how educators can help students to enhance their knowledge and their skills (to become more "knowledgeable" and "skillful"), but there is no analogous vocabulary or conception of *enhancing* students' *values*. Value positions may be more or less clear, coherent, or sincere, but values are treated as unsuitable for the kinds of substantive judgments educators commonly apply to the attainment of knowledge and skills. Values are treated as if positively given, either as the beliefs, preferences, or dispositions of individuals, or as cultural givens to be followed and applied.

Thus, for all practical purposes, even social educators who denounce positivism have remained trapped within a framework of educational discourse that preserves the positivist dichotomy of facts and values. Within this framework, the substantive selection of "core values" (or "countersocialization" values) has no real *educational* basis, but must be determined on some philosophical or social basis that is extrinsic and prior to the educators' work, properly speaking, *as educators*. As noted in the next section, John Dewey took a different approach with his "method of intelligence." Later, we will see how Dewey and others help provide a nondualistic view of the human mind and the education of mental capabilities, which we see as the basis for a nonpositivistic framework for democratic social education.

Dewey's "Method of Intelligence"

Dewey agreed that the schools should participate in the process of social transformation. "It is not whether the schools shall or shall not influence the course of future social life, but in what direction they shall do so and how" (Dewey, 1937, p. 236). If we fail to develop students' critical skills of inquiry and reflective thought, they might leave school "without power of critical discrimination, at the mercy of special propaganda, and drifting from one plan and scheme to another . . . " (1935b, p. 334). Dewey saw the schools exercising such influence not just by enhancing the knowledge and instrumental cognitive skills of students as individuals, but by raising the level of collective intelligence with which the democratic public deals with problems affecting its own progressive formation as a social polity (cf. Westbrook, 1991, pp. 312–318).

Dewey did not support the proposal by some reconstructionists to use the schools for countersocialization aimed at building a predetermined "new social order." In fact, Dewey even resisted John Childs's desire to use education to conserve democratic values and adjust students to sociocultural change (Dennis, 1989). When Dewey and Childs (1933) collaborated, they argued that the central aim of education was

> to prepare individuals to take part intelligently in the management of conditions under which they will live, to bring them to an understanding of the forces which are society, to equip them with the intellectual and practiced tools by which they can themselves enter into direction of these forces. (p.71)

The core of Dewey's educational project was what he termed the method of intelligence, a form of human behavior that would help to clarify social issues and achieve desirable social ends. He rejected the assertion by reconstructionist critics that his approach to education was neutral, mechanical, aloof, or merely intellectual in its analysis of social conflict. In fact, it was the application of reflective thought that has helped to reveal the nature of social problems and conflict and to pose new social orientations (Dewey, 1935a, p. 9). Thus, the reconstructionist calls for the schools to impose the values and practices of a new social order was both unnecessary and potentially detrimental.

> The upholders of indoctrination rest their adherence . . . , in part, upon the fact that there is a great deal of indoctrination now going on in the schools, especially with reference to the dominant economic regime. These facts unfortunately *are* facts. But they do not prove that the right course is to seize upon the method of indoctrination and reverse its object. (Dewey, 1937, p. 238)

The only form of imposition acceptable to Dewey was the assertion that the method of intelligence was the preferred approach to education: "If the method we have recommended leads teachers and students to better conclusions than those which we have reached—and surely it will if widely and honestly adopted—so much the better" (Dewey and Childs, 1933, p. 72). To impose preconceived conclusions would serve to undermine the method of intelligence; and Dewey had a deep faith in the potential of this method to serve democratic interests.

III. A NONDUALISTIC FRAMEWORK FOR DEMOCRATIC EDUCATION

Dewey's "method of intelligence" reflects a *monistic* view of mind-within-the-world, contrasting with the *dualistic* view of mind-versus-the-world articulated by Descartes and inherited through Locke, Hume, and Kant. The latter provides the unexamined framework that constrains and distorts scholarly as well as popular thinking about education—including education for democracy. We have briefly considered how progressive social educators, in some ways inspired by Dewey, appropriated some of his ideas to projects that were still framed by the sort of positivistic dichotomies that Dewey sought to challenge at a more fundamental level; and we have indicated some of the problems we see ensuing in proposed rationales for social education. We now turn our attention more directly to examine what we see as the received underlying dualistic view of mind, and a nondualistic alternative perspective afforded by a range of nonpositivist philosophical traditions including Dewey and the pragmatists. After that we will return to problems in social education, to consider implications of the nondualistic view for education of the democratic mind.

The implications for social education include important possibilities for recovering an understanding of how the real social and civic competence that must be developed in democratic education essentially involves aspects and dimensions that cannot be understood within a framework that misrepresents human abilities as nothing more than technical skills. We believe that the proper goal of social education is the development of *practical social competence,* and especially the intellectual dimensions of such competence (see, e.g., Stanley and Whitson, 1992; Stanley, 1992). In saying this, we are referring to fully *practical* competence, and not to merely *technical* knowledge or skill. Truly practical competence must be recognized as nothing less than the full competence required for human *praxis,* which has been understood for millennia as being fundamentally different from the kind of activity that can be seen as requiring nothing more than technical knowledge and skill.

In a democracy, the conduct of all citizens—in our private as well as in our public social lives—is bound up in the inescapably social praxis of determining our personal and social destinies. The fundamentally social, interpretive, and ontogenerative nature of our social praxis means that the required competence can never be reduced to the form of technical knowledge or skill (i.e., the kind of knowledge or skill that may be adequate for achieving the kinds of outcomes that can, in principle, be specified in advance of the purely instrumental activity that is sufficient to realize such outcomes). Traditional, nonpositivist philosophy uses "phronesis" (originally a Greek word) for this fully practical—and fundamentally social and interpretive—competence, as distinct from "technē," or instrumental skill.

This distinction between practical competence and instrumental skill has been suppressed to the point of extinction in the positivistic culture of education in the United States. The culture in which educational theory, research, and policy discourse takes place in this country seems to have lost even the vocabulary for understanding those kinds and aspects of human competence that cannot be represented as merely technical knowledge and skill. We believe that the failure to recognize the difference between technical and nontechnical abilities (even by those who have invoked "the practical" for other purposes[4]) is due, at least in part, to the more fundamental framework within which we now construe the nature of our selves, our minds, and the outcomes of human learning and development.

Learning outcomes are routinely separated into discontinuous "cognitive" and "affective" domains, as in the "taxonomy of educational objectives" that is so pervasively used and presumed as the unquestioned framework for instruction in our schools (Bloom et al., 1956; Krathwohl et al., 1964; Gose, 1986). Within this framework, "cognitive" objectives are construed as technical abilities, while objectives that are not acquired or used through technical means are not conceived of as abilities at all, but are consigned to the separate "affective" domain of values, attitudes, and subjective personal preferences.

This framework obviously is rooted in the positivist dualism separating the realm of "facts" from that of "values." It is true that some education theorists in recent years have tried to reassert the priority of values and have claimed that, in so doing, they are challenging the stranglehold of positivist thought in education. They do not realize, however, that positivism never did disparage values as opposed to facts. Quite the contrary: Early positivists such as Thomas Hobbes and David Hume saw values as primary determinants of political and moral conduct, and as important influences on how facts themselves are understood and used. Their essential positivism, however, lay in seeing facts and values as having *positive* (i.e., independent rather than *relational*) existences, such that facts and values could be said to exist positively within separate realms of being.

The positivist dualism of facts and values can be seen to emerge from the even more fundamental Cartesian dualism separating incorporeal mind from the material world. This view of mind as the true essence of "man," estranged from the material world, is itself not just a logical conclusion of philosophers: Robin Schott (1988), for example, shows how such a bias in epistemology has been a legacy of socially and historically situated material practices of asceticism, ascetic practices specifically intended to liberate the minds of male philosophers from bondage to the bodily demands of the material world sustained by slaves and women.

Our legacy in education is the framework tacitly presupposed by a broad range of conflicting theories, a framework that posits (indeed, "posits" with a vengeance!) cognitive knowledge and skill, or affective values and attitudes, as positivities existing within separate domains—just as the mind is considered as something that performs formal cognitive (or "mental") operations on symbolic information that has been abstracted from the data of sensory input from the world. Thus, we have reached a point at which even those who argue against elimination or neglect of the emotions in education do so by arguing that the emotions play an important role in the discovery or acquisition of knowledge (e.g., Wagner, 1990), rather than understanding our emotional responses to things in our world as part of our knowledge of those things, i.e., not just as aids to cognition, but as essential elements of cognition itself.

Dualistic Views of Mind

The general framework of Cartesian dualism appears in two different forms, both having severe ramifications for social education. Both forms presuppose a radical duality between mind and the world. In the more classically Cartesian form, a duality between

the nonmateriality of mind and the materiality of world is emphasized. Factual knowledge and "thinking skills" are supposed to
develop the mind's cognitive ability to process information from
the social world, while debates take place over the need for parallel
efforts to develop character, to teach values for directing one's
conduct and the *use* of one's mental abilities, or to balance "social-
izing" education with the right dose of "countersocializing" education. Values, attitudes, dispositions, and allegiances are viewed
as inhabiting an "affective" characterological domain, apart from
the "cognitive" or mental domain. This closely follows a view of
the mind itself as an agency that processes symbolic propositional
information *from* and *about* the world, using operations of formal
logic which (as, strictly speaking, *mental* operations) are thought
of as taking place (or rather, as *not* taking any *place*, but simply as
operating) *outside* of the material and social world.

In this form of the dualistic framework, the mind is portrayed
as being essentially logical (in the restricted sense of formal propositional logic), and as being altogether alien to social as well as to
emotional and physical phenomena. This is not to say that mental
performance or development are *unaffected* by physical, emotional, and social processes, but only that these are *outside* the activity
of mind *as such*. It is this idea of mind that supports critics who
attack progressive democratic social education by arguing that attention to personal attitudes, to self-esteem, to social processes
within the classroom or the school community, or to multicultural
or countersocializing values can only come at the expense of dis-
tracting us from the intellectual or cognitive objectives which are
the more proper and legitimate concern of public schools. Less
obvious, but more important for our purposes, however, is the
point that this same idea of mind underlies the rationales and
pedagogy of social educators who would include social and "affective" learning, but in a manner that treats such concerns as matters
of assisting the development of mental abilities, guiding the use of
mental abilities, or as matters otherwise contributing from outside
of the development of mental abilities as such.

The general framework of dualism between mind and world
appears also in a second, more Kantian form. In this form, the
conception of mind is broadened to admit the involvement of bodily elements and social processes within humans' mental "construction" of reality. But this reality is then regarded as a construction,

an extension, a product (and, to some extent, a funhouse mirror) of the human mind, again existing separately from any real world that might exist outside constructions of the human mind itself. This form of dualism between mind and world underlies a variety of Romanticist conceptions of education. In one conception (which has its advocates as well as its opponents), education is essentially a process of vanquishing unruly subjectivity by imposing more objective order (even if the only "objectivity" available is that of constructed social consensus). An alternative conception celebrates the triumph of subjective, passionate imagination and moral fervor or commitment, over the restraints and injustices of the established order. Even when Romanticism celebrates unification (for example, between reason and passion, self and society, nature and culture, etc.), it construes this as a reconciliation of principles presumed to arise from some primordially separate and opposed modes of being. This form of the dualism underlies uncritical relativism (since subjective personal or cultural world views cannot be criticized by appeal to the reality of the world itself), as well as oppositional approaches in which criticism is regarded as a matter of acting in opposition to the world's established order on the basis of personal or group values formed against and from outside of that world.

A Monistic Alternative

It is significant that a journal called *The Monist* was an important publication vehicle for both Peirce and Dewey. Completely different from Cartesian dualism, Peirce's approach revealed the principles of relation and mediation constituting the natural world *as including* thought, language, and culture—in which we find the logical potentials of those principles most fully realized. Dewey followed with his own logic of human inquiry, which agreed with Peirce's understanding of logic as addressing something far more substantial and extensive than the empty, formalistic, and non-worldly "logic" of philosophers like Bertrand Russell. Dewey's work on aesthetic, social, and educational concerns was crucially informed by his understanding of human *experience*, which he described *monistically*, i.e., as involving activity by the human mind intrinsically *within* (not *dualistically alien to*) the material and social world.

While Peirce and Dewey contributed unique insights into the nature of logic, thought, experience, and understanding, they were not alone in dealing with mind and world in non-Cartesian, nondualistic ways. In Europe, thinkers as diverse as Heidegger, Gadamer, Arendt, and Habermas all treated human beings as beings in the world (and even as "*Dasein*," or "Being-in-the-world," for the Heideggerians). They had no need and no reason to worry about the kind of radical difference between mind and world that had been presumed within the problematic dualisms of Descartes, Hume, and Kant.

Despite important differences among Peirce, Dewey, and others, important commonalities can also be observed. None of these nondualistic thinkers would accept an analysis of human conduct in which *cognitive abilities* include only technical skills, to be deployed under the direction of essentially subjective *values* and *attitudes*. Instead of analyzing beliefs as being objectively known "facts" or else subjectively preferred "opinions," these thinkers recognize that beliefs involve the complex varieties of *judgments* that people can become more or less competent to make (cf. Lipman, 1991). Some judgments concern matters that can be described in purely technical terms; but many judgments concern irreducibly *practical* matters, requiring implicit or explicit socially informed interpretations of possibilities for the well-being of oneself and others. Such judgments—and the conduct that ensues—depend upon the competence for *praxis*. From Aristotle to Arendt, the widest variety of thinkers outside the line of dualist problematics from Descartes to Hume to Kant have recognized that praxis requires a competence involving more than merely technical ability, but that this is still an educable worldly competence that can be developed through the mind's involvement in the reflective practices of social life (which, we hasten hopefully to add, ought to include the practices of social studies education for citizenship in a democracy).

IV. IMPLICATIONS: EDUCATION OF THE DEMOCRATIC MIND

An approach that aims for practical competence and is informed by a nondualistic view of mind would have far-ranging implications for education for democratic citizenship. Here, we suggest a few illustrative examples.

From *"Values"* to Value

One of the more obvious implications lies in the treatment of issues involving "values." Instead of treating democratic values as positive, a priori given attributes of individuals or of societies, to be "analyzed" and "clarified," or to be directly taught, observed, applied, and inculcated, "values" would be open to reflective and critical consideration as *judgments* that have been formed over time as to the real, demonstrable, *value* of the principles or practices in question, or the *value* that commitment to those principles or practices is believed to have in relation to real personal and social human interests.[5] Even such "core" values as freedom, justice, and equality would be open to sincere questioning which, we have no doubt, would lead to fresh reaffirmation of the value of those principles. This requires a faith in the principles themselves —a confidence that questioning would lead to a compelling demonstration of the value of those principles.

We also believe that the experience of critically re-cognizing the truth of these values[6] when they are challenged on the basis of some genuine doubt is exactly the kind of educational experience in which those values really can be learned as part of the ongoing development of the students' practical competence. While we do have confidence in this approach to teaching the real value(s) of our nation's basic principles, we also fear that the alternative approach too often teaches only pious ways of talking about values that are not truly believed—if they are even understood. Indeed, if core values are held out as immune from critical examination, that might even teach the student that these values are being preached dogmatically out of an implicit fear that they could not withstand critical scrutiny.

"Critical Thinking" and Reflective Inquiry

"Correctly" drawing distinctions between "facts" and "values" is itself one of the "skills" that students have been taught to master in some approaches to the teaching of "critical thinking skills." This is just one aspect of what happens in attempts to replace real critical thinking with something that has been reduced to merely technical procedures. Since real critical thinking cannot be reduced to technical analysis, artificial technical procedures are invented tailor-made for teaching, but without any use or relevance outside the phony teaching situation.

Typically, such artificially concocted "thinking skills" are then substituted for real practical abilities. One out of many possible examples is the "skill" of "identifying bias," where "bias" is operationally defined as characterizing statements or positions expressed (for example) in emotionally charged language. Since it is easy to teach techniques for identifying emotionally charged language, that makes this an attractive definition of "bias"—if, that is, the only relevant criterion is conduciveness to being taught as a technique requiring no practical judgment.

The problem is that outside of such bogus teaching situations, "bias" refers to something different, something real and important, something that students do need to be able to recognize and deal with—something else, which is the real concern of those who would applaud and support efforts to address such issues in social studies. Following the criteria of bogus technical definitions of "bias," students would conclude, for example, that Defense Secretary Robert S. McNamara was the most unbiased actor in the Vietnam War, since his positions always were expressed in cold, hard, unemotional statistics—until, that is, he himself had to deal (emotionally, and otherwise) with the realization that his statistical arguments had been flawed by fatal bias all along.

In the real world, "bias" refers to whatever leaning or inclination might tend to prejudice one's judgment on the question at issue. Especially when practical judgments concerning practical questions are at issue, the ability to discern bias requires far more than the kind of technical analysis called for by the definitions and criteria concocted by some gurus of "critical thinking skills." We maintain that democratic education should aim for nothing less than the real mental competence for making practical judgments of this kind.

It is in this sense that the "reflective inquiry" tradition comes closest to the approach we recommend, with its emphasis on relatively open-ended inquiry on matters of real practical concern. Some of our differences with elements within that tradition have been suggested earlier, including differences over "values" and "countersocialization." In general we see these differences resulting from conceptions of "reflective inquiry" that are, in a sense, overdetermined by social or political commitments that are not necessary a priori for the framing of reflective inquiry as such.

What we are proposing is that practical social competence, and mental competence in particular, entails more ambitious goals for democratic educators than is generally recognized, provided that we come to understand "competence" and "mind" in ways that are more adequate for the realities to which those words are meant to refer. We do not fear for principles that are so compelling on their merits that they will be recognized by *competent* "inquiring minds," without needing to be built a priori into the very definition of "inquiry" as such.

Social Science Disciplines and "The Social Imagination"

Our focus on the mental competence for social praxis also guides our approach to the role of social science disciplines in the development of democratic minds. As described by Barr, Barth, and Shermis (1977), one tradition in social studies has favored teaching the social science disciplines as themselves defining the nature, scope, and purposes of social studies. Meanwhile, teachers have shown less support for teaching knowledge and methods of the social sciences, as compared with other purposes for social studies (Fontana, 1980, p. 8). If the issue of defining social education centers on the question of what students need for social competence, then the necessary role of social science disciplines as resources becomes apparent, although not as the ends of social education in themselves. Again, one point will be suggested here to illustrate a more general position that cannot be more fully developed in this chapter.

We believe that what C. Wright Mills (1959) described as "the sociological imagination" is a good example of one form of social competence that is essential for developing the democratic mind. Mills was troubled by the widespread lack of ability for people to understand the private troubles, circumstances, and affairs of individuals in terms of larger social and historical forces and processes that decisively determine the constraints and opportunities that impinge on individuals; or, conversely, to understand the larger-scale phenomena in terms of how they result from and in turn affect the practices of daily life; or, finally, to conceive of how to act in ways that might effectively improve our situation and our prospects, taking both levels of our historical and quotidian lives into account.

Beyond sociology, we might generalize this capability as one of "social imagination," or consider also the "historical," "geographic," "political," "economic," "anthropological," and "psychological" imaginations, in particular. The key point is to understand these disciplinary capabilities as aspects of practical competence, not ends in themselves. When people think of their situations only in terms of their own immediate familiar circumstances, they might be faulted for being selfish or for lacking the right democratic values. From our perspective, however, what this calls for is not so much a socialization (or countersocialization) into a more democratic set of "values." Instead, we propose looking at the consciousness of social causes, consequences, and relationships as an attribute of social competence and democratic mind that requires social education informed by the social science disciplines.

Socialization and "Countersocialization"

Indeed, we believe that socialization itself should be understood as the development of social competence. Our view is consistent with the sociological conception of socialization as the development in individuals of the competence afforded as members of their society (see, e.g., Inkeles, 1966), including the practical competence for critical thinking capable of fundamentally challenging and transcending the practices and understandings currently prevailing within society.

When progressive educators argue that social studies should include some kind of balance between socialization and an opposing "countersocialization," they seem to be construing "socialization" differently, as the inculcation of established norms—i.e., as a debilitating training for conformity, rather than the habilitating, enabling, and empowering formation of competence to act effectively within the particular society. While we support many of the practices recommended by the advocates of countersocialization,[7] we cannot see why countersocialization would be invoked as the purpose of these practices, when it seems to us these are the practices required to provide students with the socialization that they need for competence as effective citizens within their society.

After all, as Gee (1990) argues partly through linguistic examples, development as a member of a language community or a society is fulfilled only at a stage where one is competent to improvise and to participate in fundamental transformations (cf. Habermas, 1979, especially pp. 69–94). A competent writer is not someone who is merely skilled at rewriting things that have been written before, or even at writing only within the limits of recognized conventions. Along the same lines, we do not think that the socialization of young scientists is limited to training in the replication of past findings or conventional procedures. Fresh thinking and the challenging of established paradigms are not regarded as antiscientific, and thus requiring some kind of "countersocialization" opposed to their socialization as members of their disciplines. No more should we describe as "countersocializing" those educational experiences in which students acquire the abilities to challenge social norms or policies; for these abilities also are not antisocial, but are essential aspects of the educated democratic mind.

V. CONCLUSION

When critical pedagogy advocates[8] insist, either explicitly or by their rhetoric, that an a priori value commitment to an insurgent social agenda must come first, before their specifically pedagogical proposals can be considered, this unfortunately suggests that their proposals are of interest or value only to those who share such specific substantive value commitments in advance. We believe this is unfortunate, because we believe that the curriculum and teaching practices proposed by such advocates could be understood by a broader community as the kind of pedagogy that would promote formation of the democratic mind.

The rhetoric of insurgency unfortunately (and falsely, we believe) suggests that a *truly* democratic mind can be formed only on the basis of "values" chosen by the mind in opposition to the established order of the world—one more instantiation of the post-Kantian Romanticist form of the dualistic opposition between mind and world. When "values" are treated as something separate, as matters of preference or commitment determined in advance of and apart from "factual" determinations which are then supposed to be dependent on those a priori value preferences, this is merely an instantiation of another form (perhaps the "postmodern" form) of the positivistic dualism separating facts and values.

We believe that competent engagement in the world itself, including the kinds of pedagogical engagement needed for formation of such competence, will lead to recognition of the principles and practices that have real worth, or value, in relation to real personal and social interests. In this view, the practical social competence required in the formation of the democratic mind is something that can be meaningfully and fruitfully pursued without need for prior consensus on a specific substantive political theory of what would constitute an ideal democratic society.

In this, we feel affinity with Dewey's commitment to, and faith in, what he referred to as "the method of intelligence." Dewey also believed that it was possible to cultivate formation of the democratic mind by attending to requirements of competence for social action, without the need to direct instruction toward more specific social outcomes. We believe that, as in Dewey's case, it is a non-positivistic, nondualistic view of mind that enables us to see formation of the democratic mind as something that can be meaningfully and fruitfully pursued without the need to have first come to a consensus on our substantive conceptions of democracy.

We began by noting that the tradition of discourse on education of the democratic mind has been dominated by arguments over the true nature of democracy, and that crucial background assumptions about mind itself have been relatively unexamined. We hope that we at least have demonstrated the importance of examining those assumptions, and that alternatives to the long-prevailing dualistic and positivistic view of mind are not only available, but available even in the tradition from which Dewey himself wrote.

NOTES

1.   We realize that others might disagree with our description of this category of reform. For example, Elizabeth Ellsworth (1989) contends that feminist pedagogy should be understood as distinct from critical pedagogy. For the purpose of this discussion we prefer to include feminist pedagogy within the larger framework of critical pedagogy.

2.   Barr, Barth, and Shermis (1977) have posed one of the most influential ways of defining social studies education as citizenship education dominated by three major traditions (i.e., citizenship transmission, social science education, and reflective inquiry), which are seen as providing three alternative rationales for social studies purposes, content, and teaching methods.

3.   In the view of reflective inquiry apparently favored by Barr, Barth, and Shermis, for example, what a student sees as problems will be determined by that student's personal values, interests, and needs: "There is no externally existing body of knowledge that must be learned either for its own sake or for use in later life" (1977, p. 80).

4. Traditionally, practical competence (i.e., *"phronēsis"*), or the competence for human *doing* or action, (i.e., *"praxis"*), was understood in terms of how it differed fundamentally in its nature and its development from a purely technical ability (i.e., "technē") which is sufficient for human *making* or production (i.e., "poiēsis"). See Whitson and Stanley (1990), Stanley and Whitson (1992). Within our positivistic intellectual culture, however, even those who have invoked this tradition to call for renewed attention to the "practical" (generally in opposition to crude notions of "practice" as an algorithmic application of abstract "theoretical" knowledge) have been oblivious to the essential differences between the kinds of nonalgorithmic skill that they describe as "art" or "artistry" (which, described as such, remain within the sphere of technē) and the fully practical competence that is required for human praxis (i.e., the kind of *doing* which can bring to light new possibilities for our very *being* in the world, so that the *ends in view* which orient our praxis are continuously subject to reformulation *in view of* such possibilities generated in the very course of that reflective *doing*—as distinguished from a merely "poietic" *making* of products or outcomes that could be specified in advance). See, for example, Schön (1983), Westbury (1972a, 1972b), and even Schwab (1978).

5.   Note here how the differences in syntax for the word "value" can serve as a key to understanding the difference between "values" signified as positive counterparts to "facts," and *values* as *relations,* i.e., as the real *worth* or *value* of principles or practices in relation to real interests.

6.   We understand that generations schooled in English philosophy since Hume have been taught that values are by nature neither true nor false. A *fact* claim may be true or false, but a *value* claim is a different kind of claim. The claim that "he was born in 1930" is a purely factual claim that can be meaningfully characterized as true or false. Insofar as the claim that "he is a good father" depends on values, however, it would be said that this is not a claim of fact that can be true or false, but rather an expression of the speaker's values (and, even if I say "No, he's not," my statement is not really a denial of factual truth, but only an expression of my own conflicting values).

7.   As, indeed, we have ourselves used Engle's and Ochoa's (1989) text enthusiastically since the first semester that it was available.

8.   E.g., as discussed in chapter 4 of Stanley (1992).

REFERENCES

Barr, R. D., Barth, J. L., & Shermis, S. S. (1977). *Defining the social studies*. Bulletin 51. Arlington, VA: National Council for the Social Studies.

Bestor, A. E. (1985). *Educational wastelands: The retreat from learning in our public schools* (2nd ed.). Urbana: University of Illinois Press. (Originally published 1953).

Bloom, B. S., Englehart, M. D., Furst, E. J., Hill, W. H., & Krathwohl, D.R. (1956). *Taxonomy of educational objectives. Handbook I: Cognitive domain.* New York: David McKay.

Brubaker, D. L. (1967). *Alternative directions for the social studies.* Scranton, IL: International Textbook.

Callahan, R. E. (1962). *Education and the cult of efficiency: A study of the social forces that have shaped the administration of the public schools.* Chicago: University of Chicago Press.

Cuban, L. (1991). History of teaching in social studies. In J. P. Shaver (Ed.), *Handbook of research on social studies* (pp. 197–209). New York: Macmillan.

———. (1993). *How teachers taught: Constancy and change in American classrooms, 1890–1990* (2nd ed.). New York: Teachers College Press.

Dennis, L. J. (1989). *Beyond Dewey: The social reconstructionism of George S. Counts and John L. Childs.* Paper presented at the annual meeting of the American Educational Research Association, San Francisco, March.

Dewey, J. (1899). *The school and society.* Chicago: University of Chicago Press.

———. (1902). *The child and the curriculum.* Chicago: University of Chicago Press.

———. (1935a). The crucial role of intelligence. *The Social Frontier, 1*(5): 9–10.

———. (1935b). The need for orientation. *Forum, 93*(6): 333–335.

———. (1937). Education and social change. *The Social Frontier, 3*(26): 235–238.

Dewey, J. & Childs, J. L. (1933). The social-economic situation and education. In W. H. Kilpatrick (Ed.), *Educational frontier* (pp. 32-72). New York: D. Appleton-Century.

Ellsworth, E. (1989). Why doesn't this feel empowering? Working through the repressive myths of critical pedagogy. *Harvard Educational Review, 59*(3): 297–324.

Engle, S. & Ochoa, A. (1989). *Social studies for a democracy: An alternative view.* New York: Teacher's College Press.

Fontana, L. (1980). *Status of social studies teaching practices in secondary schools.* Research Report no. 79. Bloomington, IN: Agency for Instructional Television.

Fraenkel, J. (1973). *Helping students think and value.* Englewood Cliffs, NJ: Prentice Hall.

Gee, J. P. (1990). *Five stages of individual and socio-historical development.* Paper presented at the Annual Meeting of the American Educational Research Association, Boston.

Giroux, H. A. (1988). *Schooling and the struggle for public life: Critical pedagogy in the modern age.* Minneapolis: University of Minnesota Press.

Gose, M. D. (1986). Citation studies: Influential curriculum writers. *Journal of Curriculum and Supervision, 1*(4): 341–343.

Haas, John D. (1979). Social studies: Where have we been? Where are we now? *Social Studies, 70*(4): 147–154.

Habermas, J. (1979). *Communication and the evolution of society.* Boston: Beacon Press.

Hertzberg, H. W. (1989). History and progressivism: A century of reform proposals. In P. Gagnon & The Bradley Commission on History in the Schools (Eds.), *Historical literacy: The case for history in American education* (pp. 69-99). New York: Macmillan.

Hirsch, E. D. (1987). *Cultural literacy: What every American needs to know.* Boston: Houghton Mifflin.

Hunt, M. P., & Metcalf, L. E. (1968). *Teaching high school social studies* (2nd ed.). New York: Harper and Row.

Inkeles, A. (1966). Social structure and the socialization of competence. *Harvard Educational Review, 36*(3): 265–83.

Kliebard, H. M. (1986). *The struggle for the American curriculum, 1893–1958.* Boston: Routledge and Kegan Paul.

Krathwohl, D. R., Bloom, B. S., & Masia, B. B. (1964). *Taxonomy of educational objectives. Handbook II: Affective domain.* New York: David McKay.

Leming, J. S. (1989). The two cultures of social studies education. *Social Education, 53*(6): 404–408.

———. (1992). Ideological perspectives within the social studies profession: An empirical examination of the two cultures thesis. *Theory and Research in Social Education, 20*(3): 293–312.

Lipman, M. (1991). *Thinking in education.* Cambridge: Cambridge University Press.

Lyotard, J. F. (1984). *The postmodern condition: A report on knowledge,* Minneapolis: University of Minnesota Press.

Massialas, B. G., & Cox, B. (1966). *Inquiry in the social studies.* New York: McGraw-Hill.

Mills, C. W. (1959). *The sociological imagination.* New York: Oxford University Press.

Nelson, J. L., & Michaelis, J. U. (1980). *Secondary social studies.* Englewood Cliffs, NJ: Prentice-Hall.

Newmann, F. M. (1975). *Education for citizen action: Challenge for secondary curriculum.* Berkeley, CA: McCutchen.

Newmann, F. M., & Oliver, D. W. (1970). *Clarifying public controversy: An approach to teaching social studies.* Boston: Little, Brown.

Oliver, D. W., & Shaver, J. P. (1966). *Teaching public issues in the high school.* Boston: Houghton Mifflin.

Schön, D. A. (1983). *The reflective practitioner: How professionals think in action*. New York: Basic.

Schott, R. M. (1988). *Cognition and eros: A critique of the Kantian paradigm*. Boston: Beacon.

Schwab, J. J. (1978). The practical: A language for curriculum. In I. Westbury & N. J. Wilkof (Eds.), *Science, curriculum, and liberal education*. Chicago: University of Chicago Press.

Shaver, J. P., & Strong, W. (1982). *Facing value decisions: Rationale-building for teachers* (2nd ed.). New York: Teachers College Press.

Stanley, W. B. (1985). Recent research in the foundations of social education: 1976–1983. In W. B. Stanley (Ed.), *Review of research in social studies education: 1976–1983* (pp. 309–400). Washington, DC: National Council for the Social Studies.

———. (1992). *Curriculum for utopia: Social reconstructionism and critical pedagogy in the postmodern era*. Albany: State University of New York Press.

Stanley, W. B., & Whitson, J. A. (1992). Citizenship as practical competence: A response to the new reform movement in social education. *The International Journal of Social Education, 7*(2): 57–66.

Wagner, P. A. (1990). Will education contain fewer surprises for students in the future? In V. A. Howard, (Ed.) *Varieties of thinking* (pp. 142–173). New York: Routledge.

Westbrook, R. B. (1991). *John Dewey and American democracy*. London: Cornell University Press.

Westbury, I. (1972a). The Aristotelian "art" of rhetoric and the "art" of curriculum. *Philosophy of Education, 28:* 126–136.

———. (1972b). The character of a curriculum for a "practical" curriculum. *Curriculum Theory Network* (Fall), 25–37.

Whitson, J. A., & Stanley, W. B. (1990). *Developing practical competence in social studies education*. Paper presented at the 70th Annual Meeting of the National Council for the Social Studies, Anaheim, CA.

Zilversmit, A. (1993). *Changing schools: Progressive education theory and practice, 1930–1960*. Chicago: University of Chicago Press.

CHAPTER 16

Global Perspectives

Ann V. Angell and Carole L. Hahn

In this chapter we consider democratic education from a comparative and global perspective. As the two of us have moved beyond the context of the United States to live in other democratic societies and study democratic education in differing cultural contexts, we have come to see how ideas such as *democracy, participation, community,* and *citizenship education* are rooted in culture. To illustrate ways in which understanding about democratic participation and citizenship education may vary across cultures, we present three case studies. We elaborate on cultural values, political traditions, and educational processes that contribute to educating democrats in three nations—the United Kingdom, Denmark, and Japan[1].

We focus particularly on the relationship between the role of controversial issues discussion in schools and traditions of democratic discourse and participation in the wider society—themes that are central to this book—in each of three postindustrial societies. We then compare our characterizations of the societies to highlight issues that may be relevant to other democracies at similar stages of democratic and economic development. Ultimately, a comparative perspective illuminates our own culturally embedded experience by helping make problematic aspects of citizenship preparation that we tend to take for granted. It is in this role that comparative education, like anthropology, can serve as a mirror to reflect our own culture back to us (Kluckhohn, 1949).

The three postindustrial nations studied here all have traditions of democratic institutions and universal free education for students to age 15 or 16. There is, however, considerable diversity in the expectations the three societies hold for adult citizens and the ways they prepare youth for their role as citizens.

THE UNITED KINGDOM

Political Culture

Evolving slowly over 800 years, political institutions and culture in the United Kingdom today emphasize tradition and indirect citizen participation. Through a gradual process the individual's status shifted from subject to citizen (Heater, 1990).

The United Kingdom, consisting of England, Scotland, Wales, and Northern Ireland, is a constitutional monarchy, with an unwritten constitution, a monarch who retains the position of head of state, and a prime minister who heads the government. The unwritten constitution[2] rests on legal precedents; there is no Bill of Rights. No single document asserted the rights and responsibilities of the citizen in relation to the government until the recent development of a Citizens Charter, which specifies rights of citizens to good service in dealing with public agencies. Legislative, executive, and judicial powers are centered in Parliament. The bicameral Parliament, consisting of the House of Commons and the House of Lords, is the legislative body for the country. The political party that obtains the majority of seats in the House of Commons selects the prime minister and cabinet, who perform the executive function of the government. "The loyal opposition" is an important institution in Britain, such that the major political parties have a shadow cabinet with shadow ministers monitoring the work of the government ministers. The value placed on the vigilance of the opposition is reflected in the fact that, like the official cabinet, their offices are supported by taxpayers. The House of Lords, in addition to being the second house for legislative purposes, also serves as the highest court of appeal[3]. Its members either inherit their position (peerage) or are appointed lifetime peers by the monarch upon the recommendation of the prime minister.

In addition to paying taxes, obeying laws, and serving on juries or in the military when called, the citizen's primary role is to vote for a member of Parliament and local officials about every four or five years, depending upon when a government calls an election.

When voter dissatisfaction is sufficiently strong, policies may change even before voters replace one Parliamentary majority with another. Nevertheless, for the most part, political elites have the primary tasks of governing or being in active opposition; the media, multiple political parties, and interest groups serve a mediating role; and citizens retain the ultimate power to change governments through periodic elections.

Alongside these shared institutions, variations within the United Kingdom are of major importance. For example, Scotland has a separate legal and educational system; and the Scottish National Party regularly is successful in winning seats in Parliament. In Wales, religious nonconformity and nineteenth century liberalism remain strong influences, whereas in Northern Ireland political culture is rent by religious allegiances.

Nevertheless, in all parts of the country, political culture has been characterized by a tradition of strong political parties. An individual voter casts his or her ballot for the person nominated by the party. The assumption is that one is voting for a party rather than for a person. Once in Parliament, a Member of Parliament (MP) usually votes with other members of his or her party. With the dominance of party bloc voting on most issues, an MP faces the problem of whether to vote with one's party or constituency less often than does a member of the United States Congress. MPs hold weekly "surgeries" or meetings in their constituency where citizens can express concerns, but it is rare that a citizen would write, call, or fax their MP with advice on how to vote on a bill.[4]

British citizens vote for local district councilors as well as for MPs—but again they usually vote for a party rather than for an individual. Both local and Parliamentary campaigns, which last only about one month, are characterized by party workers distributing party positions, or manifestos, door to door. During the month leading up to an election, television commercials carry party messages, which, with the recent influence of North American marketing companies, have begun to focus more on the personalities of the candidates than they did in the past. Annually, each major party holds a conference, out of which is published party positions on issues; and throughout the year, the television carries "party political broadcasts" that present the party's position on issues. The average citizen debates party positions during the brief campaign period, votes, and the remaining time follows news coverage of political issues before Parliament. A minority of activists join a party and attend local party meetings. In general, "politics" is perceived as the differences in political ideology among competing parties and as debates between opposing Parliamentarians—not the work of average citizens. Ian Lister likened British students' perceptions of politics to passively observing gladiatorial contests (Lister, 1991).

As a consequence of increased education, social mobility, the influence of the media, and weakening allegiance of voters to a particular party, a new style of British citizen is emerging, one who applies participation to himself or herself and is less likely to rely on political elites than were earlier generations (Dalton, 1988, p. 239).[5] In earlier days, protests were the last resort of desperate people trying to overthrow a regime, but since the 1960s the use of planned political protests has become an accepted form of political activity. The Campaign for Nuclear Disarmament (CND), numerous environmental groups, and animal rights groups regularly protest at such places as missile sites and NATO bases, nuclear energy plants, or in front of stores that sell products that were tested on animals. Protests against a proposed poll tax a few years ago went so far as to become riots. Many interest groups appeal particularly to young people, and some of their recommendations eventually appear in political party manifestos. Individuals, many working through interest groups, demand to be heard. Although there is still no experience with initiatives, and referenda are used only rarely, when British citizens followed news of the French and Danish referenda on the Maastricht Treaty, some individuals began to demand that their Parliament also put the issue to a vote of the people. However, tradition and power won out, and the decision to move toward closer union in the European community was made by Parliament.

Britain's role in the European Union raises other issues related to citizenship. For example, some scholars are wondering whether Britons can develop a feeling of European citizenship simultaneous to their national citizenship (Heater, 1990). British voters now elect members to the European Parliament (MEPs) and are affected by decisions made in Brussels. To the average citizen, an additional layer of government, geographically removed from them, may reinforce a notion of passive citizenship.

In democratic political cultures, rights that assure open inquiry in a "free marketplace of ideas" as well as forms of citizen participation are essential. Over the past 200 years in Britain, courts developed the doctrine that the individual is free to do anything not forbidden by a specific law, and the state cannot interfere with the civil and political liberties of its citizens unless Parliament authorizes such interference. It is assumed, therefore, that citizens generally enjoy freedom of association, speech, conscience, and movement. In recent years skeptics have questioned limits imposed on such freedoms by the government (Oliver, 1991). In a series of incidents in the 1980s, the government—under the protection of the Official Secrets Act—prevented former officials from speaking or writing on various topics deemed to be threats to national security. The words of IRA members could not be carried on television or printed in newspapers. Antiracist legislation limits speech and press in some cases, and tabloid newspaper editors increasingly are being challenged not only for libel but also for invading individuals' privacy. Interestingly, the topic of free speech and related controversial cases are not addressed in schools, perhaps because there is not a subject called "civics" in which it might fit, or because, as Oliver (1991) argues, "citizenship" is not a clearly developed concept in the United Kingdom.

Although citizenship and civic education have not been major concerns in the United Kingdom, for brief periods there was some interest in them. In the 1930s the Association for Education in Citizenship was formed to prevent the rise of totalitarian tendencies that were becoming evident on the continent, but it failed to have much sustained influence. To counter the lack of political awareness in youth in the 1970s, the Politics Association and its offspring, the Programme for Political Education, promoted "political literacy," which included the investigation of issues in school. The political literacy movement was followed in the 1980s by movements on the Left for peace education, environmental education, and antiracist education, which in turn were followed by countermovements against what the Right called "appeasement education" and for a return to "the basics."

In the years 1988–90 the concept of citizenship entered the political agenda. The three major political parties talked about it from the perspectives of their respective political ideologies. Prime Minister Thatcher and other Conservative leaders called for a return to "active citizenship" by which they encouraged individual voluntary efforts to assist the needy and to fight crime through neighborhood watch schemes. They encouraged businesses to become active citizens by contributing money and in-kind support to local schools and hospitals. Labour leaders, on the other hand, emphasized that a basic principle of democratic socialism was that citizens' obligations to the community are best fulfilled when government improves social welfare provisions. The new center party which brought together former Liberals and Social Democrats called for constitutional reforms, such as a written constitution; a Bill of Rights based on the European Convention on Human Rights; adoption of proportional representation of Parliamentary seats; a definition of entitlements to health, education, housing, and welfare; and devolution of power to national assemblies in Scotland and Wales and to regional assemblies in England (Heater, 1991; Oliver, 1991). By 1990, however, *The Guardian* newspaper noted that "the Active Citizen had vanished from public debate as if he had never been" (Heater, 1991, p. 144).

Civic Education

In the United Kingdom, politics and education have been viewed as two distinct and separate realms (Harber, 1987). Citizenship education was suspected of being indoctrinating, both by the Right and the Left. The few people who became professional politicians —the gladiators—were trained either in the British public schools (independent, expensive boarding schools) or through their union activity. Thus, class was a powerful variable in understanding political socialization as well as other features of society. For the most part, pupils received their political education through their families, the media, or through the hidden curriculum of the school. As described by Lister, "in the elite public schools, Eton and Harrow, for example, the select few—the silver spooners—learned leadership, and in the mass elementary schools the majority—the wooden spooners—learned followership" (Lister, 1987, p. 47). Whether one accepts the notion that the masses were prepared to be followers, it is clear that the vast majority of youth received their preparation for citizenship incidentally, rather than deliberately (Hahn, 1987; Lister, 1991).

The interest in citizenship preparation expressed during the political literacy movement was not heard during the political debates over the active citizen's role nor those over the 1988 Education Reform Bill, which instituted radical changes in the control of education. The previous autonomy of local education authorities diminished as schools were permitted to "opt out" of the local authority and receive funding directly from the office of the Secretary of State for Education. Whereas curriculum had been determined by individual school staffs and local authorities, under the 1988 act all state schools became responsible for teaching a national curriculum and for administering national assessments at four key stages (ages 7, 11, 14, and 16). The national curriculum includes the teaching of the specific subjects of history and/or geography, which are assessed. "Citizenship" is identified as a cross-curricular theme—along with environmental education and health education—to be infused into subjects, and is not assessed.

A visitor to an English school is almost immediately struck by the influence of the hidden curriculum. Upon first entering the school one notices that British students dress rather formally in school uniforms or uniform colors. Girls wear skirts and sweaters and boys wear trousers, leather shoes, and sweaters; neckties and blazers are required in some schools. Secondary students usually begin the morning with registration in their tutor groups (like homeroom) and then go off to an assembly. Traditionally the assemblies were the "corporate act of worship" required by the school law of 1945. Today, students in the same year group (e.g., Year 10 is like tenth grade in the United States) often attend an assembly once or twice a week to hear a Bible reading and inspirational message by a school administrator, a talk by a local religious leader, or programs that feature a charity or a Christian rock group. In a eas with large numbers of immigrants, the assemblies as well as the religious education courses may emphasize a multi-faith them .

The hool prospectus, which is given to visitors, is likely to say that all Year 9 students follow a common curriculum that includes all subjects in the national curriculum (history, geography, maths, English, technology, a foreign language, and science). In Year 10, students begin their two year "options" that prepare them for General Certificate in Secondary Education (GCSE) exams.

History and geography classes are the subjects in the national curriculum that might be expected to carry messages related to citizenship. However, their purpose is primarily t teach the academic subjects, not to achieve another end such as preparing citizens for democratic participation (Lister, 1991). In history and geography classes, teachers typically review material that is on the syllabus for the exam that the particular class will take. History teachers are masters at telling stories and historical anecdotes to hold their young pupils' attention. Geography teachers draw on their deep knowledge of the discipline to explain geographic theories and information such as that on energy use in Britain. Students take notes and "revise" (study) for exams given at the end of each year. Some schools require religious education (RE) as a separate subject for one or two lessons a week; others integrate it with personal and social education.

Like many schools, St. Peter's School, in northwest England, requires that in addition to national curriculum subjects, all pupils have one lesson per week in "personal and social development" (PSD). The course contains lessons in religion, health, sex education, and careers preparation. As part of the course, Year 10 students do one week of work experience in a local business or service agency. The PSD course is typical of courses for students in Years 9–11 at many state schools. It is often taught under titles such as "personal and social education" (PSE) or "individual and society." The class usually meets for two 45-minute periods per week. Activities focus on personal decision-making. There are no textbooks for the subject; photocopied exercises and videos are the stimulus for small-group discussions. The personal and social education programs are often coordinated by the schools' career officer because much attention is given in the course to career awareness and preparation for work. Lessons related to the Universal Declaration of Human Rights, gender stereotyping, traffic safety, alcohol and drug abuse, and careers are found in PSD and PSE courses in many schools. Sometimes local MPs are invited as guest speakers when the students "do politics."

At both the independent and state schools, exposure to controversial public-policy issues occurs primarily in a course called "General Studies" for students who stay in school past age 16. Such a course, which is not assessed, is the one common experience for "sixth formers" (Years 12 and 13), with the remainder of the two-year program devoted to preparing for Advanced- (A-) level exams. At one independent boarding school, sixth formers in one classroom discussed a newspaper editorial about violence in society while in another classroom students engaged in role-play scenarios about youth and the police. At the nearby state school, sixth-form students heard differing views on nuclear energy presented by speakers from a nuclear energy plant and the Friends of the Earth organization.

There is a strong pastoral system in British schools. Tutor groups of about twenty students each are the responsibility of one teacher, who provides student guidance, contacts parents, and often teaches the personal and social education component of the curriculum. Because tutor groups are often the basis for personal and social education, a mathematics or foreign-language teacher is as likely to teach the subject as a history or health teacher. Often tutor groups elect members to a year or school council, which plans parties, raises money for charity, and discusses uniform, homework, and discipline problems. Some schools no longer have such councils.

When students in six secondary schools in different parts of England were interviewed in 1993, most students said they were not interested in politics, government, or current events. Most said that they watch television news, and about half claimed to read newspapers regularly; for some, however, the newspapers they read were tabloids rather than those with serious news analysis. As for talking about politics, government, or current events in school, most said they did not. A few said Parliament was mentioned in history, but that was all. When asked about controversial issues, several said they talked about racism in personal and social education. Others mentioned the Maastricht Treaty as a controversial issue they had heard about in the news, but said that it was not mentioned in school and they did not know what it was about. The few exceptions to this were four pupils who took Business Studies for one of the GCSE options; they reported that in the unit on farming they learned about the common agricultural policy of the European Community. They learned about subsidies and quotas, but they had not learned about the debate over the Maastricht Treaty that was in the news at the time they took the course.

One student who was quite well informed about political and international news, including the Maastricht debate, was Chris. Chris attended an expensive independent boarding school. He was taking A-level Business Studies and was applying to a university to read (specialize in) Economics and Politics. His uncle was an MP and Chris described himself as being very interested in politics. In particular, he explained that he got his information about the EC and Maastricht not from school, but from reading newspapers and his own general interest.

Observations and talks with English youth confirmed the truth of Lister's claim (1987) that in Britain political education is caught, not taught; incidental rather than deliberate. Despite the Government policy that citizenship was to be a cross-curricular theme in the national curriculum, in visits to secondary schools in 1993, no teacher mentioned the government publication of citizenship guidelines, and the published guidelines were not visible in any of the classes.

DENMARK

Political Culture

Denmark is similar to the United Kingdom in that its constitutional monarchy evolved over hundreds of years. Unlike the British system, however, the modern Danish political system was established in a written constitution in 1849, then amended several times until the current constitution was written in 1953. The 1953 constitution confirms that Denmark is a democratic constitutional monarchy. The monarch is the head of state, the executive power is granted to the government headed by the prime minister, the legislative power is assigned to the unicameral legislature, the *Folketing*, to which members are elected by a process of proportional representation; and there is an independent judiciary. The constitution further creates an office of ombudsperson—a feature of Scandinavian political systems—to investigate citizens' complaints against national and local administrations.[6] Characteristic of Denmark and other Scandinavian countries is the periodic use of the referendum, which in recent years focused public attention on the pros and cons of Danish participation in the European Community. The constitution guarantees basic rights and fundamental freedoms, such as freedom of speech and assembly; and it guarantees declaratory social rights such as rights to work and to social welfare assistance.

Danish culture is characterized by cooperation and negotiation, as opposed to confrontation. Denmark never experienced a revolution and even the transfer of central power from a monarch to the people was achieved relatively calmly. The country was neutral in World War I and was occupied by the Nazis in 1940, with an agreement that the Danes would remain in control of their major institutions. (An underground Danish resistance movement grew after the occupation.) After the Second World War, Denmark jointed NATO and the Council of Europe, but referenda on their participation in the European Community/Union have been opposed in part because of a reluctance to join other nations in a common defense policy, reservations about a single European currency, and fears of losing cultural identity. Cooperation and negotiation are essentials, particularly within the realities of Danish political life in which multiple political parties are forced to form coalitions in order to govern. Four of the political parties have existed since the turn of the century, with other parties growing and waning from one election to the next. Since the 1920s, the Social Democrats have obtained a plurality of votes in most elections, but after each election parties seek others to form a coalition, sometimes leaving the largest single party out of the Government. At other times the Social Democrats are successful in forming coalitions with other parties either to its left or right. Citizens thus cast votes for a particular party's positions, giving it power to form coalitions. When a coalition government is formed, the parties decide how many posts (ministries) and which ones will go to each of the governing parties. A similar process is followed by the multiplicity of parties that vie for voters' support at the local, or *Kommune*, level with the largest party being assigned the most important local committees, or Councils, one of which is responsible for schools, and others for various social welfare programs.

There is a multiplicity of newspapers and newsmagazines, each representing a different political viewpoint. National radio and television was a state monopoly until 1988. Now media are regulated along public service lines by public service authorities, irrespective of revenue source (the Danish Broadcasting Corporation, a license fee, and some advertising on selected channels). Equal time is assured to all of the political parties during a three-week election campaign, but the rest of the time primary attention is given to the views of the largest parties. Although class perception was a major determinant of voting behavior in the past, and most people identified with the party of their parents, in Denmark as in other European countries and the United States, party membership and loyalty has been on the decline in recent years (Fitzmaurice, 1981). Nevertheless, young people are constantly exposed to the diverse messages of a variety of political parties. Focused issues such as tax reform, the environment, immigration policies, and closer union in the European Community/Union have generated support for new parties at the same time that older parties adjust to changing concerns. Although there have been widely differing political and economic policies advocated by different parties, it must be recognized that Denmark is culturally a very homogeneous society. Until recently, there were few immigrants and no deep religious or ethnic cleavages. Deciding among competing public policy choices within the context of shared cultural values is the task for which Danish schools prepare future citizens.

Civic Education

Danish students attend a *folkskole* until age 16, when they make the choice to stay an additional year, to go to work, or to begin their further studies in a commercial school or a gymnasium. The folkskole law emphasizes that a primary purpose of the school is to model democracy in order to prepare citizens for participation and decision-making. Toward that end, from the first grade on, by law there is a scheduled weekly class meeting in which students discuss and resolve class and school problems, hear from and advise their representatives to the student council, and decide on topics to be studied and methods to be used. The student council has a budget from the school council or board. Further, the student council elects two student representatives to the school board. Student representatives have equal voice with the two teacher representatives and five to seven parents on the board.

A visit to one ninth-grade folkskole class revealed the pervasive atmosphere of democratic learning. In this class as in most, the students call their teacher by her first name; and students and teacher alike are dressed in jeans, running shoes, and have their ubiquitous book bags on the floor by their desks. Mette's class has been together with her for nine years. After the optional tenth grade, students will leave the school and Mette will begin the ten-year sequence again with another group of students in the first grade. When the children were in the primary grades, Mette and a colleague taught all subjects, but in recent years she specialized in history, Danish, biology, and the required course in "contemporary studies"[7] while other specialists taught English, physical education, art, and religion. In Mette's class, students used the scheduled "class time" for deliberation and decision-making. For example, during that time, they decided what topics to study in contemporary studies, they planned their yearly class trips, and they advised their school council representatives on such controversial school issues as whether to use their money for a new bike shed or to repair damage to a building by some unknown student vandals. In prior years the students decided to conduct research on pollution in local lakes and to make peace games about environmental issues. At the end of the eighth grade when they were to decide on the topics for contemporary studies in the ninth grade, they debated between studying about the conflict in the former Yugoslavia or the debate over the Maastricht Treaty. They decided to investigate the Yugoslavian conflict first and then Maastricht. Another class decided to investigate the topic of video violence.

After grade 9 or 10, about 40 percent of Danish 16–17-year-olds enter a gymnasium, where they specialize in either a mathematics sciences line or a languages line. Regardless of line or track, students take a course in history in their first year, 20 percent of which is social science. In the languages line students may take social science at a medium or high level in their second or third year, which leads to their having a varied number of lessons per week in preparation for an oral or written examination. The social science courses must include attention to sociology, economics, political science, and international relations; and part of the course is based on a major social science investigation. Instead of attending a gymnasium, some students choose to take a two-year program to prepare for an exam, which includes history and social science.

At Anderson Gymnasium, about an hour from Copenhagen, a second-year medium-level social science class was doing a social science project. The class considered investigating the Yugoslavian conflict, but decided instead to investigate various aspects of the Maastricht Treaty, particularly as it was presented by the media prior to the second referendum. Two students compared the treatment in various newspapers, two others compared the Maastricht and Edinburgh versions of the treaty, and five others analyzed a survey they gave to students at two different gymnasia. At another gymnasium a high-level social science class was doing a social science project on topics related to socialization. They too had divided into groups, with each group investigating a different issue related to the topic.

At one gymnasium, students sitting in the commons area with cups of coffee and cigarettes explained that their student council decided to sell condoms, and decided on the location of the smoking and no-smoking areas. The council also worked on a national effort to raise money for refugees by encouraging students to take a day from school to earn money baby-sitting and doing other jobs for people The students said that they were interested in politics, the environment, racism, and the Maastricht referendum. Their teacher, Niels, later explained that it's not cool for gymnasium students to say they aren't interested in politics and international issues. When asked about the fact that in class discussion, on practice exams, and in projects students seemed to present several opinions and express their own opinions, he laughed and said, "Well, they know they have to do it to get a good mark. It's the Danish system."

In the seven Danish schools visited in 1993, students said they studied about the European Community because they chose that topic for their investigations. There was so much interest in the topic that every time the interviewer would encourage them to talk about some other issue in politics or the news, they would bring the conversation back to the EC, expressing divergent opinions:

> JAN: There are many reasons to be against it—one is that we would just be a member of Germany or France. Another reason is that fisherman have been hurt by it, even though they supported it in the beginning, and the Danish farmers now will be hurt in the future too.
> INGE LISE: I will vote no because the EC is for the economy, not the environment. The other countries don't have as strict laws as Denmark about pollution.
> LISBETH: The first treaty was about the common market and that was good for the economy, but the Maastricht and Edinburgh treaties go further to a more integrated union and that is not good because too many decisions are made by bureaucrats who aren't elected.
> SØREN: I have another view. I will vote yes because I think it will help the economy. For the past ten years we have had unemployment and the Danish farmers are having a difficult time and I think it will help.

KIRSTEN: We can't be certain what the consequences will be—as some say we could lose our national identity, but I think it is important to vote "yes" for economic reasons.

JAPAN

Political Culture

Japan has all the furnishings of a parliamentary democracy. The Constitution of 1946 declares the people sovereign, guarantees fundamental human rights, and provides for a parliamentary system of government. The House of Councillors and the House of Representatives make up the Diet, whose members are elected as representatives of the people; party-identified candidates compete freely in periodic elections; and all adult citizens are eligible to vote. Executive power is vested in the cabinet, which consists of the prime minister, selected from the Diet by its members, and the ministers of state, appointed by the prime minister. The emperor has no governmental powers; he is a symbol of the unity of the people. Moreover, the August 1993 election of a coalition government broke a string of thirty-eight consecutive years of one-party rule by the Liberal Democratic Party, providing some evidence of democratic pluralism in Japan.

Many observers of Japanese society and politics, however, question the degree to which Japan's postwar democracy has taken root, arguing that aspects of the sociopolitical climate in Japan contradict liberal democratic principles. Critics point to a high level of conformity that characterizes life in both public and private domains; passivity of the people in regard to public issues; weakness of unions; a single-voiced press; oppressive treatment of suspects and disregard for due process in the legal system; a Supreme Court controlled by bureaucrats; and a school system that fosters loyalty to the status quo, sorting students for placement in hierarchical bureaucracies (McCormack and Sugimoto, 1986; van Wolferen, 1989). In a critique of Japan's enigmatic political system, van Wolferen asserted that "[t]he concept of democracy in Japan is not a pragmatic concept guiding actual political processes . . . [but] a radical concept, valued in an abstract, normative sense . . . outside existing politics and history" (1989, p. 310).

For the Japanese to have taken on the forms of liberal democracy without necessarily ascribing to its content would be consistent with their tradition of cultural borrowing. Just as the Japanese borrowed many Chinese pictographs for their phonetic value without adopting their meanings, so also they may have nominally adopted democratic institutions to appease the West after World War II without embracing the underlying principles of liberal democracy. Japanese teachers who were interviewed consistently associated the origin of Japanese democracy with the Meiji Restoration of 1868, suggesting a prevailing belief that Japan had been democratized before the postwar reforms. During the Meiji period, a coalition of feudal lords reinstated the emperor and organized a new government that set Japan's course for modernization, empowering local governments, establishing universal access to schooling (boys and girls, upper and lower classes), and outlawing the tradition of rigid social-class separation. Modern Japanese teachers emphasized that the elimination of social-class restrictions constituted the essence of freedom. One teacher summarized the points made by many:

> Democracy means freedom and being equal. Freedom, equality. When we think of life in the old times, they didn't have freedom. It was a hard time. Japanese were divided into four classes: Samurai, Farmers, Craftsmen, Merchants. If I was born as a merchant, I couldn't go to be a craftsman. They stayed in one place all their lives.

Another said, "Democracy is important for women. Women didn't vote in politics, but from the Meiji era—no, World War II—they vote."

Junior high school students' responses to a civic attitudes questionnaire indicated strong support for the principle and practice of free speech (Angell, 1990a). That support seemed ironic, however, in light of students' classroom behavior, which was consistently passive and nonparticipative. Even when asked a question directly and pressed by the teacher for an answer, the habit of the students was either to mumble an answer that was barely audible or to confer hastily with classmates in the immediate vicinity until consensus on the answer was reached—and *then* mumble the answer. A teacher explained the conflict:

> In Japan we should say what we think freely, but if a person is my senior I can't speak freely. [T]o speak frankly has no relationship to good citizenship or to the good Japanese. In Japan we can't

speak frankly because it's rude. It's not a good custom, but it's a custom. I want to speak frankly, but I can't.

Respect and obedience, loyalty to family, and contributing to social harmony are basic civic values in the Japanese political culture. Student responses to questions of personal and political efficacy reflected commitment to group goals and a desire to avoid situations that would make any individual prominent within the group. Individual aspirations were seldom expressed except in relation to honoring one's family. The group loyalty that eclipsed thinking about individual action framed the students' concept of participation. A social studies teacher tried to clarify the meaning of political participation:

> In Japan what is most important is participation. Everyone participates in the meeting. What they talk about isn't so important. Of course they exchange views, but finally they agree with the plan. No opposition. The final decision is always up to the boss or someone in charge. Being present in the place is very important.

Rohlen, whose ethnographic study of Japanese high schools provided one of the clearest windows on modern Japanese education, noted in an essay on order in Japanese society that:

> Participation is the measure of acceptance, openness, and satisfaction. It is part of a reciprocal arrangement, the individual's contribution to the whole. Not joining in, on the other hand, is a rejection, an act of defiance, and a sign of alienation. (1989, pp. 28–29)

In response to questions about their future participation in politics, most students indicated that they would probably vote; few thought they would belong to a political party. Responses overall suggested low levels of expected future participation, with the females having lower levels of expected participation than the males. Conversations with teachers and school officials suggested a widespread belief that politics should be left to politicians, just as shoe repair is left to shoemakers. Political scandals, however, frequently made headline news, and the low levels of political trust expressed by the junior high students indicated some level of student awareness that was not acknowledged by teachers. Responses to questions about democratic citizens influencing public policy suggested conflict about the advisability of writing to a Diet member or participating in public demonstrations. With a political history that has traditionally demanded obedience and abhorred opposition, it is hardly surprising that neither Japanese adults nor young people could readily imagine how civil disobedience might constitute desirable political participation (Benedict, 1946; van Wolferen, 1989).

A citizen's responsibility, from the perspective of the Japanese junior high school students polled, is to obey contemporary laws and traditional standards of conduct (especially honoring one's family), to know how taxes are spent, and to vote. Some teachers were openly supportive of the teacher's union, but none seemed to equate that kind of activity with citizenship. One appointed representative to the teacher's union did say, however, that she had become much more interested in politics since serving on the union council.

The good citizen, according to most Japanese, is one who does what is expected—by the family, work group, community, and state. Contentment with prevailing conditions is regarded as a mark of character; complaints and criticism are regarded as childish. Traditionally, families have been responsible for developing character and patriotism in their offspring, with the idea that the parent-child and emperor-subject relationships are analogous. Representing all that is noble in the national tradition, the family has long been regarded as the most appropriate context for the training of loyal citizens (Dore, 1958).

Civic Education

Leaders of the Meiji government established a system of schooling for the explicit purpose of using modern technical knowledge to promote Japan's economic prosperity and to insure competitiveness with the West. The Meiji constitution, however, promoted allegiance to traditional Confucian values, emphasizing cultural transmission and deference to authority, both of which inhibited creativity and contributed to the rise of political despotism.

The postwar constitution of 1946 mandated compulsory schooling through the ninth grade and redefined the mission of Japanese schools as the fostering of peace and the preservation of a democratic social order. In an effort to quell nationalism, the moral education component of the prewar school curriculum was abolished by American occupation advisors. Civic education was instituted as the standard social studies course for the ninth-grade year, divided into three units of study—the Japanese constitution, the structure and function of government (including the "political participations of the citizen"), and the national economy.

Rohlen (1983) pointed out that the efforts of American postwar reformers to redirect Japanese educational goals towards educating citizens rather than subjects "never captured the popular imagination" (p. 74). He found that contemporary teachers generally accepted citizenship as a desirable goal, but felt it was their duty to teach citizenship through traditional methods of firm guidance, discipline, and control.

The director of a city cultural center recalled the postwar period of reform in Japanese schools, when he had been class president in his junior high school. During that time, he had been invited as a student representative to meetings of U. S. advisors with local teachers and administrators about instituting and safeguarding democracy through the school curriculum. Student councils had sprung up in every school and deliberation of issues in the classroom had been expected, along with encouragement of student questions, voting on school issues, and more autonomy for individuals within the system. The teacher's union was formed, as were the popular after-school clubs, which extend each schoolday by several hours. The director explained, however, that most of the reforms were short-lived:

> For awhile there were many discussions in classrooms. All schools had student advisory councils. At first they were asked to discuss policy issues related to the school. However, in time the primary responsibilities of student councils became the planning of events such as "Culture Day" or "Sports Day." As for the discussions in classes, teachers found that they didn't have time to teach everything and it was discovered also that students weren't learning the necessary material. So there has slowly been a return to the old way. Now the teacher talks all the time and the students just take notes and memorize the facts.

By 1958 moral education had been reinstated by the Ministry of Education, despite opposition from the Japan teacher's union. Most Japanese parents supported the reinstatement, expressing beliefs that traditional values were endangered and should be taught by the school (Singleton, 1967). Moral education is now a separate subject taught one period each week in all schools at all grade levels (1–9). The list of values to teach is specified by the Ministry of Education, but local school districts have considerable autonomy in choosing particular themes and designing lessons. Although moral education is described as a forum for discussion of personal and school problems, Japanese teachers have little experience in conducting discussions; and students, who are accustomed to listening to lectures and taking notes, have no experience participating in discussions (Rohlen, 1983; Singleton, 1967). Western observers often note that Japanese students almost never ask questions.

In a moral education lesson, the eighth-grade teacher gave explicit directions for conducting a two-sided discussion. All the students read the same story (girls seated in their desks in rows on one side of the classroom, boys on the other). Then the teacher presented questions that represented the concerns of opposing viewpoints on the topic—"modesty and generous attitude toward others." The scenarios suggested a Kohlberg moral dilemma; and in fact, moral reasoning questions were raised, the teacher trying to elicit from students some statement of opinion or position; and then, again with limited success, trying to get the students to make statements to support the other side. At no time was there discussion among the students; a labored dialogue transpired between teacher and one student after another.

In conversations about discussion as a viable pedagogical practice, Japanese teachers' questions for American educators suggested their skepticism about the relevance and practicality of discussions in the classroom: "How do you grade discussions? How do you start them? How do you get students to disagree with one another? Why do you have discussions?" they asked. Another commented that "Discussions are useless. They don't help you pass entrance examinations."

The current stated goals for social studies issued by the Ministry of Education include, for all levels of schooling, the development of citizens capable of perpetuating a democratic and peaceful society. However, the social studies curriculum beyond the elementary school has become increasingly segmented; classes are designed to impart knowledge about Japanese history, geography, government, or economics. Pedagogical practices in social studies classes beyond the seventh grade, although occasionally punctuated by student presentations of current events or a video program, are usually confined to lecture, note-taking, and limited recitation (Berman, 1990).

Whereas civic education might be formally associated with the ninth-grade civics course, the shaping of socially responsible Japanese is of paramount importance to teachers from the preschool level through the junior high homeroom teachers. Preschoolers are given considerable freedom in their social interactions to promote good social problem-solving skills, personal responsibility for the success of group functions, and a sense of dependence on the peer group for personal satisfaction (Lewis, 1989; Tobin, Wu, and Davidson, 1989). Embedded in the Japanese approach to elementary school education are some distinctly democratic principles. The elementary school is organized to give every individual child an equal opportunity, which takes the form of a highly standardized national curriculum across every district and prefecture in the country. *All* Japanese first graders learn to cultivate morning glories; second graders cultivate sunflowers; third graders, heikima; fourth graders, potatoes; fifth graders, rice; and sixth graders, pumpkins. The national curriculum dictates what is studied and how fast, to the extent that it is possible to visit one school in the city on Tuesday where the seventh graders are on Lesson 7 in their social studies book and another school in the countryside on Wednesday where the seventh graders are on Lesson 8.

The notion that each child should have equal access to the curriculum extends to all areas of the curriculum—physical education, art, and musical training included—and the expectation is that each child is capable of succeeding (White, 1987). From this perspective, which seems highly egalitarian, the classification and education of special children is problematic; and in fact, the Japanese have been slow to develop special-education settings for the variety of disabilities that occur in a normal population—visual impairment, hearing impairment, mental disability, and others. Although there has been some change in a small percentage of progressive city schools, in most schools all children, regardless of special needs, are mainstreamed and expected to succeed under normal conditions. By the time many of these special students reach middle school, they have dropped so far behind that they have been socially marginalized by peers and are ignored by teachers, despite often highly disruptive behaviors.

Another democratic principle that seems operative at the elementary level is participative group decision-making. Students are given carefully defined areas of school life within which they can operate with a high degree of peer-group autonomy. Within the group, individualism quickly withers; but student groups do plan special events, maintain their own physical school environment, and determine how free time will be spent together. The student councils that were established in the postwar reforms still exist in most schools, but the agendas are prescribed by tradition and are typically limited to planning school events such as Culture Day or waging clean-up campaigns.

In the junior high school, school rules demand a high level of conformity to dress and behavior codes, with the homeroom teachers taking full responsibility for students' decorum both in school and beyond. If a student is seen in a public establishment that is considered improper, the homeroom teacher (rather than a parent) is generally notified and takes strong action to correct the behavior, sometimes visiting the student's home to administer punishment. Scoldings and physical punishments are also meted out regularly in the teachers' room where all the faculty witness the humiliation of the offender. Occasionally there are reports of student resistance to school rules—a ninth grader refuses to get his hair cut, or a small group of students propose new lunch routines. However, seldom do those protests result in any real change of school policy, even when they are followed by the press and appear to have some parent or public support (Angell, 1990b).

Interviews with teachers suggested that politics bordered on being one of the closed areas in social discourse, and certainly was not an appropriate topic for junior high school students to think or talk about. The Japanese school official who made revisions on the civic attitudes questionnaire before giving final approval to the project changed the item that asked if different points of view were encouraged in class discussions to read "class discussions of school life," insisting that those were the only discussions students would be asked to engage in. Another closed area appeared to be the status and treatment of minorities—Koreans, the indigenous Ainu, the historically outcast Burakumin. The same school official reacted strongly to questions about discrimination and insisted that they be deleted from the instrument, while admitting that discrimination problems did exist in Japan:

Actually [discrimination] is true in daily life in Japan. It is a big problem in [another prefecture] and some other areas. The teachers in [that prefecture] would especially be angry at such a question. Here in [our prefecture] they would be very, very nervous about it. Teachers do not want students to answer questions like this because all people in the world should be equal. They think it is better not to talk about it.

Rohlen (1983) observed that Japanese students were even more politically apathetic than American high schoolers. Recent statistics indicate that dropouts and absenteeism are both on the increase in Japanese schools. Most Japanese young people, however, are studying hard to pass examinations that will gain them a place in higher education and assure subsequent employment with good companies. They are learning to conform to expectations, they remain relatively remote from the political process, and they expect to follow in the tradition of becoming good Japanese rather than active citizens.

COMPARISONS

The British, the Danish, and the Japanese all describe their political tradition as democratic, but their meanings for underlying principles such as good citizenship, political participation, and civic education differ widely. Moreover, their political cultures differ along two fundamental dimensions of democracy, described by Dahl (19⁻1) as "participation" and "contestation." The value placed on these two dimensions of democracy influences the nature of civic education, its practice in schools, and attitudes towards citizenship.

Most western political scholars associate political participation with citizen actions taken for the purpose of influencing government—voting, discussing issues, mobilizing others to vote, and involvement with groups that lobby to influence policymakers (Huntington and Nelson, 1976; Powell, 1982). Powell (1982) proposed that the extent to which elections precipitate change in government be used as an index to the meaningfulness of political participation. According to Powell's index, political participation is highly meaningful when governments regularly change as a result of elections. When there is only occasional, but some change, political participation is moderately meaningful; and when there is no change, political participation has little meaning for voters. Based on this index, among the three countries studied, political participation has the most meaning for voters in Denmark. Danish elections regularly produce changes in the government through the formation of new coalitions. In the United Kingdom, the Conservative Party has been in power since 1976 (eighteen years in 1994); in Japan the Liberal Democratic Party controlled the government from 1945 until the 1993 election, except for a brief period of socialist government in 1947–1948. Accordingly, both the United Kingdom and Japan rank lower than Denmark on Powell's index of meaningful political participation.

The three societies also differ in the extent to which contestation is expected, tolerated, and exercised in the political process. In Japan, with the Liberal Democratic Party having dominated for almost fifty years, civic virtue is associated with compliance rather than contestation. In the British Parliament, contestation is institutionalized through the appointment and maintenance of the loyal opposition; the people expect contestation on their behalf, but do not personally exercise it.[8] In Denmark, contestation is almost synonymous with participation. The Danish people respond to contested issues through participation in referenda and sociopolitical criticism. Contestation is commonplace in the government, where multiple political parties with competing points of view build coalition governments and an ombudsperson is institutionalized to represent the people's complaints against the administration of government polices.

The empowerment of the individual within the Danish political culture suggests a concept of active democratic citizenship that incorporates high levels of participation and contestation. A respectable voter turnout in the United Kingdom suggests active citizenship with relatively high levels of participation, but the British tradition of republicanism, or indirect democracy, has meant leaving government up to the professional politicians. Contestation at the grassroots level is largely absent. For the Japanese, political participation means simply to be present and counted—but without contesting, which is regarded as impolite or lacking in self-discipline. Good citizenship is nonpolitical; civic virtue consists in working hard, obeying the law, paying taxes, and doing one's best. However, recent changes in government leadership and public protests about corruption in politics may signal a change in the direction of more active and critical citizenship in Japan.

To what extent do these three democracies approach Dewey's democratic ideal of promoting increasingly free, numerous, and varied interactions among diverse social groups? Although diversity is naturally limited within the homogeneous populations of both Denmark and Japan, the two societies are quite different in the way existing diversity is managed.[9] In Denmark the interaction of diverse sociopolitical groups is fostered and encouraged; what is expected is a forging of common purposes and policies that will serve all well. In contrast, the hierarchies that continue to exist in both formal and informal Japanese society reduce interaction between different social groups. In recent years management approaches have instituted quality circles to establish communication lines between levels within a factory or service operation. Traditional family life, however, is still based on narrow bands of social interactions that tend to keep individuals with peers and people most like themselves. Moreover, insularity has been a hallmark of Japanese history. In Britain the persistent awareness of class difference is a deterrent to free and multiple interactions among the many different groups within that society. The history of British interaction with groups beyond their own society, however, has made British culture less insular than Japanese.

Civic Education Across the Three Nations

Although citizenship is a stated goal of schooling in the three countries studied here, their approaches to civic education reflect different interpretations of citizenship. Moreover, the differing value placed on political participation and contestation within each culture is reflected in the practices of civic education, which result in substantively different outcomes.

The role of teachers in preparing Japanese citizens is understood as a moral responsibility to instill the values of hard work, loyalty, obedience, and cooperation as a group member—of the family, class, neighborhood, nation. Participation is taught as a form of group cooperation; contestation is largely absent from school behavior. The British, with their resistance to formal political education in the school curriculum, also take a values approach to civic education. Teachers provide pastoral guidance for their class, religious education plays a role, and the formal curriculum sets aside regular school time for counseling on matters of personal and social development. Political participation and contestation are not represented as civic virtues.

In Denmark, where citizenship education is regarded as the primary aim of schooling, participation and contestation are both regarded as essential preparation for decision-making about public policy issues. Students are expected to learn about democratic participation and contestation through models provided in their school experience. In contrast to students in Japan, where there is no provision for discussions of public policy and an absence of criticism or differing views on an issue, Danish students are expected to participate and practice the skills of democratic deliberation, critically examining issues from different points of view, debating competing positions, and expressing their opinions. Whereas student councils appear to have only perfunctory roles in both the United Kingdom and Japan, the student and school councils on which students serve in Denmark empower students to deal with real issues—both those that directly affect their school environment and those that expand into the public realms of community and state. The approach to the education of democratic citizens in Denmark epitomizes Engle's ideal of decision-making as the heart of civic education.

The unintentional or hidden civic curriculum within each of the cases described is worth noting. The tradition of wearing uniforms in the British and Japanese schools may serve to conceal economic inequalities among students and to foster group pride. At the same time, however, uniforms suggest the indirect transmission of values such as order, conformity, and discipline. In both the British and Japanese systems, the power of examinations to sort students into strata based on academic competition also functions as part of the political socialization process. In neither system is citizenship education assessed, reducing its importance from both students' and teachers' point of view. Whereas tracking students based on their exam performance is common in the United Kingdom and Japan, folkskole law in Denmark permits ability grouping only under rare circumstances. The Japanese emphasis in school on memorization, external rewards, and acceptance rather than critical thought closely fits the authoritarian model of schooling criticized by Apple and others (Aronowitz, 1973; Bernstein, 1977; Bowles and Gintis, 1976; Giroux and Penna, 1979). The social climate of the Danish school, however, suggests more intentional planning of routines, social habits, and arrangements that might foster the development of participatory skills and deliberations of contested issues.

How do the outcomes of civic education in these cases differ? In Japan, high school students indicated apathy towards public affairs, and junior high school students reported low levels of political trust, political interest, and political efficacy; moreover, they did not expect to participate in politics as adults. English students also indicated lack of interest in politics, along with very little knowledge about public affairs. Only the Danish students indicated interest, knowledge, and intent to participate in politics. There was also evidence that the students were already well informed and skilled critical thinkers with regard to social and political affairs.

The value placed on political participation and contestation in Danish civic education not only reflects the political culture but lays the foundation for the high levels of participation and contestation that characterize the political culture of Denmark. In her theory of democratic education, Gutmann (1987) emphasized that the ideal of a democratically sovereign society can only be realized if education aims at developing the habits of participation and critical thought:

> Children must learn not just to *behave* in accordance with authority but to *think* critically about authority if they are to live up to the democratic ideal of sharing political sovereignty as citizens. (p. 27)

The Danish students' ability to think critically appears to develop through their frequent participation in discussions of controversial issues. Research has associated the discussion of controversial issues in an open intellectual climate with higher levels of political interest, political efficacy, political knowledge, and antiauthoritarian attitudes (Almond and Verba, 1963; Hahn, Tocci, and Angell, 1988; Hahn & Tocci, 1990; Torney, Oppenheim and Farnen, 1975).

There is considerable evidence to support Thomas Jefferson's conviction that people must be educated for their role as sovereign citizens if a democracy is to endure. Moreover, there is a relationship between the kind of civic education a state provides, the kind of citizen that it produces, and the civic culture that develops. Participation in open discussion of controversial issues, the encouragement of dissent, and critical thought are essential if the goal of civic education is to foster participation, contestation, and commitment to furthering democratic ideals.

NOTES

1.   Much of the data for these case studies was drawn from studies conducted by the two authors. In 1986–87 and again in 1992–93 Carole Hahn conducted research in England and Denmark as well as in several other European democracies (Hahn, 1987, 1993; Hahn and Tocci, 1990; Hahn, Tocci and Angell, 1988; Torney-Purta and Hahn, 1989). With grants from the Spencer Foundation and the Emory University Research Committee, she surveyed adolescents, observed secondary social studies classes, and interviewed teachers and students. In 1988–90 Ann Angell conducted research in junior high schools in Japan (Angell, 1990a, 1990b). During the eighteen months of living in Japan, she surveyed students, observed classes, and interviewed teachers and students. The surveys used in the three countries were translated into British English, Danish, and Japanese, and back-translated to ensure comparability of meaning. Interviews were conducted in English or with translators present to interpret when necessary. Data were obtained in a variety of schools in different parts of each country over an extended period of time so that our understandings represent more than first impressions of the traveler. However, our outsider perspectives enabled us to see things that might have been taken for granted by members of the culture. Because our goal was to capture the meanings of the participants in the schools and cultures, several colleagues in each culture reviewed our interpretations at various points in the evolution of our understanding. In this chapter we illustrate themes with data obtained in particular schools that are typical of what we observed in many places. Except where full names are specifically given, the names of teachers and schools used here are pseudonyms. We are grateful to Mette Morck, Jorgen Lerche Nielsen, Tom Lancaster, Lesley Smith, Randy Strahan, Christine von Lersner, and Roy Williams, who read earlier drafts of the manuscript and gave us helpful suggestions.

2.   Although it is generally referred to as unwritten, it includes laws affecting institutional structures and rules, as well as precedents.

3.   The Law Lords on the Judiciary committee are the highest court of appeal; there is no constitutional court.

4. There is considerable divergence of opinion over how rare this is; nevertheless, students are not taught in school that part of the role of the citizen is to contact MPs to voice their opinion on legislation.

5. Democratic ideals that emphasize rule by elected elites in a republican or representative system may be shifting to a greater emphasis on grassroots participation.

6. The United Kingdom has also adopted this Scandinavian concept whereby complaints against the administration of local government or national services can be filed with the appropriate ombudsperson for investigation.

7. In autumn 1994 a new law for **folkskoles** came into effect whereby Contemporary Studies was no longer required but taught as part of social studies. It remains to be seen whether students will continue to help select controversial public policy issues for investigation. Under the new law, class decision-making is to be handled spontaneously rather than during a scheduled weekly period.

8. The poll tax riots were an exception to this.

9. Traditionally both Japanese and Danish societies have been characterized by ethnically homogeneous populations in which cultural values are shared. However, in both countries the recent influx of immigrants from diverse racial, religious, and cultural backgrounds may pose new challenges to the civic culture.

REFERENCES

Almond, G., & Verba S. (1963). *The civic culture*. Princeton: Princeton University Press.

Angell, A. V. (1990a, November). *Civic attitudes of Japanese middle school students: Results of a pilot study*. Paper presented at the College and University Faculty Assembly of the National Council for the Social Studies, Anaheim, CA.

_____. (1990b, November). *The rights of children in Japan: A teaching unit for the upper elementary grades*. Paper presented at the National Council for the Social Studies, Anaheim, CA.

Aronowitz, S. (1973). *False promises: The shaping of the American working class consciousness*. New York: McGraw-Hill.

Benedict, R. (1946/1974). *The chrysanthemum and the sword*. New York: New American Library.

Berman, D. M. (1990). Social studies education for the new Japan. *Social Education, 56*(4): 242–243.

Bernstein, B. (1977). *Class, codes and control*. London: Routledge and Kegan Paul.

Bowles, S., & Gintis, H. (1976). *Schooling in capitalist America*. New York: Basic.

Dahl, R. A. (1971). *Polyarchy: Participation and opposition*. New Haven: Yale University Press.

Dalton, R. J. (1988). *Citizen politics in western democracies*. Chatham, NJ: Chatham House.

Dore, R. P. (1958). *City life in Japan: A study of a Tokyo ward*. Berkeley: University of California Press.

Fitzmaurice, J. (1981). *Politics in Denmark*. New York: St. Martin's Press.

Giroux, H. & Penna. (1979). Social education in the classroom: The dynamics of the hidden curriculum. *Theory and Research in Social Education*, 7: 21–42.

Gutmann, A. (1987). *Democratic education*. Princeton: Princeton University Press.

Hahn, C. L. (1987). Right to a political education. In N. B. Tarrow (Ed.), *Human rights and education* (pp. 173–187). Oxford: Pergamon Press.

———. (1991, November). *Classroom climate: The complementary roles of quantitative and qualitative data*. Paper presented at the National Council for the Social Studies, Washington, D. C.

———. (1993, November). *Preparing citizens: A preliminary report of a cross-national study*. Paper presented at the National Council for the Social Studies, Nashville, TN.

Hahn, C. L. & Tocci, C. (1990). Classroom climate and controversial issues discussions: A five nation study. *Theory and Research in Social Education*, 18: 344–362.

Hahn, C. L., Tocci, C., & Angell, A. (1988). *Five nation study of civic attitudes and controversial issues discussions*. International Conference on the Social Studies, Vancouver, British Columbia.

Harber, C. (1987). Introduction. In C. Harber (Ed.), *Political education in Britain* (pp. 1–8). London: Falmer.

Heater, D. (1990). *Citizenship: The civic ideal in world history, politics, and education*. New York: Longman.

———. (1991). Citizenship: A remarkable case of sudden interest. *Parliamentary Affairs*, 44: 140–156.

Huntington, S. P., & Nelson, J. M. (1976). *No easy choice*. Cambridge: Harvard University Press.

Kluckhohn, C. (1949). *Mirror for man*. New York: McGraw-Hill.

Lewis, C. C. (1989). From indulgence to internalization: Social control in the early school years. *Journal of Japanese Studies*, 15(1): 139–157.

Lister, I. (1987). Global and international approaches in political education. In C. Harber (Ed.), *Political education in Britain* (pp. 47–62). London: Falmer.

_____. (1991). Research on social studies and citizenship education in England. In J. P. Shaver (Ed.), *Handbook of research on social studies teaching and learning* (pp. 602–609). New York: Macmillan

McCormack, G. & Sugimoto, Y. (1986). *Democracy in contemporary Japan*. Armonk, NY: M.E. Sharpe.

Oliver, D. (1991). Active citizenship in the 1990s. *Parliamentary Affairs*, 44: 157–171.

Powell, G. B., Jr. (1982). *Contemporary democracies: Participation, stability, and violence*. Cambridge: Harvard University Press.

Rohlen, R. P. (1989). Order in Japanese society: Attachment, authority, and routine. *Journal of Japanese Studies, 15(1)*: 5–40.

Rohlen, T. P. (1983). *Japan's high schools*. Berkeley: University of California Press.

Singleton, J. (1967). *Nichu: A Japanese school*. New York: Holt, Rinehart and Winston.

Stevens, O. (1982). *Children talking politics*. Oxford: Martin Robertson.

Stradling, R., Noctor, M., & Baines, B. (1984). *Teaching controversial issues*. London: Edward Arnold.

Tobin, J. J., Wu, D. Y. H., & Davidson, D. H. (1989). *Preschoolers in three cultures: Japan, China, and the United States*. New Haven: Yale University Press.

Torney, J. V., Oppenheim, A. N., & Farnen, R. F. (1975). *Civic education in ten countries: An empirical study*. New York: John Wiley & Sons.

Torney-Purta, J. (1991). Cross-national research in social studies. In J. P. Shaver (Ed.), *Handbook of research on social studies teaching and learning* (pp. 591–601). New York: Macmillan.

Torney-Purta, J., & Hahn, C. L. (1989). Values education in the Western European tradition. In W. Cummings, S. Gopinathan, & Y. Tomoda (Eds.), *The revival of values education is Asia and the West* (pp. 31–57). Oxford: Pergamon Press.

van Wolferen, K. (1989). *The enigma of Japanese power: People and politics in a stateless nation*. New York: Alfred A. Knopf.

White, M. (1987). *The Japanese educational challenge*. New York: Free Press.

CONTRIBUTORS
OF NEW WORKS

Ann V. Angell teaches in the upper elementary grades at First Montessori School in Atlanta, Georgia. She holds a Ph.D. in educational leadership from Emory University (1991) and taught social studies education at the University of Houston before returning to elementary classroom teaching.

Jane Bernard-Powers is Associate Professor of Elementary Education at San Francisco State University. She is a founding member of the Special Interest Group for Gender and Social Justice (National Council for the Social Studies) and is interested in women's educational history and multicultural, gendered social studies education. Her publications include *The Girl Question in Education: Vocational Education for Young Women in the Progressive Era* (Falmer, 1992).

Carole L. Hahn is Professor of Social Studies Education at Emory University, where she teaches courses in social studies methods and research, and comparative education. She is past president of the National Council for the Social Studies and for ten years has been conducting research on civic education in five western democracies.

David Mathews is president of the Charles F. Kettering Foundation, a research foundation that works on problems in education, international affairs, policy development, and government problem-solving—all with an emphasis on the role of the public. He was U. S. Secretary of Health, Education, and Welfare (1975–77) and president of the University of Alabama (1969–80). His publications include *Politics for People* (University of Illinois Press, 1994).

Walter C. Parker is Professor and Chair of Social Studies Education at the University of Washington in Seattle. He is interested in curriculum for democracy, particularly deliberation and critical thinking. His publications include *Renewing the Social Studies Curriculum* (Association for Supervision and Curriculum Development, 1991).

William B. Stanley is Chair of the Department of Educational Development at the University of Delaware and Professor of Social Studies and Curriculum Theory. He is interested in the foundations of social education, curriculum theory, and concept formation. His publications include *Curriculum for Utopia* (State University of New York Press, 1992).

James Anthony Whitson is Associate Professor of Education at the University of Delaware, where he teaches social studies education and curriculum theory. His publications include *Constitution and Curriculum: Hermeneutical Semiotics of Cases and Controversies in Education, Law, and Social Science* (Falmer, 1991).

INDEX

Printed in the United States
19559LVS00002B/398